W9-ATP-566

EMMA BOVARY

Gustave Flaubert's *Madame Bovary* first appeared as
a serialization in the *Revue de Paris* in 1856, and was
published in book form the next year. Its magazine
appearance formed the occasion of a celebrated trial for
obscenity, which was finally decided in Flaubert's favor.
The trial is only one indication of the powerful emotions
stirred by Flaubert's masterwork, dealing as it does with
the hidden passions of Emma Bovary as she seeks to
escape her unhappy marriage and her stultifying country
environment with a series of passionate affairs.

In a review of the novel, Charles Baudelaire defended
the work against charges of obscenity. Early English
critics such as George Saintsbury and Matthew Arnold
clearly felt uncomfortable with the novel's sexual frank-
ness, but Henry James championed Flaubert's characterization of Emma. Such later critics as Edmund Wilson,
Erich Auerbach, Mary McCarthy, and Susan J. Rosowski
approach Emma from political, mythic, and feminist
perspectives. Mario Vargas Llosa writes provocatively on
Emma's androgynous qualities.

Frank D. McConnell discusses the novel in conjunction with Flaubert's *Dictionary of Received Ideas*, while
Margaret Lowe suggestively compares Emma with
Psyche and other mythic figures. Sarah Webster Goodwin studies the metaphor of dancing in the novel,
Nathaniel Wing focuses on Emma as narrator, and
William VanderWolk examines the function of memory
in *Madame Bovary*. These and other varied approaches
reveal the multifaceted nature of Emma Bovary, one of
the richest characters in one of the greatest novels in
Western literature.

Major Literary Characters is a series of fifty-one
titles bringing together the best criticism on the most
enduring and widely studied fictional figures from world
literature. With original introductory comments by
Harold Bloom as well as thorough documentation and
editorial notes on the essays he has selected, these
volumes offer an invaluable reexamination of a recently
neglected critical approach—the study of character.

CHELSEA HOUSE PUBLISHERS

New York • Philadelphia

EMMA BOVARY

Major Literary Characters

CHELSEA HOUSE PUBLISHERS

Major Literary Characters

DAVID COPPERFIELD
Charles Dickens, *David Copperfield*

ROBINSON CRUSOE
Daniel Defoe, *Robinson Crusoe*

DON JUAN
Molière, *Don Juan*
Lord Byron, *Don Juan*

HUCK FINN
Mark Twain, *The Adventures of Tom Sawyer, Adventures of Huckleberry Finn*

CLARISSA HARLOWE
Samuel Richardson, *Clarissa*

HEATHCLIFF
Emily Brontë, *Wuthering Heights*

ANNA KARENINA
Leo Tolstoy, *Anna Karenina*

MR. PICKWICK
Charles Dickens, *The Pickwick Papers*

HESTER PRYNNE
Nathaniel Hawthorne, *The Scarlet Letter*

BECKY SHARP
William Makepeace Thackeray, *Vanity Fair*

LAMBERT STRETHER
Henry James, *The Ambassadors*

EUSTACIA VYE
Thomas Hardy, *The Return of the Native*

TWENTIETH CENTURY

ÁNTONIA
Willa Cather, *My Ántonia*

BRETT ASHLEY
Ernest Hemingway, *The Sun Also Rises*

HANS CASTORP
Thomas Mann, *The Magic Mountain*

HOLDEN CAULFIELD
J. D. Salinger, *The Catcher in the Rye*

CADDY COMPSON
William Faulkner, *The Sound and the Fury*

JANIE CRAWFORD
Zora Neale Hurston, *Their Eyes Were Watching God*

CLARISSA DALLOWAY
Virginia Woolf, *Mrs. Dalloway*

DILSEY
William Faulkner, *The Sound and the Fury*

GATSBY
F. Scott Fitzgerald, *The Great Gatsby*

HERZOG
Saul Bellow, *Herzog*

JOAN OF ARC
William Shakespeare, *Henry VI*
George Bernard Shaw, *Saint Joan*

LOLITA
Vladimir Nabokov, *Lolita*

WILLY LOMAN
Arthur Miller, *Death of a Salesman*

MARLOW
Joseph Conrad, *Lord Jim, Heart of Darkness, Youth, Chance*

PORTNOY
Philip Roth, *Portnoy's Complaint*

BIGGER THOMAS
Richard Wright, *Native Son*

CHELSEA HOUSE PUBLISHERS

Major Literary Characters

EMMA BOVARY

Edited and with an introduction by
HAROLD BLOOM

CHELSEA HOUSE PUBLISHERS
New York ◊ Philadelphia

Jacket illustration: Engraving by Albert Fourié and D. Mordant from
Madame Bovary (Paris: A. Quantin, 1885) (courtesy of General Research
Division, New York Public Library, Astor, Lenox and Tilden Foundations).
Inset: Title page from the first edition of *Madame Bovary* (Paris:
Lévy Frères, 1857) (courtesy of Rare Books and Manuscripts Division,
New York Public Library, Astor, Lenox and Tilden Foundations).

Chelsea House Publishers

Editorial Director   Richard Rennert
Executive Managing Editor   Karyn Gullen Browne
Picture Editor   Adrian G. Allen
Art Director   Robert Mitchell
Manufacturing Director   Gerald Levine

Major Literary Characters

Senior Editor   S. T. Joshi
Copy Chief   Robin James
Designer   Maria Epes

Staff for EMMA BOVARY

Picture Researcher   Wendy Wills
Senior Designer   Rae Grant
Editorial Assistant   Robert Green
Production Coordinator   Marie Claire Cebrián-Ume

Library of Congress Cataloging-in-Publication Data

Emma Bovary / edited and with an introduction by Harold Bloom.
p.   cm.—(Major literary characters)
Includes bibliographical references.
ISBN 0-7910-0935-1.—ISBN 0-7910-0990-4 (pbk.)
1. Flaubert, Gustave, 1821–1880. Madame Bovary.   2. Flaubert, Gustave,
1821–1880—Characters—Emma Bovary.   3. Women in literature.
I. Bloom, Harold.   II. Series.
PQ2246.M3E47   1993
843'.8—dc20
93-2916
CIP

CONTENTS

THE ANALYSIS OF CHARACTER

Harold Bloom

"Character," according to our dictionaries, still has as a primary meaning a graphic symbol, such as a letter of the alphabet. This meaning reflects the word's apparent origin in the ancient Greek *charactēr*, a sharp stylus. *Charactēr* also meant the mark of the stylus' incisions. Recent fashions in literary criticism have reduced "character" in literature to a matter of marks upon a page. But our word "character" also has a very different meaning, matching that of the ancient Greek *ēthos*, "habitual way of life." Shall we say then that literary character is an imitation of human character, or is it just a grouping of marks? The issue is between a critic like Dr. Samuel Johnson, for whom words were as much like people as like things, and a critic like the late Roland Barthes, who told us that "the fact can only exist linguistically, as a term of discourse." Who is closer to our experience of reading literature, Johnson or Barthes? What difference does it make, if we side with one critic rather than the other?

Barthes is famous, like Foucault and other recent French theorists, for having added to Nietzsche's proclamation of the death of God a subsidiary demise, that of the literary author. If there are no authors, then there are no fictional personages, presumably because literature does not refer to a world outside language. Words indeed necessarily refer to other words in the first place, but the impact of words ultimately is drawn from a universe of fact. Stories, poems, and plays are recognizable as such because they are human utterances within traditions of utterances, and traditions, by achieving authority, become a kind of fact, or at least the sense of a fact. Our sense that literary characters, within the context of a fictive cosmos, indeed are fictional personages is also a kind of fact. The meaning and value of every character in a successful work of literary representation depend upon our ideas of persons in the factual reality of our lives.

Literary character is always an invention, and inventions generally are indebted to prior inventions. Shakespeare is the inventor of literary character as we know it; he reformed the universal human expectations for the verbal imitation of personality, and the reformation appears now to be permanent and uncannily inevitable. Remarkable as the Bible and Homer are at representing personages, their characters are relatively unchanging. They age within their stories, but their habitual modes of being do not develop. Jacob and Achilles unfold before us, but without metamorphoses. Lear and Macbeth, Hamlet and Othello severely modify themselves not only by their actions, but by their utterances, and most of all through *overhearing themselves,* whether they speak to themselves or to others. Pondering what they themselves have said, they will to change, and actually do change, sometimes extravagantly yet always persuasively. Or else they suffer change, without willing it, but in reaction not so much to their language as to their relation to that language.

I do not think·it useful to say that Shakespeare successfully imitated elements in our characters. Rather, it could be argued that he compelled aspects of character to appear that previously were concealed, or not available to representation. This is not to say that Shakespeare is God, but to remind us that language is not God either. The mimesis of character in Shakespeare's dramas now seems to us normative, and indeed became the accepted mode almost immediately, as Ben Jonson shrewdly and somewhat grudgingly implied. And yet, Shakespearean representation has surprisingly little in common with the imitation of reality in Jonson or in Christopher Marlowe. The origins of Shakespeare's originality in the portrayal of men and women are to be found in the *Canterbury Tales* of Geoffrey Chaucer, insofar as they can be located anywhere before Shakespeare himself. Chaucer's savage and superb Pardoner overhears his own tale-telling, as well as his mocking rehearsal of his own spiel, and through this overhearing he is emboldened to forget himself, and enthusiastically urges all his fellow-pilgrims to come forward to be fleeced by him. His self-awareness, and apocalyptically rancid sense of spiritual fall, are preludes to the even grander abysses of the perverted will in Iago and in Edmund. What might be called the character trait of a negative charisma may be Chaucer's invention, but came to its perfection in Shakespearean mimesis.

The analysis of character is as much Shakespeare's invention as the representation of character is, since Iago and Edmund are adepts at analyzing both themselves and their victims. Hamlet, whose overwhelming charisma has many negative components, is certainly the most comprehensive of all literary characters, and so necessarily prophesies the labyrinthine complexities of the will in Iago and Edmund. Charisma, according to Max Weber, its first codifier, is primarily a natural endowment, and implies a primordial and idiosyncratic power over nature, and so finally over death. Hamlet's uncanniness is at its most suggestive in the scene of his long dying, where the audience, through the mediation of Horatio, itself is compelled to meditate upon suicide, if only because outliving the prince of Denmark scarcely seems an option.

Shakespearean representation has usurped not only our sense of literary character, but our sense of ourselves as characters, with Hamlet playing the part of the largest of these usurpations. Insofar as we have an idea of human disinterestedness, we tend to derive it from the Hamlet of Act V, whose quietism has about it a ghostly authority. Oscar Wilde, in his profound and profoundly witty dialogue, "The Decay of Lying," expressed a permanent insight when he insisted that art shaped every era, far more than any age formed art. Life imitates art, we imitate Shakespeare, because without Shakespeare we would perish for lack of images. Wilde's grandest audacity demystifies Shakespearean mimesis with a Shakespearean vivaciousness: "This unfortunate aphorism about art holding the mirror up to Nature is deliberately said by Hamlet in order to convince the bystanders of his absolute insanity in all art-matters." Of *Hamlet's* influence upon the ages Wilde remarked that: "The world has grown sad because a puppet was once melancholy." "Puppet" is Wilde's own deconstruction, a brilliant reminder that Shakespeare's artistry of illusion has so mastered reality as to have changed reality, evidently forever.

The analysis of character, as a critical pursuit, seems to me as much a Shakespearean invention as literary character was, since much of what we know about how to analyze character necessarily follows Shakespearean procedures. His hero-villains, from Richard III through Iago, Edmund, and Macbeth, are shrewd and endless questers into their own self-motivations. If we could bear to see Hamlet, in his unwearied negations, as another hero-villain, then we would judge him the supreme analyst of the darker recalcitrances in the selfhood. Freud followed the pre-Socratic Empedocles, in arguing that character is fate, a frightening doctrine that maintains the fear that there are no accidents, that over-determination rules us all of our lives. Hamlet assumes the same, yet adds to this argument the terrible passivity he manifests in Act V. Throughout Shakespeare's tragedies, the most interesting personages seem doom-eager, reminding us again that a Shakespearean reading of Freud would be more illuminating than a Freudian exegesis of Shakespeare. We learn more when we discover Hamlet in the Freudian Death Drive, than when we read *Beyond the Pleasure Principle* into *Hamlet*.

In Shakespearean comedy, character achieves its true literary apotheosis, which is the representation of the inner freedom that can be created by great wit alone. Rosalind and Falstaff, perhaps alone among Shakespeare's personages, match Hamlet in wit, though hardly in the metaphysics of consciousness. Whether in the comic or the modern mode, Shakespeare has set the standard of measurement in the balance between character and passion.

In Shakespeare the self is more dramatized than theatricalized, which is why a Shakespearean reading of Freud works out so well. Character-formation after the passing of the Oedipal stage takes the place of fetishistic fragmentings of the self. Critics who now call literary character into question, and who proclaim also the death of the author, invariably also regard all notions, literary and human, of a stable character as being mere reductions of deeper pre-Oedipal desires. It

becomes clear that the fortunes of literary character rise and fall with the prestige of normative conceptions of the ego. Shakespeare's Iago, who wars against
being, may be the first deconstructionist of the self, with his proclamation of "I
am not what I am." This constitutes the necessary prologue to any view that
would regard a fixed ego as a virtual abnormality. But deconstructions of the self
are no more modern than Modernism is. Like literary modernism, the
decentered ego came out of the Hellenistic culture of ancient Alexandria. The
Gnostic heretics believed that the psyche, like the body, was a fallen entity,
mechanically fashioned by the Demiurge or false creator. They held however
that each of us possessed also a spark or pneuma, which was a fragment of
the original Abyss or true, alien God. The soul or psyche within every one of
us was thus at war with the self or pneuma, and only that sparklike self could be
saved.

Shakespeare, following after Chaucer in this respect, was the first and remains
still the greatest master of representing character both as a stable soul and a
wavering self. There is a substance that endures in Shakespeare's figures, and there
is also a quicksilver rendition of the unsettling sparks. Racine and Tolstoy, Balzac and
Dickens, follow in Shakespeare's wake by giving us some sense of pre-Oedipal
sparks or drives, and considerably more sense of post-Oedipal character and
personality, stabilizations or sublimations of the fetish-seeking drives. Critics like Leo
Bersani and René Girard argue eloquently against our taking this mimesis as the only
proper work of literature. I would suggest that strong fictions of the self, from the
Bible through Samuel Beckett, necessarily participate in both modes, the sublima-
tion of desire, and the persistence of a primordial desire. The mystery of Hamlet
or of Lear is intimately invested in the tangled mixture of the two modes of
representation.

Psychic mobility is proposed by Bersani as the ideal to which deconstructions
of the literary self may yet guide us. The ideal has its pathos, but the realities of
literary representation seem to me very different, perhaps destructively so. When
a novelist like D. H. Lawrence sought to reduce his characters to Eros and the
Death Drive, he still had to persuade us of his authority at mimesis by lavishing upon
the figures of *The Rainbow* and *Women in Love* all of the vivid stigmata of
normative personality. Birkin and Ursula may represent antithetical and uncanny
drives, but they develop and change as characters pondering their own pronouncements and reactions to self and others. The cost of a non-Shakespearean representation is enormous. Pynchon, in *The Crying of Lot 49* and *Gravity's Rainbow,*
evades the burden of the normative by resorting to something like Christopher
Marlowe's art of caricature in *The Jew of Malta.* Marlowe's Barabas is a marvelous
rhetorician, yet he is a cartoon alongside the troublingly equivocal Shylock. Pynchon's personages are deliberate cartoons also, as flat as comic strips. Marlowe's
achievement, and Pynchon's, are beyond dispute, yet they are like the prelude and
the postlude to Shakespearean reality. They do not wish to engage with our hunger
for the empirical world and so they enter the problematic cosmos of literary
fantasy.

No writer, not even Shakespeare or Proust, alters the available stock that we agree to call reality, but Shakespeare, more than any other, does show us how much of reality we could encounter if only we retained adequate desire. The strong literary representation of character is already an analysis of character, and is part of the healing work of a literary culture, which implicitly seeks to cure violence through a normative mimesis of ego, *as if it were stable,* whether in actuality it is or is not. I do not believe that this is a social quest taken on by literary culture, but rather that we confront here the aesthetic essence of what makes a culture *literary,* rather than metaphysical or ethical or religious. A culture becomes literary when its conceptual modes have failed it, which means when religion, philosophy, and science have begun to lose their authority. If they cannot heal violence, then literature attempts to do so, which may be only a turning inside out of the critical arguments of Girard and Bersani.

I conclude by offering a particular instance or special case as a paradigm for the healing enterprise that is at once the representation and the analysis of literary character. Let us call it the aesthetics of being outraged, or rather of successfully representing the state of being outraged. W. C. Fields was one modern master of such representation, and Nathanael West was another, as was Faulkner before him. Here also the greatest master remains Shakespeare, whose Macbeth, himself a bloody outrage, yet retains our imaginative sympathy precisely because he grows increasingly outraged as he experiences the equivocation of the fiend that lies like truth. The double-natured promises and the prophecies of the weird sisters finally induce in Macbeth an apocalyptic version of the stage actor's anxiety at missing cues, the horror of a phantasmagoric stage fright of missing one's time, of always reacting too late. Macbeth, a veritable monster of solipsistic inwardness but no intellectual, counters his dilemma by fresh murders, that prolong him in time yet provoke him only to a perpetually freshened sense of being outraged, as all his expectations become still worse confounded. We are moved by Macbeth, however estrangedly, because his terrible inwardness is a paradigm for our own solipsism, but also because none of us can resist a strong and successful representation of the human in a state of being outraged.

The ultimate outrage is the necessity of dying, an outrage concealed in a multitude of masks, including the tyrannical ambitions of Macbeth. I suspect that our outrage at being outraged is the most difficult of all our affects for us to represent to ourselves, which is why we are so inclined to imaginative sympathy for a character who strongly conveys that affect to us. The Shrike of West's *Miss Lonely-hearts* or Faulkner's Joe Christmas of *Light in August* are crucial modern instances, but such figures can be located in many other works, since the ability to represent this extreme emotion is one of the tests that strong writers are driven to set for themselves.

However a reader seeks to reduce literary character to a question of marks on a page, she will come at last to the impasse constituted by the thought of death, her death, and before that to all the stations of being outraged that memorialize her own drive towards death. In reading, she quests for evidences that are strong representations, whether of her desire or her despair. Such questings constitute the necessary basis for the analysis of literary character, an enterprise that always will survive every vagary of critical fashion.

EDITOR'S NOTE

This volume gathers together a representative selection of the best criticism that has been devoted to Flaubert's Emma Bovary, centering upon her as a literary character. The critical extracts and the essays each are reprinted here in the chronological order of their original publication. I am grateful to S. T. Joshi for his erudition and judgment in assisting the editing of this book.

My introduction charts some of the differing stances taken toward Emma Bovary's vitality by Flaubert and by his narrator in the novel.

The critical extracts begin with Flaubert himself, and his contemporaries Sainte-Beuve and Baudelaire, and proceed through Matthew Arnold and Henry James to such eminent modern critics as Edmund Wilson, Erich Auerbach, R. P. Blackmur, and Leo Bersani. The distinguished novelists, Mario Vargas Llosa and Vladimir Nabokov, offer very contrasting views of the pathos of Emma Bovary's fictive existence.

Full-scale critical essays commence with Frank McConnell's incisive analysis of Flaubert's subversion of some key words that are used to describe Emma's passional life. Barbara Smalley sketches an Emma caught in a dialectical interplay of human illusion and an indifferent exterior reality.

In Charles Bernheimer's subtle meditation, the authorial ecstasy of Flaubert is contrasted with the incommunicable sensual ecstasies of Emma Bovary. A fascinating discussion by Margaret Lowe finds in Emma Flaubert's goddess of the Eternal Feminine, somewhat akin to a naturalistic version of the Dantean Beatrice.

Sarah Webster Goodwin concentrates upon the negative epiphany that follows Emma's waltz or "dance of death," while Carla L. Peterson emphasizes the quixotic element in Emma's character. In Nathaniel Wing's exegesis, Emma's fantasies and dreams are seen as fetishistic exercises, after which Bruce E. Fleming gives us an Emma who is scarcely so much a human personality as simply a course in seductions.

William VanderWolk establishes the differences in the function of memory in Emma and in her creator, Flaubert. This volume concludes with Michael Danahy's feminist argument that Emma Bovary is murdered, not so much by Flaubert the novelist, as by the anxieties of patriarchal authority.

INTRODUCTION

One need hardly be a feminist to observe that Flaubert murders Emma Bovary. What is his motive? Self-punishment of course is involved, but Flaubert was too tough to be destroyed, prematurely, by the reality principle. Emma is at once far less tough and far more vital than her creator. I am afraid that the motive for murder is envy of her vitality, so that authorial sadism becomes as crucial in Emma's tragedy as is authorial masochism. The Flaubert who was to compose the dreadfully magnificent *Salammbô* (1858–62) is already present in the making of *Madame Bovary* (1852–56). Sensations are more extreme in *Salammbô*, the colors are far gaudier, the temperature extravagantly rises, and yet desire, ours and Flaubert's, seems less prevalent. As a hopelessly old-fashioned literary critic, who remembers falling in love with Marty South in Thomas Hardy's *The Woodlanders* when he was a boy, I continue to lust after Emma Bovary each time I reread Flaubert's master-work. This seems to me as valid an aesthetic experience as being moved to desire by staring at a Renoir nude. Emma may be the most persuasively sensual of all fictive beings. Shakespeare's Cleopatra, like his Falstaff, is too witty not to be ironic about her own capacities, but poor Emma is a literalist of her own sexual imagi-nation. Clearly this is a very different mode of fantasy than that of the narrator of *Madame Bovary* or of Flaubert himself. The narrator is considerably less fond of Emma than Flaubert is (or we are), and yet Flaubert, and not the narrator, is the murderer. One might transpose the novel into Shakespearean terms by seeing the narrator as Iago, Flaubert as Othello, and Emma as Desdemona. Of these three identifications (all knowingly outrageous), that of the narrator as Iago is the least fantastic. I have the same uneasy respect for Flaubert's narrator that I have for Iago; both of them propose emotions to themselves, and only then experience the emotions.

Emma, despite her hysterias, is not the heroine of a tragicomedy. The narrator intends otherwise, but Emma has the greatness of her vitality, the heroic intensity of her sexuality, and that eminence makes her an oddity, a tragic heroine in a literary work stoical, ironic, and sometimes grotesquely comic. Flaubert's savage and superb artistry conveys an embodied image of desire that is close to universal;

Emma's aura is comprehensive enough to subsume both female and male sexuality. The objects of her desire do not much matter, whether to Flaubert or to the reader. They may mean more to the narrator than they do to Emma, whose concern is only that there always be one, or at least another one beyond, in a series not to be ended. Emma is thus representative of both the average sensual male and the average sensual female, though the sensual is the one domain in which she is above average. She is to the ideal of erotic passion what Don Quixote is to the ideal of playfulness, and like the Don she is at last murdered by reality, whose name is Flaubert, or Cervantes. Human playfulness is a much wider realm than erotic fantasy, and the Don certainly dwarfs Emma in aesthetic dignity. But her own aesthetic dignity remains considerable; whom can we prefer to her in Flaubert's major fictions? She was the best available to Flaubert's imagination, and her progeny necessarily are with us still. Emma has fed herself on the erotic debasement of popular romances even as Don Quixote has sustained himself upon romances of knight-errantry. The Don is sublimely crazed, in terms of the order of reality, but he is Sublime in the order of play. No order of play is available for Emma, and in the world of reality-testing she is almost absurdly suicidal. Her self-immolation contrasts weirdly with that of Tolstoi's Anna Karenina. Tolstoi's apocalyptic moralism destroys Anna, and yet there is a tragic relief we experience at Anna's death; her sufferings are too large to be allowed to continue. Emma's sufferings seem petty in comparison, and yet Emma is too pleasure-loving to sustain them. Her death lacks grandeur, and yet we are grandly moved because such a loss of sexual vitality is a defeat for the Biblical sense of the Blessing, which is: more life. The death of Emma means less life, less possibility of natural pleasure for almost all of us, less of ourselves that we can spend in the days remaining to us.

One feels that, on a much muted level, Emma belongs in a poem by Keats or by Wallace Stevens. Her narcissism is a value, but Flaubert's novel declines to provide her with contexts in which her self-absorption can acquire any aura of radiance. Hopelessly drab in mind and spirit, incapable of singling out a proper object of desire, she cannot bore us because she herself, despite everything, remains an image of desire. We are endlessly moved by that element in her that cannot accept erotic loss. We suffer our losses, and either we sublimate them, or we harden with them. Emma is as far as she can be from Nietzsche's admirable apothegm, "That which does not destroy me strengthens me." Her losses weaken her, and then destroy her. She represents therefore something stubborn in all of us, perhaps something childlike, that refuses to believe any object is lost forever. What Freud beautifully called "the work of mourning" is not available to her. But it is available to Flaubert, and through Flaubert to his readers. Though he murders her, Flaubert performs the work of mourning for her, a work that takes the shape of his masterpiece, the purest of all novels in form, economy, and the just representation of general nature.

—H. B.

CRITICAL EXTRACTS

GUSTAVE FLAUBERT

I must love you to write you tonight, for I am *exhausted*. My head feels as though it were being squeezed in an iron vise. Since two o'clock yesterday afternoon (except for about twenty-five minutes for dinner), I have been writing *Bovary*. I am in the midst of love-making; I am sweating and my throat is tight. This has been one of the rare days of my life passed completely in illusion from beginning to end. At six o'clock this evening, as I was writing the word "hysterics," I was so swept away, was bellowing so loudly and feeling so deeply what my little Bovary was going through, that I was afraid of having hysterics myself. I got up from my table and opened the window to calm myself. My head was spinning. Now I have great pains in my knees, in my back, and in my head. I feel like a man who has ———ed too much (forgive me for the expression)—a kind of rapturous lassitude. And since I am in the midst of love it is only proper that I should not fall asleep before sending you a caress, a kiss, and whatever thoughts are left in me. Will what I write be good? I have no idea—I am hurrying a little, to be able to show Bouilhet a complete section when he comes to see me. What is certain is that my book has been going at a lively rate for the past week. May it continue so, for I am weary of my usual snail's pace. But I fear the awakening, the disillusion that may come from the recopied pages. No matter; it is a delicious thing to write, whether well or badly—to be no longer yourself but to move in an entire universe of your own creating. Today, for instance, man and woman, lover and beloved, I rode in a forest on an autumn afternoon under the yellow leaves, and I was also the horse, the leaves, the wind, the words my people spoke, even the red sun that made them half-shut their love-drowned eyes. Is this pride or piety? Is it a silly overflow of exaggerated self-satisfaction, or is it really a vague and noble religious instinct? But when I think of these marvelous pleasures I have enjoyed I am tempted to offer God a prayer of thanks—if only I knew he could hear me! Praised be the Lord for not creating me a cotton merchant, a vaudevillian, a wit, etc.! Let us sing to Apollo like the ancient bards, and breathe deeply of the cold air of Parnassus; let us strum our

3

guitars and clash our cymbals, and whirl like dervishes in the eternal pageant of Forms and Ideas.

—GUSTAVE FLAUBERT, letter to Louise Colet (December 23, 1853),
The Selected Letters of Gustave Flaubert, ed. and tr. Francis Steegmuller
(New York: Farrar, Straus, 1953), pp. 165–66

C. A. SAINTE-BEUVE

So Emma has become Mme. Bovary and has moved into the little house at Tostes. She occupies cramped quarters; there is a little garden, longer than it is wide, beyond which are open fields. She at once introduces order, cleanliness, and a certain elegance into the establishment. Her husband, who is bent on granting her every wish, buys a carriage, a secondhand buggy, so that she can take the air in it whenever she likes on the highway or in the surrounding countryside. For the first time in his life he is happy, and he feels it; busy all day with his patients, when he comes home at night he is ecstatic with joy: he is in love with his wife. He asks no more of life than that his peaceful domestic happiness should last. But she, who has dreamed of better things, and as a young girl in moments of boredom had more than once wondered how happiness could be achieved, realizes fairly promptly, during the honeymoon, that she is not happy.

Now begins a deep, thorough, subtle analysis, a cruel dissection that ends only with the book. We are led step by step into Mme. Bovary's heart. What is she really like? She is a woman; at first she is merely romantic, she has not been in the least corrupted. As he limns her for us, M. Gustave Flaubert does not spare her. Describing her dainty ways as a little girl and at school with the nuns, and showing her as given to extravagant daydreams, he exposes her pitilessly, and—shall I confess it?—we feel more indulgent toward her than he himself seems to be. Emma is unable to adjust herself to her new situation because she has one quality too many and one virtue too few: therein lies the root of all her transgressions, all her unhappiness. The quality is that she not only is a romantic nature but also has emotional and intellectual needs and ambitions, that she aspires to a higher, more refined, more elegant life than the one that has fallen to her lot. The virtue she lacks is that she never learned that the first condition of a good life is ability to endure boredom. She has a vague sense of something missing, the feeling that life ought to be more pleasant, more to her taste, and she is unable to resign herself in silence without showing anything, to create for herself an interest, a protective armor, a goal, a way of spending her time whether in her love for her child or in making herself useful to those around her. To be sure, she struggles, she does not turn away from the straight and narrow in a day: before plunging into evil, she will make many an attempt over many years to keep her head. However, every day she comes one step closer to her destiny, and in the end she has gone astray beyond recovery. But I am making a dry summary, whereas the author of *Madame Bovary* shows us his character's thoughts and actions day by day, minute by minute. ⟨...⟩

Although I appreciate the author's point of view—the keystone of his method, his poetics—I must reproach his book for the fact that there is no goodness in it. Not a single character represents goodness. The only person capable of disinterested, silent love—little Justin, M. Homais' apprentice—barely counts. Why has the author failed to include a single character capable of comforting and soothing the reader by a good action? Why is there no sympathetic character? Why lay oneself open to the reproach, "You know all there is to know about human nature, but you are cruel?" To be sure the book has a moral, one which the author has by no means dragged into it and which the reader must discover for himself. It is a rather terrible moral. But is it the duty of art to refuse all consolation to the reader, to reject every element of clemency and kindness under the pretext of being more truthful? Even granting that truth alone is a worthy goal, truth does not lie entirely with wickedness, with stupidity and perversity. These provincial lives may well abound in bickering, minor persecutions, mean ambitions, and pettiness of every variety. But there are also good people, people who have retained their innocence, perhaps more intact and more genuine than elsewhere. Modesty, resignation, devotion extending over long years—who among us has not seen examples of these virtues in the provinces? No matter how true to life your characters may be, they reflect the author's choice: it is he who has skillfully arranged the pattern of their shortcomings and absurdities. Why not arrange a pattern of good qualities—show us at least one character who captivates us or earns our respect? I once knew, in the depths of a province in central France, a woman still young, superior in intelligence, ardent of heart, and bored. Married but not a mother, having no child of her own to educate and love, what did she do to occupy the overflow of her mind and soul? She adopted the children about her. She became a benefactress, a civilizing influence in the somewhat wild country in which fate had placed her. She taught children to read, instructed them in moral culture. The villages were often far distant; at times she went a league and a half on foot; her pupil walked as far; and meeting, they had their lessons beside a path, beneath a tree, on a heath. There are such souls as that in the provinces, in the country: why not depict them, as well? This is uplifting, comforting, and makes for a more complete picture of mankind.

—C. A. SAINTE-BEUVE, "*Madame Bovary* by Gustave Flaubert" [1857],
Selected Essays, tr. Francis Steegmuller and Norbert Guterman
(Garden City, NY: Doubleday, 1963), pp. 263–65, 272–73

CHARLES BAUDELAIRE

Several critics had said: "this work, truly beautiful in the detail and liveliness of its descriptions, does not contain a single character who represents morality, who expresses the author's inmost thought. Where is the proverbial and legendary character charged with explaining the story and with guiding the reader's understanding? In other words, where is the indictment?"

What nonsense! Eternal and incorrigible confusion of functions and genres! A true work of art need not contain an indictment. The logic of the work satisfies all the claims of morality, and it is for the reader to draw his conclusions from the conclusion.

The adulteress is unquestionably the profound and intimate character of the story; she alone, the dishonored victim, possesses all the graces of the hero.—A moment ago I said that she was almost male, and that the author had endowed her (unconsciously perhaps) with all the virtues of a man.

Let us examine them carefully:

1. Imagination, that supreme and despotic faculty, replacing the heart, or what is called the heart, from which reasoning is usually excluded and which generally dominates in a woman, as it does in an animal;

2. Sudden energetic action, quickness of decision, mystical fusion of reason and passion which characterize men created to act;

3. Excessive taste for seduction, for domination, and even for the most vulgar means of seduction, descending to affectation of dress, perfume, and cosmetics—all of it summed up in two words: dandyism and exclusive love of domination.

And yet, Madame Bovary does give herself; carried away by the sophisms of her imagination, she gives herself magnificently, generously, in an altogether masculine way, to contemptible men who are not her equals, just as poets surrender to contemptible women.

Another proof of the altogether virile quality that flows in her veins is the fact that this ill-fated woman cares less about the visible, external imperfections and the glaring provincialisms of her husband than about that total lack of genius, that spiritual inferiority so clearly demonstrated by the stupid operation on the clubfoot.

And in this connection re-read the pages containing this episode which, though unjustly termed extraneous, really brings the whole character of the person into sharp focus.—A black anger, long repressed, breaks loose in Emma's whole being; doors slam; the astonished husband, who has been unable to give his romantic wife any spiritual enjoyment, is relegated to his room; the ignorant culprit is in disgrace, and Madame Bovary in despair cries out like a lesser Lady Macbeth mated with an incompetent master: "Ah! why couldn't I *at least* be the wife of one of those bald and stooped old scientists whose eyes, shielded by green eyeshades, are always fixed on scientific documents! I could lean on his arm with pride; at least I would be the companion of an intellectual king; but to be chained to this idiot who can't even straighten the foot of a cripple! Oh!"

Truly this woman is very sublime in her way, given her limited environment and the small horizon by which she was bound.

4. Even in her convent education I find proof of Madame Bovary's equivocal temperament.

The good sisters noticed in this young girl an astonishing capacity for life, for getting the best out of life, for suspecting its pleasures; there you have the man of action!

Meanwhile the young girl reveled in the color of the stained glass, in the oriental hues which the tall, elaborately designed windows cast on her convent school prayerbook; she gorged herself on the solemn vesper music and, by a paradox which may be credited to nerves, she replaced the real God in her heart by the God of her imagination, the God of the future and of chance, a picture-book God with spurs and a mustache; and there you have the hysterical poet!

Hysteria! Why couldn't this physiological mystery be made the sum and substance of a literary work—this mystery which the Academy of Medicine has not yet solved and which, manifesting itself in women by the sensation of a lump in the throat that seems to rise (I am mentioning only the chief symptom), shows itself in excitable men by every kind of impotence as well as by a tendency toward every kind of excess?

In short, this woman is truly great and above all pitiable. Despite the systematic severity of the author, who has made every effort to remain outside of his book and to assume the role of a manipulator of marionettes, all *intellectual* women will be grateful to him for having raised the female to so high a level—so far from the pure animal and so near to the ideal man—and for having made her share in that combination of calculation and reverie which constitutes the perfect being.

It is said that Madame Bovary is ridiculous. It is true that at one moment she mistakes for a Walter Scott hero a silly gentleman—shall I say a country gentleman?—wearing hunting jackets and flashy suits, and that at still another moment she is in love with a junior clerk in a lawyer's office (who isn't even clever enough to commit a dangerous action for his mistress), and that finally the poor spent creature, a strange Pasiphaë, isolated within the narrow enclosure of a village, pursues the ideal in the low dance halls and the taverns of the prefecture. Yet, what does it matter? We may as well admit it frankly—she is like Caesar at Carpentras, she is seeking the Ideal!

I shall certainly not say, like the Lycanthrope of revolutionary fame [Pétrus Borel]—that rebel who abdicated: "In the face of all the platitudes and stupidities of the present day, don't we still have cigarette paper and adultery?" But I shall maintain that after all, everything considered, even with the most accurate scales, our world is very cruel for having been begotten by Christ, that it is hardly entitled to cast a stone at adultery; and that a few Minotaurized persons more or less will not hasten the rotating speed of the spheres or advance by one second the final destruction of the universe. It is time to put an end to an increasingly contagious hypocrisy and to consider it ridiculous for men and women, deeply corrupted as they are, to denounce an unfortunate author who in modest and reserved language has deigned to cast an aureole over bedroom adventures, always repulsive and grotesque when Poetry does not soften them with the gleam of its opaline nightlight.

If I allowed myself to go on in this analytical vein, I should never have done with *Madame Bovary;* this essentially suggestive book could inspire a volume of observations. For the time being I shall confine myself to pointing out that several of the most important episodes were originally either ignored or abusively attacked by the critics. Examples: the episode of the unsuccessful operation on the clubfoot, and the one, so remarkable, so full of desolation, so truly *modern,* where the future adulteress—for the unhappy woman is still only at the beginning of the downward path!—goes to ask help of the Church, of the divine Mother, of Her who has no excuse for not being always ready, of that Pharmacy where no one has the right to slumber! The good priest Bournisien, concerned only with the scamps in his catechism class, jumping around among the choir stalls and chairs of the church, answers in all innocence: "Since you are ill, Madame, and since M. Bovary is a doctor, *why don't you go and find your husband?"*

What woman confronted by the inadequacy of the priest wouldn't go, like someone released from a madhouse, to plunge her head into the whirling waters of adultery—and who among us in troubled circumstances and at a more unsophisticated age has not inevitably come to know the incompetent priest?

—CHARLES BAUDELAIRE, "*Madame Bovary* by Gustave Flaubert" [1857], *Baudelaire as a Literary Critic,* tr. Lois Boe Hyslop and Francis E. Hyslop, Jr. (University Park: Pennsylvania State University Press, 1964), pp. 144–48

GEORGE SAINTSBURY

I never myself read *Madame Bovary* without thinking of another masterpiece of French fiction; and I have no doubt that the comparison has occurred to others also. *Madame Bovary* and *Manon Lescaut* are both histories of women whose conduct no theory of morality, however lax, can possibly excuse. Both are brought to ruin by their love of material luxury. Both are not only immoral, but cruelly unfaithful to men who in different ways are perfectly true and faithful to them. Both perish miserably, not in either case without repentance. Why does Emma Bovary repel while Manon Lescaut irresistibly attracts us? I think the answer is to be found in the ignoble character of the former as compared with Manon. The mistress of Desgrieux loves wealth, splendour, sensuous gratification of all sorts, for themselves, with a kind of artistic passion. They are the first necessity to her, and everything else comes second to this passionate devotion. On the other hand, Madame Bovary sets up lovers, spends her husband's money, cheats and deceives him, because it seems to her the proper thing to do. Her countesses and duchesses all had lovers and gorgeous garments, so she must have gorgeous garments and lovers too. Her first reflection after transgressing is almost comic—"J'ai un amant!" She has a sort of Dogberry-like conviction that a pretty woman ought to have a lover and everything handsome about her, the same sort of conviction which more harmlessly leads her English sisters to be miserable if they have not a drawing-room with a couch and chairs, and a chimney-glass, and gilt books on the table. Her excesses come from a variety of feminine snobbery, and are not prompted by any frank passion or desire.

—GEORGE SAINTSBURY, "Gustave Flaubert" [1878], *Collected Essays and Papers* (London: J. M. Dent, 1924), Vol. 4, pp. 37–38

MATTHEW ARNOLD

Much in *Anna Karénine* is painful, much is unpleasant, but nothing is of a nature to trouble the senses, or to please those who wish their senses troubled. This taint is wholly absent. In the French novels where it is so abundantly present its baneful effects do not end with itself. Burns long ago remarked with deep truth that it *petrifies feeling*. Let us revert for a moment to the powerful novel of which I spoke at the outset, *Madame Bovary*. Undoubtedly the taint in question is present in *Madame Bovary*, although to a much less degree than in more recent French novels which will be in every one's mind. But *Madame Bovary*, with this taint, is a work of *petrified feeling*; over it hangs an atmosphere of bitterness, irony, impotence; not a personage in the book to rejoice or console us; the springs of freshness and feeling are not there to create such personages. Emma Bovary follows a course in some respects like that of Anna, but where, in Emma Bovary, is Anna's charm? The treasures of compassion, tenderness, insight, which alone, amid such guilt and misery, can enable charm to subsist and to emerge, are wanting to Flaubert. He is cruel, with the cruelty of petrified feeling, to his poor heroine; he pursues her without pity or pause, as with malignity; he is harder upon her himself than any reader even, I think, will be inclined to be.

—MATTHEW ARNOLD, "Count Leo Tolstoi" [1887], *Essays in Criticism: Second Series* (London: Macmillan, 1888)

EMILE FAGUET

Mme. Bovary's eternal aspiration was to live beyond the horizon. Now, as she advances in life, the same yearning remains, but the horizon grows nearer, and the 'beyond' is no longer so far away. At first, Emma used to dream of distant journeyings, exotic scenery, gondolas and jungles. Later, she dreamt of Paris and its splendours. Now, her 'beyond the horizon' is at Rouen, a room in an inn on the quay, with a notary's clerk.

And she is unconscious of this diminishing, this lowering of her ideals; we only suspect that she feels it in a confused way. It would seem so when we look at her constant pursuit after excitement, and at the need, so new in her, *not to dream*, but to flee from herself in a sort of turmoil. Emma is very far now from what she was without having ceased to be the same person; the last effects of the adventures into which her temperament has dragged her both modify that temperament itself and give it the lie. Then the crash comes. Ruined, led into debts unknown to her husband by her extravagance and the carelessness of her housekeeping, Emma finds herself face to face with death or with deepest degradation. She chooses death. Why? It must be acknowledged that there is no very decisive reason. Mme. Bovary *might* have slipped to the bottom of the incline. She *might* have fled, leaving her husband and her child, and thrown herself into a life of prostitution. And it is precisely in order to show that it *might* have been so that Flaubert has led her to the very edge of that path, and has even made her take a few steps along it. It is like a prostitute to say to Léon: 'Money! If I were you I should know where to find some. In your office.' It is like a prostitute to go and implore the notary whom she knows to be an admirer of pretty women. It is like a prostitute to go and beg money of Rodolphe, her former lover, who has forsaken her. By all this, Flaubert points out that Emma very nearly fell to the lowest depths, and that, if it was not to be her fate, it is that of women who resemble her. However, he has stopped her just as she was entering this path, partly on account of her horror at entering it.

He was right. Emma was not born a courtesan. She was born with a romantic turn of mind which brought her to become almost a courtesan; yet she must stop and draw back when her life unfolds itself to her as being henceforth that of a courtesan *without any romantic features*. Emma, deprived of all element of romance, even merely apparent, can only die. For what would her life become henceforth? It would be a *real* life, as hopelessly real as the *bourgeois* life which she so hated. It is reality that Mme. Bovary never could admit. There are four stages: the period of dreams without a precise object; the period of dreams arrested and fixed on the man who is thought capable of realising them; the period of sensual folly and voluptuous delirium still mingled with some poetry in pleasure, and a feeling that a romance is still being lived, howbeit a vulgar one; finally the period of merely lucrative *amours,* which are a trade like that of M. Lheureux. This last stage opens before Mme. Bovary and she does not enter it. She feels that here she would really be deprived of her breathing atmosphere, that is, the feeling she has for brilliant or remarkable things, literary things that one could put in a book. When her romantic soul is killed by the necessities of Reality, Emma dies wholly. Her reason for living has now entirely disappeared. Her suicide is not caused by remorse, not exactly by despair; it is the outcome of a long bruising of dreams, of dreams suppressed and disappointed, until the feeling is reached that they will never arise again.

—EMILE FAGUET, "The Realist: *Madame Bovary," Flaubert* [1899],
tr. Mrs. R. L. Devonshire (London: Constable, 1914), pp. 122–25

HENRY JAMES

His imagination was great and splendid; in spite of which, strangely enough, his masterpiece is not his most imaginative work. *Madame Bovary,* beyond question, holds that first place, and *Madame Bovary* is concerned with the career of a country doctor's wife in a petty Norman town. The elements of the picture are of the fewest, the situation of the heroine almost of the meanest, the material for interest, considering the interest yielded, of the most unpromising; but these facts only throw into relief one of those incalculable incidents that attend the proceedings of genius. *Madame Bovary* was doomed by circumstances and causes—the freshness of comparative youth and good faith on the author's part being perhaps the chief—definitely to take its position, even though its subject was fundamentally a negation of the remote, the splendid and the strange, the stuff of his fondest and most cultivated dreams. It would have seemed very nearly to exclude the free play of the imagination, and the way this faculty on the author's part nevertheless presides is one of those accidents, manœuvres, inspirations, we hardly know what to call them, by which masterpieces grow. He of course knew more or less what he was doing for his book in making Emma Bovary a victim of the imaginative habit, but he must have been far from designing or measuring the total effect which renders the work so general, so complete an expression of himself. His separate idiosyncrasies, his irritated sensibility to the life about him, with the power to catch it in the fact and hold it hard, and his hunger for style and history and poetry, for the rich and the rare, great reverberations, great adumbrations, are here represented together as they are not in his later writings. There is nothing of the near, of the directly observed, though there may be much of the directly perceived and the minutely detailed, either in *Salammbô* or in *Saint-Antoine,* and little enough of the extravagance of illusion in that indefinable last word of restrained evocation and cold execution *L'Éducation sentimentale.* M. Faguet has of course excellently noted this—that the fortune and felicity of the book were assured by the stroke that made the central figure an embodiment of helpless romanticism. Flaubert himself but narrowly escaped being such an embodiment after all, and he is thus able to express the romantic mind with extraordinary truth. As to the rest of the matter he had the luck of having been in possession from the first, having begun so early to nurse and work up his plan that, familiarity and the native air, the native soil, aiding, he had finally made out to the last lurking shade the small sordid sunny dusty village picture, its emptiness constituted and peopled. It is in the background and the accessories that the real, the real of his theme, abides; and the romantic, the romantic of his theme, accordingly occupies the front. Emma Bovary's poor adventures are a tragedy for the very reason that in a world unsuspecting, unassisting, unconsoling, she has herself to distil the rich and the rare. Ignorant, unguided, undiverted, ridden by the very nature and mixture of her consciousness, she makes of the business an inordinate failure, a failure which in its turn makes for Flaubert the most pointed, the most *told* of anecdotes. ⟨. . .⟩

And yet it is not after all that the place the book has taken is so overwhelmingly explained by its inherent dignity; for here comes in the curiosity of the matter. Here comes in especially its fund of admonition for alien readers. The dignity of its substance is the dignity of Madame Bovary herself as a vessel of experience—a question as to which, unmistakably, I judge, we can only depart from the consensus of French critical opinion. M. Faguet for example commends the character of the heroine as one of the most living and discriminated figures of women in all literature, praises it as a field for the display of the romantic spirit that leaves nothing to be desired. Subject to an observation I shall presently make and that bears heavily in general, I think, on Flaubert as a painter of life, subject to this restriction he is right; which is a proof that a work of art may be markedly open to objection and at the same time be rare in its kind, and that when it is perfect to this point nothing else particularly matters. *Madame Bovary* has a perfection that not only stamps it, but that makes it stand almost alone; it holds itself with such a supreme unapproachable assurance as both excites and defies judgment. For it deals not in the least, as to unapproachability, with things exalted or refined; it only confers on its sufficiently vulgar elements of exhibition a final unsurpassable form. The form is in *itself* as interesting, as active, as much of the essence of the subject as the idea, and yet so close is its fit and so inseparable its life that we catch it at no moment on any errand of its own. That verily is to *be* interesting—all round; that is to be genuine and whole. The work is a classic because the thing, such as it is, is ideally *done,* and because it shows that in such doing eternal beauty may dwell. A pretty young woman who lives, socially and morally speaking, in a hole, and who is ignorant, foolish, flimsy, unhappy, takes a pair of lovers by whom she is successively deserted; in the midst of the bewilderment of which, giving up her husband and her child, letting everything go, she sinks deeper into duplicity, debt, despair, and arrives on the spot, on the small scene itself of her poor depravities, at a pitiful tragic end. In especial she does these things while remaining absorbed in romantic intention and vision, and she remains absorbed in romantic intention and vision while fairly rolling in the dust. That is the triumph of the book as the triumph stands, that Emma interests us by the nature of her consciousness and the play of her mind, thanks to the reality and beauty with which those sources are invested. It is not only that they represent *her* state; they are so true, so observed and felt, and especially so shown, that they represent the state, actual or potential, of all persons like her, persons romantically determined. Then her setting, the medium in which she struggles, becomes in its way as important, becomes eminent with the eminence of art; the tiny world in which she revolves, the contracted cage in which she flutters, is hung out in space for her, and her companions in captivity there are as true as herself.

I have said enough to show what I mean by Flaubert's having in this picture expressed something of his intimate self, given his heroine something of his own imagination: a point precisely that brings me back to the restriction at which I just now hinted, in which M. Faguet fails to indulge and yet which is immediate for the alien reader. Our complaint is that Emma Bovary, in spite of the nature of her consciousness and in spite of her reflecting so much that of her creator, is really too small an affair. This, critically speaking, is in view both of the value and the fortune of her history, a wonderful circumstance. She associates herself with Frédéric Moreau in *L'Éducation* to suggest for us a question that can be answered, I hold, only to Flaubert's detriment. Emma taken alone would possibly not so directly press it, but in her company the hero of our author's second study of the "real" drives it home. Why did Flaubert choose, as special conduits of the life he proposed to depict, such inferior and in the case of Frédéric such abject human specimens? I insist only in respect to the latter, the perfection of Madame Bovary scarce leaving one much warrant for wishing anything other. Even here, however, the general scale and size of Emma, who is small even of her sort, should be a warning to hyperbole. If I say that in the matter of Frédéric at all events the answer is inevitably detrimental I mean that it weighs heavily on our author's general credit. He wished in each case to make a picture of experience—middling experience, it is true—and of the world close to him; but if he imagined nothing better for his purpose than such a heroine and such a hero, both such limited reflectors and registers, we are forced to believe it to have been by a defect of his mind. And that sign of weakness remains even if it be objected that the images in question were addressed to his purpose better than others would have been: the purpose itself then shows as inferior. L'Éducation sentimentale is a strange, an indescribable work, about which there would be many more things to say than I have space for, and all of them of the deepest interest. It is moreover, to simplify my statement, very much less satisfying a thing, less pleasing whether in its unity or its variety, than its specific predecessor. But take it as we will, for a success or a failure—M. Faguet indeed ranks it, by the measure of its quantity of intention, a failure, and I on the whole agree with him—the personage offered us as bearing the weight of the drama, and in whom we are invited to that extent to interest ourselves, leaves us mainly wondering what our entertainer could have been thinking of. He takes Frédéric Moreau on the threshold of life and conducts him to the extreme of maturity without apparently suspecting for a moment either our wonder or our protest—"Why, why *him?*" Frédéric is positively too poor for his part, too scant for his charge; and we feel with a kind of embarrassment, certainly with a kind of compassion, that it is somehow the business of a protagonist to prevent in his designer an excessive waste of faith. When I speak of the faith in Emma Bovary as proportionately wasted I reflect on M. Faguet's judgment that she is from the point of view of deep interest richly or at least roundedly representative. Representative of what? he makes us ask even while granting all the grounds of misery and tragedy involved. The plea for her is the plea made for all the figures that live without evaporation under the painter's hand—that they are not only particular persons but types of their kind, and as valid in one light as in the other. It is Emma's "kind" that I question for this responsibility, even if it be inquired of me why I then fail to question that of Charles Bovary, in its perfection, or that of the inimitable, the immortal Homais. If we express Emma's deficiency as the poverty of her consciousness for the typical function, it is certainly not, one must admit, that she is surpassed in this respect either by her platitudinous husband or by his friend the pretentious apothecary. The difference is none the less somehow in the fact that they are respectively studies but of their character and office, which function in each expresses adequately *all* they are. It may be, I concede, because Emma is the only woman in the book that she is taken by M. Faguet as *femininely* typical, typical in the larger illustrative way, whereas the others pass with him for images specifically conditioned. Emma is this same for myself, I plead; she is conditioned to such an excess of the specific, and the specific in her case leaves out so many even of the commoner elements of conceivable life in a woman when we are invited to see that life as pathetic, as dramatic agitation, that we challenge both the author's and the critic's scale of importances. The book is a picture of the middling as much as they like, but does Emma attain even to *that?* Hers is a narrow middling even for a little imaginative person whose "social" significance is small. It is greater on the whole than her capacity of consciousness, taking this all round; and so, in a word, we feel her less illustrational than she might have been not only if the world had offered her more points of contact, but if she had had more of these to give it.

—HENRY JAMES, "Gustave Flaubert" [1902], *Notes on Novelists* (New York: Scribner's, 1914), pp. 75–77, 79–84

PERCY LUBBOCK

As for his subject, it is of course Emma Bovary in the first place; the book is the portrait of a foolish woman, romantically inclined, in small and prosaic conditions. She is in the centre of it all, certainly; there is no doubt of her position in the book. But *why* is she there? The true subject of the novel is not given, as we saw, by a mere summary of the course which is taken by the story. She may be there for her own sake, simply, or for the sake of the predicament in which she stands; she may be presented as a curious scrap of character, fit to be studied; or Flaubert may have been struck by her as the instrument, the victim, the occasion, of a particular train of events. Perhaps she is a creature portrayed because he thinks her typical and picturesque; perhaps she is a disturbing little force let loose among the lives that surround her; perhaps, on the other hand, she is a hapless sufferer in the clash between her aspirations and her fate. Given Emma and what she is by nature, given her environment and the facts of her story, there are dozens of different subjects, I dare say, latent in the case. The woman, the men, all they say and do, the whole scene behind them—none of it gives any clue to the right manner of treating them. The one irreducible idea out of which the book, as Flaubert wrote it, unfolds—this it is that must be sought.

Now if Emma was devised for her own sake, solely because a nature and a temper like hers seemed to Flaubert an amusing study—if his one aim was to make the portrait of a woman of that kind—then the rest of the matter falls into line, we shall know how to regard it. These conditions in which Emma finds herself will have been chosen by the author because they appeared to throw light on her, to call out her natural qualities, to give her the best opportunity of disclosing what she is. Her stupid husband and her fascinating lovers will enter the scene in order that she may become whatever she has it in her to be. Flaubert elects to place her in a certain provincial town, full of odd characters; he gives the town and its folk an extraordinary actuality; it is not a town *quelconque,* not a generalized town, but as individual and recognizable as he can make it. None the less—always supposing that Emma by herself is the whole of his subject—he must have lit on this particular town simply because it seemed to explain and expound her better than another. If he had thought that a woman of her sort, rather meanly ambitious, rather fatuously romantic, would have revealed her quality more intensely in a different world—in success, freedom, wealth—he would have placed her otherwise; Charles and Rodolphe and Homard and the rest of them would have vanished, the more illuminating set of circumstances (whatever they might be) would have appeared instead. Emma's world as it is at present, in the book that Flaubert wrote, would have to be regarded, accordingly, as all a *consequence* of Emma, invented to do her a service, described in order that they may make the description of *her*. Her world, that is to say, would belong to the treatment of the story; none of it, not her husband, not the life of the market-town, would be a part of the author's postulate, the groundwork of his fable; it would be possible to imagine a different setting, better, it might be, than that which Flaubert has chosen. All this—*if* the subject of the book is nothing but the portrait of such a woman.

But of course it is not so; one glance at our remembrance of the book is enough to show it. Emma's world could not be other than it is, she could not be shifted into richer and larger conditions, without destroying the whole point and purpose of Flaubert's novel. She by herself is not the subject of his book. What he proposes to exhibit is the history of a woman like her in just such a world as hers, a foolish woman in narrow circumstances; so that the provincial scene, acting upon her, making her what she becomes, is as essential as she is herself. Not a portrait, therefore, not a study of character for its own sake, but something in the nature of a drama, where the two chief players are a woman on one side and her whole environment on the other—that is *Madame Bovary*. There is a conflict, a trial of strength, and a doubtful issue. Emma is not much of a force, no doubt; her impulses are wild, her emotions are thin and poor, she has no power of passion with which to fight the world. All she has is her romantic dream and her plain, primitive appetite; but these can be effective arms, after all, and she may yet succeed in getting her way and making her own terms. On the other hand the limitations of her life are very blank and uncompromising indeed; they close all round her, hampering her flights, restricting her opportunities. The drama is set, at any rate, whatever may come of it; Emma marries her husband, is established at Yonville and faced with the poverty of her situation. Something will result, the issue will announce itself. It is the mark of a dramatic case that it contains an opposition of some kind, a pair of wills that collide, an action that pulls in two directions; and so far *Madame Bovary* has the look of a drama. Flaubert might work on the book from that point of view and throw the emphasis on the issue. The middle of his subject would then be found in the struggle between Emma and all that constitutes her life, between her romantic dreams and her besetting facts. The question is what will happen.

But then again—that is not exactly the question in this book. Obviously the emphasis is not upon the commonplace little events of Emma's career. They might, no doubt, be the steps in a dramatic tale, but they are nothing of the kind as Flaubert handles them. He makes it perfectly clear that his view is not centred upon the actual outcome of Emma's predicament, whether it will issue this way or that; *what* she does or fails to do is of very small moment. Her passages with Rodolphe and with Léon are pictures that pass; they solve nothing, they lead to no climax. Rodolphe's final rejection of her, for example, is no scene of drama, deciding a question that has been held in suspense; it is one of Emma's various mischances, with its own marked effect upon *her*, but it does not stand out in the book as a turning-point in the action. She goes her way and acts out her history; but of whatever suspense, whatever dramatic value, there might be in it Flaubert makes nothing, he evidently considers it of no account. Who, in recalling the book, thinks of the chain of incident that runs through it, compared with the long and living impression of a few of the people in it and of the place in which they are set? None of the events really matter for their own sake; they might have happened differ-ently, not one of them is indispensable as it is. Emma must certainly have made what she could of her opportunities of romance, but they need not necessarily have appeared in the shape of Léon or Rodolphe; she would have found others if these had not been at hand. The *events,* therefore, Emma's excursions to Rouen, her forest-rides, her one or two memorable adventures in the world, all these are only Flaubert's way of telling his subject, of making it count to the eye. They are not in themselves what he has to say, they simply illustrate it.

What it comes to, I take it, is that though *Madame Bovary,* the novel, is a kind of drama—since there is the interaction of this woman confronted by these facts—it is a drama chosen for the sake of the picture in it, for the impression it gives of the manner in which certain lives are lived. It might have another force of its own; it might be a strife of characters and wills, in which the men and women would take the matter into their own hands and make all the interest by their action; it might be a drama, say, as *Jane Eyre* is a drama, where another obscure little woman has a part to play, but where the question is how she plays it, what she achieves or misses in particular. To Flaubert the situation out of which he made his novel appeared in another light. It was not as dramatic as it was pictorial; there was not the stuff in Emma, more especially, that could make her the main figure of a drama; she is small and futile, she could not well uphold an interest that would depend directly on her behaviour. But for a picture, where the interest depends only on what she *is*—that is quite different. Her futility is then a real value; it can be made amusing and vivid to the last degree, so long as no other weight is thrown on it; she can make a perfect impression of life, though she cannot create much of a story. Let Emma and her plight, therefore, appear as a picture; let her be shown in the act of living her life, entangled as it is with her past and her present; that is how the final fact at the heart of Flaubert's subject will be best displayed.

Here is the clue, it seems, to his treatment of the theme. It is pictorial, and its object is to make Emma's existence as intelligible and visible as may be. We who read the book are to share her sense of life, till no uncertainty is left in it; we are to see and understand her experience, and to see *her* while she enjoys or endures it; we are to be placed within her world, to get the immediate taste of it, and outside her world as well, to get the full effect, more of it than she herself could see. Flaubert's subject demands no less, if the picture is to be complete. She herself must be known thoroughly—that is his first care; the movement of her mind is to be watched at work in all the ardour and the poverty of her imagination. How she creates her makeshift romances, how she feeds on them, how they fail her—it is all part of the picture. And then there is the dull and limited world in which her appetite is somehow to be satisfied, the small town that shuts her in and cuts her off; this, too, is to be rendered, and in order to make it clearly tell beside the figure of Emma it must be as distinct and individual, as thoroughly characterized as she is. It is more than a setting for Emma and her intrigue; it belongs to the book integrally, much more so than the accidental lovers who fall in Emma's way. They are mere occasions and attractions for her fancy; the town and the *curé* and the apothecary and the other indigenous gossips need a sharper definition. And accordingly Flaubert treats the scenery of his book, Yonville and its odd types, as intensely as he treats his heroine; he broods over it with concentration and gives it all the salience he can. The town with its life is not behind his heroine, subdued in tone to make a background; it is *with* her, no less fully to the front; its value in the picture is as strong as her own.

Such is the picture that Flaubert's book is to present. And what, then, of the point of view towards which it is to be directed? If it is to have that unity which it needs to produce its right effect there can be no uncertainty here, no arbitrary shifting of the place from which an onlooker faces it. And in the tale of *Madame Bovary* the question of the right point of view might be considerably perplexing. Where is Flaubert to find his centre of vision?—from what point, within the book or without, will the unfolding of the subject be commanded most effectively? The difficulty is this—that while one aspect of his matter can only be seen from within, through the eyes of the woman, another must inevitably be seen from without, through nobody's eyes but the author's own. Part of his subject is Emma's sense of her world; we must see how it impresses her and what she makes of it, how it thwarts her and how her imagination contrives to get a kind of sustenance out of it. The book is not really written at all unless it shows her view of things, as the woman she was, in that place, in those conditions. For this reason it is essential to pass into her consciousness, to make her *subjective;* and Flaubert takes care to do so and to make her so, as soon as she enters the book. But it is also enjoined by the story, as we found, that her place and conditions should be seen for what they are and known as intimately as herself. For this matter Emma's capacity fails.

Her intelligence is much too feeble and fitful to give a sufficient account of her world. The town of Yonville would be very poorly revealed to us if Flaubert had to keep within the measure of *her* perceptions; it would be thin and blank, it would be barely more than a dull background for the beautiful apparition of the men she desires. What were her neighbours to her? They existed in her consciousness only as tiresome interruptions and drawbacks, except now and then when she had occasion to make use of them. But to us, to the onlooker, they belong to her portrait, they represent the dead weight of provincial life which is the outstanding fact in her case. Emma's rudimentary idea of them is entirely inadequate; she has not a vestige of the humour and irony that is needed to give them shape. Moreover they affect her far more forcibly and more variously than she could even suspect; a sharper wit than hers must evidently intervene, helping out the primitive workings of her mind. Her pair of eyes is not enough; the picture beheld through them is a poor thing in itself, for she can see no more than her mind can grasp; and it does her no justice either, since she herself is so largely the creation of her surroundings.

It is a dilemma that appears in any story, wherever the matter to be represented is the experience of a simple soul or a dull intelligence. If it is the experience and the actual taste of it that is to be imparted, the story must be viewed as the poor creature saw it; and yet the poor creature cannot tell the story in full. A shift of the vision is necessary. And in *Madame Bovary,* it is to be noted, there is no one else within the book who is in a position to take up the tale when Emma fails. There is no other personage upon the scene who sees and understands any more than she; perception and discrimination are not to be found in Yonville at all—it is an essential point. The author's wit, therefore, and none other, must supply what is wanting. This necessity, to a writer of Flaubert's acute sense of effect, is one that demands a good deal of caution. The transition must be made without awkwardness, without calling attention to it. Flaubert is not the kind of story-teller who will leave it undisguised; he will not begin by "going behind" Emma, giving her view, and then openly, confessedly, revert to his own character and use his own standards. There is nothing more disconcerting in a novel than to *see* the writer changing his part in this way—throwing off the character into which he has been projecting himself and taking a new stand outside and away from the story.

Perhaps it is only Thackeray, among the great, who seems to find a positively wilful pleasure in damaging his own story by open maltreatment of this kind; there are times when Thackeray will even boast of his own independence, insisting in so many words on his freedom to say what he pleases about his men and women and to make them behave as he will. But without using Thackeray's licence a novelist may still do his story an ill turn by leaving too naked a contrast between the subjective picture of what passes through Emma's mind—Emma's or Becky's, as it may be—and the objective rendering of what he sees for himself, between the experience that is mirrored in another thought and that which is shaped in his own. When one has lived *into* the experience of somebody in the story and received the full sense of it, to be wrenched out of the story and stationed at a distance is a shock that needs to be softened and muffled in some fashion. Otherwise it may weaken whatever was true and valid in the experience; for here is a new view of it, external and detached, and another mind at work, the author's—and that sense of having shared the life of the person in the story seems suddenly unreal.

Flaubert's way of disguising the inconsistency is not a peculiar art of his own, I dare say. Even in him it was probably quite unconscious, well as he was aware of most of the refinements of his craft; and perhaps it is only a sleight of hand that might come naturally to any good storyteller. But it is interesting to follow Flaubert's method to the very end, for it holds out so consummately; and I think it is possible to define it here. I should say, then, that he deals with the difficulty I have described by keeping Emma always at a certain distance, even when he appears to be entering her mind most freely. He makes her subjective, places us so that we see through her eyes—yes; but he does so with an air of aloofness that forbids us ever to become entirely identified with her. This is how she thought and felt, he seems to say; look and you will understand; such is the soul of this foolish woman. A hint of irony is always perceptible, and it is enough to prevent us from being lost in her consciousness, immersed in it beyond easy recall. The woman's life is very real, perfectly felt; but the reader is made to accept his participation in it as a pleasing experiment, the kind of thing that appeals to a fastidious curiosity—there is no question of its ever being more than this. The *fact* of Emma is taken with entire seriousness, of course; she is there to be studied and explored, and no means of understanding her point of view will be neglected. But her value is another matter; as to that Flaubert never has an instant's illusion, he always knows her to be worthless.

—PERCY LUBBOCK, *The Craft of Fiction* [1921] (New York: Jonathan Cape & Harrison Smith, 1931), pp. 78–89

MRS. HAROLD SANDWITH

'She rejected everything which did not lend itself to being immediately consumed by her heart.'

With this single sentence, culled haphazard from amongst a number of no less pregnant ones, Flaubert—the great master-painter of the feminine heart—throws for us upon the canvas of fiction a vivid portrait of Emma Bovary.

If Becky Sharp is the type of the woman without a heart, Emma Bovary is the type of the woman who makes an idol of her heart; who, to this insatiable Moloch, recklessly sacrifices her honour, her principles, her chances of happiness in this world and the next; whose career ends in tragedy more complete, more terrible—but more noble also—than that of Becky, because it is never tainted by any sordid motive.

'Je suis à plaindre mais non pas à vendre.' In these redeeming words from her own lips we find the keynote of Emma Bovary's life.

For those who come to grief by their hearts there always seems to remain a hope of ultimate redemption. Their ruin appears at once more final and less so, because the human heart holds infinite possibilities for regeneration, even beyond this mortal sphere.

Emma, waving goodbye to Charles Bovary as she stands on her father's doorstep—with the melting snow falling in heavy drops upon her pigeon-breast coloured sunshade—Emma, the youthful bride, lost in melancholy reflections before her predecessor's wedding bouquet—Emma, the wife, smiling farewell to her husband over the flowering plants at her window—whose heart has not yearned over her?

What heart of man or woman has not ached for the struggles and sufferings of this passionate woman's soul—for this woman who sees her dream of love fade into the cruel reality of a commonplace marriage—who sees her lover and hero of romance transformed by the crude light of everyday life into the husband 'whose conversation is as flat as a pavement on which everybody's opinions are trotting about'; into the husband who, after exchanging his muddy boots for his house slippers and enjoying a full meal, kisses his wife at 'stated times,' and falls asleep placidly, with his cotton nightcap all awry upon his ruffled hair.

How many a sensitive, nobly planned woman—how many an exceptional man—how many, alas, relive in the perusal of these masterly pages of Flaubert's the tragedy of their own lives.

Emma, the little girl who, in the country inn, had gazed with almost intuitive understanding and wonder upon the plates depicting scenes from Madame Lavallière's life—Emma, who had prayed with such fervour among the nuns at her convent school, who had grieved so extravagantly for the loss of her mother, trying at that early age even, to introduce some dramatic element into the monotony of her life—this Emma is the same incorrigible romantic Emma still who naïvely, and alas vainly strives with her music and poetry to instil some poetic ardour into her commonplace husband's soul. And this Emma, despite the underlying hardness and selfishness of her nature, and even though absorbed in an egotistic quest for happiness, is not without a strange nobility and magnanimity of her own.

She does not, after the approved manner of wives, lay the blame for the failure of her married life at her husband's door. Not until long after, not until she feels the need for self-justification. No, with unconscious pathos she comes to the conclusion (how many of us have not been tempted to arrive at it likewise), that 'the poets must have exaggerated,' that love—such as we all dream of—is for the elect only, for the favoured few, for those who dwell in castles, in mansions, and in the antechambers of kings. That love is reserved for lords and their ladies, for knights and their chatelaines, that love—like some exotic plant—requires a special soil for its growth.

How was she—the simple farmer's daughter—to know that this special soil is to be found in the heart of each one of us, who may care to cultivate it.

But Emma Bovary, like Becky Sharp, is a woman of infinite possibilities.

In this fact lie both her condemnation and her justification.

From the first it is evident that the woman who, in the words of the shrewd apothecary, 'would not have been out of place in a *sous-préfecture,*' is utterly wasted upon Charles Bovary, although (oh wasteful and ironic tragedy of life) he, too, with the rest, has to go to his doom through her.

Like all women of her type Emma is destined to become '*la femme fatale*' for both high and low, indiscriminately. None can escape her charm. All must in the end be the victims of her fateful spell.

A glamour—unearthly, intangible, spiritual almost—seems to hover around this passionate woman.

Who is there that could have withstood her charm? Who that would have resisted her, running recklessly at dawn through the dew-damp meadows to her lover's home, bursting like the radiance of a spring morning into his chamber—with the dewdrops sparkling in her dark locks and upon her fine lashes?

What man would not, like Rodolphe himself, have taken her to his heart? Ah! but what man, having once held such a woman to his breast—so passionate, so romantic, so sensuous and so spiritual, so baffling, so bewitching a creature—what man could ever after think of another, could dare to profane such a memory?

The history of Emma Bovary is not the history of the ordinary disappointed married woman who, seeking an outlet for her pent-up nature, falls an easy prey to the first-comer.

In the description of her life Flaubert shows himself the great moralist that he is.

Like his English contemporary—the portrayer of Becky Sharp—he never for an instant confounds evil with the condonation of evil. But more than this. As written by Flaubert, the life-story of Emma Bovary is the story of a woman who almost to the last wrestles like Jacob of old with the angel of a higher self. ⟨...⟩

If Emma, in the place of the gentle and pious nuns, whose somewhat sentimental morality and utter ignorance of the realities of woman's life and duties and temptations in the world, made of them but ill-suited guardians for a girl of so complex and dangerous a temperament, if instead of them Emma had by her side a strong personality, endowed with sound moral principles and with common sense, yet not lacking in lofty ideals and in understanding for her conflicting nature, she might then have turned the failure of her married life into success.

Is not this what Flaubert suggests with subtlety in every line of his incomparable psychological analysis of this complex woman's nature?

But Emma's childhood and youth had been spent without any such guiding and invigorating influence. And now, stranded between the shattered dreams of girlhood romance and the sordid realities of life, in the uncongenial surroundings of a little market town, with all her finer instincts in revolt, the subtle poison imbibed in that fateful visit to the Marquis de La Vaubesseyard, in that glimpse of a world beyond her reach, had ample opportunity to work its way into her nature, into a nature crying out to be satisfied, crying out for fuller knowledge of life and of its possibilities.

Doubtless, in a common-place woman the birth of her child would have killed all romantic dreams and aspirations, would, at any rate, have regulated and directed them into normal channels. But for a woman of Emma's temperament, of her fineness and justice of instinct, motherhood—robbed of all romance and poetry, of all spiritual meaning by the contact with an inferior partner—could only intensify the suffering, could only be an additional drop in her cup of bitterness.

Is not this one of the tragic ironies of life, that the ideal citizens, those least disposed to rebel against the 'common task,' those most likely to fulfil it satisfactorily, are also likely to be the man and woman devoid of finer instincts, devoid of everything which makes the human heart a priceless possession, devoid of all that sanctifies life and reconciles us to its suffering?

The universe is not planned for the exceptional man or woman. These have to achieve success, in spite of being exceptional.

Before unfolding to us the real drama of Emma Bovary's life, Flaubert, in masterly fashion, shows us the tempter at work in the character of Léon, the young lawyer's clerk.

The innocency of this episode, which brings like a ray of sunshine into Emma's dreary existence, is not due to timidity alone. There is about these two the innate chastity, the *pudeur d'âme,* characteristic of all idealistic and romantic natures, the chastity of soul which is a stronger safeguard far than the most complete knowledge of the dangers of evil.

It is when this brief friendship, fringed with the possibilities of love, has faded away into a mere memory, when Emma's heart lies fallow once more, it is not until then that Rodolphe comes upon the scene.

From the first we know that Emma is doomed.

In the experienced hands of this unscrupulous man of the world, she is like wax. As Eugénie Grandet does her worthless cousin, so does Emma Bovary endow Rodolphe with all the virtues, with all the delicacy of her woman's heart.

And so irresistible is the spiritualising influence of woman's passion, so purifying its fire, that even this coarse and brutal lover, this hopeless sensualist, 'whose heart resembled the well-worn flagstones of a courtyard,' falls under its spell: that there are moments when we almost hold our breath, when we wait, hoping against hope, for his regeneration by the magic power of her love.

'... Where you are, Rodolphe,' she cries in rapture, 'there is my home ... there is my country....' And the hardened cynic, standing alone in the darkened meadow, with his heart beating to suffocation, remains dazed and lost in wonder at her ineffable charm, until her white figure has vanished in the night.

And oh the bitter irony of life. In playing false to her, in abandoning her, Rodolphe commits the only meritorious action perhaps, of his unworthy life, and sends her to her doom.

After having loved with so great a love there can be no hope left for Emma.

As she sinks down unconscious in the sun-flooded garret over her lover's note of farewell, we feel that her fate is sealed. Love henceforth is dead in her breast, although Nature will still exact her toll. For Nature 'is not mocked.'

A less finely organised woman might have taken up the broken threads of life once more, might have sought and found comfort and compensation—many of us do—in the daily round, in the fleshpots of Egypt. But to all finer natures the knowledge of having given of their best and highest to the unworthy, brings self-loathing and despair.

The renewal, on different lines, of Emma's friendship with the now experienced Léon, is but an unimportant interlude; a natural consequence of all that has gone before—Nemesis relentlessly pursuing woman to a logical conclusion.

But in the last heartrending scene with her lost and almost regained lover, Emma rises before us once more, as she does before Rodolphe, in all her old charm, in all the beauty and strength of true passion.

It is not until this last interview that she realises, that we ourselves realise, that all is irrevocably lost.

When convinced at last of her lover's unworthiness (although there is much to be said for him, since 'of all the chilling blasts directed upon love a request for pecuniary help is the most chilling'), when she takes up the gold links from the mantelpiece and, hurling them across the room in contempt and despair, sweeps out of Rodolphe's presence for ever—it is then—not until then, that Emma Bovary realises that in losing his love she has indeed lost the world, and love itself, for love.

There is no other end possible for this woman, than that chosen for her by Flaubert with unerring psychological insight.

We wish for no other.

And who can tell? Charles Bovary—the innocent victim of her wasted love, and of his—Charles Bovary, lying dead in the deserted summer-house with a lock of her black hair clasped in his lifeless hand, may at the last himself not have wished it otherwise.

—MRS. HAROLD SANDWITH, "Becky Sharp and Emma Bovary," *Nineteenth Century and After* 91, No. 1 (January 1922): 61–64, 65–67

EDMUND WILSON

In *Madame Bovary*, Flaubert criticizes the nostalgia for the exotic which played such a large part in his own life and which led him to write *Salammbô* and *Saint Antoine*. What cuts Flaubert off from the other romantics and makes him primarily a social critic is his grim realization of the futility of dreaming about the splendors of the Orient and the brave old days of the past as an antidote to bourgeois society. Emma Bovary, the wife of a small country doctor, is always seeing herself in some other setting, imagining herself someone else. She will never face her situation as it is, with the result that she is eventually undone by the realities she has been trying to ignore. The upshot of all Emma's yearnings for a larger and more glamorous life is that her poor little daughter, left an orphan by Emma's suicide and the death of her father, is sent to work in a cotton mill.

The socialist of Flaubert's time might perfectly have approved of this: while the romantic individualist deludes himself with dreams in the attempt to evade bourgeois society and only succeeds in destroying himself, he lets humanity fall a victim to the industrial-commercial processes, which, unimpeded by his dreaming, go on.

—EDMUND WILSON, "Flaubert's Politics" [1937], *The Triple Thinkers* (New York: Harcourt, Brace, 1938), pp. 106–7

ANDRÉ MAUROIS

Does Madame Bovary remain a universal type? She probably does. I have met her even in America. There, Charles Bovary is a bank teller, a grocery clerk, an assistant professor, when Emma Rouault Bovary would want him to be President of the United States, a partner in the Morgan Bank, or a male star in Hollywood. This American Bovary seeks refuge in the fictions of the screen rather than in those of novels; she expects from life what the big films reveal of it; she is disappointed because most men, in America as elsewhere, are average beings.

Average, but not devoid of interest. Herein lies the immense, the fearful error of all the Bovarys. They are so ardent in their pursuit of romantic love that they no longer see human love, which would bring them happiness. If Emma had taken the trouble to observe Charles Bovary, if she had been content to share with him the simple joys which were within his scope, and to find in her readings other joys which she could have reserved for herself, she might have led in Yonville a quite tolerable existence. But because she committed the error of confusing the plane of art with that of life, she detested Yonville. To which it may be answered that it is not well to find Yonville tolerable, that one must surpass Yonville, and that civilizations are improved only by those who hate them.

Endless discussions, these, which Flaubert would have condemned. A novel, he would have repeated again, is not a lesson in morality.

"What seems to me the highest in art, and the most difficult, is neither to make men laugh, nor to make them weep, but to do as nature does, namely to make them dream. And this is the character of the very finest works. They are serene in aspect, and incomprehensible in their processes; they are motionless as cliffs, tumultuous as the sea, full of foliage, greennesses and murmurs like the woods, melancholy as the desert, blue as the sky. Homer, Rabelais, Michelangelo, Shakespeare, Goethe strike me as pitiless. Their work is bottomless, infinite, multiple. Through little apertures one perceives precipices; there is blackness at the bottom, dizziness, and yet something singularly troubling hovers over the whole. It is the ideal of light, the smile of the sun, and it is calm; it is calm and it is strong . . ."

Such is Madame Bovary. Was she a sinner, a fool, or a heroine? No matter! She exists. We know her. She appears to us with her little turned-down white collar, the day Charles Bovary, on the farm, sees her for the first time. She slips off her clothes with a single movement, in the room with the Turkey-red curtains in the Hôtel des Empereurs at Rouen. She slowly passes her hand through Charles's hair, as she lies dying. As Flaubert would have it, she awakens, not judgment, but revery. The philosopher Hegel, in the presence of mountains, found only this to say: "That's how it is." Before the very great works of art, this is also the only remark that comes to our lips. Because a very great artist has depicted it, we can contemplate that little Norman town and find it "bottomless, infinite, multiple". Like the great religious mystics, Flaubert, a mystic of art, found his recompense in a vision that transcends time. And as the believer, because he humiliates himself, shall be saved, the romantic Flaubert, because one day he accepted the humblest of subjects, wrote the most illustrious, and the most rightly illustrious of French novels.

—ANDRÉ MAUROIS, *"Madame Bovary," Seven Faces of Love*, tr. Haakon M. Chevalier (New York: Didier, 1944), pp. 205–8

ERICH AUERBACH

In Flaubert realism becomes impartial, impersonal, and objective. In an earlier study, "Serious Imitation of Everyday Life," I analyzed a paragraph from *Madame Bovary* from this point of view, and will here, with slight changes and abridgements, reproduce the pages concerned, since they are in line with the present train of thought and since it is unlikely, in view of the time and place of their publication (Istanbul, 1937), that they have reached many readers. The paragraph concerned occurs in part 1, chapter 9, of *Madame Bovary:*

Mais c'était surtout aux heures des repas qu'elle n'en pouvait plus, dans cette petite salle au rez-de-chaussée, avec le poêle qui fumait, la porte qui criait, les murs qui suintaient, les pavés humides; toute l'amertume de l'existence lui semblait servie sur son assiette, et, à la fumée du bouilli, il montait du fond de son âme comme d'autres bouffées d'affadissement. Charles était long à manger; elle grignotait quelques noisettes, ou bien, appuyée du coude, s'amusait, avec la pointe de son couteau, de faire des raies sur la toile cirée.

(But it was above all at mealtimes that she could bear it no longer, in that little room on the ground floor, with the smoking stove, the creaking door, the oozing walls, the damp floor-tiles; all the bitterness of life seemed to be served to her on her plate, and, with the steam from the boiled beef, there rose from the depths of her soul other exhalations as it were of disgust. Charles was a slow eater; she would nibble a few hazel-nuts, or else, leaning on her elbow, would amuse herself making marks on the oilcloth with the point of her table-knife.)

The paragraph forms the climax of a presentation whose subject is Emma Bovary's dissatisfaction with her life in Tostes. She has long hoped for a sudden event which would give a new turn to it—to her life without elegance, adventure, and love, in the depths of the provinces, beside a mediocre and boring husband; she has even made preparations for such an event, has lavished care on herself and her house, as if to earn that turn of fate, to be worthy of it; when it does not come, she is seized with unrest and despair. All this Flaubert describes in several pictures which portray Emma's world as it now appears to her; its cheerlessness, unvaryingness, grayness, staleness, airlessness, and inescapability now first become clearly apparent to her when she has no more hope of fleeing from it. Our paragraph is the climax of the portrayal of her despair. After it we are told how she lets everything in the house go, neglects herself, and begins to fall ill, so that her husband decides to leave Tostes, thinking that the climate does not agree with her.

The paragraph itself presents a picture—man and wife together at mealtime. But the picture is not presented in and for itself; it is subordinated to the dominant subject, Emma's despair. Hence it is not put before the reader directly: here the two sit at table—there the reader stands watching them. Instead, the reader first sees Emma, who has been much in evidence in the preceding pages, and he sees the picture first through her; directly, he sees only Emma's inner state; he sees what goes on at the meal indirectly, from within her state, in the light of her perception. The first words of the paragraph, *Mais c'était surtout aux heures des repas qu'elle n'en pouvait plus* ... state the theme, and all that follows is but a development of it. Not only are the phrases dependent upon *dans* and *avec*, which define the physical scene, a commentary on *elle n'en pouvait plus* in their piling up of the individual elements of discomfort, but the following clause too, which tells of the distaste aroused in her by the food, accords with the principal purpose both in sense and rhythm. When we read further, *Charles était long à manger*, this, though grammatically a new sentence and rhythmically a new movement, is still only a resumption, a variation, of the principal theme; not until we come to the contrast between his leisurely eating and her disgust and to the nervous gestures of her despair, which are described immediately afterward, does the sentence acquire its true significance. The husband, unconcernedly eating, becomes ludicrous and almost ghastly; when Emma looks at him and sees him sitting there eating, he becomes the actual cause of the *elle n'en pouvait plus;* because everything else that arouses her desperation—the gloomy room, the commonplace food, the lack of a tablecloth, the hopelessness of it all—appears to her, and through her to the reader also, as something that is connected with him, that emanates from him, and that would be entirely different if he were different from what he is.

The situation, then, is not presented simply as a picture, but we are first given Emma and then the situation through her. It is not, however, a matter—as it is in many first-person novels and other later works of a similar type—of a simple representation of the content of Emma's consciousness, of *what* she feels *as* she feels it. Though the light which illuminates the picture proceeds from her, she is yet herself part of the picture, she is situated within it. In this she recalls the speaker in the scene from Petronius discussed in our second chapter; but the means Flaubert employs are different. Here it is not Emma who speaks, but the writer. *Le poêle qui fumait, la porte qui criait, les murs qui suintaient, les pavés humides*—all this, of course, Emma sees and feels, but she would not be able to sum it all up in this way. *Toute l'amertume de l'existence lui semblait servie sur son assiette*— she doubtless has such a feeling; but if she wanted to express it, it would not come out like that; she has neither the intelligence nor the cold candor of self-accounting necessary for such a formulation. To be sure, there is nothing of Flaubert's life in these words, but only Emma's; Flaubert does nothing but bestow the power of mature expression upon the material which she affords, in its complete subjectivity. If Emma could do this herself, she would no longer be what she is, she would have outgrown herself and thereby saved herself. So she does not simply see, but is herself seen as one seeing, and is thus judged, simply through a plain description of her subjective life, out of her own feelings. Reading in a later passage (part 2, chapter 12): *jamais Charles ne lui paraissait aussi désagréable, avoir les doigts aussi carrés, l'esprit aussi lourd, les façons si communes* . . . , the reader perhaps thinks for a moment that this strange series is an emotional piling up of the causes that time and again bring Emma's aversion to her husband to the boiling point, and that she herself is, as it were, inwardly speaking these words; that this, then, is an example of *erlebte Rede.* But this would be a mistake. We have here, to be sure, a number of paradigmatic causes of Emma's aversion, but they are put together deliberately by the writer, not emotionally by Emma. For Emma feels much more, and much more confusedly; she sees other things than these—in his body, his manners, his dress; memories mix in, meanwhile she perhaps hears him speak, perhaps feels his hand, his breath, sees him walk about, good-hearted, limited, unappetizing, and unaware; she has countless confused impressions. The only thing that is clearly defined is the result of all this, her aversion to him, which she must hide. Flaubert transfers the clearness to the impressions; he selects three, apparently quite at random, but which are paradigmatically taken from Bovary's physique, his mentality, and his behavior; and he arranges them as if they were three shocks which Emma felt one after the other. This is not at all a naturalistic representation of consciousness. Natural shocks occur quite differently. The ordering hand of the writer is present here, deliberately summing up the confusion of the psychological situation in the direction toward which it tends of itself—the direction of "aversion to Charles Bovary." This ordering of the psychological situation does not, to be sure, derive its standards from without, but from the material of the situation itself. It is the type of ordering which must be employed if the situation itself is to be translated into language without admixture.

> —ERICH AUERBACH, "In the Hôtel de la Mole," *Mimesis: The Representation of Reality in Western Literature* [1946], tr. Willard R. Trask (Princeton: Princeton University Press, 1953), pp. 482–85

ELIZABETH BOWEN

Madame Bovary, in its unforeseen and imperative demand to be written, displaced an already projected book. Flaubert, off and on, had discussed with Maxime and Louis the idea of a novel that should have a Flemish setting and be about a young girl who was a mystic and died a virgin. And there had been more: the idea had begun to collect matter. From this to the story of an adulteress may seem a far cry—yet, does one not see in *Bovary*, never quite submerged, the young girl's face? That the soul of Emma should be without virtue does not make it less a palpable soul—of whose pitiful fluttering candescence, at the most carnal moments, one is aware. She is a guilty innocent, for whom rightly or wrongly one must weep. It is terrible for her, coming home to the null little roadside house at Tostes the day after the ball. It is terrible when she receives the basket of apricots; and when, at table with her husband that same evening, she sees the lights of Rodolphe's carriage driving away across Yonville square. Running through the early morning sunshine to Rodolphe's house, singing on the Seine with Leon, in the ray of moonlight coming between the iron shutters of the boat, to the metronome-sound of the oars, she is happy. Is Emma a 'character'? Not, I think, in the English novelist's sense. She consists in sentiments and sensations, in moments for their own sake.

> —ELIZABETH BOWEN, "Preface to *The Flaubert Omnibus*" [1947], *Collected Impressions* (New York: Knopf, 1950), pp. 24–25

R. P. BLACKMUR

Emma remains accessible to experience, to invasion, destruction, hysteria, to desire; she has within her the extreme possibility for metamorphosis, an absolute change in her whole system of relations. As the moth has once in its lifetime a total metamorphosis, usually the last one, for the sole purpose of procreation,

Emma has the chance of change for sex and death; she has in her an energy for change which presses till satisfied—but presses within the frame of a constructed society, and so has to deceive itself in order to survive, to transform its objects in order to act.

She has all the energy of beauty out of place with which to transform the illicit, the prodigal, the nostalgic from the low price, narrow motives, and contemptible manners in which she finds them: the maximum against which the adolescent can compete. Emma's energy is of the highest price: the high price of beauty out of place raised still higher by hysteria. Beauty out of place will always be marred; its efforts at self-assertion and self-protection must always be excessive, since it must create its object as well as its response to it, and when the object fails comes hysteria: the disease or disorder which is the convulsive effort of the womb that cannot create. Love must indeed in such persons be habit-hysteria; it cannot be anything else, since it persists in being, not a quality of experience, but experience itself.

That is why we think that it is to lovers above all that things happen; not that it is true, but that we know that to the heightened, crippled consciousness that goes with being in love experience is keener and makes a deeper mark; besides which there is the experience that hysteria adds.

Emma is one of these women to whom things happen; but she is also the normal woman, the bourgeois wife of the bourgeois functionary in the small town— like everybody she tends to sink into the pattern, the cycle; to be part of the social institution whose function it is to bridge or absorb happenings, suffering or enjoying them only at a low degree, *as a matter of course,* vicious or virtuous indiscriminately. All her energies, even her hysteria, are accidental elements of her Bovarysme: her life other than she is. She herself is a combination. Thinking of both we achieve the sense of her identity, her motive, her fate. It is the art of the novel to show this migration of being, and it is the special craft of Flaubert to reach a special sense of identity through the progressively intensive balance of the normal and of Bovarysme. Rodolphe, let us say, would have been meaningless without the club-foot; Lheureux would have been meaningless without Léon's return; there was no nostalgia without sordidness, no sordidness without hysteria. All are used to situate, to give extension to, Emma and our sense of what she is. Extension, in this sense, is only another word for verisimilitude; as intension is a name for what it is that seems true.

—R. P. BLACKMUR, "Beauty out of Place: *Madame Bovary"* [1951],
Eleven Essays in the European Novel (New York: Harcourt,
Brace & World, 1964), pp. 63–64

ALBERT COOK

Madame Bovary has been called a religious novel, and surely what undoes Emma in the novel is a kind of mortal sin. After Rodolphe her soul has still enough balance not to be drawn down by the vertigo of the lathe, but after the depravation of Léon she can submit to the horribly inky taste of arsenic. The appearances she has submitted to have left a residuum of gritty reality. The song of the blind man calls her back to a life of the whole sentiments, a life now as lost to her through the suicide that culminates her sin as the visible world is lost to him. He sings of a lost love, of a love that in the song is already lost.

Her first seduction takes place on the autumn leaves, and Flaubert describes it in terms of the lengthening shadows of twilight, the patches of light on the leaves; a vague prolonged cry on the horizon is expressly noted as the correlative of her feelings "like music." The second seduction, by deliberate contrast, takes place in a black fiacre rattling around Rouen after a tour of the cathedral. Out of the fiacre float into the air the torn up pieces of the letter refusing the Léon she has acquiesced to, "like white butterflies," the ironic simile echoing the "black butterflies" of the ashes at the back of the stove where she has long ago burned her wedding bouquet.

Here the secret history of the soul takes place in the feelings. Before her first seduction Emma reaches out to the Church, but an insensitive abbé Bournisien, counterpart to the pigheaded Homais with whom he later argues, repulses her. His moral categories are a mere appearance which uncharitably refuse to face the reality of the environment-drenched feelings Emma is struggling to account for. "Emma Bovary's poor adventures are a tragedy," James says, "for the very reason that in a world unsuspecting, unassisting, unconsoling, she has herself to distil the rich and the rare."

If we ask why Emma was seduced, we find not actions but feelings, impressions concretized in the analogical details of the detached narrative. Rodolphe's gentility calls up in her a memory of her flood of impressions at the Vaubyessard dinner party. The sensation of having lost the too timid Léon makes her more willing to listen to another. But finally she needs that 'abandonment' (s'abandonner is Flaubert's usual verb for sexual seduction) to enjoy the luxuries she has already been buying from Lheureux; refusing to go riding with Rodolphe out of decorous fear and moral soundness, her reserve is broken down by a new riding costume she has just bought. 'L'amazone la decida,' Flaubert says. She goes riding because of the luxurious jodhpurs; she is seduced because she goes riding.

Another reason she succumbs is the presence of what she thinks is Charles' revolting insensitivity. This is ironic for her past; she thought him not insensitive when he rescued her from the farm by marrying her. And it is ironic for his mute sufferings, easily as sensitive as hers to the stream of feeling. The sensitivity achingly present in the first scene of the novel, where his schoolfellows tease him, stakes its whole life on love for Madame Bovary. Hers is a true marriage, then, and only with her husband, by facing the heavy physical reality and commonplace mind which house the delicacy of his spirit, could she reach the good life she perversely allows herself to feel him stifling out of her. The title, Madame Bovary, is significant. Anna Karenina, but not Emma Bovary, because Charles is not the stultified Karenin Emma thinks him. She is his true wife, as the title hints, and her tragic flaw is in not recognizing it.

Significant, too, is what many critics have pointed out, that Charles surrounds

Emma at the beginning and at the end of the novel. The pathos of this passive 'bourgeois tragedy' is his as much as hers. We measure the effect of her sin by the depth of his sadness much more than by the brief mention of her daughter's later life as a factory worker. He is physically ugly, and she lets this fact dominate her response to him, not willing to let her feelings know, as Flaubert says metaphorically of Charles' hat at the beginning of the narrative, that "la laideur muette a des profondeurs d'expression comme le visage d'un imbécile." Charles' mute suffering is deep enough to kill him; he is completely the husband of a woman who perversely would not see his sensitivity.

In this novel the secret life accretes through a stream of sensation diffused in the physical environment; the characters themselves as well are presented almost as undeveloped images. Charles is defined, and Flaubert's detachment is aware of it, by his professional mediocrity and physical clumsiness, Emma by her purchases, reading, and music; Homais by his quack science, Rodolphe by his hunting, Léon by his poetry and law. But these characters are fixed in a kind of everyday reality which their feelings must admit, —if, unlike Homais, they have feelings. The actual, individualized town is the background against which Emma operates, and, while insensitive, it has a reality her romantic illusions will not recognize.

Flaubert's detachment, again, renders the reality of the town. He fixes each detail of town or of metaphorized feeling with a series of 'mots justes.' The division in Flaubert's own spirit between romantic feeling and documentary accuracy was united in the style: each mot juste picks up an impressionistic fact as with a pair of laboratory tweezers. His self-conscious detachment, present in every mot juste, draws the distinction between Emma's impression of the town's appearance, a kind of reality, and the everyday reality she does not realize is interacting with her impression. The possible synthesis of the romantic and the real is nowhere present in the novel but everywhere present in the narrator, so that, like Proust, Flaubert has a kind of health in his description of sickness.

—ALBERT COOK, "Flaubert: The Riches of Detachment," *French Review*
32, No. 2 (December 1958): 124–26

MARGARET G. TILLETT

The great thing in *Madame Bovary* is the impression it gives of the continual vibration of an acute sensitivity held in control, an instrument finely tuned, giving a true note. The main character lives as a series of recognizable moods conveyed with remarkable feeling and power; in these the universality of the work lies. Emma Bovary is a Romantic, and the Romantic outlook on life as it appears here, caricatured by Flaubert, is immediately recognizable to everyone, to those who suppose that it is a symptom of adolescence and must be outgrown, and to those who know, as Flaubert himself did, that at its best it is admirable, the only defence against insidious soul-destroying materialism. There is no real opposition between Romantic and Realist; the great adversary is the Materialist, the anti-poet. Unfortunately

Romanticism is all too often represented in life by such as poor Emma Bovary, shoddily pursuing a shoddy ideal, a piece of imitation jewellery if ever there was one. This bastard Romanticism is what Flaubert is satirizing in *Madame Bovary*. Emma, possessing beauty and some intelligence, lacks one quality which is essential to the genuine Romantic—warmth of heart, which her creator did possess and which he endeavoured to conceal from his readers. Emma's capricious acts of material 'generosity' have little significance:—

> ... elle jetait parfois aux pauvres toutes les pièces blanches de sa bourse, quoiqu'elle ne fut guère tendre cependant, ni facilement accessible à l'émotion d'autrui, comme la plupart des gens issus de campagnards, qui gardent toujours à l'âme quelque chose de la callosité des mains paternelles.

And in fact she is completely selfish. Another of the worst tendencies of the Romantic disposition—the tendency to self-dramatization—is very marked in her. But she has such intelligence and taste that she adapts herself easily to the society of the aristocracy, at La Vaubyessard. The picture of Emma at the ball, dancing with a vicomte, is the one that has to be constantly called to mind if the full measure of her increasing misery and degradation is to be brought home, and if the reader is to feel for her any sympathy at all. Flaubert therefore recalls it, with delicate touches, throughout the book, the last reminder of it coming towards the end, when she is in Rouen making a desperate attempt to find money to pay her debts:

> Elle s'arrêta pour laisser passer un cheval noir, piaffant dans les brancards d'un tilbury que conduisait un gentleman en fourrure de zibeline. Qui était-ce donc? Elle le connaissait.... La voiture s'élança et disparut.
>   Mais c'était lui, le Vicomte!

> —MARGARET G. TILLETT, *"Madame Bovary," On Reading Flaubert* (London: Oxford University Press, 1961), pp. 14–15

HARRY LEVIN

In sharpest contradistinction to Don Quixote, whose vagaries were intellectual, Emma Bovary's are emotional. Hence they are counterweighted by no earthbound Sancho Panza, but by the intellectually pretentious M. Homais. The comic relief that he injects into Emma's tragedy is later to be elaborated into the unrelieved comedy of *Bouvard et Pécuchet*. Because it is herself that she misconceives, where Don Quixote's misconception of actuality could be corrected by reference to his fellow men, she remains incorrigibly tragic. This paranoiac attitude of Emma's, this self-hallucination induced by overreading, this "habit of conceiving ourselves otherwise than as we are," is so epidemic that Jules de Gaultier could diagnose the weakness of the modern mind as *Bovarysme*. The vicarious lives that film stars lead for shop-girls, the fictive euphoria that slogans promise and advertisements promote, the imaginary flourishes that supplement and garnish daily existence for all of us, are equally Bovaristic. If to Bovarize is simply to daydream, as everyone does to a greater or lesser extent, the criterion is not how much we do so, but whether our daydreams are egoistic like Emma's or altruistic like Don Quixote's. Every epoch depends upon some verbal medium for its conception of itself: on printed words and private fictions, if not on public rituals and collective myths. The trouble came when, instead of the imitation of Christ or the veneration of Mary, readers practised the emulation of Rastignac or the cult of Lélia. Yet, whatever their models, they were romanticizing a reality which would otherwise have been formless and colorless; for when nature has established norms of conduct, art is called upon to publicize them. "There are people who would not fall in love if they had never heard of love," said La Rochefoucauld. Denis de Rougemont has tried to substantiate that epigram by arguing that the erotic motive was superimposed upon the West through medieval romance. Paolo might never have loved Francesca, in Dante's memorable episode, had not the book of Galeotto acted as a go-between.

But the writer, if not the reader, cannot afford to be swept off his feet by emotions involved in a given story. Thus Flaubert, in his first *Education sentimentale*, describes the youthful reading of his poet, Jules:

> He reread *René* and *Werther*, those books of disgust with life; he reread Byron and dreamed of the solitude of his great-souled heroes; but too much of his admiration was based on personal sympathy, which has nothing in common with the disinterested admiration of the true artist. The last word in this kind of criticism, its most inane expression, is supplied to us every day by a number of worthy gentlemen and charming ladies interested in literature, who disapprove of this character because he is cruel, of that situation because it is equivocal and rather smutty—discovering, in the last analysis, that in the place of such a person they would not have done the same thing, without understanding the necessary laws that preside over a work of art, or the logical deductions that follow from an idea.

It follows that Emma Bovary and her censors, though their ethics differed, shared the same esthetic approach. Jules on the other hand would learn, as did Flaubert, to differentiate a work of art from its subject-matter and the artist from his protagonist. The anecdote of Cervantes on his deathbed, identifying himself with his hero, has its much quoted Flaubertian parallel: *Madame Bovary c'est moi.* But this equivocal statement was not so much a confession as a cautious disclaimer of certain resemblances which Madame Delamare's neighbors, without indulging in unwarranted gossip, might have suspected. In so far as Flaubert lived the part, as any novelist enters into his fully realized characterizations, it was a *tour de force* of female impersonation. The identification was not nearly so close as it had been with Saint-Antoine or would become with Frédéric Moreau. It is true that, on summer days, he worked in the arbor where he stages trysts between Emma and Rodolphe; that the cigar-case, the seal inscribed *Amor nel cor*, and other relics actually commemorate his own affair with Louise Colet; that Louise may well have suggested aspects of Emma, and Emma's lovers and husband may have embodied aspects of Gustave. But the very first premise of the book was the suppression of his own personality, and his later pronouncements adhere with stiffening conviction to the principle of *ne s'écrire.* Empathy is seasoned with antipathy whenever he writes about Emma to Louise; he repeatedly complains that the bourgeois vulgarity of his material disgusts and nauseates him. He would much prefer to write a book without a subject; or rather, he would like to abolish the transitions and obstacles between thought and expression; and he prophesies that literary convention, like the Marxian concept of the state, will some day wither away.

—HARRY LEVIN, "Flaubert," *The Gates of Horn: A Study of Five French Novelists* (New York: Oxford University Press, 1963), pp. 249–51

MARY McCARTHY

On the one hand, Flaubert declared *he* was Emma. On the other, he wrote to a lady: "There's nothing in *Madame Bovary* that's drawn from life. It's a *completely invented* story. None of my own feelings or experiences are in it." So help him God. Of course, he was fibbing, and contradicting himself as well. Like all novelists, he drew on his own experiences, and, more than most novelists, he was frightened by the need to invent. When he came to do the ball at Vaubyessard, he lamented. "It's so long since I've been to a ball." If memory failed, he documented himself, as he did for Emma's school reading, going back over the children's stories he had read as a little boy and the picture books he had colored. If he had not had an experience the story required, he sought it out. Before writing the chapter about the agricultural fair, he went to one; he consulted his brother about club foot and, disappointed by the ignorance manifest in Achille's answers, procured textbooks. There is hardly a page in the novel that he had not "lived," and he constantly drew on his own feelings to render Emma's.

All novelists do this, but Flaubert went beyond the usual call of duty. Madame Bovary was not Flaubert, certainly; yet he became Madame Bovary and all the accessories to her story, her lovers, her husband, her little greyhound, the corset lace that hissed around her hips like a slithery grass snake as she undressed in the hotel room in Rouen, the blinds of the cab that hid her and Léon as they made love. In a letter he made clear the state of mind in which he wrote. That day he had been doing the scene of the horseback ride, when Rodolphe seduces Emma in the woods. "What a delicious thing writing is—not to be you any more but to move through the whole universe you're talking about. Take me today, for instance: I was a man and woman, lover and mistress; I went riding in a forest on a fall afternoon beneath the yellow leaves, and I was the horses, the leaves, the wind, the words he and she spoke, and the red sun beating on their half-closed eyelids, which were already heavy with passion." It is hard to imagine another great novelist—Stendhal, Tolstoy, Jane Austen, Dickens, Dostoievsky, Balzac—who would conceive of the act of writing as a rapturous loss of identity. Poets have often expressed the wish for otherness, for fusion—to be their mistress' sparrow or her girdle or the breeze that caressed her temples and wantoned with her ribbons, but Flaubert was the first to realize this wish in prose, in the disguise of a realistic story. The climax of the horseback ride was, of course, a coupling, in which all of Nature joined in a gigantic, throbbing *partouze* while Flaubert's pen flew. He was writing a book, and yet from his account you would think he was *reading* one. "What a delicious thing reading is—not to be you any more but to flow through the whole universe you're reading about . . ." etc., etc.

> —MARY MCCARTHY, "On *Madame Bovary*" [1964], *The Writing on the Wall and Other Literary Essays* (New York: Harcourt, Brace & World, 1970), pp. 77–78

VICTOR BROMBERT

Emma's characteristic pose is at, or near, a window. This is indeed one of the first impressions Charles has of her: ". . . il la trouva debout, le front contre la fenêtre." Windows which are "ajar" are part of her literary reveries in the convent. The image, from the very outset, suggests some manner of imprisonment as well as a longing for a liberation. After her marriage, her daily routine brings her to the window every morning. When she goes through one of her nervous crises, she locks herself up in her room, but then, "stifling," throws open the windows. Exasperated by a sense of shame and contempt for her husband, she again resorts to the typical gesture: "She went to open the window . . . and breathed in the fresh air to calm herself" (I.9). The sense of oppression and immurement is further stressed after Rodolphe abandons her: the shutter of the window overlooking the garden remains permanently closed. But the imprisonment in her own boundless desire is intolerable. Emma's sexual frenzy, which reaches climactic proportions during her affair with Léon, is probably the most physical manifestation of her need to "liberate" herself. The window, as symbol, offers an image of this release. It is revealing that she first glimpses her future lover, Rodolphe, from her window. Similarly, she watches Léon cross the Yonville square. And it is characteristic also that, upon Léon's departure from Yonville, Emma's first gesture is to open her window and watch the clouds. The space-reverie at first corresponds to a sense of hope: either the surge toward emancipation, as after the Vaubyessard ball (Emma "opened the window and leant out"); or the process of convalescence (Emma, recovering from her nervous depression, is wheeled to the window in her armchair). But the space-hope is even more fundamentally a space-despair. From the garret where she reads Rodolphe's letter and almost commits suicide, all the surrounding plain is visible. The garret-window offers the broadest panorama. But it is a dreary view; the endless flat expanse provides a hopeless perspective.

   Chronic expectation turns to chronic futility, as Emma's élans toward the elsewhere disintegrate in the grayness of undifferentiated space. Daydreams of movement and flight only carry her back to a more intolerable confinement within her petty existence and her unfulfilled self. But expectation there is. Just as the chatelaines in her beloved Gothic romances wait for the dashing cavalier on his black horse, so Emma lives in perpetual anticipation. "At the bottom of her heart ... she was waiting for something to happen" (I.9). Flaubert insists, somewhat heavily at times, on this compulsive expectance of the conclusive event. The frustrated local barber, dreaming of a shop in the theater district of some big town, thus walks up and down "like a sentinel on duty" waiting for customers. And Emma, casting despairing glances upon her life's solitude, interrogates the empty horizon. Each morning, as she wakes up, she hopes that this day will bring a three-decker, laden with passion to the portholes. Every evening, disappointed, she again longs for the morrow.

Images of movement reinforce the theme of escapism. Emma enjoys taking lonely walks with her greyhound and watching the leaps and dashes of the graceful animal. Restlessness and taste for aimless motion point to the allurement of a mythical *elsewhere*. Once again, the theme is ironically broached early in the novel, in pages concerned with Charles. "He had an aimless hope. ..." Images of space and motion—the two are frequently combined—serve, throughout the novel, to bring out the vagrant quality of Emma's thoughts. Departure, travel and access to privileged regions are recurring motifs. The "immense land of joys and passions" exists somewhere beyond her immediate surroundings: the more accessible things are, the more Emma's thoughts turn away from them. Happiness, by definition, can never be *here*. "Anywhere out of the World"—the title of Baudelaire's prose poem—could sum up Emma's chronic yearning for the exotic. "It seemed to her that certain places on earth must yield happiness, just as some plants are peculiar to certain places and grow poorly anywhere else" (I.7). By a skillful, and certainly far from gratuitous touch, Flaubert concludes Emma's initiatory stay at the Vaubyessard residence with a visit to the hothouses, where the strangest plants, rising in pyramids under hanging vases, evoke a climate of pure sensuality. The exotic setting becomes the very symbol of a yearned-for bliss. The "coming joys" are compared to tropical shores so distant that they cannot be seen, but from where soft winds carry back an intoxicating sweetness.

Travel and estrangement come to symbolize salvation from the immurement of ennui. Emma believes that change of abode alone is almost a guarantee of happiness. "She did not believe that things could be the same in different places ..." (II.2). The unseen country is obviously also the richest in promises of felicity. Paris remains sublimely alluring precisely because—contrary to his original intentions—Flaubert does not grant Emma access to this promised land. Her first conversation with Léon typically exploits the Romantic cliché of the "limitless" expanse of the ocean, which "elevates the soul" through suggestions of the ideal and of infinity. And Léon's blue eyes seem beautiful to Emma because they appear more limpid than "those mountain-lakes where the sky is mirrored." The culmination of the travel imagery coincides with plans for Emma's elopement with Rodolphe ("... il fera bon voyager ..." II.12) and with her visions of life in gondolas or under palm trees, to the accompaniment of guitars, in far-off countries with splendent domes and women dressed in red bodices. The very concept of emancipation is bound up with the notion of voyage. During her pregnancy Emma hopes to have a son, because a man is free: "he can travel over passions and over countries, cross obstacles, taste of the most far-away pleasures." And part of Rodolphe's prestige when she meets him is that he appears to her like a "traveler who has voyaged over strange lands." As early as her disappointing honeymoon (which, she feels, ought to have led to "those lands with sonorous names"), she knows that Charles did not, and could not, live up to her ideal of man as initiator to remote mysteries. She yearns for the inaccessible with a naïve but pungent lyricism: ". . . she was filled with desires, with rage, with hate" (II.5). Her desperate escapism, which ultimately alarms and alien-ates both her lovers, is of an almost sacrilegious nature. It is significant that sex is repeatedly associated with mystico-religious images (the remarkable death scene pushes the association to its logical conclusion), and that the assignation with Léon takes place in the Rouen cathedral, which Emma's distorted sensibility views as a "gigantic boudoir." Emma's tragedy is that she cannot escape her own immanence. "Everything, including herself, was unbearable to her" (III.6). But just as her walks always lead back to the detested house, so Emma feels thrown back into herself, left stranded on her own shore. The lyrical thrust toward the inaccessible leads back to an anesthetizing confinement.

—VICTOR BROMBERT, *"Madame Bovary:* The Tragedy of Dreams," *The Novels of Flaubert* (Princeton: Princeton University Press, 1966), pp. 58–61

HAROLD KAPLAN

Emma Bovary is the protagonist in a great example of modern fiction, building itself upon the dramatic isolation of an individual consciousness in a world which resists both her will and understanding. Emma is surrounded by a cold light, she is seen objectively, almost clinically, a fragment of life spinning on its separate path. The reader knows Emma, but as he might know a sick, mad, or otherwise self-absorbed person who cannot return communication. He knows as a scientist knows, not in a dialogue, but as in the observation of an unanswering thing. This drama, typically naturalistic, splits the point of view so that to be the actor in life is one thing, and to *know* life, quite another thing, is to be the spectator of it. Emma's consciousness cannot deal equally with that of the reader. This is the key of the work and its effects. In that sense it is a modern novel, one of the most remorseless in method and brilliant of modern novels. No one went further than Flaubert, except perhaps Joyce, in administering an epistemology that we understand so deeply. This defines knowledge as solipsistic and private when it is knowledge in action. Emma is alive in her own context, but her life is a distant flicker so long as the point of view is truly given up to a neutral omniscience.

A literary empiricism or positivism is in the position of the laboratory. It remains outside the object of experiment, and pursuing its own interest, widely outside the fatal personal interests of the agents in the drama. In that sense there is no dialogue, as I put it, between character and reader. Flaubert concentrates on the stage, as if the only hold we have on truth is the immediate scene, and every secondary report is a subjective distortion. When the report comes we are interested in it *because* of its subjective distortion. A context of coldest, precise objectivity is prepared for Emma's illusions. As protagonist, locked in her private world, she is mocked by the contrast, and the straining of desire is shown against the indifference of facts. This makes a drama of cross-purposes, working itself out brutally, pathetically, toward the final silencing of the consciousness and will. The terms must be brutal and pathetic because the antagonists are not evenly matched. Emma is defeated by the premises of the conflict; her antagonist is not so much inexplicable as non-communicating. It is not a personality, it does not respond, and as an antagonist it merely exists in her perception of the array of time, matter, circumstance set against her. It is, abstractly, a blind principle of resistance.

The objectivity of fate is recorded in the objectivity of the narrator. Like a spectator god he refuses to intervene, and he will not allow the dramatic loneliness of the protagonist to be comforted. He asserts nothing to give her life a share in a world of significant meaning, nor will he allow her illusions to wrest something from extinction at the end. ⟨. . .⟩

In Flaubert's work then we find the expression of realism at its philosophic extreme, the effort to report things as they are with a scrupulously neutral teleological point of view. The most austere realism can successfully avoid the effect of satire or of polemic, but it cannot avoid the implications of irony and pathos. These will arise in dramatic presentation in proportion, in fact, to the distance or neutrality of the point of view. The removal of the author from value judgments has the effect of stressing and isolating the values of his protagonists, now seen clearly in dramatic collision with things as they are. The contrast is with things as they *might be,* in this case imagined in the subjective or solipsistic world of Emma Bovary. The center for ironic treatment is not the world as found so much as the human consciousness itself, moved by idealization and desire, destined for self-deception and failure. The reality which surrounds consciousness has a kind of neutral undebated existence which in fact tends to be as awe-inspiring as the traditional metaphysical power of God. It has dignity at the expense, we might say, of the principle of subjectivity. Nature is not a benevolent god in typical modern naturalism, but it is a god nonetheless, to whose omnipotence has been added the impressive attribute of indifference or incommunicability insofar as the human interest is concerned. There is a school of naturalism, in Zola and Dreiser for instance, more typical of the nineteenth than the twentieth century, which suggests that the God of nature is comprehensible at least, and when its *diktat* is known men can achieve some fulfillment in their living. That combination of scientific method and humanitarian purpose was long ago expressed by the Goncourt brothers (as Erich Auerbach points out) in their preface to *Germinie Lacerteux:* "Today when the Novel is broadening and growing, when it is beginning to be the great, serious, impassioned, living form of literary study and social investigation . . . ; today when the Novel has imposed upon itself the studies and duties of science, it can demand the freedoms and immunities of science. And if it seek Art and Truth, if it disclose troubles which it were well the happy people of Paris should not forget . . . ; human suffering, present and alive, which teaches charity; if the Novel have that religion to which the past century gave its broad and vast name: Humanity;—that consciousness suffices it; its right lies there." But this is not the quality of Flaubert's naturalism, neither polemic, nor moral exposure, nor affirmation.

Emma Bovary, like any protagonist, is an agent of the sensuous, ethical and esthetic human imagination. When the content of that imagination becomes the object of neutral study rather than either assent or denial, then the normative function itself becomes depreciated and is patronized by the intelligence. The dialogue traditionally conducted between the reader and the protagonist of the narrative is broken. It is the way, as I have said, in which Emma's motivated consciousness is isolated from productive correspondence with her environment, and isolated in addition from a consensus of values; it is this isolation from world, audience, and author which strikes the characteristic quality of the novel, and I believe, the dominant tradition of naturalistic writing which grows from it. It is necessary at this point to offer some illustrations of the effects I have generally described.

Emma has begun to be bored in her marriage, and here is an example of her early dreaming:

> Didn't love, like Indian plants, require rich soils, special temperatures? Sighs in the moonlight, long embraces, hands bathed in lover's tears—all the fevers of the flesh and the languors of love—were inseparable from the balconies of great idle-houred castles, from a silk-curtained, thick-carpeted, be-flowered boudoir with its bed on a dais, from the sparkle of precious stones and the swank of liveries.
>
> The hired boy at the relay post across the road, who came in every morning to rubdown the mare, walked through the hall in his heavy wooden shoes; his smock was in holes, his feet were innocent of stockings.

There is the immediate counterpoint. The hired boy in his heavy wooden shoes echoes outside Emma's dreams, illustrating the characteristic tension in Flaubert's writing. The brilliantly concise objective scene records itself.

> Charles jogged back and forth across the countryside under snow and rain. He ate omelettes at farmhouse tables, thrust his arm into damp beds, had his face spattered with jets of warm blood at bleedings; he listened to death rattles, examined the contents of basins, handled a lot of soiled underclothing.

Those tingling sensations define a reality. Its coldness presses against Emma's luxurious imagination, where the intense vagueness of desire moves in ratio with the resistless tendency toward solipsism. Her images . . .

> lived on a higher plane than other people, somewhere sublime between heaven and earth, up among the storm clouds. As for the rest of the world,

it was in some indeterminate place beyond the pale; it could scarcely be said to exist. Indeed the closer to her things were, the further away from them her thoughts turned.

The force of the romantic imagination is passion searching for its objects. In that sense, as Denis de Rougemont stressed in his study of the theme ⟨Love in the Western World⟩, romantic passion grows from resistance, its basis is frustration from which it moves out to the limitless, the unrealizable where all terms are its own. Experience is self-generated; wave after wave of private impulse moves outward to meet resistance, which serves only to send the flight higher or make a total collapse. There is no coming to terms because there is no communication of terms. The climaxes of the romantic experience are passive, in the sense that desire is separated from action and confined to itself. The most extreme of personal demands alternate with the passive retreat. The dynamics of Keats' "Ode to a Nightingale," for instance, might illustrate the subjective flight and fall. Desire finds its essence in imagined experience, the image taking perfection into itself. The climax moves into the fall, reality intervenes, and the fall into reality forces help-lessness. The final position is inert, the will has lost its objects, the consciousness is lost between dream and reality. The poem plausibly ends, "Do I wake or sleep?"

The "fictional" basis of Emma's consciousness attaches her naturally to in-vented and transcendental worlds, romantic novels, the theatre, the church. Emma at the theatre is Emma in life, thoroughly absorbed in artificial forms. She identifies herself simply with the woman on the stage, though "no one had ever loved her with such a love." The experience is interrupted by the arrival of Leon, and Emma moves without a break, forgetting the opera completely, into her love affair with him as if to illustrate the continuity of her fantasies.

The church is more impressively the source for subjective experience, and the best themes for Emma's internal climaxes are religious. The images are absolute but they remain sensual, they are Emma's.

> . . . she gently succumbed to the mystical languor induced by the perfumes of the altar, the coolness of the holy water fonts, the gleaming of the candles. . . . The metaphors constantly used in sermons—'betrothed,' 'spouse,' 'heavenly lover,' 'mystical marriage'—excited her in a thrilling new way.

In these ironic metaphors Flaubert seems to put religion at the apex of the expressive human fallacy. In his story, "Un Coeur Simple" the consummation of Félicité's locked-in emotional consciousness is a vision of the Holy Ghost in the form of her stuffed and moth-eaten parrot, the latter intruding into her fantasy directly as the sign of the mundane and opaque reality of her existence.

After the illness provoked by her frustrations, Emma goes through something very like a religious experience which seems to spiritualize her excess of desire, but inexorably Flaubert turns it back. The lovers meet at the church itself, which to Leon "was like a gigantic boudoir suffused with her image," and again without much transition, religion reduces itself to a private sensuous fantasy. Leaving the church, in the same confused trance as it were, Emma passes into the arms of her lover and the process of her self-seduction is completed.

Here idealization is seen as close as it can be to its physical sources. The realism is reductive and man is viewed as a dreaming animal, his dreams a symptom of his biology. It is not irrelevant that Charles is a physician. He is part of the reality trap for Emma, and he brings its naturalistic aspect to the foreground. The image of Charles examining the contents of basins and listening to death rattles is a forecast of the end. Meanwhile as Emma surrenders to her first lover, Rodolphe, his hyperbolic seduction speech is counterpointed by the political speaker at the country fair, with his praise of scientific agriculture, with the awards for the best breeding and the best manures.

Flaubert's intentions are clear in the lingering over the physical details of Emma's death. The blind beggar comes to Emma as the messenger of fate, and he exhibits fate with his shredded flesh and open wounds. His voice is the last sound in Emma's ears. Whatever principle of meaning it has, nature answers irrelevantly to the question of the consciousness. This is expressed in the "scientific" discussion among the medical men, while they eat a good lunch at Homais' house and Emma lies dying. "First we had a sensation of siccity in the pharynx, then intolerable pain in the epigastrium, superpurgation, coma." This is the hammering emotionless tone of fact, idiotic in its factualness. The scientific report speaks a language unintelligible to the subjective life at its extreme; pain, grief, fear, these are terms that have lost utterly their ground of reference. Their source, their only knower, has herself become extinct.

The ironies of irrelevance are climaxed in the final argument between the priest and Homais as they sit with the dead body. At cross-purposes, unintelligible to each other, the dead body is their audience, and religion and liberal science make their claims in the heaviest resisting silence. Enforcing the point, they both finally fall asleep.

> They sat opposite one another, stomachs out, faces swollen, both of them scowling—united, after so much dissension, in the same human weakness; and they stirred no more than the corpse that was like another sleeper beside them.

Although Christianity might have spoken to Emma's last flicker of consciousness, it has been betrayed by the object she has become, it now speaks in a world she no longer inhabits. Science, as expressed by the vulgar pharmacist to be sure, has some crude validity in describing the object she was and has become, but as a language, never has it been less in communication with the sentient spirit which made use of language.

The truth the novel has to tell is that Emma, the sentient, subjective being, is alone, and very few have pursued this insight with as much clarity and courageous finality as Flaubert. Emma chooses her death when the people in her life, one might say, have all become bill collectors, when they refuse her what she wants, when they ask for payment. Her desires require what is not freely given. She loves but

Lheureux pays the bills and he says, "Do you expect me to pay your bills indefinitely?" A material arrangement has to be made, a physical power won before the will can be satisfied. An impersonal and abstract machine, in society as well as nature, has power over life, and it cannot answer Emma's language of desire.

In this way the novel ends with the progressive beleaguerment of the protagonist. She is overwhelmed by externality, both social and natural. There is a climactic series of refusals ending in total failure to impose her will. Leon, Lheureux, the notary, Rodolphe, these with the absence and silence of Charles, force Emma to the wall. She has purified the issue of being at odds. This is the acute psychological position and the one which suggests suicide.

Flaubert follows the stages of disintegration to the end, for he knows that it is the ruin of the great theatre of meaning itself, the theatre of the consciousness. He enacts in his writing the incoherence and disorientation of her mind; her subjectivity has closed in completely.

> Madness began to take hold of her; she was frightened, but managed to control herself—without, however, emerging from her confusion, for the cause of her horrible state—the question of money—had faded from her mind. It was only her love that was making her suffer, and she felt her soul leave her at the thought—just as a wounded man, as he lies dying, feels his life flowing out with his blood through the gaping hole.
>
> Night was falling; crows flew overhead. It suddenly seemed to her that fiery particles were bursting in the air, like bullets exploding as they fell, and spinning and spinning and finally melting in the snow among the tree branches. In the center of each of them appeared Rodolphe's face. They multiplied; they came together; they penetrated her; everything vanished.

Flaubert stresses at that moment the refusal of love, the greatest subjective claim itself. Like the wavering of a single light in the dark, the poignant principle of life is that its meaning is self-generated, the light has its source within itself.

—HAROLD KAPLAN, *"Madame Bovary:* The Seriousness of Comedy," *The Passive Voice: An Approach to Modern Fiction* (Athens: Ohio University Press, 1966), pp. 23–24, 27–34

LEO BERSANI

The unresponsiveness of Emma's environment to her dreams of glamor produces the "symptoms" which give her a deceptively complex psychology and obscure the highly original thinness of her character. I'm thinking especially of two agitated but empty periods of her life: the year and a half between the ball at La Vaubyessard and the Bovarys' decision to leave Tostes, and the time between Emma's realization that Léon loves her and Léon's departure from Yonville. At the beginning of each section, something thrilling has happened; at the end of both, we see Emma in a kind of catatonic stupor. But nothing happens in between; her sickness is purely imaginary. The excitement she felt at la Vaubyessard keeps her busy for a while: she dreams of Paris and even begins to buy the clothes and luxury objects she has seen in the fashion magazines. But the vulgarity of Charles and of Tostes debases and trivializes these fragments from a more glamorous world, and we watch Emma slowly sink into discouraged passivity. She abandons music, drawing and reading ("—I've read everything, she would say"), stares vacantly out of the window at the uneventful life on the streets of Tostes, becomes capricious, develops palpitations and a dry cough and remains "without speaking, without moving" after equally inexplicable outbursts of feverish talk. This instability is even more marked during the period following her discovery of Léon's love. Her immediate reaction is a voluptuous self-satisfaction which she enjoys by curious self-denials: she admires her economy in refusing the scarves and slippers Lheureux tempts her with, and she exasperates Léon by suddenly playing the role of the devoted wife. "Full of covetous desires, of rage, of hatred," hoping for some catastrophe that would reveal her love to Léon, but held back by "laziness or terror," she consoles herself by taking "resigned poses" in front of a mirror and congratulating herself on her virtue. But the strain is too much, and instead of seeking an escape from her suffering, she forces herself to think of it, "arousing herself with her pain and looking everywhere for opportunities to suffer." She abandons herself to wild adulterous fantasies, blames Charles for all her unhappiness and wishes that he would beat her so that she might hate him more intensely. When she thinks of running away with Léon, "a vague abyss, full of obscurity, opened in her soul," and she finally seeks help from the town priest, who has no idea what she's talking about. Her last hope gone, she returns home in a stupor, knocks her daughter down in a fit of irritation, frantically worries about the bruise on Berthe's cheek, but later that evening stares coldly at the sleeping child and thinks how strange it is that Berthe should be so ugly.

The absence of events thus produces rich enough psychological sequences. But there are already signs in *Madame Bovary* that psychological detail is merely incidental to what interests Flaubert most deeply in novelistic character. The most original passages in the first of the two sections I have been referring to are not analyses of Emma's feelings, but rather some coolly precise descriptions of Tostes. Emma watches, at an incalculable distance, the most ordinary events:

> How sad she was on Sundays when the church bell rang for vespers! She listened to each dull stroke with a kind of dazed attention. A cat walking slowly across the roofs would arch its back in the pale sunlight. The wind blew trails of dust along the highway. Sometimes a dog would howl in the distance. And the regular, monotonous tolling would continue to float from the belfry, dying away over the surrounding countryside.

More than Emma's self-punishing or sadistic fantasies, this kind of thoughtless stupor in front of the world dramatizes the anxiety of a consciousness living entirely off itself. Nothing in her fantasies *connects with* her environment, and the juxtaposition of her dreams with literal descriptions of that environment produces the effect of disconnectedness (it even accounts for the often awkward, enigmatic divisions among chapters) characteristic of the Flaubertian narrative. And not only is the world alien to Emma's dreams of romance; it also offers no images which she can use as a relatively appeasing spectacle of her anguish. When she returns from her fruitless visit to church, she is struck by the calm immobility of the objects in her house, "while she felt in herself so much turmoil." Flaubert's extraordinarily detailed and extraordinarily literal descriptions deprive Emma of what might be called any metaphorical relief. Things simply *are there*, much more so than in *La Nausée*, where the supposedly alien nature of objects is belied by the sickening richness of their metaphorical viscosity, a viscosity clearly projected on them by a highly particularized psychology. If it is true, as Jean-Pierre Richard has said, that Flaubert fears a perhaps similar absorption in a pasty world of undifferentiated liquid matter, this phenomenological obsession is largely irrelevant to his art. For the "solution" of writing (which, by giving the world sharply defined forms, also keeps it at a distance) immediately creates a problem of being which can be accounted for *only* by the inventions of art. True, Emma occasionally experiences a sense of oneness with the world: in the form of an ecstatic synchronization with the rhythms of nature when Rodolphe makes love to her for the first time in the forest, and, just before she takes the poison, in the form of a terrifying, vertiginous confusion between her frantic mind and a suddenly spinning countryside. But in a sense these "natural" illusions, even the terrifying ones, are privileged moments of exception. The deeper horror in *Madame Bovary* is Flaubert's stunning achievement of describing a world which represents nothing; for in the anxiety Emma feels in front of the most banal aspects of an astonishingly banal environment, Flaubert indicates the more profound mystery of a totally abstract sickness, that is, of an agony and a death whose insignificant cause is merely the exercise of imagination.

The profundity of Emma Bovary as a figure in literature has been obscured by her intellectual and psychological triviality as a "character." I would associate that profundity first of all with what may seem like a sign of her imaginative mediocrity: her indifference to, and curious irritability over occasions which seem to realize her dreams. For, even in this mortally boring province, occasions *do* present themselves: there are, after all, the adventures with Léon and Rodolphe. But, significantly, Emma is never more exasperated than during her love affairs. The affair with Rodolphe could, one imagines, have gone on indefinitely; it's *Emma* who ends it with her frantic insistence on transporting it to other, more "suitable" climates. And Léon doesn't really break with her; with docility and terror, he plays the pathetic games of an extravagant, brutal sexuality meant to deaden Emma's constant sense of "the insufficiency of life," of that "instant decay of the things she leaned on." And, even during their discreet, unavowed love at Yonville earlier in the novel, Léon's presence destroys the pleasure of thinking of him. "Emma trembled at the sound of his footsteps: then, in his presence, her emotion fell, and afterwards there remained only an immense astonishment which ended in sadness."

What are the reasons for that sadness? Superficially, they are obvious enough: Rodolphe and Léon are hopelessly mediocre, and Emma's dreams of romance are so absurd that *no* lover could help her to realize them. But how important is the content of her dreams? The novels that have corrupted her are, on the whole, third-rate imitations of the great romantic works, but while Flaubert is obviously mocking those literary clichés of romance, nothing in any of his own works suggests that so-called superior art can provide more accurate images of reality. It matters very little that Emma's thought is trivial; we might even say that her mediocrity is an advantage in the novel in that it helps Flaubert to dramatize the essentially insignificant nature of imagination. James, who obscured the insubstantiality of imagination with the conjectures of enormously ingenious centers of consciousness, understandably felt that Emma is not an interesting or perceptive enough "vessel of experience"; her consciousness is "really too small an affair" even for "a picture of the middling." But Flaubert, as his later work shows even more clearly, is fundamentally unresponsive to the appeal of a psychological or intellectual richness to which he is still making some concessions in *Madame Bovary*. Emma's trivial mind ideally carries the weight—or the weightlessness—of the novel's self-destructive meaning. The astonishingly sympathetic identification between Flaubert and Emma can be explained by the simple fact that she lives in fantasy (any fantasy will do). The mediocrity of her thought is less important than the artistic rigor of her refusal to accept *any* equivalence between imagination and reality. She intuitively understands what was for Flaubert the central fact about literature: its fictions *resemble nothing*. The anxiety produced by that awareness makes her an object of subtle clinical observation, but her symptoms are irrelevant to the disease of imagination itself. So is her limited intelligence: method and discrimination have nothing to do with the life of the mind in its purest form, which explains why Bouvard and Pécuchet are the ideal Flaubertian heroes. The fact that they live only for knowledge explains Flaubert's uneasy sympathy for them; their grotesqueness is part of their unenviable integrity, that is, of their touchingly foolish attempt to derive a "truth" from the aleatory, arbitrary, infinitely rich and infinitely futile universe of words and ideas.

—LEO BERSANI, "The Anxious Imagination," *Partisan Review* 35, No. 1
(Winter 1968): 59–62

MARIO VARGAS LLOSA

Emma is a basically ambiguous character, in whom contrary sentiments and appetites coexist—at one point the narrator says that in her "one could no longer distinguish selfishness from charity, or corruption from virtue"—and this fundamental trait, which at the time of the book's appearance seemed absurd to critics accustomed to the Manichaean distribution of vices and virtues among separate and distinct characters, seems to us today to be the best proof of her humanity. But her lack of precise definition is not only moral and psychological; it also applies to her sex, for beneath the exquisite femininity of this young woman a strong-willed, determined male lies hidden.

Emma's tragedy is that she is not free. She sees her slavery as not only a product of her social class—the petty bourgeoisie as mediatized by certain modes of life and prejudices—and of her provincial milieu—a tiny world where the possibilities of accomplishing anything of note are few—but also, and perhaps most importantly, as a consequence of her being a woman. In the fictional reality, to be a woman is to be tied down, to find doors closed, to be condemned to more mediocre choices than those open to a man. During the amorous exchange with Rodolphe that has the agricultural fair as its background, when the seducer speaks of the class of beings to which he belongs, to whom dreams and action, pure passions and furious pleasures, are indispensable, Emma stares at him as though he were someone who had traveled through "exotic lands," and answers bitterly, in the name of her sex: "We poor women don't even have that distraction!" This is true: in the fictional reality not only are amorous escapades forbidden the woman; dreaming as well appears to be a masculine privilege, since those who seek to escape by way of the imagination, by reading novels, for example, as Madame Bovary does, are looked down upon, are considered to be *"évaporées,"* females who are featherbrained and flighty. Emma is well aware of the inferior status in which women find themselves in the fictional society—a typical "male-chauvinist phallocracy," as it would be called in today's feminist vocabulary—as becomes even more evident when she finds herself pregnant. She ardently hopes the baby will be a boy, "and this idea of having a male child was like the potential revenge of all her past frustrations." Immediately thereafter, using the *style indirect libre* with its elusive transitions, the narrator sets down the following reflection, undoubtedly Emma's, describing the sexual discrimination of the day: "A man is free, at least; free to range passions and the world, surmount obstacles, taste the most exotic fruits of pleasure. Whereas a woman is constantly thwarted. At once inert and compliant, she has both the weaknesses of the flesh and legal subjection to contend with. Her will, like the veil tied to her hat, quivers with every breath of wind; there is always a desire that leads her on, a rule of decorum that holds her back." Being a woman—above all, if one has imagination and a restless temperament—is a real curse in the fictitious reality: it is not surprising that on learning that she has given birth to a daughter, Emma, her hope deceived, faints dead away.

But Emma is too rebellious and active to content herself with dreaming of a vicarious "revenge," by way of a possible male child, for the powerlessness to which her sex condemns her. Instinctively, gropingly, she combats this feminine inferiority in a way that anticipates certain forms chosen a century later by a number of women fighting for the emancipation of their sisters: by assuming attitudes and dress traditionally considered masculine. A tragic feminist—because her battle is an individual one, more intuitive than logical, a contradictory one since it in fact seeks what it rejects, and one doomed to failure—deep in her heart of hearts Emma would like to be a man. It is thus more than by chance that in her visits to the château de La Huchette, her lover's home, she plays at being a man—"she combed her hair with his comb and looked at herself in his shaving mirror"—and (in a gesture of frustration that a psychoanalyst would label a characteristic sign of penis envy) even falls into the habit of clenching between her teeth "the stem of a large pipe" of Rodolphe's. Nor are these the only occasions on which Emma acts in ways that transparently reveal the unconscious wish to be a man. Her biography abounds in details that make this attitude a constant from her adolescence to her death. One of them is her manner of dress. Emma often adds a masculine touch to her attire, and takes to wearing men's clothes; what is more, the men in her life find this attractive. When Charles meets her for the first time, at Les Bertaux, he observes that "a pince-nez framed in tortoise shell, like a man's, was tucked between two buttons of her bodice." On her first horseback ride with Rodolphe, that is to say, on the day that her liberation from the bonds of matrimony begins, Emma is symbolically wearing "a man's hat." As her affair with Rodolphe goes on and she becomes more daring and imprudent, these outward signs of her identification with the virile begin to be more and more noticeable: as though to "shock everyone," the narrator says, Emma goes about with a cigar in her mouth, and one day we see her step out of the Hirondelle "wearing a tight-fitting vest, like a man's": this masculine attire strikes the villagers as being so outlandish that those who had given her the benefit of the doubt as to her infidelity "doubted no more."

This propensity of Emma's for going beyond the limits of the second sex and invading the territory of the first betrays itself, naturally, in ways less evident than her style of dress. It is implicit in her dominating nature, in the swiftness with which, the moment she notices any sign of weakness on the part of the male, she imme-diately takes over from him and forces him to assume female attitudes. In her relations with Léon, for example, their respective roles change very soon, and it is always she who takes the initiative: it is she who goes to Rouen to see him, rather than vice versa; it is she who asks him to dress in a certain way so as to please her, she who advises him to buy new curtains for his rooms, she who more or less orders him to write poems to her. Because Léon is tightfisted and has inhibitions about indulging himself, Emma ends up sharing the expenses of the hotel where they make love. Léon is the passive element, she the active one, as the narrator points out: "he never disputed any of her ideas; he went along with all her tastes; *he was becoming her mistress, more than she was his.*" But precisely because Léon plays the feminine role that his energetic mistress forces upon him, Emma feels frustrated and is contemptuous of him, *because in her eyes he behaves like a woman;* her identification with the male mentality is thus total. The day comes when Léon stands her up because he can't manage to shake Homais; the thought then crosses her mind that the notary's clerk is "incapable of heroism, weak, common, *more spineless than a woman,* and a penny-pincher and a coward be-sides." (All italics in these quotations mine.) Emma is forever doomed to frustration: as a woman, because the woman in the fictional reality is a subjugated being to whom the world of dreams and passion is forbidden; as a man, because she can reach that world only by turning her lover into a nonentity, incapable of arousing in her an admiration and a respect for the so-called *virile* virtues, which she has failed to find in her husband and seeks in vain in her lovers. This is one of the insoluble contradictions that make Emma a pathetic character. Heroism, daring, prodigality, freedom are, apparently, masculine prerogatives; yet Emma discovers that the males in her life—Charles, Léon, Rodolphe—become weaklings, cowards, mediocrities, and slaves the moment she assumes a "masculine" attitude (the only one that allows her to break the bonds of slavery to which those of her sex are condemned in the fictional reality). Thus there is no solution. Her horror at having borne a daughter, so bitterly criticized by the self-righteous, is the horror of having brought a feminine being into a world in which life for a woman (one like herself at least) is simply impossible.

In her marital relations too, the male-female roles are very soon reversed; Emma becomes the dominant personality and Charles the dominated. She sets the tone, everything is always done her way, at first only about the house, but later in other domains as well: Emma takes over the task of making out the patients' bills, obtains a power of attorney that will enable her to make all the decisions, and gradually becomes the lord and master in the family. She obtains this status with little difficulty, for all it takes to turn her weak-willed husband into a tool is a little guile or a bit of wheedling; but if necessary she does not hesitate to use forceful means, as when she backs her husband into a corner by demanding that he choose between her and her mother-in-law. Emma's hold over Charles does not end with her death, for it grows even stronger following her suicide. The first thing Charles does after she has breathed her last is to decide to have a splendid, romantic funeral, as would suit her tastes. Later on, he contracts her spendthrift habits, her fancy notions, thus bringing on his ruin, exactly as Emma has brought catastrophe upon herself. The narrator sums up this situation in a moving image: "She was corrupting him from beyond the grave."

Moreover, in the fictitious reality Emma's case is not unique; there are two other women who assume masculine roles without feeling as frustrated as Madame Bovary by so doing. In both instances the women are matriarchs who take over the man's role in the marriage because of the husband's weakness. Charles Bovary's mother becomes the head of the household when the couple meets financial ruin, and in like manner Charles's first wife, the narrator tells us, "was the master" from the moment the couple married. There is a difference, naturally. These matriarchs are not feminists in the usual sense of the word; their reversal of the roles is in no way a sign of rebellion; on the contrary, it implies resignation. They take over the role of the man because there is nothing else they can do, given the fact that their husbands have rejected it and someone in the household must make decisions. In Emma's case, masculinity is not only a function she assumes in order to fill a place left empty but also a striving for freedom, a way of fighting against the miseries of the feminine condition.

—MARIO VARGAS LLOSA, "Emma Bovary, a Man," *The Perpetual Orgy: Flaubert and Madame Bovary* [1975], tr. Helen Lane (New York: Farrar, Straus, & Giroux, 1986), pp. 140–45

SUSAN J. ROSOWSKI

Flaubert's *Madame Bovary* is a prototype for the novel of awakening. Emma Bovary, a character who has learned the nature of the world through romantic fiction, struggles to acquire an art of living in accord with those fictional values.

Conflict is largely internal, between two selves: an inner, imaginative self of private value is at odds with an outer, conventional self of social value. Movement is from an initial childhood separation between the two selves to an illusion of synthesis in marriage, followed by an awakening to the impossibility of such a union and a return to separation. Finally, like many other protagonists in the novel of awakening, Emma Bovary is essentially passive. Tension results from the reader's awareness of the impossibility—even undesirability—of her efforts: we ask what will happen to Emma Bovary, not what will she bring about, and we measure her greatness—her soul—by the extent to which she awakens to impossibilities.

In her childhood, Emma Rouault experienced a separation between two basic elements in herself—her private, imaginative self and her public, social self. Early she began to live a dual life: at school, the outward asceticism of a convent was at odds with inner excesses of religious mysticism and romantic dreams; at home, the realism and simplicity of farm life conflicted with dreams of luxury and bliss. Romantic fiction promises that separation between these two lives will end with marriage, when a girl will combine passionate love with public duties as a wife and mother. And so Emma Rouault, believing "qu'elle possédait enfin cette passion merveilleuse qui jusqu'alors s'était tenue comme un grand oiseau au plumage rose planant dans la splendeur des cieux poétiques," marries Charles Bovary.

Almost immediately disparity between dream and reality is evident, for Emma "ne pouvait s'imaginer à présent que ce calme où elle vivait fût le bonheur qu'elle avait rêvé." Tension builds as her imaginative self, shaped by romantic fantasies, finds no outlet in her role as a wife. By the time the Bovarys are invited to a ball given by a neighboring Marquis at la Vaubyessard, Emma has recognized that all her efforts to insert passionate love into her marriage have failed. Bored with her everyday existence, she perceives the ball as an incarnation of her earlier fantasy life, but with a difference. At the ball, imaginative value is maintained only by a complete separation from the human reality of time; and Emma ceases to perceive herself in terms of a past and a future: "sa vie passée, si nette jusqu'alors, s'évanouissait tout entière, et elle doutait presque de l'avoir vécue. Elle était là; puis autour du bal, il n'y avait plus que de l'ombre, étalée sur tout le reste."

It is against this fact of separation that Emma Bovary concentrates her resources. As a woman, however, her possibilities for action are limited: she believes her sex is dependent upon a man to initiate her "aux énergies de la passion, aux raffinements de la vie, à tous les mystères." No longer expecting to be satisfied by vicarious existence through her husband, Emma turns to other men—to a son and, finally, to lovers. While she is pregnant, "cette idée d'avoir pour enfant un mâle était comme la revanche en espoir de toutes ses impuissances passées. Un homme, au moins, est libre; il peut parcourir les passions et les pays, traverser les obstacles, mordre aux bonheurs les plus lointains. Mais une femme est empêchée continuellement. Inerte et flexible à la fois, elle a contre elle les mollesses de la chair avec les dépendances de la loi."

With the birth of a daughter, even this dream of vicarious extension is disproved, and Emma turns to imaginative value through lovers. Entering an affair with a neighboring landowner, Rodolphe Boulanger, Emma revels "à cette idée comme à celle d'une autre puberté qui lui serait survenue.... Elle entrait dans quelque chose de merveilleux où tout serait passion, extase, délire." More specifically, Emma again imagines release from the limitations of space and time: "une immensité bleuâtre l'entourait, les sommets due sentiment étincelaient sous sa pensée, et l'existence ordinaire n'apparaissait qu'an loin, tout en bas, dans l'ombre, entre les intervalles de ces hauteurs." Separation between her two lives remains complete: Emma imagines not joining her fantasy with everyday existence, but rather leaving everyday existence and entering a dream world of romantic love: "Elle devenait elle-même comme une partie veritable de ces imaginations et réalisait la longue rêverie de sa jeunesse, en se considérant dans ce type d'amoureuse qu'elle avait tant envié."

Tension in the novel of awakening results from the reader's awareness that the protagonist's attempts to escape human realities are impossible. Flaubert reminds us of this impossibility by counterposing characters that represent worldly concerns to Emma's dream of escape. Lheureux, a usurer, pursues Emma as a hunter pursues his victim, tightening his net about her as she becomes ensnared in debts taken on in desperate attempts to reproduce the luxurious life of her imagination; and the blind man symbolically pursues her, a stark reminder of the sickness, decay, and death that are inevitable elements of human existence.

Finally, then, change disproves Emma Bovary's dreams of romantic bliss. Her vision of a future with Rodolphe, "infini, harmonieux," ends when he abandons her. Her initial happiness with the clerk, Léon, ends when she rediscovers "dans l'adultère toutes les platitudes du mariage." Through change, Emma Bovary realizes the "impossibilitié" of her dream of everlasting bliss, for "tout plaisir [a] son dégoût, et les meilleurs baisers ne vous laissaient sur la lèvre qu'une irréalisable envie d'une volupté plus haute." Eventually, the tension between Emma's two lives becomes intolerable. Still seeking to satisfy the imaginative self formed in her childhood and wishing to escape "comme un oiseau, aller se rajeunir quelque part, bien loin, dans les espaces immaculés," Emma takes poison. In her last moments, the narrator comments, she undoubtedly rediscovers "au milieu d'un apaisement extraordinaire la volupté perdue de ses premiers élancements mystiques, avec des visions de béatitude éternelle qui commençaient."

—SUSAN J. ROSOWSKI, "The Novel of Awakening," *Genre* 12, No. 3
(Fall 1979): 314–16

VLADIMIR NABOKOV

The ups and downs of Emma's emotions—the longings, the passion, the frustration, the loves, the disappointments—a chequered sequence, end in a violent self-inflicted and very messy death. Yet before we part with Emma, we shall mark the essential hardness of her nature, somehow symbolized by a slight physical flaw, by the hard dry angularities of her hands; her hands were fondly groomed, delicate and white, pretty, perhaps, but not beautiful.

She is false, she is deceitful by nature: she deceives Charles from the very start before actually committing adultery. She lives among philistines, and she is a philistine herself. Her mental vulgarity is not so obvious as that of Homais. It might be too hard on her to say that the trite, ready-made pseudoprogressive aspects of Homais's nature are duplicated in a feminine pseudoromantic way in Emma; but one cannot help feeling that Homais and Emma not only phonetically echo each other but do have something in common—and that something is the vulgar cruelty of their natures. In Emma the vulgarity, the philistinism, is veiled by her grace, her cunning, her beauty, her meandering intelligence, her power of idealization, her moments of tenderness and understanding, and by the fact that her brief bird life ends in human tragedy.

—VLADIMIR NABOKOV, *"Madame Bovary* (1856)," *Lectures on Literature,*
ed. Fredson Bowers (New York: Harcourt Brace Jovanovich, 1980), p. 142

DOMINICK LaCAPRA

Emma was the central figure in the novel for both the prosecution and the defense at the trial. She is also the character in whom metaphysical desire for an absolute—desire which ennobles and sets one apart—is endangered, even hopelessly contaminated, by banal and pathetic attempts at evasion that are symptomatic of the milieu they would transcend. She has velleities of purity and a thirst for something better: she makes demands on her environment. Yet she is a narcissistic creature of her romantic dreams and longings with little or no concern for the needs or the existence of others. She oscillates between boredom and hysteria, recognizes only what comes in cliché, and unites the "pleasure principle" with a deadly pattern of repetition. "Incapable . . . of understanding what she did not experience or of believing anything that did not take on a conventional form," Emma "rejected as useless whatever did not contribute to the immediate satisfaction of her heart's desire—being of a temperament more sentimental than artistic, looking for emotions, not landscapes."

The narrator who can analyze her ironically and critically is also fascinated with her—as are the other men who come into contact with her. When narratorial fascination reaches the limit of identification, it approaches the emulation of Emma that marks Charles at the end of the novel. The sense that the narrator in relating to Emma is also relating to himself—and beyond his fictive role to the authorial or biographical Flaubert—makes his ambivalence all the more difficult to pin down. Emma is manifestly, as the prosecutor at the trial (who himself courted becoming "involved" with her) observed, the most forceful creature in the book—more forceful perhaps than the author-narrator who gives birth to her. Men cannot handle her; she cannot handle herself. And "Flaubert" threatens to be overwhelmed by her less sophisticated, less sublimated, and in certain respects more powerful desires and demands. She insistently wants something out of life and is willing to take major risks to get it. If one can speak of her "problem," it is in no sense a simple problem, and it is perplexingly bound up with the "problems" of her world.

Indeed the figure of Emma represents a crucial breakdown in the circuits of sexual, socioeconomic, and linguistic exchange and reproduction. Given the interference of these circuits with one another, she also signals a more general short-circuiting in society and culture at large.

Sexually, Emma's position is not fixed: it is far from stable in any regard. She is a woman who refuses to play the traditional woman's role. And, despite her own weaknesses, she is the most active and "masculine" figure in the novel, dominating not only other characters but threatening to dominate the author-narrator as well. For Baudelaire, Flaubert poured his own masculine blood into Emma's veins, while for Sartre, in a kind of reverse transfusion, Emma is Flaubert feminized. This chiasmic criss-crossing of perspectives—each turn of which is equally plausible or equally exorbitant—indicates that Emma's masculinity is not a question of ordinary role reversal and that her relation to Flaubert is implicated in a tangled web of involvements. Indeed Baudelaire saw Emma's hysteria in terms that broached the problem of androgeny:

> The Academy of Medicine has not as yet been able to explain the mysterious condition of hysteria. In woman, it acts like a stifling ball rising in the body (I mention only the main symptom), while in nervous men it can be the cause of many forms of impotence as well as of a limitless ability at excess. Why could this physiological mystery not serve as the central subject, the true core, of a literary work?

The image of a ball rising in the body might suggest that of a cat that chokes "hysterically" on a fur ball caused by licking the self, and it metaphorically links hysteria and narcissism. The relation between impotence—for example, that felt by the epigone—and excess points to the interplay between lack and limitlessness that preoccupied Flaubert in the world he represented and in his own narrative practice.

Emma herself is in character neither for the traditional man nor for the traditional woman, for her desires both exceed and fall short of the expectations of both. She does at times affect masculine dress and behavior, but she does not simply want to be a man in the traditional sense. Nor does she want to have this kind of man, assuming that he exists in her world. The man of whom she dreams transcends ordinary incarnations of "manhood" to the point of becoming vaguely utopian.

Nor will Emma assume the role of traditional housewife. Her activity in the family departs from the conventional code in an extravagant way. She performs her duties with obsessive finesse, or she abandons them with peremptory negligence. In both cases, she really seems to be elsewhere. She does wish that her child were a boy, and she loses interest in the poor creature who has the misfortune to be born a girl. "George" might have had the chances denied to Emma and provided her with a vicarious sense of fulfillment—at least as long as "George" remained as imaginary as Emma's other longed-for men. The girl child is an absence in the novel, almost a literal figure of castration. Emma takes leave of the role of *"mère de famille"* before the standard Oedipal triangle has a chance to get started, for the child is a blank in her life. In this sense, even her pregnancy was hysterical, and its product, which is not an object of imaginary investments or narcissistic identification, loses all interest for her.

Equally significant for the rupture of the generational cycle is the fact that Emma's mother is dead as the story opens, and she does not seem to play a significant part in Emma's life. Far from identifying with her mother, Emma escapes motherhood and behaves in a way that establishes an association between the position of her mother and that of her child: both are absences. Indeed the first explicit reference to Emma's mother in the novel comes from the mouth of her father, and it is an analogy between the woman and Charles's first wife. The analogy is situationally ironic, for it is intended to console Charles after the passing of the unlamented Héloïse—herself a widow he had married under false pretenses. The second and last reference to Emma's mother recalls that Emma cried much the first few days when her mother died, and she sent her father a letter "full of sad reflections on life" and requesting that she be buried in her mother's grave. This reference is followed by her father's anticlimactic reaction (the "old man" thinks she is ill and comes to see her) and by Emma's own self-satisfaction in attaining "at a first attempt the rare ideal of delicate lives, never attained by mediocre hearts"—an ideal immediately linked to "Lamartine, . . . harps on lakes, . . . all the songs of dying swans, . . . the falling of the leaves, the pure virgins ascending to heaven, and the voice of the Eternal discoursing down the valleys." Thus Emma reduces and assimilates her mother's death to her ordinary romantic musings.

Economically as well as socially, Emma has no productive or reproductive function. She is a pure consumer in a world where commodities tend to be reduced to counters in a largely imaginary game. And her pattern of consumption, which is more heedless and imprudent than wasteful, creates financial difficulties that adulterate the purity of "romantic" fate—the one thing she would like to attain, perhaps even in its more elevated tragic form. In fact, her financial mismanagement is itself paradoxically traditional rather than modern: she behaves like a displaced *grande dame* in her desire to give gifts, unconcerned with mere money matters, and like a good *bourgeoise* in her will to possess fully what she has bought. Yet her lack of prudence is capitalized upon by those, such as Lheureux, who are more in tune with existing economic demands in their own small scale and petty fashion. Emma is less a victim of Capitalism than someone whose desires cannot be accommodated within its limits—and perhaps within any limits, even largely technical or formal ones. But the system she chooses to disdain returns to her with a vengeance, bringing her both to the verge of prostitution and to the absurdly virtuous and highly conventional affirmation that she cannot be bought. Emma is a scandal both to the traditional bourgeois family and to its modern economic setting.

Linguistically, Emma herself disrupts the code of realistic representation. Her primary use of language is incantatory. Her magical clichés and rhythmic repetitions create their object—one that can never be attained in the world of mundane realities. Indeed an "other" attains reality for her only when it may be perceived as the incarnation of a memory recast through the imagination. A perverse Platonist, she is also a small-town Proustian *avant la lettre.* Rodolphe registers as a lover only after the event of seduction when Emma may intone him into imaginary existence through an appeal to an evanescent but transcendent archetype.

> She repeated: 'I have a lover! a lover!' delighting at the idea as if a second puberty had come to her. So at last she was to know those joys of love, that fever of happiness of which she had despaired! She was entering upon a marvelous world where all would be passion, ecstasy, delirium. She felt herself surrounded by an endless rapture. A blue space surrounded her and ordinary existence appeared only intermittently between these heights, dark and far away beneath her.
>
> Then she recalled the heroines of books that she had read, and the lyric legion of their adulterous women began to sing in her memory with the voice of sisters that charmed her.

Cliché and stereotype are as much the vehicles of Emma's dreams as they are the powers that help to create them. The one thing they are not is a simple representation of a preexistent reality. Emma herself is both utterly conventional and insistently unconventional—so much so that it becomes difficult to distinguish between what is and is not "ordinary" in her behavior. Her disaffection for her child is the conventional response of a "narcissistic" woman who would have her progeny be what she is not but would like to be. But her reaction goes beyond the limits of convention in its hyperbole. And her various "men" always have something dubious about them: Rodolphe is a hackneyed, hollow phallus that crudely signifies the imaginary; Léon is her mistress; and Charles as fool and saint is both less and more than the average man.

Emma herself is strangely above and below the level of her time—above it, however equivocally, in the magnitude and insistence of her claims and below it, however pathetically, in her willingness to sacrifice everything—others as well as self—in trying hopelessly to make those claims good. I have intimated that, in one sense, her demands cannot be fulfilled because they are of such an exorbitant nature that nothing could conceivably satisfy them. In another sense, they cannot be made good because the concrete forms they take are so trite that they coalesce confusingly with that to which they are presumably opposed. Metaphysics turns maudlin as Emma's quest for an absolute becomes excessively compromised by its continuous contact with vulgar desires and realities. Her claims cave into the same subsoil of empty repetition from which they would escape until they are terminated—not meaningfully ended—by death. Both the divided nature of her demands and the fact that they subside into an order that is itself on the verge of exhaustion prevent her suicide from attaining the grandeur of tragic protest. To the extent that it makes a statement, that statement is itself threatened by trivialization and cliché. Yet the nature of her quest prevents reducing her to her milieu, and it allegorically raises questions about its relation to the project of pure art itself.

—DOMINICK LACAPRA, "Aspects of the Novel," Madame Bovary *on Trial* (Ithaca, NY: Cornell University Press, 1982), pp. 178–83

JULIAN BARNES

Madame Bovary has a dog, given to her by a game-keeper whose chest infection has been cured by her husband. It is *une petite levrette d'Italie:* a small Italian greyhound bitch. Nabokov, who is exceedingly peremptory with all translators of Flaubert, renders this as whippet. Whether he is zoologically correct or not, he certainly loses the sex of the animal, which seems to me important. This dog is given a passing significance as … less than a symbol, not exactly a metaphor; call it a figure. Emma acquires the greyhound while she and Charles are still living at Tostes: the time of early, inchoate stirrings of dissatisfaction within her; the time of boredom and discontent, but not yet of corruption. She takes her greyhound for walks, and the animal becomes, tactfully, briefly, for half a paragraph or so, something more than just a dog. 'At first her thoughts would wander aimlessly, like her greyhound, which ran in circles, yapping after yellow butterflies, chasing field-mice and nibbling at poppies on the edge of a cornfield. Then, gradually, her ideas would come together until, sitting on a stretch of grass and stabbing at it with the end of her parasol, she would repeat to herself, "Oh God, why did I get married?" '

That is the first appearance of the dog, a delicate insertion; afterwards, Emma holds its head and kisses it (as Gustave had done to Nero/Thabor): the dog has a melancholy expression, and she talks to it as if to someone in need of consolation. She is talking, in other words (and in both senses), to herself. The dog's second appearance is also its last. Charles and Emma move from Tostes to Yonville—a journey which marks Emma's shift from dreams and fantasies to reality and corruption. Note also the traveller who shares the coach with them: the ironically named Monsieur Lheureux, the fancy-goods dealer and part-time usurer who finally ensnares Emma (financial corruption marks her fall as much as sexual corruption). On the journey, Emma's greyhound escapes. They spend a good quarter of an hour whistling for it, and then give up. M. Lheureux plies Emma with a foretaste of false comfort: he tells her consoling stories of lost dogs which have returned to their masters despite great distances; why, there was even one that made it all the way back to Paris from Constantinople. Emma's reaction to these stories is not recorded.

What happened to the dog is also not recorded.

—JULIAN BARNES, "The Flaubert Bestiary," *Flaubert's Parrot* (New York: Knopf, 1984), pp. 63–64

FREDERICK ALFRED LUBICH

In his portrayal of Emma Bovary—of whom Flaubert said "Madame Bovary, c'est moi"—the author establishes a case history of romantic illusionment and disillusionment, whose psychological mechanisms he analyses with the detached objectivity of a scientist. Emma Bovary spends the formative years of her adolescence in a convent, where the mysticism and sensuality of the religious rituals awakens in her a deep yearning for a world of exotic and luxurious self-enchantment. Once again and for the last time the heroine of a novel falls under the spell of other romantic novels of her time: "They were all about love, lovers, sweethearts, persecuted ladies fainting in lonely pavilions . . . and . . . gentlemen brave as lions, gentle as lambs, virtuous as no one ever was, always well dressed and weeping like fountains." It is in particular the Gothic novels of Walter Scott that make her long to "live in some old manor-house, like those long-waisted chatelaines who, in the shade of pointed arches, spent their days leaning on the stone, chin in hand, watching a white-plumed knight galloping on his black horse from the distant fields."

Emma's marriage to the provincial and pedestrian country doctor Charles Bovary turns out to be in every imaginable aspect the exact opposite of all her romantic dreams and aspirations. Unwilling to awake to reality, Emma at first tries to instill her listless marriage with some magic of romance by reciting "passionate rhymes" and singing "melancholy adagios" to her husband in their moonlit garden. This sentimental ruse, however, proves to be a complete failure. After having "for a while struck the flint on her heart without getting a spark"—this cutting metaphor works like an incision into Emma's indulgent imagination—she grows increasingly despondent.

Since the reality of her life will not deliver the high promises of her novels, Emma looks for romantic redemption in extramarital affairs. Rodolphe, a leisure-class virtuoso of numerous erotic adventures, seems to match all her dreams of a heroic lover. He, however, is nothing but a skillful impersonator of Emma's grand illusions. Using all the romantic lines that he knows would strike a chord in her, he carefully prepares the stage for his erotic conquest. It is, of all places, the local agricultural fair, where he begins to utter his romantic stock phrases of eternal love and betrayal, while being constantly interrupted by the endless announcement of prizes for livestock and vegetables:

> "A hundred times I tried to leave; yet I followed you and stayed . . ." / "For manures!" . . . "And I will never forget you." / "for a merino ram." . . . "Tell me there can be a place for me in your thoughts, in your life, can't there?" / "Hog! first prize equally divided between Messrs. Lehérissé and Cullembourg, sixty francs!"

This contrapuntal juxtaposition of meat prizes and passionate entreaties amounts to parody in the most literal and original sense of the word, that is, a pure form of antiphony. Rodolphe's declaration of love at the agricultural fair thus sets the tone for their ensuing love affair. After they have both paid the romantic price of mutual self-deception and consumed their passion, it soon loses its novelty and becomes an everyday commodity to alleviate their provincial boredom. Emma's desperate attempts to raise their relationship above a routine back-door adultery and imbue it with an aura of romantic grandeur comes to an anticlimactic end; and again Flaubert cannot refrain from twisting it into a parody of ludicrous proportions. Instead of eloping with Emma in the grand style of romance, as originally planned, Rodolphe changes his mind at the last moment. Sitting at his desk "under the stag's head that hung as a trophy on the wall," he rummages through a thick stack of love letters from his former conquest. Getting bored with reading them, Emma's would-be hero decides to cancel the elopement, writes a final farewell letter, and as he cannot shed any tears over it, lets a big drop of water fall on the paper: "Whereupon he smoked three pipes and went to bed."

Emma is so deeply distraught over Rodolphe's betrayal that she falls seriously ill. With the sharp eyes of a caricaturist who sees through the follies of human illusions, Flaubert discovers—or better, rediscovers—at the bottom of Emma's lovesickness the mysticism of her Catholic religion, in which her imagination had been nourished from early childhood. Exploiting all the traditional erotic undertones of man's *unio mystica* with God, Flaubert grants Emma at the height of her sickness the ecstatic illusion of a divine seduction: "Tasting the joy of weakness, she saw within herself the destruction of her will opening wide the gates for heavenly grace to conquer her." After she had "fainted with celestial joy as she advanced her lips to accept the body of *the Savior*"—a kiss with Flaubert's tongue in cheek—Emma feels "the existence of a bliss that could replace happiness, another love beyond all loves, without pause and without end." Emma's lovesickness is a psychological case history in which all human physical and metaphysical longings coalesce into a sublime form of parody. The climax of her religious cum romantic self-deception is also the turning point for her ensuing disillusionment: "When she knelt on her Gothic prie-Dieu, she addressed to the Lord the same suave words that she had murmured formerly to her lover in the outpourings of adultery. She was searching for faith; but no delights descended from the heavens, and she arose with aching limbs and the vague feeling that she was being cheated."

Barely recovered from her spiritual lovesickness, Emma resumes her relationship with Leon, the young poetaster-clerk, with whom she once shared her obsession for lyrical reverts. Jaded by her attempts at sentimental and spiritual salvation, Emma now veers toward instant gratification, which of course turns her former platonic ties with Leon almost immediately into a passionate tangle. Whereas in her youth Emma had dreamt of "carriages, gliding through parks ... driven at a trot by two small postilions in white breeches," she now finds herself in a rattling coach behind whose drawn curtain her romance turns into a desperate rampage. While the coachman is driven into a frantic ride, which makes him circle the bumpy streets of the city until he is "almost weeping with thirst, fatigue and despair," Emma and Leon indulge in their passion, a passion that cannot be anything else but a grotesque struggle against the odds of a permanent and involuntary coitus interruptus. Flaubert, who in writing his novel became fascinated with what he called the "double abyss of lyricism and vulgarity," has certainly plumbed the depths of both in this coach scene. From this experience Emma will no longer fully recover. Whereas the young Leon continues to idolize her as the "mistress of all the novels, heroine of all the dramas, the vague 'she' of all the volumes of verse," the admirer himself begins to fall short of the heroic expectations Emma cherishes in him. Her rapidly growing disillusionment with him unravels in an endless litany of paradoxes: "Everything was a lie. Every smile concealed a yawn of boredom, every joy a curse, every pleasure its own disgust." Paradox—once the paradigm of Schlegel's universal poetry and romantic parody—has become Emma's source of growing mental derangement. In her final letter, in which she blames Leon for her disappointed hopes, her accusations blend with new infatuations. Out of the ashes of her burned-out love for Leon rises a new "phantom fashioned out of her most ardent memories, of her favorite books . . . and at last he became so real . . . like a god, he was hidden beneath the abundance of his attributes. He dwelt in that azure land where silken ladders swung from balconies in the moonlight, beneath a flower scented breeze." In this apotheosis of kitsch, Emma's romantic imagination has reached not only pathetic but above all pathological proportions.

Emma's death through arsenic poisoning is filled with all the tragedy of suicide, but it is neither a melodramatic *Liebestod* nor a romantic act of insanity; rather it is the desperate solution to her ever increasing financial problems. And even in her last hour, Emma is not spared a final parodistic stab, which pokes fun at her fate. At her extreme unction she experiences her last relapse into the "lost bliss of her mystical flights, mingling with the visions of eternal beatitude," only to be rudely awakened by the raucous voice of a blind beggar. The incantation of his frivolous song is a parody—again in the original sense of the word—of the religious dirges of *Misereatur* and *Indulgentiam,* sung at her deathbed. It begins with a couplet, which turns out to be the leitmotif proper of Emma's lifelong emotional immaturity:

Often the heat of a summer's day
Makes a young girl dream her heart away.

Then it swells up to a more contemplative stanza on the transitoriness of all life and concludes with a highly burlesque couplet:

The wind blew very hard that day
It blew her petticoat away.

The ironic parallels between a petticoat blowing away and a soul leaving its dying body behind are not lost on Emma. She breaks into an "atrocious, frantic, desperate laugh"—what else could better express the shattering of her lifelong romantic and religious illusions than this last penetrating laugh—and with a final spasm that throws her back on the mattress she dies.

—FREDERICK ALFRED LUBICH, "The Parody of Romanticism: Quixotic
Reflections in the Romantic Novel," *European Romanticism: Literary
Cross-Currents, Modes, and Models,* ed. Gerhart Hoffmeister (Detroit:
Wayne State University Press, 1990), pp. 322–26

CRITICAL ESSAYS

Frank D. McConnell

THE LEXICOGRAPHY OF *MADAME BOVARY*

NOVELS: Corrupt the masses. Are less immoral in serial than in volume form. Only historical novels should be allowed, because they teach history. Some novels are written with the point of a scalpel (Ex: *Madame Bovary*). Others revolve on the point of a needle.[1]

Flaubert's *Dictionary of Accepted Ideas* is, in its peculiar fashion, one of his most important documents—more so, perhaps, than even the letters. For while the letters give us a consistently complex and often paradoxical record of the artist's struggle toward and evaluation of his position as artist, the *Dictionary* is in fact a minimal reduction, an imaginative paradigm, of that art itself. The cranky result of a lifetime's attraction-repulsion by the brutal ignorance of the French bourgeoisie, it is marked by the gusto of neither satire nor aestheticism, but by the willed verbal exhaustion which is characteristic of Flaubert and the poetic tradition of which he is a central figure: the tradition of Byron, Kafka, Sartre, and Genet. What critics like Jean-Pierre Richard and Jean Rousset have seen as Flaubert's tendency to drive intelligence toward its own negation in a process of liquescent entropy[2]—manifest at the end of *The Temptation of St. Anthony* in the cry, "To be matter!"—is manifest in the *Dictionary* as the horrified and fascinated penchant of the lexicographer for the sheer stupidities implicit in language. And it is precisely the pose of lexicographer which allows the "narrator" of the *Dictionary* to maintain the necessary distance from his perversely treasured vulgarities. To realize *how* necessary—and how difficult—this distance was for Flaubert, one need only remember the mawkishly elephantine eroticism of the early letters to Louise Colet, or the vulgar collectorship of the letter to Maxime du Camp (23 March 1846) where, much in the manner of his own Rodolphe Bourlanger, the author tells about such objects as the shawl and lock of hair that he acquired at his sister Caroline's funeral. The "scientific" pseudo-structure of the dictionary is one of the most efficient of Flaubert's psychic disguises.

For the definitions of the *Dictionary* are not simply clichés brought together in a list of exhibits against the silliness of the nineteenth century: they form instead a random sampling, damning in its very randomness, of the wastage of history and the perishability of the Word. Much like the "language games" of Wittgenstein's late thought, they present a complete but absurdly finite set of terms from which an entire—and absurd—culture may be extrapolated:[3]

From *Novel* 3, No. 2 (Winter 1970): 153–66.

GOTHIC: Architectural style which inspires religious feeling to a greater degree than others.

JEWS: "Sons of Israel." All Jews are spectacle vendors.

LIGHT: Always say: *"Fiat lux"* as you light a candle.

The flatness of the definitions comes cumulatively to mark a terminal stage of energy in language itself. And the dictionary "order" equally reflects a minimized verbal control, alphabetizing without compunction "Denture, Derby, Descartes, Desert, Dessert," and "Device: Obscene word" for one randomly inane series. In form and motive, the *Dictionary* mediates between an austere and annihilative control of language and the half-conscious surrender to that grotesquerie which was the obverse of Flaubert's lyricism. And in this manner it is far more than simply the whimsical and unfinished appendix to *Bouvard et Pécuchet:* it is a brilliant element in a crucially modern tradition.

In one subtle form or another, the lexicographer and the collector are important subtypes in post-Romantic literature: the lexicography being always bogus and the collection always incomplete. Byron, Flaubert's early hero and perhaps the first fully conscious post-Romantic, sends the narrator of *Don Juan* again and again off into lengthy digressions on philosophy, poetry, and his own speech—digressions which are reductive "definitions" of the Wordsworthian and Shelleyan ideal of the self-creative Word:

Oh! ye immortal Gods! what is Theogony?
   Oh! thou, too, mortal man! what is Philanthropy?
Oh! World, which was and is, what is Cosmogony?
   Some people have accused me of Misanthropy;
And yet I know no more than the mahogany
   That forms this desk, of what they mean;—*Lykanthropy*
I comprehend, for without transformation
Men become wolves on any slight occasion.   (IX, 20)

In *Don Juan,* as this process of narrative reduction continues, we gradually become aware that the "subject" of the poem is precisely the act of verbal reduction itself: the weary, obsessively confessional narrator is literally trapped by his own speaking voice and by the incipient gigantism of his poem. He is forced to continue until he bores himself (himself being both Byron and "Byron") to death.[4] This is the Byron whom the young Flaubert said he valued with Rabelais above all other writers because he had written "in a spirit of malice toward the human race and with the intention of laughing in its face":[5] an appraisal which, in spite of its jejune cynicism, was to bear important imaginative fruit in the younger author's career.

Byron's friend and Flaubert's immediate master Stendhal belongs to the same general line of descent, although his celebration of Romantic egotism renders his sense of language ambiguous, at once more exuberant and less terminally self-conscious.[6] Frequently, however, Stendhal's paragraphs move in much the same way as the characteristic stanza of *Don Juan,* systematically emptying a term or an event of its assumed nobility of "meaning"; as in Julien Sorel's first view of the ramparts of Besançon:

> He had gotten some street clothes at Fouqués, and in this costume he passed the drawbridge. Filled with the history of the siege of 1674, he wanted to see, before burying himself in the seminary, the ramparts and the citadel. Two or three times he was almost stopped by the guards; he penetrated into those places that military wisdom forbids to the public, in order to sell twelve or fifteen francs'-worth of hay a year.[7]

And, of course, the whole career of the *jeune ambitieux* Sorel is a tragicomic attempt to locate and "define" the meanings of those Napoleonic terms which have formed the matrix of his boyhood imagination: terms which he constantly finds do not function in the bureaucratized France of the 1820's. The word most frequently on Julien's lips is some form of *devoir:* and the divisive ambiguity of the word, alternating between the senses of obedience to an abstract ethical paradigm (Napoleon) and celebration of imperiously individual moral energy, is what finally exalts and destroys Julien. As he says of himself after being condemned to death: "The duty (*devoir*) I have prescribed for myself, right or wrong, has been like the trunk of a strong tree I grasped during a storm. . . . Finally I was only a man . . . but I have not been blown away."[8]

In both Byron and Stendhal, the particularly post-Romantic technique of lexicographic reduction easily blends with a much older motif, that of the novel-trained *naif* who discovers that "real life" is not lived as it appears to be from fiction (Don Quixote, Werther, Marianne Dashwood). But there is a recognizable difference between the two motives: not really qualitative so much as imaginatively quantitative, an upping of the ante in the more recent line. The critical testing of "plot," or of fiction's natural tendency to crystallize the structure of experience, is in fact a prime genetic impulse of the novel as a form. The structure of most novels can, in fact, be discussed as a variation of Cervantes' use of the "plot" of medieval romance, and of his ambiguously respectful and scoffing handling of his "source," Cide Hamete Benengeli. But the act of sheer lexicographic devaluation, the testing of the power of words themselves, at whatever level of complexity, to preserve and control our ideational life, is a performance set up *against* the inherited structure of the novel. It is a distinctive energy of the last two centuries, with their growing realization that, as E. M. Cioran says, *"Sous chaque formule gît un cadavre."*[9] In this century the sense of the negative dictionary is raised to full consciousness: Wittgenstein's language games, and indeed his whole thought from the *Brown Book* to the *Philosophical Investigations,* are perhaps the most brilliant explorations of its possibilities. And Kafka's fables frequently operate as "language games" in a nearly Wittgensteinian sense: a completely "naturalistic" plot working out the implications of one absurd premise, and finally demonstrating the innate absurdity of the normal premises assumed by "naturalistic" language itself.[10] But it is in Sartre and Genet that the technique is used with the fullest deliberation. Roquentin's horrifying discovery, in *La Nausée,* that words are only desperate bulwarks against the disgusting

plenitude of existence, is counterpointed by the desiccated humanism of the Au-
todidact who, replaying the dark comedy of Flaubert's *Dictionary*, is educating
himself by reading through the Library in alphabetical order: "Today he's at L. K
after J, L after K. He's come lurching from the study of coleoptera to quantum
theory, from a work on Tamerlane to a Catholic pamphlet against Darwinism: not
disconcerted for a moment."[11] And Genet, lovingly detailing the speech of the
prison queens in *Our Lady of the Flowers*, projects a designedly interminable web
of debased metaphors and gutter-slang "poems"—the verbal equivalent of that
imaginative nihilism for which his chief image is his own homosexuality.

Flaubert's role is central to the line of descent I have been tracing. For in both
the *Dictionary* and, even more strikingly, in *Madame Bovary*, one can see the older
motif of "testing the plot" emerging into the radically critical motif of "testing the
Word," of a consciously negative lexicography. There are, in fact, many points
(most of them listed in the appendix to Lea Caminiti's 1966 collation) at which the
Dictionary, no less than *A Simple Heart*, appears to cast a retrospective glance at
the author's early triumph. The definition of "Novels" at the beginning of this essay
contains a wry memory of Lemot's 1859 cartoon depicting Flaubert dissecting
Madame Bovary's heart. And the definition of "Decoration" is a reminiscence of the
armchair liberal, Homais: "The Legion of Honor: make fun of it, but covet it. When
you obtain it, say it was unsolicited." And two important definitions both complement each other and cast a grim afterglow on one of the most important imagistic
matrices of *Madame Bovary*, that of food-sex-poison-intoxication:

> ABSINTHE: Extra-violent poison: one glass and you're dead. Newspaper-
> men drink it as they write their copy. Has killed more soldiers than the
> Bedouin.
> ARSENIC [the poison with which Emma kills herself]: Found in everything.
> Bring up Mme. Lafarge. And yet certain peoples eat it.

But by far the most revealing connection between the two books is the passage in
Madame Bovary (I, v) where Emma begins to contemplate her marriage to Charles
and her disappointed expectations. It is a crucial passage, coming at the end of a
crucial chapter: for this is the point, as the couple enter their home at Tostes, that
the narrator makes his startling transition from Charles' to Emma's point of view.
That transition is made with a symmetry as deliberate as that of classic psychoma-
chia. After two opening paragraphs describing the house and its garden, the third
paragraph describes Emma's entry:

> Emma went upstairs. The first room was not furnished, but in the second,
> the conjugal bedroom, was a mahogany bedstead in an alcove with red
> drapery. A shell-box adorned the chest of drawers, and on the secretary near
> the window a bouquet of orange blossoms tied with white satin ribbons stood
> in a bottle. It was a bride's bouquet: the other one's [*C'était un bouquet de
> mariée, le bouquet de l'autre!*] Charles noticed; he took the bouquet, carried
> it to the attic, while Emma seated in an armchair (they were putting her things

down around her) thought of her bridal flowers packed up in a bandbox, and wondered, dreaming, what would be done with them if she were to die.[12]

(23)

The four verbs relating to Emma in this passage mark a progressive narrative penetration from action through simple perception to that nearly-hallucinatory sensibility which is to be the hallmark of Emma's interior monologue: *Emma montait ... regarda ... songeait ... et se demandait, en revant.* ... After a second paragraph from Emma's point of view there follow three paragraphs reverting to Charles', in which his already bovine self-consciousness begins to narrow to the obsessive cynosure of his new wife's regard: "His own eyes lost themselves in these depths and he could see himself mirrored in miniature, down to his shoulders, with his scarf round his head and the top of his shirt open" (23–24). And finally, after Charles' unsuspecting bliss has been catalogued, the last paragraph of the chapter announces Emma's definitive reaction to the marriage and her now total control of the narrator's point of view:

> Before marriage she thought herself in love; but since the happiness that should have followed failed to come, she must, she thought, have been mistaken. And Emma tried to find out what one meant exactly in life by the words *bliss, passion, ecstasy,* that had seemed to her so beautiful in books [*Et Emma cherchait à savoir ce que l'on entendait au juste dans la vie par les mots de* félicité, *de* passion *et d'*ivresse, *qui lui avait paru si beaux dans les livres*].
>
> (24)

Here, at the carefully planned moment of Emma's first major revelation of consciousness, she appears not merely as the traditional novel-trained *naïve,* but as a lexicographer of experience; for it is not simply a plot she is testing against the "real" world, but those three ironically loaded words, *félicité, passion,* and *ivresse,* which among themselves finally come to encompass the whole of her disastrous career.

To understand fully the range and importance of the verbal motto *félicité, passion, ivresse,* it is necessary to examine their potential grammar. All three may be understood as both intransitive and relational terms, depending upon the sense in which we decide to take them. *Félicité*—"bliss," "luck," "joy," or a kind of benign capacity for grace, is either a serenely full good humor or a dynamic equilibrium of circumstance and spirit. *Passion* is both *le grand passion,* the English "passion," and also a "passive" suffering, a state of being painfully objective to another person or to the world. And *Ivresse* is both "ecstasy" and, simply, "drunkenness" or "intoxication": taken most generally, the use of an object—or the objectification of a subject—for the artificial transcendence of one's subjective consciousness. This last sense, of course, aligns most immediately with the sex-food-poison matrix I have mentioned before, but all three words, in their contrary grammars, play throughout the course of Emma's experience.

The importance of the relational-nonrelational ambiguity of these three key words is made plain in a passage following close upon the one I have just cited.

Chapter vi of Part One is a recitation of the young Emma's reading—*Paul et Virginie,* Chateaubriand, and the Abbé Frayssinous—in the conventional novelistic motif already mentioned. But the effect of her romantic reading is given a deeper articulation than the conventional; she is shown committed to the "romance" view of life in terms not only of projected action, but of willed perception:

> Accustomed to the quieter aspects of life, she turned instead to its tumultuous parts. She loved the sea only for the sake of its storms, and the green only when it was scattered among ruins. She had to gain some personal profit from things and she rejected as useless whatever did not contribute to the immediate satisfaction of her heart's desires [*elle rejetait comme inutile tout ce qui ne contribuait pas à la consommation immédiate de son coeur*]— being of a temperament more sentimental than artistic, looking for emotions, not landscapes.   (25–26)

Like earlier novelistic heroes and heroines, Emma is engaged in trying to work out of her own life the form—the plot—of the romances she has been trained on. But unlike earlier characters, she, and the narrator, carry this activity consciously to the level of the perceiving eye itself, to the level of the use and abuse of *things* in their relationship to the imagination. The alternatives are the artist's concern for "landscapes without emotion," the realization that past a certain point the world of the seen is intractable to the "use" of words or perceptions; and the sentimentalist's drive for a private profit from things, that urge to reduce objects to tools which has a sinister tendency to turn on itself and reduce the perceiver to the slave of the objects which surround him.[13] The key phrase in the passage is *la consommation immédiate de son coeur:* a phrase whose overtones range from the "satisfaction" to the "consumption" or "destruction" of Emma's heart, from her "eating" things to her being eaten by them, with the full ambiguity of relationship of the words, *félicité, passion,* and *ivresse* which the book develops.

It is not enough, however, simply to say that Emma represents the sentimentalist's sense of words and perception, and Flaubert the artist's; for the third term that subsumes both author and creation is that of *homo rhetor,* man enlivened and limited by his language, which implies a complex relationship between all three elements. Flaubert himself was profoundly aware of this relationship when he wrote to Louise Colet, of the composition of *Madame Bovary:* "The less you feel a thing, the fitter you are to express it as it is (as it *always* is, in itself, in its essence, freed of all ephemeral contingencies). But you must have the capacity to *make yourself feel it.* This capacity is what we call genius; the ability to *see,* to have your model constantly posing in front of you."[14] Here is the relationship between landscape and emotion at its fullest articulation; the heart of that simultaneous detachment from and obsessive involvement with his characters which Charles DuBos and others have found at the heart of Flaubert's creative power. And the "genius" which balances these two forms of perception is the genius of words, and of the creative devaluation of words. Flaubert continues in the next paragraph, "That is why I detest so-called poetic language. When there are no words, a glance is enough."

"When there are no words"—or when the words exist in a grammar which criticizes their own power to contain experience, transformed from the magic terms of romantic dreaming into a desperately serious linguistic and phenomeno-logical game. The *consommation de son coeur* Emma desires is *immédiate.* But for Flaubert, here as in the *Dictionary,* the perilous experience of creation is "medi-ated" through his quizzical and existential sense of the limits of language.[15] It is not simply a brilliant result but, for Flaubert, a necessary condition of his creativity.

Félicité, passion, and *ivresse* function, then, as both the genetic and structural seeds of *Madame Bovary's* lexical nihilism. In that order, furthermore, they reflect a mounting violence of contradiction between their relational and nonrelational overtones. And as Emma moves through her career as disappointed wife, young adulteress, and experienced (and somewhat blasé) mistress, she can be seen trying disastrously to discover "what one really means in life" by each of those terms in succession. In the case of each term, her romantic sentimentalism leads her to opt for the static or nonrelational "grammar" of the word—for the use of things—only to have the arc of her experience force her into knowledge of its relational contingencies, and of the intractability of the world to her words for it. And as a kind of harmonic variation on these three key words, each Part of *Madame Bovary* involves itself with a variation of *consommation,* in its three senses of eating, sexual consummation (the most metabolic, and ambiguous, "use" we make of things), and destruction.

Part One is definitively the book of *félicité.* Emma's naive romanticism projects itself into the vision of a cozy bourgeois idyll shared with the widower Charles. It is the classic, wished-for balance of the middle-class home that she attempts to co-opt into the stuff of her dreams, and she encounters a dreadful disappointment precisely because of Charles' complete willingness to let himself be thus co-opted. Charles is happy in exactly the fashion Emma wants to obtain happiness, in a kind of blissfully ignorant, static condition which obviates his relating to Emma in any intelligent way. But this nonrelational *félicité* of his is a block to Emma's own, and she comes to see that her use of him as the object of her living fantasies reduces him finally to the status of object pure and simple: a piece of hardly necessary furniture in the Tostes home:

> Sometimes Emma tucked the red borders of his undervest into his waistcoat, rearranged his cravat, and threw away the faded gloves he was going to put on; and this was not, as he fancied, for his sake; it was for herself, by an expansion of selfishness, of nervous irritation. At other times, she told him what she had been reading, some passage in a novel, a new play, or an anecdote from high society found in a newspaper story; for, after all, Charles was someone to talk to, an ever-open ear, an ever-ready approbation [*car, enfin, Charles était quelqu'un, une oreille toujours ouverte, une approbation toujours prête*]. She even confided many a thing to her greyhound! She would have done so to the logs in the fireplace, or to the pendulum of the clock.
> (I, ix, 44)

Emma has turned Charles into a completely outfitted doll only to find the doll boring in its—for her eyes—unconsciousness. Her assertion to herself that, after all, he is *someone* is subtly contradicted by the immediate appositives of that *quelqu'un: une oreille* and *une approbation,* a feature and an attitude, but not a recognizable human *gestalt.* And by the end of the passage, he has become simply an equivalent object to those other stage-props of the ideal of bourgeois blessedness, dog, fireplace, and family clock.

Operating within the orbit of this dream of *félicité,* the overtones of *consommation* coalesce, in a phenomenon very like that of grammatical attraction, into images primarily of *consommation* = eating:[16] all of them variations of that familial meal which is the unacknowledged liturgy of the French bourgeoisie. Three meals describe the movement of the First Part: the wedding-feast in Chapter Four with its festive abundance and its absurdly overdecorated wedding-cake; the dinner-ball at Vaubyessard, which opens to Emma another possible level of experience (and introduces an innuendo of assignation, i.e. sexual *consommation*); and the complementary image of Emma's home meals with Charles in Chapter Nine, with the image of the meal completely interiorized in the landscape of Emma's boredom: "All the bitterness of life seemed served up on her plate, and with the smoke of the boiled beef there rose from her secret soul waves of nauseous disgust" (47).[17] But even before this final image, the key term of Part One has achieved its final reductive definition in Emma's experience. The housekeeper-maid whom Emma hires to replace the harassed Nastasie, and whom she trains, with a pathetic desperation for gentility, to address her in the third person and knock before entering her room, is named, with a surely conscious irony, Félicité.[18]

Having exhausted the grammar of *félicité* through her too-efficient objectification of Charles, Emma next explores the "meaning in real life" of *passion:* that state of delirious surrender for another which easily transforms itself into a relationship of tortured objectivity *to* the other. The classic articulation of this concept is the literature and tradition of courtly love, with its religious overtones of the Virgin cult and its celebration of the inaccessibility of the mistress as an essential aspect of her perfection. And the introductory interlude of Part Two, Emma's subtle flirtation with Léon Dupuis, is a deliberate imitation (on the narrator's part and, of course, Emma's) of the action of courtly love. The comically exalted tone of their dialogue, which reads as if taken from a chapbook of the romantic sublime, reaches its climax in II, v, when Léon, visiting Emma, chances to see Emma, Charles, and their daughter in a family tableau. Struck by what appears the happiness (*bonheur,* not *félicité*) of this domestic scene, he despairingly renounces all hope of attaining her: "She seemed so virtuous and inaccessible to him that he lost all hope, even the faintest. But, by thus renouncing her, he made her ascend to extraordinary heights. She transcended, in his eyes, those sensuous attributes which were forever out of his reach; and in his heart she rose forever, soaring away from him like a winged apotheosis" (76). In the original, Emma did not precisely "transcend" sensuous attributes: rather *Elle se dégagea . . . des qualités charnelles;* nor did she simply "rise forever, soaring away from him": *Elle alla . . . montant toujours et s'en détachant....* Both important verbs, *dégager* and *détacher,* emphasize the act of separation, of objectification of the loved one that is taking place in Léon's mind with Emma's complicity if not through her design.

This sort of passion, suffering oneself to take on the objectivity of the ideal, has its inversion: suffering oneself to take on the objectivity of the *thing.* This is the grammatical genesis of Rodolphe Bourlanger, certainly the most self-conscious, and deliberately factitious, character in the novel. Rodolphe is a collector of women: a semi-professional reducer of persons to objects; and Flaubert, after Emma's first meeting him in II, vii, even breaks into an uncharacteristically heraldic description of him to make the point: "Monsieur Rodolphe Bourlanger was thirty-four; he combined brutality of temperament with a shrewd judgment, having had much experience with women, and being somewhat of a connoisseur. This one had seemed pretty to him; so he kept dreaming about her and her husband" (93). One is reminded inevitably of Rodolphe's great model, the "Byron" of continental myth. And he manages Emma's seduction with all the linguistic cynicism of the real Byron. His perverse rhetorical brilliance at the Yonville Agricultural Fair (II, viii) largely constitutes that most brilliant scene of the novel, and needs no more comment at this point. But Emma's interior monologue after her first seduction, in Chapter Nine, is equally crucial to the linguistic development we are tracing: "She repeated: 'I have a lover! a lover!' delighting at the idea as if a second puberty had come to her. So at last she was to know those joys of love, that fever of happiness of which she had despaired! She was entering upon a marvelous world where all would be passion, ecstasy, delirium" (117). *Passion, extase, délire:* but this *passion* is also the suffering (hinted at in the phrase *cette fièvre du bonheur*) of becoming completely objective, absolutely a thing, to another person. It is a passion (Lat. *patior*) mirrored in the brutal comedy of Charles' attempts, at Emma's encouragement, to cure the clubfoot Hippolyte.

The presents Emma gives Rodolphe play a central role in the transvaluation of her *"passion"* from its nonrelational to its relational sense. They are objects she intends as mementos of herself, but which humiliate Rodolphe, since he can see them only as unnecessary transactions in a shoddy affair. And following immediately the failure of these gifts comes the climactic dialogue of II, xxi:

> Then she had strange ideas.
> "When midnight strikes," she said, "you must think of me."
> And if he confessed that he had not thought of her, there were floods of reproaches, that always ended with the eternal question:
> "Do you love me?"
> "Why, of course I love you," he answered.
> "A great deal?"
> "Certainly!"
> "You haven't loved any others?"
> "Did you think you'd got a virgin?" [*Crois-tu m'avoir pris vierge?*] he exclaimed laughing.   (137)

Emma's impulse is to remain permanently and ideally objective for her lover, but not to him: *tu penseras à moi*, she says: you must think *of* (not about) me.[19] And Rodolphe's cruel question, "Did you think you'd *taken me* virgin?" savagely inverts Emma's idea by reminding her that she had also participated in the seduction, that it was in fact a mutual transaction rather than a romantic quest with herself as passive goal. As Emma tearfully professes her adoration for Rodolphe, he reflects, partly in the tones of the narrator himself, on the stale linguistic of her *"passion,* that has always the same shape and the same language" (138).

The whole scene marks an important transition in Emma's experience. After this, Rodolphe's relationship to her takes on a cruder aspect of *use,* of a hinted-at depersonalization of sexual experiment which, as it continues, subtly introduces the third verbal theme of Emma's quest:

> He discarded all modesty as inconvenient. He treated her without consideration. And he made her into something at once malleable and corrupt. [*Il en fit quelque chose de souple et de corrompu*]. It was an idiotic sort of attachment, full of admiration on his side and voluptuousness on hers, a beatitude which left her numb [*l'engourdissait*]; and her soul sunk deep into this intoxication [*ivresse*] and drowned in it, all shrivelled up, like the duke of Clarence in his butt of malmsey.   (138)

Passion disappointed is already merging into the self-numbing and finally destructive *ivresse* of Part Three; sexuality depersonalized is becoming the sexuality of aphrodisiac. This is surely part of the "point" of Emma's reconversion, after her abandonment by Rodolphe, to a pietistic Catholicism. Her Eucharistic fervor and her passion for the little reliquary, set in emeralds (II, xiv) are a final attempt to realize the ideal grammar of *passion*—but an attempt which in its debased and misused sacramentalism anticipates the manic exaltation-depression of "intoxication": "When she knelt on her Gothic prie-Dieu, she addressed to the Lord the same suave words that she had murmured formerly to her lover in the outpourings of adultery. She was searching for faith [*C'était pour faire venir la vroyance*]; but no delights descended from the heavens, and she arose with aching limbs and the vague feeling that she was being cheated" (155). *C'était pour faire venir la croyance:* in trying to make faith *come* to her she is seeking a desperately idealized *passion,* and also another kind of terminally-reduced *consommation de son coeur. Consommation* as a hidden motif throughout Part Two is realized primarily as sexual consummation; but in the control of Emma's ideal of *passion* (and ultimately derived from the courtly-love figure of *danger*[20]), it becomes a sexuality of denial. Her relationship with Léon, as we have seen, is based firmly on the psychology of sexual aloofness. And during her affair with Rodolphe, she makes him the embarrassing promise not to have intercourse with her husband (II, x). And finally, in her prie-Dieu stage, she yearns for a perfectly alembicated, unresolved *consommation* of religious fervor with the lover-Jesus of excessive pietism. It is the *consommation,* really, of the *Liebestod,* and as such shades into the sense of *consommation* = ultimate dissolution which is operative throughout Part Three.

Ivresse, in the triad of terms we have been tracing, is the most dangerously ambiguous of phenomenological relationships. It is precisely a state of artificially induced rapture whose success depends upon the subject's being able to forget or deny the rapture's artificiality: the perpetually foredoomed use of phenomena to overcome the boredom of phenomena.[21] And throughout Part Three, images and verbs of drinking, of the theatre, and of aphrodisiac cluster around Emma's adultery with Léon Dupuis. For Emma is attempting to maintain a nonrelational, permanent *ivresse* by assimilating, turning into artifact, the entire world of her perception. In II, xv, she goes to the theater in Rouen to see *Lucie de Lammermoor* and is initiated into the grammar of artificial rapture:

> All her attempts at critical detachment were swept away by the poetic power of the acting, and, drawn to the man by the illusion of the part, she tried to imagine his life. . . . Every night, hidden behind the golden lattice of her box, she would have drunk in eagerly [*elle eût recuelli, béante*] the expansions of this soul that would have sung for her alone. . . . She longed . . . to cry out, "Take me away! carry me with you! let us leave! All my passion and all my dreams are yours!" [*À toi, à toi! toutes mes ardeurs et tous mes rêves!*]
>
> (163)

Immediately after this she meets Léon, for the first time in three years.

It is the expansive, rapturous side of *ivresse* which accounts for the hot-house luxuriousness with which the early idyll of Léon and Emma is described. Shifting the scene of her expectations to Rouen from Yonville, Emma encounters a landscape which in its very remoteness from her everyday life is easily assimilated and altered into an erotic intoxicant. The three-day sojourn at the Hôtel-de-Boulogne master-fully articulates this hallucinatory factitiousness:

> They were three full, exquisite, magnificent days—a true honeymoon. . . . And they lived there behind drawn blinds and closed doors, with flowers on the floor, and iced fruit syrups that were brought them early in the morning. . . . They took a covered boat and went to dine on one of the islands. . . . They sat down in the low-ceilinged room of a tavern with black fishing-nets hanging across the door. . . . It was as if nature had not existed before, or had only begun to be beautiful since the gratification of their desires.   (185)

Nature seems expansively renewed for the lovers, but the whole weight of the passage emphasizes the roofed-over, closed-in, deliberately constructed vantage-point from which they witness this illusory rebirth of the world. Emma is the efficient artificer of this hotel-room paradise, who manages everything, including Léon's own erotic rapture, and who yet must maintain the difficult belief that the ecstasy is hers and natural. Returning from Rouen to Yonville, she can surrender herself still to the induced ecstasy and shiver in the carriage, drunk with grief [*ivre de tristesse*]. But during the week between visits, she learns to exercise a now-experienced control over her passion: "His own passion was manifested by continual expressions of wonder and gratitude. Emma tasted [*goûtait*] this love discretely, and with all her being, nourished it by every tender device she knew [*l'entretenait par tous les artifices de sa tendresse*], and trembled a little that some day it might be lost" (194). The ecstatic assimilation of *ivresse* has its inevitable transformation and reversal in the image of repletion and nausea: intoxication becoming drunkenness, satiety becoming disgust. Emma's absorption of the world into her idea includes even Léon himself. And as the lovers grow bored of their overfulfillment in each other, Emma attempts to maintain the relationship's static balance by frank erotic fantasizing about the now all-but-invisible Léon. "Then she would fall back to earth again shattered; for these vague ecstasies of imaginary love would exhaust her more than the wildest orgies" (211–212). Immediately following this comes the description of the Mid-Lent *bal masqué*, at which Emma is subtly shown *really* intoxicated and disoriented, and which is the turning-point in the grammar of *ivresse* (III, vi):

> And in the morning she found herself on the steps of the theatre together with five or six other masked dancers, dressed as stevedores or sailors, friends of Léon's who were talking about going out to find some supper.... The others began to eat; she ate nothing. Her head was on fire, her eyes smarted, and her skin was ice-cold. In her head she seemed to feel the floor of the ball-room rebounding again beneath the rhythmical pulsation of thousands of dancing feet. The smell of punch and cigar smoke made her dizzy. She fainted: they carried her to the window.   (212)

Emma awakes the next morning with a carefully described hangover.

The arc of this scene is that which the remainder of the novel is to follow. For the last kind of *ivresse*, the final drug to be assimilated, is the long death of Homais' arsenic. And the extended narration of Emma's retching death agony, which it cost Flaubert so much to write, is on one level an image of metabolic elimination parallel to the phenomenological sickening and elimination she has brought about by attempting to assimilate, to "use" the intractable material of her experience. As Emma's attempt to locate the grammar "in real life" of the terms *félicité, passion,* and *ivresse* reflects a cumulative frenzy of romantic idealism, so the ambiguous grammars of those words become increasingly violent in their alternation between ideal (nonrelational) and phenomenological (relational) resonances. And the final articulation of the *ivresse*-motif of total assimilation is a savage inversion of Emma's dream of the *Liebestod*—a death not for or through, but within love itself: "The priest rose to take the crucifix; then she stretched forward her neck like one suffering from thirst [*alors elle allongea le cou comme quelqu'un qui a soif*], and glueing her lips to the body of the Man-God, she pressed upon it with all her expiring strength the fullest kiss of love that she had ever given" (237). She receives extreme unction, hears outside the window the absurd love-song of the beggar from Rouen, and dies. Having exhausted the grammar of her three key-terms for existence, all that is left her is the final *consommation de son coeur* of dissolution.

But the lexicographic thrust of *Madame Bovary* is not simply to invert, ironize, or exhaust words, but to subvert them. And the last three chapters of the novel are the final necessary appendix to the negative dictionary of Emma's career, the irrefutable demonstration that the world continues past our ability to encompass it through our words. These last chapters are reminiscent of nothing so much as the conclusion of Kafka's *Metamorphosis,* where Gregor Samsa, having exhausted the implications of the equation man = vermin, is present only through his absence, through the annihilation of his living consciousness. And Emma's absence, which broods over the end of the novel named after her, is one of the earliest and most complete explorations of nothingness and silence in a tradition which grows more and more central to the troubled imaginative life of our own century.[22]

NOTES

[1] *The Dictionary of Accepted Ideas.* The translation is that of Jacques Barzun (New York, 1968); but occasional additions are made, without notation, from Lea Caminiti's synoptic edition of the *Dictionnaire des Idées Reçues* (Paris, 1966), which Barzun was not able to use in his translation.

[2] The essays of Richard and Rousset are found conveniently translated in *Flaubert,* ed. Raymond Giraud (Englewood Cliffs, 1964), pp. 36–56, 112–131. Cf. Sartre's comments, in *Search for a Method* (New York, 1963), on Flaubert's peculiar love-hate for his bourgeois origins; and compare Sartre's comments on the same psychic mechanism in Genet, *Saint Genet* (New York, 1964).

[3] "That is to say, whether a word of the language of our tribe is rightly translated into a word of the English language depends upon the role this word plays in the whole life of the tribe; the occasions on which it is used, the expressions of emotion by which it is generally accompanied, the ideas which it generally awakens or which prompt its saying, etc., etc." Wittgenstein, *The Brown Book* (New York, 1958), p. 103.

[4] See J. R. Thompson, "Byron's Plays and *Don Juan:* Genre and Myth," in *Bucknell Review,* XV (1967), 22–38.

[5] The translation is Francis Steegmuller's *Selected Letters of Flaubert* (New York, 1957), p. 12.

[6] The parallelism of *Don Juan* and *Le Rouge et le Noir* is most apparent in the equivalence Mme. de Rênal : Mathilde :: Dona Julia : Adeline Amundeville.

[7] Stendhal, *Le Rouge et le noir* (New York, 1963); my translation.

[8] Stendhal, p. 541.

[9] *Précis de decomposition* (Paris, 1949), p. 13.

[10] See George Steiner, *Language and Silence* (New York, 1967), on Kafka and Wittgenstein.

[11] *La Nausée* (Paris, 1938), pp. 48–49; my translation.

[12] The translation is that of Paul de Man (New York, 1965).

[13] Such an enslavement by objects is, of course, at the heart of Alain Robbe-Grillet's theory of fiction: *For a New Novel* (New York, 1967).

[14] Steegmuller, p. 136; the date is 6 July 1852.

[15] "Mediation" is used here in the sense of Geoffrey Hartman, *The Unmediated Vision* (New Haven, 1967).

[16] By "grammatical attraction" is meant simply the phenomenon of a word's being employed in a form not "correct," but appropriate to the nearest governing term, e.g. "A large number of people were at the game."

[17] This is the passage on which Erich Auerbach based his famous analysis of *Madame Bovary: Mimesis* (New York, 1957).

[18] Cf. the maid Félicité in *Un Coeur simple* and the following entry from the *Dictionnaire* (Caminiti, p. 173): *Félicité. Est toujours "parfaite." "Votre bonne se nomme Félicité, alors elle est parfaite."*

[19] *à* : *de* :: of : about. The meanings are reversed in English, of course.

[20] *Danger* in Courtly Love literature is the figure of aloofness, sexual coldness. Cf. C. S. Lewis, *The Allegory of Love* (Oxford, 1960).

[21] Cf. my own "William Burroughs and the Literature of Addiction," *Massachusetts Review,* VIII (1967), 665–680.

[22] Rousset's essay, already mentioned (fn. 2) seems to imply much the same thing in speaking of *Madame Bovary* as an early antinovel.

Barbara Smalley

MADAME BOVARY: ILLUSION, COUNTERPOINT, AND THE DARKENED UNIVERSE

In the earlier stages of Emma's married life, before the appearance of Rodolphe, her illusions though often implicitly sexual in overtone are still centered in the fashionable life of Paris or the glamour of more distant places, their remoteness from her daily life constituting an important element in the fascination they have for her. The Viscount is scarcely an exception, for he is, for Emma, a perfumed symbol rather than a man of flesh and blood. It is only in the later stages of her course following the advent of Rodolphe that Emma's visions become deeply colored with sexual experience in itself. Even in her most bizarre scenes with Rodolphe and later with Léon at Rouen, *illusion* remains at the very heart of her demands, despite the increasing tones of Satanism that then color her experience. There are still times when she reverts to dreams of a lost paradise that never existed. When she has abandoned the respectable married life of Yonville so far as to dance through the night with Léon to "the wild sounds of the trombones," attired in masculine costume, with velvet breeches, carmine stockings, and a wig and a three-cornered hat—a costume that might come from the pages of the Marquis de Sade or, later, of Huysmans—Emma finds herself capable of being shocked when the voices of other women betray them as females of the "lowest class."[1] She imagines herself escaping the present through a return to youth and innocence: "Everything, herself included, was now unbearable. She would have liked to fly away like a bird, to go away to become young again somewhere far off in the regions of immaculate space."

In the early weeks of her marriage, she had tried to picture for herself an ideal setting for the first experience of married love. The scene is touchingly sentimental, distanced, and pastel: "To taste the full sweetness, one would no doubt have to travel to those lands with resounding names where the days following marriage are spent in delicious idleness. In post-chaises behind curtains of blue silk one slowly ascends the mountain roads, listening to the song of the postilion as it is re-echoed

From *George Eliot and Flaubert: Pioneers of the Modern Novel* (Athens; Ohio University Press, 1974), pp. 51–107 (abridged).

by the mountains amid the sounds of the little bells of goats and the far-off roar of waterfalls" (I.vii.56). As if she were turning pages in one of the keepsakes that supplied her with pictures of the world, Emma's fantasy leaves this lithograph of Switzerland for a more exotic setting to the south: "At sunset on the shore of a bay they would breathe the perfume of lemon trees; then in the evening on the villa terraces above they would gaze hand in hand at the stars and make plans for the future." Flaubert has already told us how, during the period of courtship, Emma in her conversations with Charles would abruptly shift from one mood to another, "her voice . . . clear, or sharp, or . . . filled with languor, trailing off" as if she spoke to herself (I.iii.31). In a similar way her fantasy takes sudden turns of scene and mood. She shifts from her vision of "regions that produce happiness" to those that induce melancholy: "Why could she not now be leaning over the balcony of some Swiss chalet, or enshrining her melancholy in a Scotch cottage, with a husband clad in a black velvet coat with long tails, and soft boots, a pointed hat and ruffles?"

Emma's wistful vision of the slow-paced carriage shared with a loved one behind silk curtains sets up ironical echoes in her later vision of galloping away in the arms of Rodolphe drawn by four horses. It resonates with greater irony, as has often been observed, to the famous scene with Léon, in which their love is consummated for the first time in a public cab with drawn blinds circulating monotonously through the streets of Rouen.

To adjust the world of her illusion to the world of Tostes, in which her husband cupped blood and prescribed pills, was, of course, an impossibility. But Flaubert (himself in his one aspect equally addicted to romantic visions) views Emma's desires for living a romance with a special delicacy at this stage of her experience, if one judges from the tone of his presentation: "Perhaps she would have wished to confide all these thoughts to some one. But how speak about an uneasiness so elusive, changing shape like the clouds, unstable as the winds? Words failed her, and also the occasion, the courage. But if Charles had only wished it, if he had guessed, if his eyes had only once read her thoughts, it seemed to her that her heart would have opened its wealth to him, suddenly, as ripened fruit falls from a tree at the touch of a hand. But even as their outward familiarity became greater, so did her aloofness from him in her inward life" (I.vii.57).

It is easy to understand how some critics have inclined to the view that Emma represents to an important degree an island of refined aesthetic and spiritual yearnings surrounded by elements not only alien but distinctly inferior to her own in the bourgeois village life in general and the dullness of her husband in particular, and that that is the way Flaubert has arranged for us to see her. The lyricism of such passages as the one last quoted seems to imply a nature attuned to delicate perceptions, a nature that, planted in finer soil, would have flowered without danger of blighting. It is necessary, however, to make a distinction: The diction and the lyrical movement of such passages are not Emma's. They are Flaubert's working as ventriloquist. It may be worth noting in the passage just quoted that when Emma thinks of confiding her fleeting visions, not only the occasion and the courage fail her, but the words as well. Flaubert's use of the indirect free style (*le style indirect libre*), his employment of various devices of phrase and structure to evoke Emma's felt presence—not merely her attitudes but an impression that we are hearing her voice in the moment of her silent speaking to herself[2]—is somewhat more complicated than it is often considered. The accents Flaubert assigns his heroine in such passages as that quoted in the preceding paragraph represent her unspoken yearnings. They conjure up for the reader an impression of overhearing a musical voice in lyrical accents quite in keeping with what we have learned of her charms of face and figure. But Flaubert is playing Cyrano for Christian de Neuvillette; we are endowing Emma (as Roxane endowed Christian) with poetical graces that belong elsewhere. And it is better so. Much later Emma is to pour out her love for Rodolphe Boulanger in words designed to represent her own idiom (at a time, it is true, when her imagination is colored by more vivid experience) and not Flaubert's translation into the language of her inward yearnings. Emma's idiom when it reaches the reader from her own lips is passionate, but it is not poetical: " 'Oh, I love you, I love you,' " she exclaims to Rodolphe (who is embarrassed by her asking him, a jaded roué, to declare he has never loved any one else). " 'I love you so much I couldn't live without you, understand? . . . I'm your slave, your concubine! You're my king, my idol! You're good! You're beautiful! You're wise! You're strong!' " (II.xii.264–265). If I have not managed here to be entirely fair to Emma's accents in my translation (the original will be found in the notes[3]), it is in any event clear that Rodolphe does not find her exclamatory language distinctive from that he is used to hearing in such situations and that Flaubert intended the passage to be full of feeling but lame in its diction and rhythms. Rodolphe for his part had "heard these things uttered so often that they had no freshness for him. Emma was like all his other mistresses; and the charm of novelty, falling away little by little like a garment, laid bare the eternal monotony of passion, that always assumes the same forms and the same language." But Flaubert, as narrator, even in his published version of his novel, in which on theory he so carefully represses remarks that might be labeled an obvious deviation from his mask of "impersonality," comments in what amounts to an open authorial intrusion on the part of the narrator: "He did not perceive, this man so versed in experience, the differences in emotions underlying the same expressions. Since libertine or venal lips had murmured to him phrases like Emma's, he believed only slightly in the sincerity of her words. One ought, [Rodolphe] thought, to discount exaggerated phrases used to cloak an ordinary love affair. . . ." And Flaubert's observation completing the passage suggests rather clearly that despite his famous avowal of purpose to Louise Colet—"no lyricism, no author's reflections, the personality of the author not present"[4]—he must at times have been conscious that he was intervening in his work as authorial commentator: ". . . as though the fullness of one's soul did not sometimes overflow in empty metaphors, since no one ever is able to give the exact measure of his needs, his concepts, or his sorrows. Human speech is like a cracked kettle whereon we beat out tunes to set a bear dancing when we would aspire to move the stars to tenderness." If Emma's speech, outside the special language of love, is of a quality above that suggested by thumping on a cracked kettle to produce rhythms for a dancing bear, it is nevertheless the narrator who supplies her oftentimes with translations in a prose that might, if a poet's hyperboles were facts, move the stars to tenderness. Flaubert, working at the one time as both realist and lyricist, had, indeed, no choice. Emma—ostensibly the mind doing the perceiving—must assume the spotlight while the author himself sings behind the scenes; for, as Donald Fanger points out, realism has to appear objective by nature and the "lyrical material has to be attributed or attributable to a character—a procedure that keeps it under narrative control, keeps it judged."[5]

A passage that occurs on the first night of the Bovarys' removal from Tostes to Yonville also suggests that Emma's familiarity with sentimental reading has not given her speech distinction—at least beyond the clichés of such literature. She and Charles converse with Léon and Homais at the chief inn of the town, and Emma and Léon find they speak a common language. Léon, it is worth observing, though like Emma he cultivates sentimental reading, is an attorney's clerk, a petit-bourgeois. He is, much later in the novel, to be her second lover. In the early months at Yonville, however, before the appearance of Rodolphe, Léon shares sentimental scenes with Emma on a Platonic level. Like Emma, he assumes his superiority to the general citizenry of Yonville because of his sensitivity to literature and to music. He dresses neatly; he cleans his fingernails. A passage near the end of the novel, after his months as Emma's lover at Rouen, synthesizes Flaubert's conception of his nature. The liaison has by that time run its course; Léon has been reprimanded by his employer for neglect of work and scandalous conduct. He promises to reform and thinks of all the trouble Emma may still stir up for him. He thinks, too, of all the jokes his fellow clerks will make: "Besides, he was going to be promoted to head clerk; it was time to be serious. So he gave up his flute, his exalted sentiments, his romantic imagination; *for every bourgeois in the warmth of his youth, were it for only a day, a moment, has believed himself capable of immense passions, of high enterprises.* The pettiest libertine has dreamed of sultanas; *every notary bears within him the debris of a poet"* (III.vi.400–401, italics mine).

There is not much reason to suppose, therefore, that when Emma enjoys a sense of communication and kinship with Léon at Yonville, she is conversing with a spirit possessed of unusual refinement, or that her own responses to Léon's words are to be thought of as those of an especially sensitive nature. Indeed the dialogue that Flaubert gives to Léon and Emma contrasts significantly with the lyrical quality that invests his language when he is translating Emma's thoughts and emotions into his own lyrical idiom for her. Charles Bovary in the scene at the inn remarks that his wife is not fond of exercise, for she " 'prefers always sitting in her room reading.' " Léon replies that he also prefers such occupation. " 'And indeed, what could be better than to sit by one's fireside of an evening with a book, with the wind beating against the window and the lamp burning?' " The words strike a ready response in Emma: " 'What, indeed?' she said, gazing at him with her large black eyes wide open."

Encouraged by such response from a woman of obvious refinement who is also very pretty, Léon expands his thought in clichés fostered by the popular book trade, clichés that Flaubert himself could only consider absurdly bourgeois: " 'You forget everything else,' he continued; 'the hours slip by. Without moving from your chair, you travel through the countries of your imagination, and your thought, blending with the fiction, relishes the details, or rushes forward with the adventures. It mingles with the characters, and it is you who are living their lives, your own heart beats in their breasts.' " Emma exclaims, "How true! how true!" It is splendid to discover one's own sentiments expressed in books, but she prefers novels to poetry, which is in the long run boring. Her delight is "stories that rush breathlessly along, that frighten one." She has no use for novels that have commonplace heroes and deal with the concerns of everyday life. (Flaubert, of course, is writing a book in that general vein as she speaks.) Léon agrees: " 'Indeed,' observed the clerk, 'since these works fail to touch the heart, they miss, it seems to me, the true aim of art. It is so sweet, amid all the disappointments of life, to be able to dwell in the imagination upon noble characters, pure affections, and pictures of happiness. For myself, living here far from the world, this is my sole distraction. Yonville has so little to offer' " (II.ii.114–115). By degrees, Flaubert tells us, while Charles and Homais talked of medical and civic matters, Léon and Emma "entered into one of those vague conversations where random turns of phrasing keep bringing you back to a core of shared sympathies." But lest the reader should think that this implies a distinguished power of intellect in Léon and Emma, Flaubert specifies the things that they discoursed about—the theaters of Paris, "titles of novels, new dance tunes, *and the world they did not know*" (italics mine).

The pains that it took Flaubert to enter into the world of Emma's reading and Emma's imagination are evident in his letters to Louise Colet while he was suffering his agonies of art in creating the earlier chapters of *Madame Bovary*. The contempt he felt for sentimentality, as opposed to sincere sentiment, was during this period very intense in him. His work on this part of the novel progressed with excruciating slowness. "Tonight I finished scribbling the first draft of my young girl's dreams. I have another fortnight to put in sailing on these blue lakes, after which I'll attend a ball and then endure the rainy winter, following which I'll close with a pregnancy" (*C*, II, 381). The "young girl's dreams" are clearly Emma's early readings and her imaginative life as they are described in retrospect between her marriage to Charles and the winter following the ball at Vaubyessard. The pregnancy of Emma spans the last months at Tostes and the first at Yonville. Such material continued to exact agonizing effort. Though Flaubert had intended to complete his novel as far as the visit to Vaubyessard in a fortnight, he had just managed to carry his manuscript that far at the end of four weeks: "I have now come to my ball, which I will commence on Monday," he wrote Louise Colet on April 24, 1852. "I hope it will go better." He had managed only twenty-five pages in the last six weeks, averaging a little more than half a page a day (*C*, II, 394). His natural inclination, he wrote in July, was not at all toward the sort of material that he was dealing with (*C*, II, 461–462); and it was only, one infers, by an enormous effort of empathy that he could manage to see through the eyes of Emma in the earlier stages of her career. Some months later but still when only a little over the first year of the four years and eight months he was to spend on *Madame Bovary* had gone by, Flaubert was still feeling the great difficulty of creating the imaginative world of his novel: "I am working fairly well, I mean with some confidence; but it is hard to express well something one has never felt" (*C*, III, 53, November 22, 1852).

Such complaining was to come to a halt. A change in tone takes place with Flaubert's letter to Louise Colet at the end of December, 1853. He has at last reached the scene of Emma's seduction by Rodolphe. She is now "my little woman" rather than the embodiment of a problem; Flaubert is able to throw himself into the scene of his narrative. He exults over his task that has overwhelmed him for nearly all of the last twelve hours, from two in the afternoon until two the next morning. "I am in the midst of lovemaking," he writes Louise Colet. "I am sweating and my throat is choked. This has been one of the rare days of my life which I have passed entirely in illusion from end to end." Flaubert is no longer occupied with the "dreams of young girls" or troubadours in caps of velvet: "At six o'clock, just as I wrote the words 'fit of hysterics,' I was so carried away, was bellowing so loudly and felt so deeply what my little woman was going through, that I was afraid of having hysterics myself." For the time the agonies of art were displaced by joy in his power to write—"to be no longer yourself but to move in an entire world of your own creating. Today, for instance, man and woman together, lover and beloved, I rode in a forest on an autumn afternoon under the yellow leaves, and I was the horses, the leaves, the wind, the words that were spoken, and the red sun that made them half-close their love-drowned eyes" (*C*, III, 404–405).

What had happened was that Flaubert had at last arrived at a point in his story where he could sometimes enter into the imaginative life of his heroine without cramping his own imagination. As Mario Praz illustrates at length in *The Romantic Agony*, Flaubert by nature had much in common with such writers as de Sade, Baudelaire, and Huysmans.[6] Even through her affair with Léon before he leaves Yonville for Paris—an affair made up of sighs and glances—there is much restraint in Emma's imaginings as well as in her conduct. Her thoughts at this point are indeed complicated; they reveal a good deal about Flaubert's agonies in trying to chart precisely his heroine's intricate moods. Emma was quite conscious, he tells us, of being enamored of Léon and entertained fancies of a physical consummation. "But the more she became aware of her love, the more she repressed it, hoping to conceal it, and make it lessen" (II.v.150). Part of her reluctance, Flaubert says, came from modesty, part from fear of consequences, and part from sheer indolence! There was also the pleasure she obtained during this affair from playing the drama of virtue under duress: "Then pride and the pleasure of saying to herself, 'I am virtuous,' and of studying herself in the mirror assuming poses of resignation con-soled her a little for the sacrifice *she thought she was making*" (italics mine). Flaubert's difficulties were to last through the departure of Léon for Paris and even (with qualification) through the early part of Emma's experience with Rodolphe.

Once Emma has surrendered to Rodolphe, there is, as has been intimated, a change in the color of her inner world, though the change is not the abrupt *volte-face* and total abandonment of bourgeois attitudes and values that she fancies it to be. She begins to identify herself with the more lurid of the heroines of history and literature—the "lyric legion of adulterous women." The life of permanent bliss she had so often read about is, she feels, soon to become her reality. "She was about to enter a world of wonders where all would be passion, ecstasy, delirium. An azure immensity surrounded her and ordinary life appeared distant and far beneath her wrapped in shade, visible only at moments from these heights" (II. ix.225). Such visions do not, however, inspire her tongue with language to suit them. She achieves expression only in traditional clichés of respectable bourgeois life that Rodolphe finds flattering but absurd. "Besides, she was getting dreadfully sentimental. She had made him exchange miniatures, handfuls of hair had been cut off, and now she was asking for a ring—a veritable wedding-ring, in token of eternal union. Often she spoke to him of the 'chimes of evening,' of the 'voices of nature.' Then she would go on and on about her mother, and his. Rodolphe's had been dead for twenty years; nevertheless Emma consoled him with affected phrases of the sort one would use with a bereaved child. Sometimes she would even say, gazing at the moon: 'I am sure that somewhere up there they both give their blessing to our love'" (II.x.235–236). Their love, far from supporting a state of permanent ecstasy as Emma had assumed, tames down in the course of six months to a routine resembling marriage. Temporarily Emma leaves off seeing Rodolphe and explores novel sensations in playing the role of virtuous wife and mother, to abandon it only after the humiliations attending Charles's disastrous operation on Hippolyte's clubbed foot. It is only during this second pursuit of ecstasy with Rodolphe that Emma's inner world assumes at last positive colorings of Satanism. When Emma dreams of eloping with Rodolphe, abandoning Charles and her re-spectable life once and for all, her fantasy, as Flaubert elaborates it, significantly parallels the pattern of her earlier fantasy (during her first weeks of marriage) of what the honeymoon would have been like if it had touched perfection. The details, however, are much altered. In the earlier fantasy she and her husband would have ridden in a post-chaise at a leisurely pace through the mountains of Switzerland while the mountains echoed to the postilion's song, the sound of goat's bells, and the far-off roar of waterfalls. Or they would have gazed hand in hand at the stars, breathing the perfume of lemon trees, or would have savored a haunting melan-choly in a Swiss chalet or (it might be) a Scotch cottage. Now, she fancied, she was soon to hurtle away with Rodolphe in a carriage drawn by four horses. They would gallop for a week toward some novel land, never to return. They would travel "on and on, their arms entwined, without speaking a word." Splendid cities would suddenly appear, with domes, bridges, ships, "whole forests of lemon trees, and cathedrals of white marble, their pointed spires bearing storks' nests." They would ride down a wide pavement where their path would be strewn with bouquets of flowers offered by women dressed in red. Chiming bells, neighing mules, strum-ming of guitars, and the hiss of fountains would greet them. Heaps of fruit would be piled in pyramids at the foot of pale statues that smiled beneath sprays of water. "They would row in gondolas, swing in hammocks, and their life would be as easy and free as their loose silken gowns, warm and star-studded as the nights they would contemplate." Days, all of them magnificent, would go on and on like waves. The vision "hovered on the horizon, infinite, harmonious, azure, and washed in sunshine" (II.xii.271–272).

This is all a long distance from Emma's early fancies. Her fantasy of life with Rodolphe is much closer to the tone of many passages in Flaubert's *The Temptation of Saint Anthony*, which he had laid aside unpublished when he started *Madame Bovary*, and still closer to the voluptuous romanticism and overt Satanism of *Salammbô*, the work that was to follow *Madame Bovary*. Emma now luxuriates in the atmosphere of illicit love, Flaubert tells us, and she increases in voluptuous beauty like a flower nourished on rain, wind, sunshine, and—the counterpointing detail claiming its place—manure. "Her cravings, her sorrows, her sensual ecstasies and her ever-youthful illusions had gradually developed her, and she blossomed out in the fullness of her nature, like a flower nourished on manure, on rain, wind, and sunshine." Her outward appearance assumes a sensual allure to match the preoccupations of her inner world. "Her half-closed eyelids seemed expressly shaped for the long amorous glances that issued from beneath them, while her sighs dilated the fine nostrils and raised the fleshy corners of her lips.... Some artist skilled in corruption seemed to have designed the shape of her hair as it fell on her neck, coiled in a heavy mass, casually rearranged after being loosened every day in adultery" (II.xii.269–270). In contrast to the eloquence of her flesh, her language has become coarsened; its plethora of lame clichés—no longer clichés of bourgeois life but now clichés of frankly erotic love—disgusts Rodolphe, who at last allows his contempt to enter even into his love-making. "He threw aside all modesty as inconvenient. He treated her as he pleased, and made her into something pliant and corrupt. It was an idiotic species of infatuation, full of admiration on his part and voluptuousness on hers, a beatitude that left her drugged; and her soul sank deep into this drunken state, drowned and shrivelled in it, like the duke of Clarence in his butt of malmsey" (II.xii.265–266). Later, in Emma's liaison with Léon at Rouen, religious symbols and connotations are fused with sexual in a manner especially reminiscent of Flaubert's *The Temptation of Saint Anthony*. Their place of assignation before the first consummation of their love is the cathedral, where Léon sees the church surrounding Emma "like a huge boudoir." Stained glass, a silver lamp, a painting of Salome dancing, sounds that resemble sighs of love, the aroma of incense set up voluptuously ambiguous overtones. "The arches bent down to shelter in their darkness the avowal of her love; the windows shone resplendent to illumine her face, and the censers would burn that she might appear like an angel amid perfumed clouds" (III.i.331).

Love gifts for Rodolphe and later for Léon account for many of Emma's debts to Lheureux, a bourgeois Mephistopheles who offers her all manner of luxuries on easy credit. She borrows recklessly until, "all absorbed in her passions, she had no more worry over money matters than an archduchess" (III.vi.393). She progresses by degrees from dunning Charles's patients and thus collecting money without his knowledge, to falsifying records. In her last desperation, she tries to force Léon to steal from his employer. As her imaginative world deepens in its colors and increasingly absorbs her, she is less and less able to face her reality; and when her resources for evading reality are gone she eventually escapes by suicide.

NOTES

[1] Gustave Flaubert, *Madame Bovary, Oeuvres complètes,* ed. Louis Conard (1910; Paris, 1930), VIII, part III, chapter vi, page 403. All quotations are keyed to the pages of this edition, in which *Madame Bovary* constitutes volume VIII. References will be made hereafter by part, chapter, and page numbers in parentheses.

[2] For definitions or descriptions of Flaubert's *style indirect libre,* see especially R. J. Sherrington, *Three Novels by Flaubert: A Study of Techniques* (Oxford, 1970), pp. 89–94; and Harry Levin, *The Gates of Horn* (New York, 1963), pp. 252ff. For a more elaborate treatment, see Stephen Ullmann, *Style in the French Novel* (Oxford, 1964), pp. 112ff. For a most interesting analysis of George Eliot's employment of a variety of indirect free style in her presentation of Dorothea Brooke, see Derek Oldfield, "The Language of the Novel: The Character of Dorothea," in *Middlemarch: Critical Approaches to the Novel,* ed. Barbara Hardy (New York, 1967), pp. 63–86.

[3] "—Oh! c'est que je t'aime! reprenait-elle, je t'aime à ne pouvoir me passer de toi, sais-tu bien? J'ai quelquefois des envies de te revoir où toutes les colères de l'amour me déchirent. Je me demande: 'Où est-il? Peut-être il parle à d'autres femmes? Elles lui sourient, il s'approche ... [sic]' Oh! non, n'est-ce pas, aucune ne te plaît? Il y en a de plus belles; mais moi, je sais mieux aimer! Je suis ta servante et ta concubine! Tu es mon roi, mon idole! tu es beau! tu es intelligent! tu est fort!" (II.xii.264–265).

[4] *Correspondance,* ed. Louis Conard (Paris, 1926), II, 361. Subsequent quotations from Flaubert's letters will be followed by volume and page number of this edition unless otherwise indicated. To make it clear that the correspondence of Flaubert is being quoted, a *C* (for *Correspondance*) will precede volume and page number.

[5] *Dostoevsky and Romantic Realism* (Chicago, 1967), p. 7.

[6] Mario Praz, *The Romantic Agony,* trans. Angus Davidson (1933; London, 1962), p. 170. "Baudelaire and Flaubert are like the two faces of a Herm planted firmly in the middle of the century, marking the division between Romanticism and Decadence, between the period of the Fatal Man and the Fatal Woman, between the period of Delacroix and that of Moreau." Elsewhere Praz treats the sadistic elements in *Madame Bovary:* "Madame Bovary, in order to excite her imagination, felt the necessity of reading 'des livres extravagants où il y avait des tableaux orgiaques avec des situations sanglantes' (an obvious allusion to de Sade)" (p. 171).

Charles Bernheimer

THE PSYCHOGENESIS OF FLAUBERT'S STYLE

In the third version of *La Tentation de Saint Antoine,* the Devil's attempt to seduce the saint climaxes in Anthony's fervent wish to become matter. This passage has attained a certain parabolic status in Flaubert criticism. Following Flaubert's sugges- tion that he was himself in the place of the saint $(2:127)$[1] and referring to the many autobiographical passages in which the novelist voices a pantheistic longing for union with the natural world, critics have interpreted Anthony's final ecstatic outburst as the expression of his creator's deepest yearning. The difficulty has been to explain just what this yearning signifies, both for the structure of *La Tentation* and for Flaubert's own creative process. Is it a mystical wish for union with the very principle of life or is it, on the contrary, a nihilistic desire for self-destruction? Or are both these apparently opposite interpretations operative within an indeterminate play of possible meanings? Whatever the answer, it is clearly no accident that the Devil is responsible for this parable of Flaubertian desire.

The appeal of this passage for a psychopoetic approach is evident: it is ana- clitically related to the vital order of Flaubert's personal experience, and that experience concerns the relation of language to desire, of metaphor to metamor- phosis. These are the relations that will concern me in this chapter. I do not propose to undertake an exhaustive analysis of *La Tentation de Saint Antoine.* Rather, I will read that text in conjunction with a number of others from *Madame Bovary* and the *oeuvres de jeunesse* in an effort to provide a psychogenetic interpretation of Flaubert's ideal of style. My focus, in other words, will be on the psychoanalytic meaning of Flaubert's rhetorical choices.

I begin with a passage from a letter Flaubert wrote to Louise Colet on the night of December 23, 1853, when he was about halfway through the composition of *Madame Bovary.* Since Flaubert describes specifically the scene he was writing that day, this letter makes possible an exact coordination between his account of the writing experience and the fictional product of that experience.

From *Flaubert and Kafka: Studies in Psychopoetic Structure* (New Haven: Yale University Press, 1982), pp. 56–101 (abridged).

I must love you to write you tonight, for I am *exhausted*. I feel as though I had an iron helmet squeezing my skull. Since two o'clock in the afternoon (apart from about twenty-five minutes off for dinner), I have been writing *Bovary*. I am at their Fucking [*Baisade*], fully, in the midst of it. One sweats and has a tight throat. This has been one of the rare days of my life passed completely in illusion from beginning to end. A little while ago, at six o'clock, as I was writing the phrase *fit of hysterics* [*attaque de nerfs*], I was so swept away, was bellowing [*gueulais*] so loudly, and feeling so deeply what my little woman was experiencing, that I was afraid of having a fit myself. I got up from the table and opened the window to calm myself. My head was spinning. Now I have great pains in my knees, in my back, and in my head. I feel like a man who has screwed too much (pardon the expression), that is, in a kind of rapturous lassitude.—And since I am *in the midst of love* [*dans l'amour*], it is only proper that I should not go to sleep without sending you a caress, a kiss, and whatever thoughts are left in me.

Will what I write be good? I have no idea (I am hurrying a little so as to show Bouilhet a complete section [*un ensemble*] when he comes). What is certain is that things have been advancing at a lively pace for the past week. May it continue so! for I am tired of my slowness! But I fear the awakening, the disillusions of the recopied pages. No matter, whether well or badly, it is a delicious thing to write! to no longer be *oneself* but to circulate within the entire creation of which one speaks. Today, for instance, man and woman together, lover and mistress all at once, I rode horseback through a forest, on an autumn afternoon, under yellow leaves, and I was the horses, the leaves, the wind, the words they said to each other, and the red sun that made them half close their love-drowned eyes.

Is this pride? or piety? Is it the silly overflow of exaggerated self-satisfaction, or a vague and noble Religious instinct, but when I ponder those pleasures [*jouissances*] after having sustained them [*les avoir subies*], I would be tempted to offer God a prayer of thanks, if I knew he could hear me.
[2:483–84]

This is probably the most exuberant account of the pleasures of writing to be found in all of Flaubert's immense correspondence. The experience is explicitly erotic on two levels: the scene being written describes seduction and sexual conquest, and Flaubert himself is seduced, "swept away," by the scene's power of illusion. The first paragraph focuses on the source of that power while the second evokes the content of the illusion. The source is identification—identification with the woman being seduced, not with the seducer. This female identification is apparent even in the sentence "On sue et on la gorge seree" ("One sweats and has a tight throat"). Francis Steegmuller's translation relates this sentence to Flaubert himself, rendering the "On" as "I," whereas in the text of the novel, as Flaubert wrote it that day, Emma is described as having "la tête en feu, la gorge étroite" ("her head on fire, her throat tight"), a phrase he later deleted.[2] Furthermore the "rapturous lassitude" that Flaubert associates with a man's feeling after lovemaking is actually a perfect description of Emma's state after intercourse with Rodolphe. Thus Flaubert is seduced into belief in illusion by his identifying with a woman being seduced.

Flaubert's female identification is furthered by his habit of giving voice to his writing as it is produced. By bellowing his sentences out loud as he writes, Flaubert feels the words to be a part of his inner being. They are exhaled in harmony with his inspiration, both physical and psychic. Expressed in this manner, language does not appear as something material, objective, distanced. It is immediately available and the agency of erotic immediacy. Oral declamation integrates written language into the rhythms of being. Written marks are removed from their alien inscription on the page and made to live in their vocal rendition. Bellowing his words, identifying with a submissive woman, Flaubert seems to feel himself nourished by language, as if its constitutive possibilities were also his.

Thus Flaubert's feminine identification becomes the agency that puts the process of identification itself in circulation within a fictional world. To write is to be transformed, not just into the things to which words refer—lovers, horses, leaves, wind, and sun—but even into words themselves, dialogue. Flaubert finds his erotic *jouissance* by exploiting the capacity of language to sustain illusion. Thereby he seems to fulfill Saint Anthony's wish to "divide [him]self everywhere, be in everything" (*OC* 1:571).[3] He is polymorphous, androgynous (the masculine identification being as fictional as the previous feminine one). The restraints of a specific self are broken—much as Flaubert felt that the violence of his *gueulades* might burst his lungs open—and his being becomes simply one term in a potentially infinite series of transformations.

The feeling of ecstatic self-dispersal that Flaubert experienced in writing this scene he then attributes to Emma as the effect of postcoital lassitude. The paragraph describing her feelings after her sexual surrender to Rodolphe is saturated with metaphorical expressions:

> The shades of night were falling; the horizontal sun passing between the branches dazzled her eyes. Here and there around her, in the leaves or on the ground, luminous patches trembled, as if hummingbirds flying about had scattered their feathers. Silence was everywhere; something sweet seemed to come forth from the trees; she felt her heartbeat return and the blood circulate in her flesh like a river of milk. Then far away, beyond the wood, on the other hills, she heard a vague prolonged cry, a voice that lingered, and she listened in silence as it mingled like music with the last vibrations of her throbbing nerves. Rodolphe, a cigar between his teeth, was mending one of the two broken bridles with his penknife. [*OC* 1:629; *MB*, p. 116][4]

The verb *circuler*, which in Flaubert's letter to Louise Colet described his substitution of one identification for another, here is explicitly linked to the process of metaphorical substitution: Emma's blood circulates "like a river of milk." The circulation of transformative possibilities further includes the sweet emanation from the trees, the musical cry from afar, and the trembling patches of light. The use of similes, three in the space of four sentences, draws the reader's attention to the process of analogy by which inside and outside, subjective feeling and natural environment, are linked in this privileged moment of erotic abandon. Boundaries collapse to such an extent in this fluid atmosphere that the vibrations of Emma's nerves seem to be of the same nature as the trembling luminous patches in the forest. Emma's own highly derivative linguistic consciousness is silent. Her eyes dazzled, her ears listening to inarticulate sounds, she seems to experience a meta-morphic extension of being. In his great study of Flaubert, *L'Idiot de la famille*, Sartre suggests, I think rightly, that Emma's state here comes close to realizing Saint Anthony's desire to become matter.[5]

But Flaubert can grant Emma this moment of freedom from the clichéd literary metaphors through which she usually interprets her experience only by creating his own metaphors in their stead.[6] This suggests the difference between Flaubert's erotic experience of writing himself into a transformative illusion and Emma's erotic experience of illusion generated by her physical surrender. Flaubert's identification with Emma cannot go so far as to reproduce her consciousness, for the erotic sensation she experiences is silent and unmediated, while his is enabled by the loud declamation of words. Her ecstasy is attained when the secondhand illusions of fiction are annihilated by the intensity of sensation, while Flaubert's *jouissances* are the result of an intensified belief in the fictional and trust in the unifying function of metaphor. As he indicates in the letter to Louise, that trust is as privileged an experience for him as is Emma's sensation of union with nature.

But he also suggests that such a giving of self to illusion is a dangerous excess that may debilitate both body and mind. When Flaubert writes of Emma's fear of an *attaque de nerfs* just at that point when he is identifying with her and believing in the illusions of fiction, his mention of this fear is not fortuitous. Emma's fear of an hysterical fit, "an anxiety of her entire being, as if an *attaque de nerfs* were going to occur" (*N.v.*, p. 378), reflects no doubt Flaubert's own fear of the consequences of his fictional femininity. Feminine identification, with its accompanying trust in the metaphorical continuities between self and nature, is associated by Flaubert with madness and death. Indeed, a few paragraphs later Emma is described as being "inert like a statue" (*N.v.*, p. 378), an image to which I shall have occasion to return. This negativity is made sensible at the close of the paragraph evoking Emma's postcoital ecstasy in the affectless metonymic presentation of the details of Rod-olphe's activity. His cigar and penknife, Freudian phallic symbols par excellence, here suggest primarily the indifference of the object world in terms of which Emma's subjective experience seems entirely delusional.

In his description of Emma's response to her first adulterous act, Flaubert evokes the process through which this potential for delusional madness is actual-ized. Alone in her room that night, Emma's memories are at first closely linked to her physical sensation and to the sense of union with nature that accompanied it: "She saw the trees, the paths, the ditches, Rodolphe, and she again felt the pressure of his arms, while the leaves rustled and the reeds whistled" (p. 629; p. 117). But then she glimpses her face in a mirror, and Flaubert conveys the effect of this sudden specular doubling in an indirect style that throws the truth of Emma's response into question: "Never had her eyes been so large, so black, or so deep. Something subtle pervading her person transfigured her." Is this transfiguration Emma's delusion or has there been some actual physical change in her appearance? The mirror image introduces the problem of representation in relation to a possible gap between physical reality and subjective apprehension, a gap that Lacan would attribute to the ego's *fonction de méconnaissance.*[7]

That this function of misknowing, or misreading, is indeed a matter of transfiguration becomes clear in the next two paragraphs (p. 629; p. 117). For here Emma loses touch entirely with the immediacy of her sensual consciousness, and her memory becomes saturated with literary models: "Then she recalled the heroines of the books that she had read and the lyrical legion of those adulterous women began to sing in her memory with the voices of sisters that charmed her. She herself became like an actual part of these imaginings." The musical voice of indefinite origin that had seemed to mingle with Emma's vibrant nerves after intercourse with Rodolphe is now drowned out by an indistinguishable plurality of literary voices. Their charm, for Emma, is their apparent offer to metamorphose her into literature and thereby make her readable to herself in terms of a conventional literary code. The appeal of this code involves a self-dispersal similar to that Emma experienced in the forest. But now that transformative dispersal no longer has an origin in physical experience. Indeed, the appeal of Emma's adulterous sisterhood is the appeal of the process of doubling, repetition, and substitution that I have called metaphoricity and associated with the death instinct.

When Flaubert writes of Emma: "She repeated to herself: 'I have a lover, a lover!'," this repetition involves a dissociation from the vital order of experience and an entry into the metaphorical order of fantasy, "something marvelous where all would be passion, ecstasy, delirium." That this entry should feel to Emma like "another puberty" suggests its close relation to sexuality as defined by Laplanche: "a movement which deflects the instinct, metaphorizes its aim, displaces and internalizes its object." Emma's taking a lover involves her less in a relationship with a real "other" than it does in an autoerotic relationship based on internalized fantasy scenarios. Those scenarios derive from an entirely impersonal and imaginary "other," and their incorporation alienates Emma's memory from its anaclitic basis in bodily experience and defines her desire in terms of a series of metaphorical substitutions.

It was precisely this kind of alienation that Flaubert feared might be the consequence of his trust in the illusory continuities of metaphor. That trust involved binding metaphor to the service of Eros so as to create ever larger wholes and more inclusive unities. In my terms, such a project could be understood as an attempt to metonymize metaphor, thereby linking its transformative activity to the binding function of the life instincts. But Flaubert was intensely aware, for reasons I will explore shortly, of metaphor's potentially subversive function, of its capacity to free itself from any unifying bond to an origin and to offer itself promiscuously as a revolutionary force to break through the constraints of contiguity. This is the offer to which Emma responds when she imagines adding herself to "the lyrical legion of those adulterous women."

The effects of her becoming her own literary model are nowhere more evident than in her own literary activity, her letter writing. As Naomi Schor has pointed out, Emma and Rodolphe together compose a kind of epistolary novel, in which the illusion of communication is created through the adherence of both writers to the same sentimental code.[8] But by the end of Emma's affair with Léon, she is actually producing an imaginary correspondent in and through her writing. She is as much seduced by this phantasmal lover as was Flaubert in writing his scene of seduction, and, like him, she is left exhausted by her excessive indulgence in illusion:

> As she wrote, she saw another man, a phantom made of her most ardent memories, of the most beautiful things she had read, of her most powerful desires; and he finally became so real, so accessible, that her heart beat wildly in admiration, even though she was unable to imagine him distinctly, for, like a god, he was lost beneath the abundance of his attributes. He dwelt in that bluish land where silken ladders swing from balconies in the moonlight, beneath a flower-scented breeze. She felt him near her; he was going to come and would ravish her entire being [*l'enleverait tout entière*] in a kiss. Then she fell back to earth, shattered [*elle retombait à plat, brisée*]; for these outbursts of imaginary love exhausted her more than great orgies.
>
> [p. 672; pp. 211–12]

Images from her experience, her reading, and her desire fuse in Emma's head to produce a composite phantasm that defies any distinct identity. What Emma considers "real" about this figure is precisely its figurality, that is, its function as a stimulus for metaphoric attribution.[9] The figure's godlike power derives from its relation to loss, to that absence of physical reference that generates the metaphorical functions of displacement and substitution. Emma would like to be carried away *tout entière* by these functions, which she associates with the erotic immediacy of a kiss. But she always falls back *à plat, brisée.* The return to the physical is at once a flattening out and a breaking into pieces. Emma looks to metaphor to give her the Erotic pleasure of totality. But she finds that she cannot sustain its expansive movement of imaginary ascription and that her return to the phenomenal world involves a kind of bodily mutilation.

This mutilation is the physical consequence of Emma's psychic fragmentation. Flaubert's distance from Emma is now clearly established: her circulation among the clichés of second-rate novels leaves him no room to create metaphors for her. Her identification with the illusions of fiction cancels the invitation he had felt to interpret her bodily ecstasy. Now her experience *is* interpretation, the already-written versions of romance.

The *plat*itudes that seduce Emma through their independence and difference from the world *à plat* cause her to lose her metonymic connection to that world. The transfiguring attractions of adultery are reduced to the same fictional status as the promised happiness of marriage: "Emma found again in adultery all the platitudes of marriage" (p. 672; p. 211). Undermined by this pervasive breakdown of difference, the world can no longer support Emma with the assurance of continuity and stability. Thus she complains about "the instantaneous decay [*pourriture*] of everything she leaned on" (p. 670; p. 206) and reflects that "everything within herself and without was abandoning her. She felt that she was lost, turning at random in undefinable abysses" (p. 675; p. 217). This random turning in the undefinable defines the subversive action of metaphoricity. It undoes the sense of personal identity, blurs the difference between inside and outside, and infects the world with a disintegrating force to which nothing is immune.[10]

Finally, after Rodolphe's refusal to help her financially, Emma experiences the *attaque de nerfs* that had threatened to occur during the initial seduction scene. The description is evidently modeled on Flaubert's own nervous attacks, the significance of which I will discuss in a later context. What interests me at present are the parallels between Emma's experience of sexual fulfillment and her experience of sexual rejection. For Flaubert is at pains to point out that Emma suffers not because of the money denied her but "in her love." In effect, her suffering is conveyed (p. 680; p. 228) in terms that explicitly echo the sense of fusion she felt after intercourse with Rodolphe, while transposing that positive illusion into the domain of delusion and death. Earlier her heartbeat had seemed in harmony with the natural environment and the vibrations of her nerves in tune with the vague, prolonged cry from afar. Now "she thought she heard the beating of her arteries breaking free like a deafening music that filled the countryside." The benign sweetness previously given off by the trees seems now to have invaded the earth making it "more soft than the sea."[11] And the sun, which had dazzled her eyes and produced luminous patches trembling like the feathers of hummingbirds, now appears as "fiery spheres [that] exploded in the air like bullets when they strike and whirled, whirled." It is as if the metaphorical analogies that had united Emma with the natural world had ruptured, leaving nature prey to uncontrollable metamorphoses ("the furrows seemed to her immense brown waves bursting into foam") and transforming her mental world into an explosive chaos of "memories and ideas." Internal and external vacillate and she feels "madness coming upon her."

In the earlier love experience, the intensely felt presence of physical sensation had cancelled any thinking process. Now love exists only as a memory, and Emma is the victim of that potential for unlimited metaphoric proliferation that Flaubert had felt to inhere in the space that had separated him from her bodily ecstasy. At present, Emma herself is experiencing the gap between psyche and soma, and she feels it as a wound, a mutilation of the remembered continuity that constitutes the body of Eros. The blood that flows from this wound is an outflow of images similar to that which Flaubert experienced in his nervous attacks. He described those attacks to Taine as "an illness of memory, a loosening of what it contains. You feel images escaping like floods of blood" (*Sup.* 2:94). Of Emma, Flaubert writes: "She suffered only in her love, and felt her soul escaping from her in this memory, even as wounded men, dying, feel their life ebb from their bleeding wound."

Paradoxically, as they enter into the death flow the remembered images are not dissolved but, on the contrary, become absolutely distinct and detached from one another. "She saw her father, Lheureux's closet, their room at home, another landscape." Since these images, and many others, supposedly exploded in Emma's head "all at once, at one bound, like a thousand pieces of fireworks," Flaubert's listing of them in this sentence gives them a false quality of temporal duration. Moreover, Flaubert told Taine that, in his own experience, when it seemed to him that "everything one has in one's head is exploding at once like a thousand pieces of fireworks, one does not have time to look at those internal images that file by in fury" (*Sup.* 2:94). Each element Emma sees is a component part of her memory and has significance only in a remembered context she alone can provide. But that context, "all the memories and ideas that she had in her head," has exploded into innumerable fragments. Memory is divorced from the continuity of lived experience to which it anaclitically adhered and is atomized into pieces lacking any integrating model. It is as if Freud's notion of the ego being "a mental projection of the surface of the body"[12] had been radicalized to the point that only projections are left. The reference to a contextual whole being lost, or nearly so, the structural and syntactic resemblance between individual metonyms becomes more significant than their semantic relation to any unifying entity. The resemblance is external to life and internal to language. It metaphorizes metonymy.

It could be said that Emma at this point is experiencing the existential equivalent of deconstruction. Her self is unraveling; she has a paranoid awareness of the other as a ubiquitous agent of persecution; her memory no longer provides the assurance of identity; she feels mutilated. This process of undoing works directly against the Erotic identification between writer and heroine that had stimulated Flaubert's creation of unifying analogies. Then Flaubert felt his blood circulating within everything of which he wrote. Language was the vehicle for an illusion that Flaubert experienced as a sensuous extension of being. But simultaneously he was aware of a potential for excess, for an explosion of madness, and this awareness produced anxiety and doubt.

"Where is the limit between inspiration and madness, stupidity and ecstasy?" he asked Louise. Is his writing a "silly overflow" or a religious effusion? Is he, in other words, guilty or innocent for taking his pleasure in illusion? Guilty, in any case, in regard to Louise herself, the flesh-and-blood mistress to whom he sends "whatever thoughts are left" after his indulgence in the imaginary debauchery of identification with her sex. But possibly guilty also in regard to the stylistic criteria of art, represented by his male friend, Louis Bouilhet. He fears "the awakening, the disillusions of the recopied pages." As well he might, since in the work of revision he eliminated the entire paragraph in which the phrase *attaque de nerfs* appeared and discarded the greater part of the paragraph describing the forest, including the only two references to the yellow color of the leaves.

In the process of copying over his writing, language appears to Flaubert at its most material. The illusion of immediacy is broken. Fiction is no longer an Erotic vehicle for metamorphosis but a collage composed of others' words, a tissue of clichés. Whereas Emma attempts to weave herself tightly into this tissue, Flaubert pulls the fabric apart thread by thread. Thus he shows that to submit to a patchwork of make-believe, to trust fiction's illusion, is itself the most clichéd of attitudes. Flaubert makes his own declaration about how delicious a thing it is to be oneself no longer and to circulate within a fictional creation seem entirely banal when it is articulated by Léon to explain the pleasure he finds in reading. Speaking to Emma, who enthusiastically agrees with his description, Léon says of the delights of novel-reading: "You think of nothing, the hours slip by. Without moving, you walk through countries you seem to see, and your thought, intertwined with the fiction, plays with the details or follows the outline of the adventures. It mingles with the characters; it seems that it is your heart that beats under their clothing" (p. 602; p. 59). Léon and Emma enjoy reading for the same reasons that Flaubert enjoys writing: the expansive metamorphosis of self, the faith in an invented world. But whereas Emma's awakening from illusion leaves her anxiously aware of the inadequacy of the real, Flaubert's awakening leaves him convinced that reality and illusion are both purely verbal effects that mirror each other. He finds himself on the outside of any linguistic performance, in an everyman's land of verbal matter. From this perspective, even his most privileged moments of ecstasy, stimulated by the vast expanse of the ocean, moments that I will show to be of crucial importance to his literary project, are reduced to the same status as the other platitudes in a formulaic code. In response to Léon's declaration that he loves the sea, Emma gives a description of the sea's effect on the observer's mind that corresponds precisely to the oceanic feeling Flaubert tried to recreate through the work of style: " 'And doesn't it seem to you,' " she asks Léon, " 'that the mind sails more freely on this limitless expanse, the contemplation of which elevates the soul and gives ideas of the infinite, the ideal?' " (p. 602; p. 58).

Thus Flaubert writes—or, with respect to *Madame Bovary*, I should say rewrites—with the blood issuing from the wound of memory, be it Emma's, his own, or the accumulated archival memory of the nineteenth century. The images that pour out of this wound are heterogeneous fragments signifying the death of whatever context used to hold them together. Flaubert, the craftsman of linguistic materiality, picks out these detached verbal elements from the death flow and juxtaposes them to form hard blocks, blocks that he wished as devoid of figuration and as smoothly polished as a perfectly blank wall of the Acropolis. When the blocks are assembled according to plan, they should form a pyramid: "Books are not made like children," Flaubert told Ernest Feydeau, "but like pyramids, on a premeditated pattern, and by laying great blocks one on top of another, by dint of effort, time and sweat, and it is useless! and it stays in the desert! but dominates it prodigiously" (2:783). From this dominating perspective, Flaubert condemns his own erotic enjoyment of illusion. Insofar as his identification with female sexuality was the vehicle of this *jouissance,* he masochistically asserts the supremacy of the male principle in literary style. "Above all else," he wrote a correspondent in 1844, "I like a sentence that is nervous, substantial, clear, with prominent muscles and a swarthy skin; I like male, not female sentences" (1:210).

NOTES

[1] References abbreviated simply 1 and 2 refer to the two volumes of Flaubert's *Correspondance* published by Gallimard in the Bibliothèque de la Pléiade and edited by Jean Bruneau. Volume 1 (1973) goes from January 1830 to April 1851, volume 2 (1980) covers July 1851 to December 1858. For letters written after this date, I will refer to the Conard edition in nine volumes (1926–33) and four in *Supplément* (1954), using the abbreviations *Cor.* and *Sup.*

[2] Gustave Flaubert, *Madame Bovary—Nouvelle version précédée des scenarios inédits,* ed. Jean Pommier and Gabrielle Leleu (Corti, 1949), p. 378. Hereinafter abbreviated *N.v.*

[3] References thus abbreviated refer to the two-volume edition of Flaubert's *Oeuvres complètes* published by Seuil in *l'Intégrale* edition (1964).

[4] *MB* refers to the best English translation I know of *Madame Bovary,* that by Eleanor Marx Aveling as revised by Paul de Man for the Norton Critical Edition (New York, 1965). Subsequent page references to this novel will be first to the text in the *Oeuvres complètes* (*OC*1), then to this translation.

[5] Jean-Paul Sartre, *L'Idiot de la famille,* vol. 2 (Gallimard, 1971), p. 1283. Sartre's monumental study, which one hopes will be read more widely in the translation currently being prepared, has been a major influence on my thinking about Flaubert. I quote only from the first two volumes. Volume 1 contains pages 1–1104; volume 2, pages 1105–2136.

[6] Leo Bersani has written brilliantly about these gratuitous verbal displays by means of which the Flaubertian narrator "fills in" for his silent, passively absorbed characters. See *Balzac to Beckett: Center and Circumference in French Fiction* (New York: Oxford University Press, 1970), pp. 181–82

[7] Jacques Lacan, "Le stade du miroir comme formateur de la fonction du Je," in *Écrits,* Vol. 1 (Seuil, 1966), p. 96.

[8] Naomi Schor, "Pour une thématique restreinte: Écriture, parole et différence dans *Madame Bovary,"* *Littérature,* no. 22 (May 1976):39.

[9] It is worth noting that Emma, in turn, plays a similar role for Léon: "She was the loving woman of all novels, the heroine of all dramas, the vague 'she' of all volumes of verse. On her shoulders he rediscovered the amber color of the *Odalisque Bathing;* her waist was long like the feudal chatelaines; she also resembled the *pale woman of Barcelona,* but above all she was an Angel!" (p. 664; p. 192). In his stimulating analysis of *Madame Bovary,* Tony Tanner observes quite rightly that Emma's function as a blank screen for the projection of alien, male-derived images serves both to smother and to fragment any distinct identity she might have attained for others (*Adultery in the Novel: Contract and Transgression* [Baltimore: The Johns Hopkins University Press, 1979], p. 311).

[10] The first version of *Madame Bovary* includes a passage describing the varied contents of Emma's letters to Rodolphe that grotesquely pictures this decay and disintegration in the most platitudinous of images: "A heap of experiences, great and small, some ordinary, some exotic, some insipid, some succulent, reappeared there [in Emma's letters], giving the passion variety, like those Spanish salads where one finds fruits and vegetables, chunks of goat meat and slices of lemon floating about in pale-blond oil" (*N.v.,* p. 383). This flotation in oil is perhaps the culinary equivalent of the metaphysical turning in abysses! Much of Flaubert's work of revision on *Madame Bovary* involved eliminating the products of his "metaphorical sense" which, he told Louise Colet, "unquestionably dominates me too much. I am devoured by comparisons as one is by lice and I spend all my time squashing them" (2:220).

[11] Flaubert had initially thought of making the transformation of the earth into an undulating surface a part of Emma's initial response to Rodolphe. The first version includes this sentence: "The earth oscillated under her steps like the deck of a boat" (*N.v.,* p. 379).

[12] Sigmund Freud, *The Ego and the Id* (New York: Norton, 1962), p. 16.

Margaret Lowe

''MADAME BOVARY, C'EST MOI''

Les bourgeois ne se doutent guère que nous leur servons notre coeur.[1]

'Madame Bovary, c'est moi, d'après moi' is probably Gustave Flaubert's most celebrated remark, allegedly made to his friend, Amélie Bosquet, novelist and historian of Norman folklore. The words ring true but surprise us coming from this apostle of detachment from the ephemeral and the accidental, for whom above all 'c'est là ce qu'il y a de moins fort au monde, parler de soi' (13, p. 290)

This remark has been much discussed, but the sense in which Flaubert means it may be illuminated by a comment made by François Mauriac who, while objecting to the biographical approach to literature and envying Shakespeare the obscurity which surrounds most of his life, has this to say: 'Un écrivain ne se confie ni à sa Correspondance ni même à ses journaux intimes. Seules ses créatures racontent sa véritable histoire.' It is a secret history, which a certain *pudeur* prevents him from enunciating openly, which he does not himself know entirely, until it can eventually find expression and arrive at its conclusion, indeed even exorcise itself, by means of representative personages and situations. The Gustave Flaubert who, at the age of roughly thirty, sat down to write *Madame Bovary,* had known a severe mental illness at the age of twenty-three, followed by the deaths in quick succession of his distinguished surgeon father, still at the height of his powers, of his only sister Caroline, to whom he had been very close, and finally, only two years later, of his beloved friend Alfred Le Poittevin. Pain and mortality, a 'plaie profonde toujours cachée' (14, p. 217) are at the heart of this tragic story, which is yet for some a comic masterpiece, set in a milieu which Flaubert chose deliberately, reflecting his overall view of modern life as well as of art.

Rarely does Flaubert speak of his sister's death in his letters. Only to his mother, writing during his journey through the East, does he say: 'Le souvenir de mon pauvre rat ne me quitte pas. J'ai toujours à son endroit une place vide au cœur

From *Towards the Real Flaubert,* ed. A. W. Raitt (Oxford: Clarendon Press, 1984), pp. 15–28.

et que rien ne comble' (13, p. 116). And arriving at Cana, he cannot bear to go into the church (10, p. 582) because of his memories of Veronese's picture in the Louvré showing Christ's first miracle, the turning at a wedding feast of water into wine, colour of the blood Christ eventually spilt on the Cross, of the blood vomited by Caroline, so recently a bride, and later by Emma, poisoned by her own hand but also as an outcome of a series of events which had begun with her marriage, and even earlier by the fact of her ever meeting Charles, an event which moreover took place on the very day of the wedding at Cana—6 January. The recurrence of the colour of blood is a basic image in the novel, as we shall see in more detail. Nor does the parallel shock, for the passion of the Son of Man prefigures the destiny of all men, and of women too. 'Tirelessly the Fates repeat a thousand times the old story of the falling night,' wrote Goethe to Zelter on the death of the latter's son. For Flaubert, the task of the writer, male or female, is to take upon himself all the passions of the world (13, p. 461).

A lofty notion of the mission of the poet is fundamental to the Romantic ethos, and in nineteenth-century literature alongside Christ Himself, 'l'éternelle victime', brother of Icarus and of Attys, who is overtly claimed by Gérard de Nerval as a prefigurement of the artist,[2] there walks another proto-Christ, Orpheus, delightful *pâtre* and singer upon the lyre. Professor Riffaterre has noted that, although never actually mentioned by Flaubert's close friend Bouilhet, Orpheus is discernible in his works.[3] It was impossible for Flaubert not to know the poetic scene of his time, given his relations with Bouilhet and with Louise, and it is the contemporary epic poem which is of particular interest here. Flaubert's first version of his *mystère Saint Antoine* had been modelled on Quinet's prose poem *Ahasvérus,* and it was Flaubert's belief, stated in the correspondence, that the latest development in literature, 's'éthérisant' as he thought it had been through the ages (that is, appealing progressively less to the senses, expressing—as we have already seen Flaubert's aim to be—the psyche in so far as possible), was the replacement of the epic in verse by the novel in prose (13, p. 158). Alfred de Vigny had said as much in his time, but, after attempts such as *Stello* and with an unfinished *Daphné* still on his hands, he had returned to verse in *Les Destinées.* For Flaubert, the very style of the new novel was to be that of the epic (13, p. 316).

Now a favourite theme in the statuary of Flaubert's period was the group Psyche and Eros. Pradier, in whose studio Flaubert had met Louise Colet, sculpted more than one Psyche, while the young Flaubert had himself been delighted with a *Psyche and Eros* by the eighteenth-century artist Canova, which he had seen in the Villa Carlotti (10, p. 377) and of which an example is now in the permanent collection at the Louvre. In the scenarios of *Madame Bovary*, an unspecified 'Canova' was to have figured in the salon at Yonville (1, p. 141). It is perhaps not too fanciful to suggest that Flaubert had the Psyche and Eros group in mind and that he repressed the statue as at the same time unrealistic in such a background and also as being too obvious a hint to us. For that matter, Canova and his pupils sculpted many a Psyche, and the presence of one of his pieces in Flaubert's original conception of *Madame Bovary* cannot but be encouraging to my point of view. Perhaps, similarly, the Pradier which (this time realistically) would stand upon the mantleshelf in Jacques Arnoux's office in *L'Éducation sentimentale* had a kindred subject? Certainly it was one which we know to have continued to charm Flaubert, for the 1931 catalogue for the Franklin-Grout sale contained a bronze mantleshelf set by Clésinger—a clock and two candelabras—which also figures Psyche and Eros and which was Flaubert's wedding present to his niece Caroline. An example of the set (Clésinger made two) can be seen at the Musée Marmottan in Paris. Subjects from the story of Psyche are also treated in paintings of the period by Gérard, Picot, and Pierre-Paul Prud'hon that are now in the Louvre. As for the literature of the period, the poet Laprade had written an epic poem *Psyché* in 1841. Moreover, the subtitle of Lamartine's epic *Jocelyn* had been *Psyché*. Given Flaubert's attitude towards Lamartine and his 'school', together with Lamartine's declared aim in *La Chute d'un ange* to describe 'la métempsycose d'une âme dégradée', we may see that Flaubert is indeed taking up a common preoccupation of his contemporaries and vying with their treatment of it. For 'la métempsycose d'une âme dégradée' describes Emma. She is, in Flaubert's own words at the time of the book's trial, 'un caractère de femme naturellement corrompu' (13, p. 548). Her lot in life denies her transcendence, notably in the 'forme convenue' which she had been conditioned to require by her reading, by the particular type of semi-mystical religiosity imparted to her at the convent, and by the general attitude towards the young ladies with whom she identifies herself after her schooling. The progress of Emma from unusual *candeur* (a key word in Flaubert's presentation of her) to what most will see as final degradation can be seen as a deliberate attempt to rival Lamartine's intention, but in prose, muscular, rhythmic, packed with content, multiple, varied, infinitely suggestive—and epic.

It is my contention, then, that the story of Psyche and Eros underpins *Madame Bovary*. Personal names can be symbolic in Flaubert's works, and indeed can form part of the patterns of imagery; they are, in Flaubert's own words, 'une chose capitale' (14, p. 460), and once incorporated into a work after much groping, they are completely unchangeable, as in an allegory. Now *Ema,* anagram of *âme,* was the name of the heroine in an eighteenth-century allegory dealing with the relationship between the soul and the senses,[4] and, although there is no proof that Flaubert read the book, the idea is shown, by its existence, to be feasible. Thus it is my belief that Flaubert has advisedly adopted the name Emma (a particularly Norman name, what is more) for this, his first relation of the Psyche myth.

A further point of interest with regard to representations of the human soul comes in a book written by Alfred Maury, Flaubert's revered friend. The book in question, *Essai sur les légendes pieuses du Moyen Age* (1843), has been proved to be an early source of *Saint Julien l'Hospitalier,* first meditated upon by Flaubert when *Madame Bovary* was still in progress.[5] In it, Maury shows how the earliest representation of the human soul in remote art was an 'androgyne', indicating a primitive view of the soul, the breath of life, before the encroachment of the artificial over-differentiation of the sexes that Flaubert summed up in these words: '*La femme est un produit de l'homme. Dieu a créé la femelle et l'homme a fait la femme;* elle est le résultat de la civilisation, une œuvre factice (13, p. 314).

What is our first view of Emma? 'Ce qu'elle avait de beau, c'étaient les yeux.'

Her lips, however, are sensual, and we see her biting them. We are back with the faces of the intellectual women noted in *Par les champs et par les grèves,* of whom, as was pointed out earlier, Flaubert wrote that their spirituality only began at the eyes: 'tout le reste est resté dans les instincts matériels' (10, p. 44). Baudelaire's words about 'une âme virile dans un charmant corps feminin' likewise stress the androgynous nature of the human spirit whose history we are to read, emphasizing indeed her early aspiration to be spirit first and foremost, by comparing her to 'Pallas, surgie tout armée de la tête de son père'.[6] We have already had occasion to notice Athene-Minerva as representing, traditionally as she always has, pure spirit and pure intelligence—striven for by certain of Flaubert's contemporary artists. Now Athene-Minerva is alone among classical goddesses in being mentioned in the text of *Madame Bovary,* where, on our first acquaintance with Emma, we find her portrait, drawn by Emma's hand when at school, framed in gold and pinned upon the kitchen wall. It was originally to have had a cracked glass, but Flaubert suppressed so obvious and premature an indication of decadence from an ideal.[7] For Emma too will attempt to emulate the bold-eyed goddess who, as Flaubert inserted into Louise Colet's poem *L'Acropole d'Athènes,* was the original 'mère d'Athènes', city of pure form and of aspiration to pure beauty, to be replaced, alas, as time wore on by 'Vénus impudique', or so Flaubert wished Louise to recount in her poem (13, pp. 300–6). The parallel will prove interesting.

Here then is Flaubert's heroine: Psyche, called Emma and evoking the androgyne, Pallas Athene, a lorgnette tucked into her corsage to stress the point. Flaubert, using one of his poetic devices, has superimposed various images one upon the other in this first view of Emma, each leading into the development of certain facets of her character: nineteenth-century intellectual woman (however inadequate her training and ability, the urge to learn is there), possessed of unusual *candeur,* that is, innocence and a basic naïveté, recalling Apuleius' description of the 'simple-hearted' Psyche. Finally Emma has pretensions and a weakness for the trappings of appearance, most important in the evolution of the psyche as seen by writers in the later ancient world. Apuleius' superlative narration of the tale of *Psyche and Eros* is the most important example. Flaubert would have read in Creuzer that for the allegorical minds of the ancients the fall of the soul in this tale away from its pristine purity is essentially an ever greater engagement in the toils of appearance, that is, of matter, the temptations of the matter which surrounds us, as Baudelaire described them.

When Flaubert mentions the 'tête de Minerve' on the kitchen wall at Les Bertaux, he notes that the inscription upon it has been written by Emma in 'lettres gothiques'. Now the medieval and later version of Psyche and Eros is, of course, *La Belle et la bête,* though Perrault was hard put to it to understand the equivalence he knew to exist between them in the preface to his seventeenth-century edition.[8] Flaubert's handbook to the study of the past, Creuzer's vast examination of ancient religions with special reference to their symbolisms, has no such difficulty. Psyche and Eros, he states with simplicity, represent the soul and the body, just as Hugo interpreted *La Belle et la bête* in the *Préface de Cromwell.*

Before looking further into this antithesis and its representation in *Madame Bovary*, let us deepen our study of the early Emma. The Gothic lettering of her interpretation we shall learn to see as an indication that, if our first sight of her with her *candeur* and her bold stare calls to mind Homer and the early Greek representation of pure spirit whose portrait hangs on her wall, by the end of the book our vision of her will have been brought up to date in the 'vieille cité normande' of Rouen with its Gothic cathedral and Gothic quarter (in Flaubert's early versions Rouen was to be described as 'la cité gothique'[9]). The colour of her eyes, for instance, will no longer be dark nearing to black. They will be blue, for she has evolved, as the book proceeds, into a Northern heroine. But was the colour of Athene-Minerva's eyes black? Hers were surely green. Was it not Venus, the blackness of whose eyes had been stressed by Homer?

Here is the parable within the parable. For when Aphrodite-Venus took upon herself to try to spin Athene's web, did the thread not break in her hands? The significance of this, so Flaubert could have read in Benjamin Constant's book on the history of religions[10] as well as in Creuzer, is the treachery and inadequacy of matter. And is not this the story of Emma? *Madame Bovary* is, at the most conceptual level, an allegory of the changes which come over the human psyche between birth and death, of a sensual being striving unsuccessfully and eventually perversely to be pure spirit, to be intellect and aspiration, as well as the 'instincts matériels' which the young Flaubert had so automatically identified as female. Through all the actions—selfish, dishonest, and plain silly—which we may find it difficult to accept in her, Emma is still, in Baudelaire's words, seeking that elusive goal so stressed in the early nineteenth century, 'l'Idéal'.[11] When writing *Madame Bovary*, Flaubert commented upon how aspirations of a noble nature—'des élans d'idéalisme . . . l'aspiration éthérée de la souveraine joie'—aimed, as in Emma's case, at deliverance from both the 'dépendances de la loi' and the 'mollesses de la chair', can become degraded to the level of 'les appétits matériels les plus furieux', 'les extravagances charnelles les plus immondes' (13, p. 661). While not exaggerating the extent of the downfall of Emma—for, thief, adulteress, and bad mother though she is, she would seem to many readers (Sartre, one presumes) no more guilty as an individual than would Faust—we appreciate the value of Flaubert's remarks on the perversion of appetite and will see their relevance for all his women characters, right through to the symbolic dance of Salome, which also begins as that of a 'Psyché curieuse' (4, p. 274). To them we may add his further words concerning the savage reactions of the unsatisfied human spirit: 'Notre âme est une bête féroce; toujours affamée, il faut la gorger jusqu'à la gueule pour qu'elle ne se jette pas sur nous.' As so often when we read Flaubert, modern society in general, as well as the history of Emma and of the past, is here tragically called to mind.

So far, then, we have seen superimposed within Emma: Psyche, Pallas Athene, and, finally, Venus striving to emulate her illustrious artist sibling. Emma, who tries to spin the web of her own life (for the importance of spinning and weaving in *Madame Bovary*, see below, Chapter Five) fails comparably. How, asks Flaubert in one of his notebooks, does it come about that the noble goddess Venus Urania (*alter ego* of Athene) descended through the ages to a depraved level, Venus 'amour de la forme' becoming a 'putain' (4, p. 424)? In the episode of the gods in *Saint Antoine,* Flaubert's Venus again retraces her own career in much the same terms. And this too, as we shall show, is the story of Emma, who, alas, declines from unusual *candeur* (such, for instance, as no other of Rodolphe's mistresses had ever possessed) to a state of mind where she is ready to sell herself 'sans se douter le moins du monde de sa prostitution'. Her failure to *recognize* what she has become is particularly noteworthy, as this is for Flaubert a feature of his whole age, as is made clear in *L'Éducation sentimentale.* Louise Colet's high-minded strictures about 'les filles', while at the same time depending on her lovers for assistance of all kinds, including money, cannot be irrelevant to this conclusion of the career of Emma-Venus.

To return to the anagram *Emma/Âme,* it is extremely interesting to note that Guignault's translation of Creuzer quotes certain nineteenth-century scholars as positing that a similar inversion of the name of the Egyptian goddess of the spirit, Neith, was the origin of the name Athene, an equivalence already suggested by Plato. For an analogical mind such as Flaubert's, this knowledge must have provided encouragement. But this would not necessarily be of any importance if it were not for the great vogue for everything Egyptian, as well as 'Orphic' (indeed, Creuzer points out that for Herodotus 'Orphic' and 'Egyptian' were synonymous) which characterized nineteenth-century France—'la rage permanente de l'Egypte', to quote Flaubert's words in *Par les champs et par les grèves* (10, p. 138). Flaubert, with his interest in ancient religions and civilizations, travelled to Egypt, as we have seen, like many other writers including Lamartine and Nerval. Now Emma is an inhabitant of Normandy, and among the great enthusiasts for Egypt and things Egyptian was the school of Norman and Breton Celticists for which Flaubert did not conceal his scorn. In *Par les champs,* after studying the question with what he assures Louise Colet is scholarly thoroughness (13, p. 178), he concludes that the Celtic contribution to historical monuments consisted entirely of 'des pierres' (10, p. 105)—unidentifiable stones of a primitive character—and that all the explanations put forward concerning their function and origin are so much nonsense. Flaubert is extremely witty about those of his contemporaries who took so seriously the putative glories of their forebears. When Bouvard and Pécuchet come to study the subject, the humour is even more scathing. What is the relevance here?

The great word which had linked both cultures in the minds of the Celticists was the place-name Sais. Now it is from Sais in Egypt that Neith travelled to Athens and became Athene, so Creuzer has it. Similarly, it is the name Saez (or Sées) in the Orne that leads the amateur Celticists whom Flaubert found so comic to see the origins of their own civilization in Egypt. Flaubert will himself travel to Saez when preparing *Bouvard et Pécuchet.*

The Egyptian Sais was, precisely, the cult-centre of Neith-Athene. What is more, another name now enters our view of this composite goddess whose development is contained within Emma. This is Isis, whose name, so we learn from Plutarch, was openly connected, again at Sais, with Athene. Plutarch alone in the ancient world systematized the religion of Isis and Osiris—in the *Moralia* which, as we have seen, Flaubert read over a long period while composing *Madame Bovary*. Plutarch tells us that at Sais there was a statue of Athene, 'whom they believe to be Isis'. Likewise, 'they oftentimes call Isis by the name of Athene'. The name Isis, so we are further informed by Plutarch, was said, like the name Athene, to mean a 'lover of wisdom'. Moreover, she is connected by Plato—for here again is this cardinal force in Flaubert's life and work—with 'essence' and 'sense', and thus often called Athene.

Like Athene (indeed, another name for her) and like Venus Urania (that is, the goddess in her stellar and non-material aspect), there is then another goddess who, in the early stages of human attempts to conceptualize Nature, stood for wisdom, essence, sense. Summing up all the goddesses (that is, visions of nature) is one further attribute with which the ancients endowed Isis, namely, that she was 'many-eyed'. Has not Flaubert superimposed upon his evocations of these androgynous goddesses aiming to attain to pure reason, their flashing eyes developing through the book from dark brown, black to blue, the ever-evolving figure of Isis, both anterior and posterior to all the others, as Nerval describes her in a near-contemporaneous text?[12]

What justification would Flaubert have for this vision, in a modern Psyche, of a composite goddess? His reading list, as indicated in his letters to Louise Colet, again lends support to our interpretation, even though a knowledge of contemporary references to Isis might in any case have made all clear to us. Does Flaubert mention Isis? Indeed he does: in 1853 he calls upon Louise Colet with great enthusiasm to read in Apuleius' *Golden Ass* Lucius' invocation to the goddess Isis and her reply to him (13, p. 285). The answer and illumination to Lucius are that Isis is in fact all the great goddesses. Many are their names, but one is their identity, the lady Isis herself:

> You can see me here, Lucius, in answer to your prayer. I am Nature, the universal Mother, mistress of all the elements, primordial child of time, sovereign of all things spiritual, queen of the dead, queen also of the immortals, the single manifestation of all gods and goddesses that are. My nod governs the shining heights of Heaven, the wholesome sea-breezes, the lamentable silences of the world below.

She is, then, queen of Heaven, earth, sea, and the underworld, and we cannot but think of Charles's view of the Emma he worshipped: 'L'univers entier n'excédait pas le tour soyeux de son jupon.'

An interesting point will very likely have struck the reader by now. Both this cardinal text, identifying all the goddesses as nature, and the beautiful telling of the tale of Psyche and Eros appear in a single book—Apuleius' *Golden Ass*. By this late period in Rome, then, heir to so much that was Greek and Egyptian, the androgynous human soul of earliest art and the androgynous prefigurations of nature have both become female as they were in the Syrian and Near Eastern religions. They are Psyche and the great goddess, who, as we have seen, contains within herself not only all the goddesses but also all the gods. All nature has thus become anthropomorphized as a female and in particular as the Mother. If woman, as Flaubert had upheld in a letter to Louise Colet, is 'une œuvre factice' (13, p. 314), so, logically, the soul as female *anima* and nature as female, the Universal Mother, are equally factitious, equally artificial, the products of civilization.

A symbolic 'culte de la mère' has thus been extended beyond woman to the human spirit itself and to nature, all of which are seen in terms one of another. Comparisons with Romanticism and the nineteenth century in general readily come to mind, as we shall see. But, before considering Flaubert's relationship with his contemporaries and with the whole tradition of the treatment in modern literature of the feminine, it is interesting to recall a few well-known facts concerning Flaubert's own conditioning and aspirations in the generation to which Emma belonged and which came in so many ways to an end with the December *coup d'état* in 1851, a theme which is made clearer in *L'Éducation sentimentale.* Emma's ardent temperament, given to revery, was Flaubert's own. His instincts for luxury in modest financial circumstances, even absurd dreams of *bayadères* upon oriental divans, contributed to his picture of Emma. He would not attempt to deny that in his own youth he had been 'parfaitement ridicule' (14, p. 40), for self-criticism is a part of self-depiction. His analysis of Emma was, he averred, based upon himself (13, p. 214). In writing, he whipped himself until he drew blood, figuratively speaking. His own high dreams, his own former agonizing boredom as a student of the law, a subject alien to him and to all his dearest interests, help to explain why Emma's collapse rings so true.

A human psyche that has learned to aspire spiritually and sensually, however inadequately, will, when deprived, flutter and die or else become degraded, as Flaubert shows in Emma and as Creuzer comments in his analysis of the Psyche story. One solution exists—that open to Flaubert himself. For, though understanding all the yearnings for a different sort of society which beset Emma, and though sharing in the pursuit of the ideal which Baudelaire discerned in her, though participating, indeed, to an even higher degree in a distaste for the onerous, purely physical side of being alive, Flaubert, conquered or, as he himself might have said, 'elevated' the Emma within him. He too knew what it was to wish to escape into 'les espaces immaculés'. But unlike her, whose temperament was, we are specifically told, 'plus sentimentale qu'artiste' and who passes from panacea to panacea, each tossed aside in a manner Flaubert noted elsewhere as characteristic of his whole generation (Du Camp, Louise Colet, and later his own creation Frédéric), Flaubert discovered his task in this life and persevered along a 'ligne droite'. Flaubert's view of mankind resembling Plato's in the *Republic,* he could declare that an ideal world would be one in which each individual, having found his personal bent, lived in accordance with it. Now for Flaubert, being born an artist meant that he studied the world and nature for their own sake and not for his own. In this he differs from Louise Colet and from so many Romantic writers who follow in the steps of Jean-Jacques Rousseau. The view of nature he applauded in the works of Apuleius is one which presents 'la Nature pour elle-même' (13, p. 215). And if

Flaubert chooses his representative woman in the mediocre surroundings he was to make his special field, he made the choice even *because* it was so repugnant to him, in search of that very probability which seemed to him more scientific, and knowing that the mediocre is, above all, the realm of that tragic state, illusion.

What of other examples of the treatment of the eternal feminine? Thus, for instance, at the first sight of Beatrice, Dante, known to Flaubert since his early teens, felt most beautifully the pricking of the growth of the wings of love. The neo-Platonists of the sixteenth century (which, in a *Carnet,* Flaubert referred to as carrying on 'la tradition' more authentically than the 'grand siècle') believed that woman might afford some glimpse of the ideal form of beauty. Much more recently, in *La Nouvelle Héloïse,* Rousseau, whose 'petit-fils' Flaubert owned that he was (14, p. 386), had invented a memorable mother-figure in Julie. At the end of Part Two of *Faust,* that 'maître homme' Goethe had shown Gretchen beckoning the hero onwards and upwards to salvation: 'Das Ewig-Weibliche zieht uns hinan.' Men are redeemed, also, by woman in the French poetry of the time as well as in Rousseau—Laprade, Ballanche, l'abbé Constant, Quinet, like Balzac and Lamartine, subscribed to the idealized notion of a 'femme-ange', embodiment for Flaubert of the false spirituality noted in the previous chapter. All three of the men in Emma's life address her in these terms. But in Flaubert's novel the word is also there so that he can deny the very notion; it is easier, so he argues, to portray an angel than a woman, because the wings dissimulate the hump. (13, p. 185). Not for Flaubert, as Goethe had confessed of himself to Eckermann, fictional women who were better than those he had met in reality. Flaubert abandoned his first idea of depicting a provincial modern mystic (though with no mission for redemption that he ever mentioned) precisely because Emma, upon whom his choice finally settled, seemed to him a woman such as one meets in actual life (13, p. 510).

In contrast to woman as redemptress and as guiding hand in transcendence upwards towards the divine and the beautiful, Emma is more like a female Don Juan, taking the character in its most interesting non-cliché form, as Flaubert had begun to do in extracts from an abandoned project later published by Maupassant (12, p. 232). The Don, another soul in search of purity, seeks it perversely and exclusively in sexual adventures, which swamp and divert some of his magnificent rebelliousness and passion for liberty. Emma, like him, is caused by Flaubert to descend, apparently damned, into the abyss, fetched and guided as he was, in her case by the blind man—'dans les ténèbres éternelles, comme un épouvantement'. Once dead, Emma, again in contrast to Gretchen, will seem to be dragging Charles down towards her. 'Elle le corrompait par-delà le tombeau.' The chaste Diana the huntress, parodied as Emma in riding-habit ('en amazone') and whom Rodolphe did not seduce without some trouble, has become Diana the infernal, that is, Hecate herself, whose dogs howl in the distance after Emma's death, for there is yet more prey left in the Bovary family.

As for Flaubert's contemporaries, his view is this: 'Il n'est pas un écrivain qui n'ait exalté la mère, l'épouse ou l'amante ... la génération endolorie larmoie sur les genoux des femmes, comme un enfant malade. On n'a pas l'idée de la lâcheté des

hommes, envers elles' (14, p. 20). We recognize a further reference to 'le culte de
la mère', here clearly identified with submission to all females—'sur les genoux des
femmes'—and ascribed to Flaubert's whole generation. Elsewhere he will go further, speaking of 'ce pauvre siècle à scrofules et à pâmoisons . . . qui se complaît sur
les genoux féminins, comme un enfant malade' (13, p. 655). A tendency of his
whole epoch is in question, and, with his affair with Louise Colet at an end and
Madame Bovary, that investigation of a female psyche, also complete, he will round
upon all women as a sex. Other sallies are well known: 'Je crois . . . qu'une des
causes de la faiblesse morale du dix-neuvième siècle vient de sa poétisation exa-
gérée' (14, p. 20). Yet all three of these attacks upon the female species were in
fact written in letters to individual women. Flaubert's hostility is towards some
element which he called symbolically rather than literally 'la femme', the enemy
within herself, as he had told Louise, 'l'élément féminin' (13, p. 402), which is, as he
also said, the work of the male. Flaubert's studies of Salammbô, supplemented by
his portraits in *L'Éducation sentimentale,* will contribute to a full understanding of his
meaning, culminating in that allegory of the Second Empire which is *Hérodias,*
where the dance of Salome expresses in terrifying fashion the power of the eternal
feminine.[13]

The equivalence between Emma and an over-poeticized figure of the eternal
feminine is made clear in a number of ways, notably in Léon's famous composite
portrait:

> Par la diversité de son humeur, tour à tour mystique ou joyeuse, babillarde,
> taciturne, emportée, nonchalante, elle allait rappelant en lui mille désirs, évo-
> quant des instincts ou des réminiscences. Elle était l'amoureuse de tous les
> romans, l'héroïne de tous les drames, le vague *elle* de tous les volumes de
> vers. Il retrouvait sur ses épaules la couleur ambrée de l'odalisque au bain; elle
> avait le corsage long des châtelaines féodales; elle ressemblait aussi à *la femme
> pâle de Barcelone,* mais elle était par-dessus tout Ange!

All these elements—Egyptian, medieval, Romantic Spanish, Romantic French—are
the invention of males—writers, painters, musicians. And although aiding and abet-
ting as women will in the confection of this vaporous persona, Emma is its victim
and will be abandoned when the time comes for 'settling down'. Neither worship
of the 'ange-femme' nor 'le culte de la mère' imply feminism. Both are accompanied
by a 'souverain mépris', as Flaubert himself once said (13, p. 181), for actual,
individual women. The relationship is false, an aspect of the *Blague* that Flaubert so
detested. The very idealization of a fictitious feminine is a lie, as we have seen in
considering Lamartine, cancelling out the treatment of a woman as an individual
reality, as a self-contained will to liberty. All this emerges from the history of Emma.
Its effect upon the character of men we shall consider later.

Baudelaire (a contemporary, it is worth stressing) found Emma 'très-sublime
. . . en face de son petit horizon'.[14] Victor Brombert has similarly admired her
dignified, *fantôme*-like figure when she overawes Justin, commanding our respect
even as she swallows the arsenic.[15] But above all, Emma appears as the eternal

feminine in her tragic relationship throughout her life with the male, presented by Flaubert in many forms, culminating in the very poison itself, the etymological sense of the word 'arsenic' being 'male'. 'Les bourgeois ne se doutent guère que nous leur servons notre cœur (13, p. 675),' wrote Flaubert to Feydeau. Flaubert's beloved sister Caroline died in childbed, that is, quite specifically as a result of the arrival of love, which is to say of the masculine in her life. So, just as certainly—and on the same day in the year—does Emma, if in a different way. In one case, the corruption has been physical infection resulting from fertility itself; in the other, the corruption is moral, following on a life which, for diverse reasons, has been spiritually sterile.

In this way did Flaubert exorcise the pain of the loss of Caroline. This is one of the causes of his famous remark: 'Madame Bovary, c'est moi.'

NOTES

[1] *Oeuvres complètes*, Paris, Club de l'Honnête Homme, 1971–6, vol. 13, p. 675 (further references to this edition will be given in the text in abbreviated form, thus: 13, p. 675).

[2] See *Le Christ aux Oliviers*, in *Oeuvres*, Paris, vol. I, 1956, p. 38.

[3] H. B. Riffaterre, *L'Orphisme dans le poésie romantique*, Paris, 1970, pp. 71 and 74.

[4] Claude de Thiard de Bissy, *Histoire d'Ema*, 2 vols., Paris, 1752.

[5] See B. F. Bart and Richard Francis Cook, *The Legendary Sources of Flaubert's 'Saint Julien'*, Toronto, 1977.

[6] *Oeuvres*, Paris, 1939, vol. II, p. 445.

[7] *'Madame Bovary', Novelle Version*, ed. Jean Pommier and Gabrielle Leleu, Paris, 1949, p. 155.

[8] *Contes*, ed. G. Rouger, Paris, 1967, pp. 3–10.

[9] *'Madame Bovary', Nouvelle Version*, p. 525.

[10] *De la religion considérée dans sa source, ses formes et ses développements*, 5 vols., 1824–30.

[11] *Oeuvres*, vol. II, p. 448.

[12] *Isis* (first published 1845), in *Oeuvres*, vol. I, pp. 324–8.

[13] See Margaret Lowe, ' "Rendre plastique . . .": Flaubert's Treatment of the Female Principle in *Hérodias'*, *Modern Language Review*, July 1983.

[14] *Oeuvres*, vol. II, p. 447.

[15] *The Novels of Flaubert*, Princeton, 1966, pp. 87–8.

Sarah Webster Goodwin

EMMA BOVARY'S DANCE OF DEATH[1]

After an inebriating waltz with the viscount at the chateau La Vaubyessard, Emma Bovary, catching her breath, leans against a wall and closes her eyes. An apparently trivial anti-climax follows:

> Quand elle les rouvrit, au milieu du salon, une dame assise sur un tabouret avait devant elle trois valseurs agenouillés. Elle choisit le vicomte, et le violon recommença. On les regardait.... Elle savait valser, celle-là![2]

> When she opened them again, in the middle of the drawing room three waltzers were kneeling before a lady sitting on a stool. She chose the Viscount, and the violin struck up once more. Every one looked at them.... That woman knew how to waltz! (38)

The passage has a narrative structure not unlike the one which Freud discusses in his essay "The Theme of the Three Caskets." Of the choices which characters often must make among three possibilities, where the "correct" one is the most attractive but represents death, Freud writes, "Choice stands in the place of necessity, of destiny. Thus man overcomes death, which in thought he has acknowledged. No greater triumph of wish-fulfillment is conceivable. Just where in reality he obeys compulsion, he exercises choice; and that which he chooses is not a thing of horror, but the fairest and most desirable thing in life" (76). Emma, the initiate, must first learn how to make the choice; for now a proxy chooses for her. Beginning with, "Emma ne savait pas valser" (86) ("Emma did not know how to waltz" [37]), and moving through Emma's envious thought, "Elle savait valser, celle-là!" ("That woman knew how to waltz!"), the last dance at the ball shows Emma just starting to cross a mental and dramatic threshold. Although she will never waltz again, she will spend the rest of her life trying to place herself in the position which she imagines the other woman occupies. Throughout the novel, Emma appropriates a freedom of choice which repeatedly unveils itself as illusory.

From *Novel* 19, No. 3 (Spring 1986): 197–215.

By this time in the novel we sense that forces we only dimly perceive have shaped the story's outcome. The forces of necessity which dictate Emma's choice and thus her death-wish are psychological and economic within the realities of her world. I will argue that another kind of force shaping her experience, one of a different order, is the popular motif of the dance of death, transformed and embedded by Flaubert in the novel's structures. Flaubert seems to have explored, in *Madame Bovary*, the way both the features and the movement of a popular motif can provide a model for understanding experience. This need not suggest that the experience precedes the model—indeed, Flaubert cannily works within a moment of inseparability. That he did so intentionally appears unlikely: it seems clear that the dance of death, as an exemplary cliché of extremist sensibility, itself represents a "thing of horror," to use Freud's phrase, a *bêtise*, that Flaubert would have wished to avoid. To explore the role of such a motif in Flaubert's writing is thus to return to the question of how he uses clichés, with what kinds of irony, and what degree of self-consciousness.

It is not clear how we can distinguish Emma's psyche from Flaubert's own, once it seems likely that the motif's presence is not fully conscious. Emma's life in fiction, Flaubert's psyche, and the sources which had suggestive power for him cannot finally be disentangled. The essay that follows begins by charting the shape of Emma's experience as it grows out of her first waltz. It then turns to Flaubert's manipulations of the contemporary dance of death. To see these two approaches synthetically is to see an essential unity between the author's imaginative life and the story he writes. The dance of death, as Flaubert transforms it into lived experience in Emma's story, is an absent paradigm of the individual's confrontation with obscure necessities, both internal and external. Thus this particular motif is not an arbitrary cliché among many, but is peculiarly appropriate to Flaubert's subject.

In the late-medieval dance of death, Death appears as a skeleton or corpse to a series of people, hierarchically arranged, and interrupts their daily lives to lead them to death. The earliest versions, in the fourteenth and fifteenth centuries, depict a round dance or line dance, in which Death is the partner. Later versions, most notably Hans Holbein's of 1538, divide the dance into realistic scenes in which Death is a fantastic intruder. In the early nineteenth century, the dance of death experienced a serious revival, in various forms: facsimiles and cheap copies, especially of Holbein;[3] bibliophiles' collections; scholarly studies; preservationist movements for the monumental versions, including the bas-relief at Rouen's cloister St. Maclou; and, finally, countless contemporary versions in the graphic arts and popular literature. The motif became especially popular as the basis for a moral tale, issuing a thinly-veiled warning to women who were disobedient or who abandoned family and domesticity for the implicit eroticism of the ball.[4] In the context of this romantic revival of the *danse macabre* Emma's own dance takes on added significance.

Although, in *Madame Bovary,* there are intimations of Emma's death as early as her wedding, she actually approaches the threshold—enters the dance, so to speak—during the ball at La Vaubyessard. Readers have often noticed that the ball represents a turning point in Emma's life: she glimpses a world at the chateau which will make it impossible for her ever again to be satisfied with her simple and limited existence.[5] The ball initiates Emma to a scene appropriate to her imagination and offers her an agent to transport her there. That agent is the viscount with whom Emma waltzes.

A second ball late in the novel matches the one at La Vaubyessard, the two standing like a pair of parentheses around Emma's life as an adultress. The second ball is a kind of unveiling of the first, a stripping away of the glittering surface. A masked ball at Rouen, it takes place during the last romantic encounter Emma has with Léon, immediately before Lheureux's nets close in on her. Léon Bopp (458) has noted a series of correspondences between the two balls, in which the second is clearly an ironic inversion of the first: Emma's costume, the mediocre breakfast in a dingy cafe, the third-rate company, and Emma's meditation before an open window at dawn all recall elements of the decisive experience at the chateau—and all are emblems of how far she has fallen. The most significant inversion is in the nature of her dance: rather than waltzing with an agent of her aspirations, "Elle sauta toute la nuit, au son furieux des trombones; on faisait cercle autour d'elle . . ." (312) ("She danced all night to the wild sound of trombones; people gathered around her" [212]). Here there is no question of knowing or not knowing how to dance, no question of a proxy. She leads the dance herself; she makes it her own. The orchestra is no longer dominated by the poignant tones of the violin, but by a trombone, whose "son furieux" has a threatening and martial intensity. We sense something like the vitality of ritual in this strange dance of which the narrator permits only a brief glimpse.

Immediately after the ball at Rouen, Emma returns home to find that the events have already been set in motion which lead ineluctably to her suicide. As she returns, she encounters the financier Lheureux, who informs her, "Il y a jugement!" (314) ("There's a judgment" [213]), and Emma submits her house to an inventory. Flaubert describes the moment with a macabre metaphor:

Ils examinèrent ses robes, le linge, le cabinet de toilette; et son existence, jusque dans ses recoins les plus intimes, fut, comme un cadavre que l'on autopsie, étalée tout du long aux regards de ces trois hommes.   (316)

They examined her dresses, the linen, the dressing-room; and her whole existence, to its most intimate details, was stretched out like a cadaver in an autopsy before the eyes of these three men.   (215)

These three men, inspecting Emma's life as though it were a corpse stretched before them, echo subtly the three men who knelt before Emma's proxy at the ball. In the narrative the men are the bailiff and two witnesses, final agents of the forces of (economic) necessity which entered Emma's life when, at La Vaubyessard, she committed herself to her desires.

Between the two balls Emma encounters a series of complements to the viscount, and each one repeats elements of her experience at the ball while unfolding an ever more complex iconographic net. The last, and most important, of the series, is *l'aveugle,* the blind beggar whose song Emma hears as she is dying. Scholars have sought ways of describing the blind man's allegorical function in the novel: the strained coincidence of his presence at Emma's death comes close to breaking the mimetic fabric. He makes the most sense as a complement to the significant moment of the waltz, that is as the "thing of horror" Emma unwittingly chooses to fulfill her desire.

The most important feature of *l'aveugle* is his voice and its effect on Emma: "Cela lui descendait au fond de l'âme comme un tourbillon dans un abîme, et l'emportait parmi les espaces d'une mélancolie sans bornes" (291) ("It went to the very depths of her soul, like a whirlwind in an abyss, and carried her away to a boundless realm of melancholy" [193]). The *tourbillon* locates Emma's response to the blind man among her responses to the viscount, Rodolphe, and Léon. Each of these figures seems to Emma to promise an escape from her confining existence; all arouse in her a mental state of confusion, a *tourbillon* whose vortex she enters with a mixture of desire and fear. The *mélancolie sans bornes* to which the blind man transports her is, in other guises, the pure infinity of her desire.

Although in many ways dissimilar characters, the viscount, Léon, and Rodolphe inspire a substantially similar set of feelings in Emma. These feelings have a source elsewhere than in the male characters. Each of Emma's amorous encounters is an attempt to find the original agent of her desires, the "cavalier à plume blanche qui galope sur un cheval noir" (72) ("a white-plumed knight galloping on his black horse" [26]) of whom she has read and dreamed as an adolescent, building her fantasies on popular romance narratives. She seeks through her *cavaliers* a sensual access to another imagined life: smelling Rodolphe's hair for the first time, Emma conflates him with the viscount and Léon, as her "désirs d'autrefois ... tourbillon-naient dans la bouffée subtile du parfum qui se répandait sur son âme" (177) ("her past desires ... swirled around in the subtle breath of the perfume that diffused over her soul" [106]).

The hurdy-gurdy man of Tostes serves to bridge the symbolic and psycho-logical gap between Emma's elegant escorts on the one hand and the blind man on the other. Physically unpleasant with his jet of brown saliva, the hurdy-gurdy man, like the blind man, lives by soliciting money in public. And yet with his tinsel-and-paper portable ballroom he has a curious power to evoke for Emma the fantasy world most vividly encountered during the waltz at La Vaubyessard. His figures, too, are waltzing, their image reflected in a fragmented mirror: "Une valse aussitôt commençait, et ... des danseurs hauts comme le doigt ... *tournaient, tournaient* entre les fauteuils ... se répétant dans les morceaux de miroir ..." (98, my em-phasis) ("A waltz began and ... dancers the size of a finger ... turned and turned between the armchairs ... reflected in small pieces of mirror ..." [46]). These words recall the moment of Emma's dance with the viscount: "Ils tournaient: tout tournait autour d'eux, les lampes, les meubles, les lambris, et le parquet, comme un disque sur un pivot" (86) ("They turned: all around them was turning, the lamps, the furniture, the wainscoting, the floor, like a disc on a pivot" [38]). And the dance anticipates Emma's last vision of Rodolphe an instant before she decides to commit suicide:

> Il lui sembla tout à coup que des globules couleur de feu éclataient dans l'air comme des balles fulminantes en s'aplatissant, et tournaient, tournaient, pour aller se fondre dans la neige, entre les branches des arbres. Au milieu de chacun d'eux, la figure de Rodolphe apparaissait. (333)

> Suddenly it seemed to her that fiery spheres were exploding in the air like bullets when they strike, and were whirling, whirling, to melt at last upon the snow between the branches of the trees. In the midst of each of them appeared the face of Rodolphe. (228)

The waltz, it becomes clear, enacts a state of mind, its origins concealed, which Emma compulsively repeats until her death.

Like the blind man's song, the hurdy-gurdy man's music transports Emma; "échos du monde qui arrivaient jusqu'à Emma" (98) ("echoes of the world that reached even to Emma" [47]), it gives her an imaginative way out. Both Léon and Rodolphe seem to promise to transport Emma more literally out of her world, on horseback and in carriages. From the moment Léon seduces her in a carriage (described, in the famous metaphor, as tomb-like, "plus close qu'un tombeau" [270]), Emma associates him with departure from Yonville. But Léon is not only inadequate as an agent of release; he brings Emma almost to the point where confinement and release merge in a substantial paradox: the carriage, emblematic vehicle of her escape from Yonville, also enacts the closure of passion, the finitude of carnal pleasure.

Emma's affair with Léon plays out terms she has already established with Rodolphe. Earlier in the novel, Emma believes that she finds in Rodolphe the *cavalier,* the horseman who will succeed in carrying her away, and in actualizing her adolescent fantasy. Just as he is about to break off with her she is entertaining her highest hopes of a kind of personal apocalypse: she dreams,

> Au galop de quatre chevaux, elle était emportée depuis huit jours vers un pays nouveau, d'où ils ne reviendraient plus. Ils allaient, ils allaient.... (223)

> To the gallop of four hourses she was carried away for a week towards a new land, from where they would never return. They went on and on.... (141)

Emma mistakes the cycle she is playing out with Rodolphe for a possible linear escape. The dream described here culminates a series of references to horses, allusions which become especially frequent during the affair with Rodolphe. The semantic traits associated with the horse are escape, eroticism, masculinity, and wealth. From the day Emma and Rodolphe become lovers while out riding, horses remain part of Rodolphe's seductive appeal, like a constant promise to remove her to another world.

Rodolphe is, of course, not the first to lead Emma to believe that her fantasy *cavalier* may present himself to her in the flesh and carry her away. The first is the viscount. During the ball references to horses form something like a subtext of peculiar intensity, working subtly on Emma's imagination.[6] On the way home after the ball, Emma has her last glimpse of the viscount. As Charles and Emma return toward Yonville with a little horse awkwardly drawing a carriage too big for it, some riders approach, smoking cigars: "tout à coup, des cavaliers passèrent en riant, avec des cigares à la bouche" (88). Later in the novel, right after Rodolphe seduces Emma, she watches him repair a broken bridle with his pocket-knife, "le cigare aux dents" (190). The cigar is one of many inconspicuous details which, compounded, suggest that the viscount and Rodolphe share an identity as types of Emma's longed-for *cavalier*.

If the series of *cavaliers* as horsemen promises a linear escape, the *cavalier* as waltzing-partner promises an agent of passion, guiding Emma into a vortex which provides another figure of escape. Music is the agency of transport: the blind man's *cri prolongé* has its counterpart in other kinds of music, beginning with the violin. During the ball at La Vaubyessard the violin's three appearances mark stages in the dance, each one progressively closer to the heart of the matter, the moment of *tourbillon* with the viscount. The first "ritournelle de violon" occurs at the beginning of the quadrilles; the second sounds while Emma dances with an unnamed *cavalier*, and "un sourire lui montait aux lèvres à certaines délicatesses du violon, qui jouait seul, quelquefois . . ." (84) ("A smile rose to her lips at certain delicate phrases of the violin, that sometimes played alone . . ." [36]). And finally, while Emma watches the envied woman who can waltz, "Elle choisit le vicomte, et le violon recommença" (87) ("She chose the Viscount, and the violin struck up once more" [38]). The violin's solitary voice assumes in this episode a peculiar power: it works as a call and as a promise. Its allure has both a sensual essence and a symbolic authority.

Later Emma hears a violin—at the theater in Rouen—and senses herself as the instrument: "Elle se laissait aller au bercement des mélodies et se sentait elle-même vibrer de tout son être comme si les archets des violons se fussent promenés sur ses nerfs" (248) ("She gave herself up to the flow [rocking movement] of the melodies, and felt all her being vibrate as if the violin bows were being drawn across her nerves" [161]). Emma submits herself imaginatively to the sound of the violin, in a sense taking on its identity. In the music's harmonies she hears the agitation of multiple imaginations "comme dans l'atmosphère d'un autre monde." The "other world" is, overtly, the fictional world of the theatrical presentation; it is also related to the many other times Emma is drawn vaguely toward another kind of being which she cannot name.

The passage recalls an earlier moment when Emma hears a sound and feels herself its instrument; it is the moment just after she and Rodolphe have made love for the first time. In both cases the music is an access to a state of mind which is at once physical (erotic, nervous), imaginative, and inarticulate. In a passage from an early version of the novel, Flaubert draws a direct parallel between erotic fulfillment and Emma's sense of herself as a violin being played by her lover:

Elle se sentait toute possédée par son caprice, comme un violon qui vibre sous les doigts d'un maître et c'était tour à tour des joyeusetés sensuelles comme dans les cavatines italiennes ou bien des harmonies à plein accord avec des repos dans le bonheur, intervalles de silence aussi chantants que la musique. Puis l'amour descendait dans les profondeurs graves; des rêveries sans cause se balançaient mollement et disparaissaient emportées sous un tourbillon d'idées confuses. Cependant, cela se dégageait, et une extase suprême allait se dégageant toujours jusqu'au haut, jusqu'a la dernière limite, comme une petite note délicate et sérieuse, qui monte, en glissant sur la chanterelle et palpite d'un son si pur, si plein, si léger, qu'il vous semble même que rien au-delà n'existe.   (Pommier and Leleu, 417)

She felt herself totally possessed by his caprice, like a violin which vibrates under the fingers of a master. By turns, it would play a gay and sensuous air, like an Italian cavatina, or again, a melody perfectly attuned to those pauses in happiness, the intervals of silence which sing as loudly as the music itself. Then love would descend the scale to a lower register; reveries without cause would hover softly and then disappear, swept away by a whirlwind of confused ideas. This too would break off, and a supreme ecstasy would mount, break off and mount again, rising to the outermost extreme, like a little note, fragile and serious, which mounts, sliding over the E string, and throbbing with a sound so pure, so full, so delicate it seems that nothing beyond that point could exist.   (de Man, 275–76)

Interestingly, the *tourbillon* here is not the end but the middle of the sensation, and the pure note, the "petite note délicate et sérieuse ... d'un ton si pur" seems the end toward which everything moves. (It is an end in which identities disintegrate, as *elle* becomes *vous* in the last sentence.) Repeatedly the *tourbillon* represents a threshold state which Emma crosses toward something. It may well be that Flaubert struck this passage at least partly to retain the pattern of incompletion in her movement. She does not reach the austere and pure other state evoked above until she has passed out of the narrative. She does long for it and try to imagine it—figuring it as *l'azur, l'espace*—countless times.

II

By the time Flaubert, as an adolescent, wrote his fantastic lyrical drama "La danse des morts," he was no longer very original in changing the motif almost unrecognizably to fit his needs. Scholars have ignored what appears to be the most significant influence; but they have noted the probable influence of Edgar Quinet's *Ahasvérus* and Gautier's *La comédie de la mort,* works which incorporate a dance of death for its eschatological connotations (Bruneau, 197n). It is certain that Flaubert knew at least Quinet's work and the fifteenth-century version from which he drew his epigraph ("Mort fait finalement/Tous aller au jugement") ("Death sends us all finally to judgment" [*Premières oeuvres,* 19]). And it is likely or possible that he knew several other contemporary works, among them Grandville's very successful and witty graphic cycle, "Voyage pour l'éternité, départ à toute heure," published in 1830;[7] Goethe's famous lyric "Der Totentanz," to which Flaubert's opening scene bears precise resemblance;[8] and two popular lyrics published in 1833 and 1836 in journals Flaubert apparently read (Bruneau, 197n). Most significantly, he probably also knew the scholarly study written by an old family friend of some importance to Flaubert, E. H. Langlois.

Flaubert's letters contain numerous references to Langlois, all of them positive, and all indicating both a neighborly intimacy and respect.[9] Furthermore, on the evening Flaubert is commonly supposed to have first conceived *Madame Bovary* (Bollème, 53n), while traveling abroad, he was thinking about Langlois' life-long influence on him:

> Nous portons en nous notre passé, pendant toute notre vie nous sentons de la nourrice. Quand je m'analyse je trouve encore fraîches et avec toutes leurs influences ... la place du père Langlois, celle du père Mignot, celle de don Quichotte, et de mes songeries d'enfant. ...   (Corr. II 5)

> We carry our pasts within us; throughout our lives we bear our nurses' imprint. When I analyze myself I find, still fresh and effective ... the place of old Langlois, Mignot, Don Quixote, my childhood reveries. ...[10]

Flaubert wrote these words in a letter to Louis Bouilhet; the letter also contains the first sketch of the novel which was to become *Madame Bovary.* The "père Mignot" was a family friend who introduced the child Flaubert to literature by reading him *Don Quixote. Madame Bovary* responds to *Don Quixote,* we know, in ways that are both obvious and very rich. But Langlois' place in Flaubert's memory, and his relation to the novel, have remained obscure.

Langlois describes in his study, published in 1832, all of the dances of death that he had found, many of which were in his private collection. They range from medieval to contemporary versions. He discusses the medieval bas-reliefs in Rouen, and he invents and illustrates his own didactic narrative version involving an initiatory ball that turns into a dance of death. It seems not only possible but likely that Langlois' personal collections and life-long enthusiasm for the motif fueled the young Flaubert's interest. After Langlois' death, friends of his (and Flaubert's) undertook to re-issue his 1832 study in a handsome, massive edition, complete with an entire volume of illustrations from his collection, his own engravings, and those of his children. It appeared in 1852—four years before the publication of *Madame Bovary*—and became one of the standard early works on the dance of death.

The similarity between Emma's story and the contemporary popular narrative versions of the dance of death would suffice, given the variety and number of these sources, to propose a footnote to the more general study of Flaubert's sources. But Flaubert's mention of Langlois in such suggestive terms and in such a crucial letter leads us to speculate on why the dance of death in particular seems to have such a resonant, though never explicit, place in the novel. To assemble Flaubert's sources in this context is to buttress an argument that the motif had an ongoing presence in his mental life. That presence accumulated over time, building a potent memory-bank which he drew on in his writing, and shaping his choices as he wrote in ways he may well not fully have known.

In 1838, at the age of sixteen, Flaubert wrote "La danse des morts." Already he makes use of the series of pairs and the vortex which becomes constitutive in *Madame Bovary:*

> Les morts dansaient et la longue file de squelettes tournait et tourbillonait en une immense spirale qui montait jusqu'aux hauteurs les plus hautes et descendait jusqu'aux abîmes les plus profonds. Là, le roi donnait la main au mendiante, le prêtre au bourreau, la prêtresse à la courtisane. . . .
>
> *(Premières oeuvres, 57–58)*

> The dead danced and the long line of skeletons turned and whirled in an immense spiral that mounted up as high as the highest heights and descended into the deepest depths. There, the king took the hand of the beggar, the priest that of the torturer, the priestess that of the courtesan. . . .

The spiral's moving force is the *tourbillon* which pairs off series of opposites and subsumes them, spinning them toward a kind of death-within-death. It is an original image.[11] These are opposites (king and beggar, priestess and courtesan) primarily by the principle of social norm. Their differences from each other are at once a condition for society and a social artifice. Within verbal expression, based on difference, there is no way to express that whose nature is perpetual identity except by implied contrast to that whose nature is difference. In the medieval motif, death and life oppose each other in pairs of figures; in Flaubert's "Danse des morts" they oppose each other in the formal contrast between increment (the basis of episode in linear narrative) and vortex (the figure of moving towards fusion, the dense moment which subsumes all others). The vortex is not death itself but is the narrative principle corresponding to death.

In *Madame Bovary* the same schema operates implicitly. Episodes take the place of the pairs, and the *tourbillon,* we have seen, recurs at crucial moments, counterpointing narrative development. Critics have commented frequently on the episodic nature of the novel and its relation to Emma's experience. Georges Poulet, for example, in *Les métamorphoses du cercle,* describes the form of *Madame Bovary* in a well-known passage as that of a series of pools, into each of which a stone is thrown, whose expanding centers he sees as the dynamic form of human consciousness (381).[12] Poulet's insight into the relation of literary form to consciousness is an important one; and he describes succinctly how the novel's movement by episodic increment is significant for the narration of consciousness, with sensation and memory rippling out from the center of events. Emma performs, it is true, a kind of mental *bricolage* with her surroundings, as any object becomes potentially an agent of meaning; Flaubert forces the reader to do the same. The text acquires a memory-bank of images which is elusively distinguishable from Emma's fictional consciousness. Episodes, organizing clusters of images, are as natural an increment in narrative as they are in a remembered life.

It is precisely the episode as such which is missing from "La danse des morts": it attempts—and fails—to create a narrative from within the vortex, having shed already the perceptual clutter that makes its opposite, emptiness, perceivable. There is a kind of bad faith in the text; it uses unquestioningly some of the very clichés whose phenomenal aspects Flaubert so probingly, and ironically, documents in the novel. In "La danse des morts," for example, Death rides a splendid horse. Transversing the heavens in the manner of an apocalyptic horseman, Death cries to its mount,

> Comme tu cours sur le monde, comme ton sabot d'acier retentit bien sur les têtes que tu broies dans ton galop, ô mon cheval! . . . penchée sur tes crins, sur ton cou que s'allonge, je n'entends que le vent qui siffle à mes oreilles et fait résonner ma faulx et mes flèches suspendues à ta croupe. . . .   (40)

> How you run over the world, how your steeled hoof resounds on the skulls which you crush as you gallop, O my steed! . . . leaning on your mane, on your straining neck, I hear only the wind which whistles in my ears and makes my bow and arrows resonate as they hang at your haunches. . . .

The horse is clearly part of Death's power, cruelty, and beauty; Death partakes of the strength in its haunches. It is a strength which is essentially erotic and which culminates in motion, in supernatural freedom and departure. But we see in *Madame Bovary* that the same erotic power has mundane and natural sources, related directly to money and social status.

Death the Horseman, like Death as fiddler or the Grim Reaper, is a motif that is related to the traditional dance of death, but only in modern (eighteenth-century and later) versions conflated with it.[13] In "La danse des morts" Flaubert is clearly drawing, in flexible ways, on the traditional iconography. To proceed to argue that he is doing so in *Madame Bovary* may seem a very large step; and the argument must indeed be of a different order. It is clearly an overstatement to argue that Rodolphe as horseman symbolizes Death, just as it is an overstatement to say that the dance of death is overtly present as a motif in the novel. Both are among several aspects of the iconography of death which do not intrude upon the mimetic fabric. But they remain like a level of the text which is in fact absent, finding its existence in the mental file of commonplaces which the reader brings to the work, a subliminal accompaniment to the manifest action.[14]

There is, in any case, iconographic precedent for an *aveugle* who is in some sense a death-figure. Langlois discusses a medieval "Dance [sic] aux aveugles" by Pierre Michaut which, he says, resembles a dance of death; the three blind men are *l'amour, la fortune,* and *la mort,* echoes perhaps for Flaubert of the three fates, which scholars have seen as resonating in the novel (Engstrom, *passim*). The other major French scholar of the dance of death, Gabriel Peignot, devotes an entire chapter of his important 1826 study to the Michaut "Dance aux aveugles."[15]

The medieval dances of death, up to and including Holbein's version, commonly establish a diachronic time reference to frame the synchrony of repeated encounters. That diachrony is central to the motif's rhetorical stance: the frame—whether Biblical images from Genesis and Revelation, or depictions of the artist or of a preaching clergyman—explicitly evokes divine judgment, warning the observer to apply what he has seen to his own standards of conduct and understanding of history. In *Madame Bovary* the chapters framing Emma's story, puzzling to commentators like Poulet, who focus on Emma's consciousness, similarly shape the novel's normative and historiographic import.[16]

At the end of "La danse des morts" Flaubert has *L'Histoire* appear and pose a question to *La Mort:*

> C'est que je t'envie, ou plutôt j'envie le monde que tu emportes chaque soir
> ... mais moi je reste. Quand donc pourrai-je me mêler à la caravane funèbre,
> moi, son conducteur et son maître?   (63–64)

> You see I envy you, or rather I envy the world which you carry off every night
> ... but I stay behind. When will I be able to join the funereal caravan, I who
> am its conductor and master?

It is the last line spoken in the work; and it revises the kind of closure typical of the medieval topos, where human event gives way to eschatology. In "La danse des morts," Flaubert announces not apocalypse but its impossibility. Bruneau (200) faults this work for being confused, for imposing a cyclical and pessimistic framework on a Christian framework. But therein, of course, lies its daring. *L'Histoire* feels itself condemned to continue indefinitely; divine and final judgment fall out of the picture. The nature of implied judgments in the work becomes problematic.[17]

In depicting a recognizable social and historical context for Emma Bovary's impulses and for the novel's elaborate literary devices, and in foregrounding that context by excluding Emma from the frame chapters, Flaubert invites us to perceive modes of behavior and to evaluate what motivates them. As in "La danse des morts," history, in *Madame Bovary,* is condemned to continue; there is no salvation, nor any prefiguration of salvation.

But there is judgment. We condemn, for example, Homais for the worst evil—small-mindedness; Bournisien for his stupidity and insensitivity; and Lheureux for his ruthlessness and greed. The novel's judgment of each of these figures carries historiographic weight. We may see the figures as metonymic emblems of, respectively, naive positivism, the Church, and unbridled capitalism.[18]

We have much greater difficulty establishing what kind of judgment to pass on Emma. It is the novel's greatest ambiguity, and one which is present thematically in the story. Lheureux, we have seen, exclaims, "Il y a jugement!" shortly before Emma commits suicide. His words echo the reader's own sentiments; Emma must be judged, no matter how much sympathy she arouses. Lheureux's words refer to a legal judgment, but it is one which had its real-life counterpart, with explicitly moral dimensions, in the post-publication trial. Emma's economic dilemmas are inextricable from her moral ones. The question is: is her fate sealed because she makes the mistake of reifying her being in the objects with which she surrounds herself? Or are Lheureux and the bailiff's men, enforcing judgment, agents of the same relentlessly and destructively materialist world whose insufficiency is the cause of Emma's suffering? We are meant to find unjust Lheureux's cold-blooded ex-ploitation of Emma. But Emma's greatest failure has been, as Ahearn has expressed it (76), her inability to distinguish between the amorous and the economic. It is at the ball at La Vaubyessard that Emma enters that confusion irreversibly.

Money is not only an instrument of Emma's destruction in the narrative, it is also, iconographically, an attribute of death. The tinkle of coins appears in an important encounter with each of the figures in our series of *cavaliers*. At La Vaubyessard the sound of *louis d'or* striking the gambling tables mingles with the violin's delicate notes (84); when Rodolphe first comes to Yonville he leaves three francs on the Bovarys' table; Léon, resurfacing in Emma's life at Rouen, pays for the Bovarys' ice cream with "deux pièces blanches qu'il fit sonner contre le marbre" (254); and both the hurdy-gurdy man and the blind man collect their coins. In one object, the coin, Flaubert concentrates iconographic, mimetic, and normative functions.

Emma's personal failure has a historiographic dimension as well. As Ahearn (79) and Tanner (262ff.) have pointed out, a series of references to spinning appears in the novel. The references juxtapose the conventional imagery of fate with the contingency of history, as industrialized processes take over the homely craft that makes it possible for Mère Rolet, spinning as she presides over Emma's final panic, to seem a dream-like allegory as well as a living woman. A failed mother-figure characterized otherwise mainly by her mercenary pleas, the Mère Rolet here enacts another kind of motherhood which continued to fascinate Flau-bert: the matrix of death. The Mère Rolet has her counterpart in "La danse des morts": "La Mort" herself says, "Je suis la nourrice du monde, qui l'endort chaque soir dans une couche chérie" (38, 39) ("I am the world's nurse, who rocks it to sleep each night in a beloved bed"); and "on eut dit une vieille mère qui rappelait à elle ses enfants" (47) ("she resembled an aged mother who called her children back to her"). In *Madame Bovary,* fate has psychological as well as historical resonance.

A prescience of fate, of necessity, then, hangs over the novel, but does not substitute for judgment. Indeed we suspect that, just as "Mort fait finalement/Tous aller au jugement," so too does the narrated life: begun and ended, it is spread out before us to be examined. In Freud's essay on the theme of the three caskets quoted earlier, the character who chooses among three possibilities believes he overcomes death because he replaces necessity or fate with choice. Freud implies the figure is not in any obvious way morally responsible for choosing death or bringing it on himself; the motif's *normative* aspect is culture- or context-specific. But Freud directs his attention mainly to the observation that, as he puts it, "There are forces in mental life tending toward the replacement of the opposite" (75) and to the dramatic configuration required to depict those forces. It is precisely this aspect of the mental life that renders moral judgment, distinctions between good and evil, difficult at best. Not only in respect to death do those forces hold sway, as Emma's life attests.

Flaubert could not have known that Emma's envy of the waltzing woman bears a subtle relation to the legend of the three caskets, but he could have intuited that it amounts to a death-wish. One of the peculiar strengths of Flaubert's writing is the way he strips commonplaces of their allegorical veneer but retains their psychological significance in narrative. Such an observation runs counter to one strain of contemporary Flaubert criticism, a strain perhaps best represented by Shoshana Felman, who has written with great ingenuity on Flaubert's use of the *lieu commun*. In one article in particular Felman describes Flaubert's use of cliché in terms not uncommon to recent Flaubert criticism:

> Car si dans le cliché, le contenu est preconçu et stéréotypé, le contenu, du coup, importe moins que l'action formelle et la structure du signifiant, l'énoncé importe moins que le *fonctionnement, l'effet* de l'énonciation.... Le lieu commun sera, dès lors, repris par l'écriture non plus comme signe ou comme sens, mais comme signal: signal du code.   (37)

> Because if in the cliché, the content is preconceived and stereotyped, the content, suddenly, is less important than the *function,* the *effect* of the enunciation.... The cliché or commonplace thenceforth will be used by writing not as a sign or as significance, but as signal: signal of the code.

Felman is right, of course, and Flaubert's critical sense that *all* of language is a cliché permeates to a greater or lesser extent all of his works. But in *Madame Bovary* there is a tension which Felman does not allow for. However critical and ironic, Flaubert is not indifferent to signification, nor does he ever empty words of their sense. We may counter Felman's observation with the famous passage in *Madame Bovary* where the narrative voice breaks in with an unusual note of sincerity, when Rodolphe "ne distinguait pas ... la dissemblance des sentiments sous la parité des expressions.... [C]omme si la plénitude de l'âme ne débordait pas quelquefois par les métaphores les plus vides" (219) ("He was unable to see ... the variety of feelings hidden within the same expressions.... [A]s though the abundance of one's soul did not sometimes overflow with empty metaphors" [138]). The different sentiment will be the sincere one, the overflowing of the soul's plenitude: hardly a statement we expect from an author whose sole concern is to signal the code. While this passage is exceptional in Flaubert's mature works, we need not dismiss it. Flaubert encourages us to sympathize at least with a longing for meaning. And we are meant to see that passion, eternally monotonous, will not provide it, any more than material objects will.

Cliché, then, becomes another way of signalling *la parité des expressions*— but, at the same time, it is what must be said. Flaubert's solution is to use commonplaces ironically; or, quite otherwise, to use them in such a way that he sheds the *signal du code,* the elements alerting the reader to the presence of the cliché, and retains the *signifié* substantially in the narrative. In doing so he returns necessarily to the experienced moment out of which the commonplace grows metonymically: the wet-nurse spinning as one's life runs out, or the waltz in another world.

The German critic Manfred Hardt has written on another such *lieu commun* in *Madame Bovary:* the image of the shipwreck. He calls it a *Bildreihe,* which works as a microtext paralleling the narrative (151). The shipwreck commonplace in Flaubert, like the dance of death, can work both ways, that is, both ironically and seriously; and when it is serious it is unobtrusive. Flaubert has one of the speakers during the *comices agricoles* resort to the shipwreck cliché in the course of his empty rhetoric (M. le Conseiller speaks of the "roi bien-aimé ... qui dirige à la fois d'une main si ferme et si sage le char de l'État parmi les périls incessants d'une mer orageuse ..." [172]) ("beloved king ... who directs with a hand at once so firm and so wise the chariot of the state amid the incessant perils of a stormy sea" [102]). But the same cliché is also a serious paradigm of confusion in Emma's movement toward death. In his discussion Hardt concentrates on the way in which—and the reasons why—Flaubert uses cliché obliquely, as though concealing it from the reader. Hardt resorts to a metaphor which Flaubert used repeatedly in his correspondence, that of levels in the text, quoting letters where Flaubert writes of "troisièmes et quatrièmes plans en prose," of the "surface lisses" of the text, and of a prose which must be "bourrée de choses et sans qu'on les aperçoive" (173).

Those "hidden levels," we have seen, are of several different kinds, and not necessarily comparable. One is the body of the reader's presuppositions, the judgments and narrative elements with which he or she will fill in the blanks. Another is the psychological complexity of the characters, a "level" Flaubert must have intuited as much as planned. Yet another—and here we see that the "levels" metaphor imposes limits, just as "latent" and "manifest" are problematic in Freud's usage—is the enactment in various formal terms of the cliché's elements.

One such formal enactment of the dance of death is the narration of a series of encounters. Two important ones, Emma's early conversations with Léon and with Rodolphe, show that what she has in common with them is an uncritical view of cliché. But Emma's sincerity also counts for something; her willingness to abandon everything for the chance of realizing her hopes is what distinguishes her in our sympathies from her two lovers. Our difficulty in judging her is part of the larger problem that clichés pose for literature: that of recognizing sincerity and, pushing further, that of *original* feeling. Emma's feelings may be derivative in the extreme, but no more than those of most others in the novel; and she submits herself imaginatively to her perceptions in a way that no other character does.

Such submission is the experiential equivalent of the *tourbillon.* While it is fatal to Emma it is the matrix of the novel. Albert Cook has remarked in *The Meaning of Fiction* that Flaubert in *Madame Bovary* thematizes point of view. One might add that at no time is point of view unrelated to the problem of cliché: who is using it, with what motivation, with how much sincerity or irony or *bêtise,* and with what audience in mind.

Emma's waltz with the viscount provides an excellent example of the way

Flaubert manipulates point of view to move us in and out of the clichéd understanding which is the scene's paradigm, and which informs Emma's unconscious
perceptions as she moves through the ball:

> Cependant, un des valseurs qu'on appelait familièrement *Vicomte*, dont le gilet
> très ouvert semblait moulé sur la poitrine, vint une seconde fois encore inviter
> Mme Bovary, l'assurant qu'il la guiderait et qu'elle s'en tirerait bien.
>   Ils commencèrent lentement, puis allèrent plus vite. Ils tournaient: tout
> tournait autour d'eux, les lampes, les meubles, les lambris, et le parquet,
> comme un disque sur un pivot. En passant auprès des portes, la robe d'Emma,
> par le bas, s'ériflait au pantalon; leurs jambes entraient l'une dans l'autre; il
> baissait ses regards vers elle, elle levait les siens vers lui; une torpeur la prenait,
> elle s'arrêta. Ils repartirent; et, d'un mouvement plus rapide, le vicomte, l'en-
> traînant, disparut avec elle jusqu'au bout de la galerie, où, haletante, elle faillit
> tomber, et, un instant, s'appuya la tête sur sa poitrine. Et puis, tournant
> toujours, mais plus doucement, il la reconduisit à sa place; elle se renversa
> contre la muraille et mit la main devant ses yeux.   (86–87)

One of the waltzers, however, who was addressed as Viscount, and whose
low cut waistcoat seemed moulded to his chest, came a second time to ask
Madame Bovary to dance, assuring her that he would guide her, and that she
would get through it very well.

> They began slowly, then increased in speed. They turned; all around
> them was turning, the lamps, the furniture, the wainscoting, the floor, like a
> disc on a pivot. On passing near the doors the train of Emma's dress caught
> against his trousers. Their legs intertwined; he looked down at her; she raised
> her eyes to his. A torpor seized her and she stopped. They started again, at
> an even faster pace; the Viscount, sweeping her along, disappeared with her
> to the end of the gallery, where, panting, she almost fell, and for a moment
> rested her head upon his breast. And then, still turning, but more slowly, he
> guided her back to her seat. She leaned back against the wall and covered her
> eyes with her hands.   (37–38)

It would be hard to find a passage which thematizes point of view more carefully;
Flaubert uses more than his standard strategies here to play with a shifting of
perspectives. Here as always he uses the imperfect—Proust called it, admiringly,
"cet éternel imparfait"—in an ambiguous voice hovering on the boundary between
indirect discourse and third person narrative. The viscount assures Emma "qu'elle
s'en tirerait bien": his phrasing. But what about: "Ils tournaient: tout tournait autour
d'eux"? We cannot assume Emma is thinking these words, although with their
rhythmic repetition of the *tou* phoneme they both depict her impressions and bring
the reader into them, and into the center of her experiential vortex (Tanner,
257ff.). In the next sentence we are within Emma's voice; "s'ériflait," Bopp points
out (95), is a *normandism,* and we may assume the awkward grammar of "les
jambes entraient l'une dans l'autre" (which Bopp calls "insupportable") reflects
Emma's phrasing and perceptions. But Emma is sensing and feeling a great deal

which the narrator does not convey to us. In the phrase, "une torpeur la prenait," the dance reaches a climax where the significant details (for example, the aroma of the viscount's pomade, of which we learn much later) are silenced. We are meant to guess the intensity of excitement but to retain some distance from it.

The *passé simple* which ends that sentence—"elle s'arrêta"—removes us from Emma's point of view. As if to insist on the issue, the narrator removes the couple bodily from our sight: "le vicomte . . . disparut avec elle. . . ." For an instant we may wonder where we are: with Charles, perhaps, watching them silently? But the narrative stays in the *passée simple,* its neutral tense, and recounts briefly the rest of the couple's movements. When Emma puts her hand before her eyes, we see her do it, without knowing what prompts the gesture.

Why, at the moment of Emma's greatest excitement, does she drop suddenly out of sight? Why does the narrator say so little about her impressions during these moments which are so decisive for her? One simple reason may be that we are meant to feel Emma's perceptions are so confused and intense as to be indistin-guishable; during the rest of the ball she has time to observe and savor minute details, from the maraschino ice to, later, the humid breeze outside her window. The nature of the waltz, as a dance described here mimetically, is to take one's breath away and confuse one's equilibrium and perceptions.

Its nature is also, however, to be an image which Emma imagines herself realizing. That is, part of Emma's excitement is the internalizing of an observer's—or a reader's—point of view as she enacts unreflectingly what she has read or nar-rated to herself.

When Emma puts her hand before her eyes she removes herself from us. She seeks her balance; she may be trying to retain or to picture what has just happened; no matter, the motivation is the same: her intense and disturbing desire to live the story she imagines, modeled on clichés she does not consciously recognize. Open-ing her eyes, then, her first sight is the woman choosing among three partners, and Emma is again on the outside looking in. Both states of mind are essential to Emma's dance of death: the confused ecstasy of the *tourbillon;* and the linear desire, the sense of being different from what she wants to be, that drives her through her narrative. Most important, the narrator himself seems drawn to the fusion of voices and sensations which accompanies Emma's most intense experiences, while at the same time conveying the dangers of unexamined desire—the desire which unveils itself as a manipulative *idée recue.*

Clearly it is not only Emma who performs a *bricolage* with her world, building a rich half-conscious memory. To trace the paradigmatic dance of death embedded by Flaubert in *Madame Bovary* back to Langlois or to contemporary popular sources is not to discover its origin, but to interrupt a chain at one possible point. Flaubert writes, reminiscing about Langlois, "pendant toute notre vie nous sentons de la nourrice": but the *nourrice,* we have seen, may also be, for Flaubert, *La Mort.* As he writes this sentence Flaubert is also struggling to launch a novel and to choose his subject. It seems that he both chooses it and conceals it; or that, to return to Freud's phrase, choice stands in the place of necessity.

If Emma Bovary *is* Flaubert, then she is *his* proxy in the waltz. Perhaps her drive through memory to her *cavalier* is analogous to Flaubert's drive through his memory to his *nourrice,* and the reader stands before the text as before an infinitely regressing mirror. If the *tourbillon,* the instant of gratified desire, fuses the fragments of the image, then it does so at the cost of self-conscious reflection. The dance of death, with its inherently contradictory logic of horror and desire, makes us the spectators as we watch others face the forces of necessity. But the spectator must also be inward-turning.

NOTES

[1] Work on this article was supported by a Skidmore Faculty Research Grant.

[2] Gustave Flaubert, *Madame Bovary,* ed. Jacques Suffel (Paris: Garnier-Flammarion, 1966), p. 87. Translations of passages from *Madame Bovary* are by Paul de Man; all other translations are my own, unless otherwise noted.

[3] Facsimiles and imitations of Holbein's version have appeared unceasingly from its first printing. It is the most famous (and most frequently reproduced) version of the motif. An edition, with commentary, appeared in Paris in 1842; and a copy of Holbein's "alphabet of death" was published in Paris in separate French, English, and Italian versions in 1856. Some twenty other separate editions appeared in England and Europe between 1770 and 1850.

[4] Douce (188) recounts a typical popular ballad published in Paris in 1832:

> A girl named Lise is admonished by her mother not to dance on a Saturday, the day on which Satan calls the dead to the infernal Sabbat. She promises obedience, but whilst her mother is napping, escapes to the ball. She forgets the midnight hour, when a company of damned souls, led by Satan, enter the ball-room hand-in-hand, exclaiming, "Make way for Death." All the party escape, except Lise, who suddenly finds herself encircled by skeletons, who continue dancing round her. From that time, on every Saturday at midnight, there is heard underground, in the churchyard, the lamentation of a soul forcibly detained, and exclaiming, "Girls, beware of dancing Satan!"

[5] Jean Bruneau (494–99) outlines the similar patterns in several balls in Flaubert's opus, suggesting they have a common biographical source. Another critic, Manfred Hardt, says that the ball at La Vaubyessard "durchbricht ... den öden Alltag" (156). Such a movement of breaking through quotidian time is clearly relevant to my reading.

[6] Tony Tanner makes a related point as he discusses this scene: "... the aristocrats can dominate the bodies of their horses ...; it is just such a mastery over Emma's body and its movement that the Viscount exhibits in the waltz" (300). In this and other points Tanner's astute reading of *Madame Bovary* has influenced my own.

[7] Grandville's version was an immediate success, receiving high praise from Balzac in the *Silhouette* and appearing quickly in a second, full-color edition (Sello, 29).

[8] Flaubert is known to have read Goethe widely and with enthusiasm as an adolescent, although it is difficult to ascertain exactly what works he read. See Bruneau, 17–31 and 49n.

[9] Several letters strongly imply that Langlois was a significant influence on Flaubert. In one, for example, Flaubert writes to his niece Caroline, "... j'ai écrit (en trois jours!) une demi-page du plan de la 'Légende de Saint Julien l'Hospitalier.' Si tu veux le connaître, prends *L'Essai sur la peinture de verre,* de Langlois" ("... I've written [in three days!] a half-page of the outline of the 'Legend of St. Julian the Hospitaler.' If you want to know the legend, pick up the *Essay on Stained Glass* by Langlois"). He also writes elsewhere that he would like to use Langlois' drawing of the windows to illustrate his own story (Bollème, 266–67, 285).

[10] Steegmuller's translation (110). The phrase "nous sentons de la nourrice" is untranslatable.

[11] And a recurrent one. Compare Flaubert's letter to Louise Colet, March 3, 1852: "Mes voyages, mes souvenirs d'enfant, tout se colore l'un de l'autre, se met bout à bout, danse avec de prodigieux flamboiements et monte en spirale" ("My travels, my childhood memories, all color each other, come together, dance in immense flame-like pulses and mount into a spiral"). He resorts to the metaphor to explain an emotion so intense as to fuse the distinct images from his memory which inspired it. Cited from Bollème (66).

[12] Poulet also sees the spiral form as an expansion of the circle in Flaubert; he points to numerous direct references to spirals in the works and correspondence (385). In a recent article John O'Connor enlarges

upon Poulet's observations, arguing that a form he calls a "double cone" serves as a "motive form" in Flaubert's narrative, and especially in the *Trois Contes*. Tanner also includes some discussion of the vortex as an important narrative principle of *Madame Bovary*.

[13] Grandville's dance of death, for example, presents a carriage as a vehicle of death in several images besides its title-page. In one, a dapper Death reassures a fashionably-dressed woman, "Oui, Madame, ce sera bien la promenade la plus délicieuse! Une voiture qui fend l'air, et le meilleur groom de France!" Perhaps the most influential conflation of Death as Horseman and the dance of death is Bürger's ballad "Lenore," written in 1773; it was popular throughout Europe (and often illustrated) as a paradigmatic romantic ballad, and it features a dashing horseman turned death figure who brings the innocent Lenore to a macabre death-dance. Finally, Alfred Rethel's cycle of engravings entitled "Auch ein Totentanz aus dem Jahre 1848" features Death as a horseman and was immensely popular in France around 1848 (Kastner, 124).

[14] For a similar approach to clichés in *Madame Bovary*, see Riffaterre, who uses the word *presuppositions* rather than cliché.

[15] Another author in 1852 describes Michaut's work in some detail, claiming that it had "presque autant d'éditions que la danse macabre" (Kastner, 19). And in what may simply be a curious coincidence, Langlois notes that in Michaut's "Dance" Death is mounted not on a horse, as would have been customary, but on a cow. Roy (278–79) has proposed that Michaut chose the cow rather than a horse for its methodical, ineluctably slow movement, a complement to the frenzy of the *danse macabre*. I need hardly point to the similar connotations of the Bovary name.

[16] Commentaries which are exemplary exceptions include Tanner and Ahearn; see Ahearn (73n) for bibliography.

[17] For example, we may consider the question asked by "Les Damnés"; "Quand la Mort viendra-t-elle nous endormir pour toujours, loin des festins, des tièdes embrassements, de tout ce qui se vend et qu'on achète?" (62) ("When will Death come to put us to sleep for good, far from the banquets, the lukewarm embraces, from all that can be bought and sold?"). The judgment here is one which condemns the damned to be what they are perpetually choosing to be—and yet it is a choice, we sense, without options. "On" is a shifter pronoun here which implies a whole social and economic context.

[18] Ahearn places a strong emphasis on the novel's moral dimension in its historical context: it "shows an appalling willingness by people to destroy others, often for the sake of economic profit."

WORKS CITED

Ahearn, Edward J. "Using Marx to Read Flaubert: The Case of *Madame Bovary*," in *L'Hénaurme Siècle: A Miscellany of Essays on Nineteenth-Century French Literature*, ed. Reihe Siegen. Heidelberg: Carl Winter, 1984, pp. 73–91.

Bollème, Geneviève, ed. *Gustave Flaubert: Extraits de correspondance ou Préface à la vie d'écrivain*. Paris: Seuil, 1963.

Bopp, Léon. *Commentaire sur Madame Bovary*. Neuchâtel: Éditions de la Baconnière, 1951.

Bruneau, Jean. *Les Débuts littéraires de Gustave Flaubert*. Paris: Armand Colin, 1962.

Cook, Albert. *The Meaning of Fiction*. Detroit: Wayne State University Press, 1960.

Douce, Francis. *The Dance of Death in Elegant Engravings on Wood with a Dissertation on the Several Representations of That Subject*. London: Bohn, 1833.

Felman, Shoshana. "Modernité du lieu commun: En marge de Flaubert: *Novembre*." *Littéraire* 20 (1975), pp. 32–48.

Engstrom, Alfred. "Vergil, Ovid, and the Cry of Fate in *Madame Bovary*." *Studies in Philology* 46 (1949), pp. 470–95.

Flaubert, Gustave. *Madame Bovary*, ed. Jacques Suffel. Paris: Garnier-Flammarion, 1966.

———. *Madame Bovary*, trans. and ed. Paul de Man. New York: Norton, 1965.

———. *Premières oeuvres*, 2 vols., II: 1838–1842. Paris: Charpentier, 1925.

Freud, Sigmund. "The Theme of the Three Caskets," in *Character and Culture*. New York: Collier, 1963, pp. 67–79.

Hardt, Manfred. *Das Bild in der Dichtung*. Munich: Wilhelm Fink, 1966.

Kastner, Georges. *Les Danses des morts: dissertations et recherches [. . .].* Paris: Brandus, 1852.

Kermode, Frank. *The Sense of an Ending.* Oxford: Oxford University Press, 1966.

Langlois, Eustache Hyacinth. *Essai historique, philosophique et pittoresque sur les danses des morts.* Rouen: Lebrument, 1852.

O'Connor, John. "Flaubert: *Trois Contes* and the Figure of the Double Cone." *PMLA* 95 (1980), pp. 812–25.

Peignot, Gabriel. *Recherches historiques et littéraires sur les danses des morts [. . .].* Dijon, Paris: Lagier, 1826.

Pommier, Jean, and Gabrielle Leleu, eds. *Madame Bovary: Nouvelle version.* Paris: Jose Corti, 1949.

Poulet, Georges. *Les Métamorphoses du cercle.* Paris: Plon, 1961.

Riffaterre, Michael. "Flaubert's Presuppositions." In *Flaubert and Post-Modernism,* ed. Naomi Schor and Henry Majewski. Omaha: University of Nebraska Press, 1984, pp. 177–91.

Roy, Bruno. "La Mort sur un boeuf." In *Le Sentiment de la mort au moyen âge.* Montreal: L'Aurore, 1979, pp. 278–79.

Sello, Gottfried, ed. *Grandville: Das Gesamte Werk.* Munich: Rogner and Bernhard, 1969.

Steegmuller, Francis, trans. and ed. *The Selected Letters of Gustave Flaubert.* New York: Farrar, Straus, 1953.

Carla L. Peterson

MADAME BOVARY: DIONYSIAN RITUALS

Flaubert's *Madame Bovary* is, of course, the nineteenth-century novel that is most often associated with book reading, with the notion of a quixotic character who finds in romantic books specular images with which to identify, turns to reality for corroboration of romantic illusions, fails in that quest, and dies disillusioned. Such is indeed the plot of *Madame Bovary*, but the novel is also much more: it is Flaubert's portrayal of the artist in the post-Romantic period, who embodies the failure of earlier Romantic aspirations toward organic synthesis and the reconciliation of opposites.

Many narrative details from Stendhal's *Lamiel* reverberate in *Madame Bovary*, suggesting interesting parallels between the two novels. Both novels begin with a first-person narrator who attempts to legitimize his narrative presence by asserting his authority as an eyewitness but then gradually gives way to the impersonal voice of the historian. Both novels take place in Normandy, and Flaubert's description of the countryside surrounding Yonville bears a striking resemblance to Stendhal's earlier description of the countryside around Carville. Both novels have at their center a female protagonist who is a reader and whose reading is directly tied to issues of identity, sexuality, energy (of a somewhat criminal nature), and artistry. Both heroines have a rather ambiguous tie to an eccentric older man (Sansfin, Homais) who aspires to social acceptability and power but who is essentially marginal to society, occasionally even dabbling in criminal activity. Both heroines establish relationships with lovers in which they adopt the masculine role and become the dominant partner. Finally, in the expression of their energy and their sexuality, both Lamiel and Emma come to represent the intoxicated Dionysian artist, the "poète hystérique" who has lost all sense of Apollonian measure.

If *Madame Bovary* can be seen as an extension of Stendhal's antiromantic tendencies and ironic realism, it can also be seen as a revision of that seminal Romantic text, Balzac's *Louis Lambert*. Flaubert himself commented on the

From *The Determined Reader: Gender and Culture in the Novel from Napoleon to Victoria* (New Brunswick, NJ: Rutgers University Press, 1986), pp. 132–79 (abridged).

similarity between the two novels in a letter to Louise Colet: *"Louis Lambert commence, comme Bovary,* par une entrée au collège, et il y a une phrase qui *est la même."*[1] Thus, if Charles's school experiences—alienation from classmates, mockery of teachers, repeated punishments—are drawn in part from Flaubert's memories of his own school experiences at the collège de Rouen with his friend Alfred Le Poittevin, they are also reminiscent of Louis's school days. However, Flaubert's revision of Louis's school life is, for the most part, ironic. Thus, Louis's intimate relationship with his narrator-friend is ironically transposed in *Madame Bovary* into Charles's distanced relationship with the eyewitness narrator who opens the novel. Charles's intellectual failings—his confused speech, bewilderment over terminology, unimaginative use of dictionaries, strict adherence to rules, re-liance on copying and repetition—may be seen as an ironic revision of Louis Lambert's prodigious genius. Even more important, the figure of the Romantic female genius, represented by Balzac in the person of Mme. de Staël, ridiculed as a monstrosity, and summarily dismissed, is now reintroduced in Flaubert's novel in the character of Emma Bovary. If Louis Lambert represented the Romantic genius in search of historical and cultural origins, endeavoring to reconcile a divided and fragmented cultural tradition, Emma Bovary testifies to Flaubert's belief in the failure of this Romantic attempt at synthesis, and to the triumph of analytical modes of thought in the post-Romantic period.

Like some of our earlier reader-protagonists, Emma Bovary is a half-orphan. Her mother having died, Emma is brought up by her father—a down-to-earth and easygoing farmer—who admires his daughter and indulges her but remains at a considerable emotional distance, taking little part in her upbringing. Emma herself is detached not only from her father but from the larger community around her as well. Bored with provincial life and impatient with the narrow-minded attitudes of Tostes and Yonville, she sets herself apart from society, asserts herself as different from the other women she knows, and aspires to break out of the narrow domestic sphere to which she has been confined. With the encouragement of her father, who believes that she has "trop d'esprit pour la culture,"[2] she comes to think of herself as superior in intelligence, imagination, and emotional capacity. Emma's aspirations to difference and to greatness are manifested most especially in her reading, which she considers to be a true sign of superiority; thus she scorns all those people, including her husband Charles, who never read. But Emma's society is fundamentally hostile to books, so that her reading sets her even farther apart from her environment. Indeed, the *bons bourgeois* of Yonville consider her reading as dangerous and evil. Madame Bovary *mère* blames Emma's caprices and dizzy spells on the influence of novels and other bad books. Likewise, Homais accuses young Justin of corrupting his children by exposing them to injurious texts: " 'Tu n'as donc pas réfléchi qu'il pouvait, ce livre infâme, tomber entre les mains de mes enfants, mettre l'étincelle dans leur cerveau, ternir la pureté d'Athalie, corrompre Napoléon!' " (p. 255).[3]

Because of such societal hostility to books, Emma's reading becomes an es-sentially private act, undertaken secretly and alone. This secretiveness leads Emma, the most spiritually isolated of all our reader-protagonists, to serious misreadings and misapplications of her texts. For books are her only means of acquiring knowledge about herself and the outside world; and she thus reads them out of pure self-interest "y cherchant des assouvissements imaginaires pour ses convoitises personnelles," and "rejet[ant] comme inutile tout ce qui ne contribuait pas à la consommation immédiate de son coeur" (pp. 59, 37).[4] Alienated from the outside world, deprived of a mature and informed guide, Emma in her lonely reading comes to many wrong conclusions.

Emma's first important encounter with books occurs at the convent in the education provided her by the nuns. Flaubert's narrator makes it quite clear that this education is sterile, meaningless, and totally unsuited to Emma's temperament. For the convent is an unnatural community composed of women only who live in an atmosphere of *tiédeur* and *langueur,* bound to empty and repetitious forms of routine and discipline, and paying strict obeisance to male authorities—the Father, the Son, and their representatives on earth. Such a community is incapable of providing Emma with an education that could properly channel her imagination, energy, and ambition. Quick to perceive the vapidity of the religious education offered her, Emma rebels against the stringencies of conventual life and places herself at odds with the community. In this her school experiences are not unlike those of Charles.[5] For although he is best suited for outdoor agricultural and manual labor, Charles is forced by his mother, an embittered woman who projects all of her frustrated ambitions onto her son, to acquire a bookish education, first at the *lycée* and then at medical school. At school Charles reveals himself incapable of dealing with either spoken or written language—he cannot articulate his name, cannot make any sense of his readings, can only learn by means of copying and repetition. Totally misplaced in a community that lives by the word, ridiculed by classmates and professors alike, Charles can escape only by losing himself in daydreams of country life. Both Emma's and Charles's education, then, reflects Flaubert's hostility to a book education based on meaningless routine, repetition, and learning of rules, in which no natural relationship between reader and text is allowed to flourish, in which ready-made interpretations are forced on the child-reader and all critical reading is discouraged.

Rejecting the conventional and meaningless education offered her by the nuns, Emma turns to secret forms of reading, immersing herself in a whole body of Romantic literature—novels, romances, keepsakes of the period. As in the case of other reader-protagonists, she views these texts as sacred, revelatory of those mysteries of existence that she believes the banality and triviality of provincial life have hidden from her. As with other reader-protagonists, Emma reads her books in search of a specular image with which to identify, to find out who she is and what she might become. Her quest for identity is bound up with the issue of sexuality, for, like Lamiel, Emma undertakes her reading of romantic literature at the time of puberty, and the primary subject of her books is explicitly that of erotic adventure and intrigue. And so Emma's reading becomes an initiation into sexuality, a secret puberty ritual. Turning from literature to life, Emma then expects to find for herself the same kind of erotic fulfillment experienced by the heroines in her novels. She marries Charles in the belief that he will bring her the *"félicité, ... passion,* et *... ivresse,* qui lui avaient paru si beaux dans les livres" (p. 36).[6] So obsessed has Emma become by her erotic texts that she starts to eroticize all the other kinds of literature that she reads, especially religious books. She reads religious texts in much the same way that she reads romances, searching for sentimental episodes and hints of eroticism: "Les comparaisons de fiancé, d'époux, d'amant céleste et de mariage éternel qui reviennent dans les sermons lui soulevaient au fond de l'âme des douceurs inattendues" (p. 37). Emma misreads these religious texts, subverting them to her own romantic and erotic purposes.[7]

Like Mathilde de la Mole, Emma engages in reading of a highly eclectic nature. If she consumes products of *le bas romantisme*—keepsakes and fashion magazines such as *La Corbeille* and *Le Sylphe des salons*—she also reads many respectable Romantic texts and authors, such as *Paul et Virginie, Le Génie du christianisme,* Sir Walter Scott, Balzac, and George Sand. But the narrator is never very specific about what Emma reads, which novels of Balzac's vast *Comédie humaine,* what portions of the many volumes of *Le Génie du christianisme.* He never cites from Emma's readings, referring to them in general terms: "Avec Walter Scott, plus tard, elle s'éprit de choses historiques, rêva bahuts, salle des gardes et ménestrels" (p. 38); "Elle étudia, dans Eugène Sue, des descriptions d'ameublements; elle lut Balzac et George Sand" (p. 59).[8] For Flaubert's narrator is just as much interested in how Emma reads, in reading as an aesthetic process, as in what she reads. Nowhere is this concern for the aesthetics of reading explicitly articulated, but it is implicit throughout the narrator's *discours,* especially in chapter 6. What we first assumed to be passages of narrative *récit*—the objective description of Emma's texts—are in fact instances of narrative *discours,* designed to analyze and comment upon the nature of Emma's reading process.

The narrator's description of Emma's reading of romantic novels and of their illustrations in chapter 6 suggests that she reads analytically, almost disintegratively, rather than synthetically.[9] For if Emma starts by contemplating the whole of a picture, she quickly comes to break it down, enumerating and analyzing its different parts. The narrator makes use of specific stylistic techniques to indicate such a reading process. In the first sentence of the paragraph describing Emma's reading of illustrations, he speaks of these illustrations quite generally. Then, using the equational formula *c'était,* he proceeds in the following sentence to define the engravings in terms of the many parts that compose them. They are broken down into a first level of figures or objects, functioning as kernels around which, on a second level, highly specific details are clustered: "C'était, derrière la balustrade d'un balcon, un jeune homme en court manteau qui serrait dans ses bras une jeune fille en robe blanche, portant une aumônière à sa ceinture; ou bien les portraits anonymes des ladies anglaises à boucles blondes, qui, sous leur chapeau de paille rond, vous regardent avec leurs grands yeux clairs" (p. 39). The description continues in this fashion with no attempt to regroup the details into a cohesive whole. The engravings thus become nothing more than a series of paratactically juxtaposed metonymic details that often possess only the barest logical connection to one another, as in the following description: "Et vous y étiez aussi, sultans à longues pipes, pâmés sous des tonnelles, aux bras des bayadères, djiaours, sabres turcs, bonnets grecs, et vous surtout, paysages blafards des contrées dithyrambiques, qui souvent nous montrez à la fois des palmiers, des sapins, des tigres à droite, un lion à gauche, des minarets tartares à l'horizon, au premier plan des ruines romaines, puis des chameaux accroupis" (pp. 39–40).[10] Emma's reading of pictures thus results in an enumeration of disparate details that have no meaningful relationship to one another; all sense of wholeness, of totality of the picture, becomes lost. And Emma never attempts the necessary synthetic reconstruction that would bring the fragmented details into a new unified whole.[11]

The narrator presents Emma's reading of texts in much the same way. He starts by describing Emma's books in narrative summary as an anonymous and undifferentiated body of literature that she reads purely for plot and for models of imitation. Once again, he portrays Emma's reading as a disintegrative process in which she repeatedly breaks down general concepts into their constituent parts that are then metonymically juxtaposed. And he resorts to the same stylistic techniques (the equational formula c'était, enumeration, the kernel with its clustered modifiers) to suggest this process: "Ce n'étaient qu'amours, amants, amantes, dames persécutées s'évanouissant dans des pavillons solitaires, postillons qu'on tue à tous les relais, chevaux qu'on crève à toutes les pages, forêts sombres, troubles du coeur, serments, sanglots, larmes et baisers, nacelles au clair de lune, rossignols dans les bosquets, messieurs braves comme des lions, doux comme des agneaux, vertueux comme on ne l'est pas, toujours bien mis, et qui pleurent comme des urnes" (p. 38).[12] Once again, Emma clings to the metonymic details that she is unable to reconstitute into a new unity.

Throughout the novel the narrator makes repeated use of such stylistic patterns to organize his descriptions of Emma reading or fantasizing on the basis of her readings; for example, her early meditation on the honeymoon that occurs right after her marriage to Charles, her vision of Paris that develops from her reading of fashion magazines after her visit to the château de la Vaubyessard, her reverie as she prepares for elopement with Rodolphe. Each passage starts with a kernel word, "la lune de miel," "Paris," "un pays nouveau," and then shifts from the central concept to those important elements that define it. These terms are in turn provided with a multitude of disparate and detailed images that are randomly grouped around them.

The narrator's stylistic strategy in these passages derives, I contend, from lexicographical procedures characteristic of the dictionary, particularly of the Dictionnaire des idées reçues that Flaubert had conceived of as early as 1843, as a catalog of received ideas designed to expose the inadequacies of bourgeois modes of thought and expression. The Dictionnaire exposes bourgeois stupidity both in the way words are proposed for definition and in the way they are then defined. First of all, words are arbitrarily ordered for definition in the dictionary, as they are juxtaposed according to sign rather than significance. The proposed terms are then

provided with multiple, paratactically juxtaposed definitions that are often contradictory or, at least, unrelated to one another; sometimes the same definitions are
used to define completely different terms. Finally, the definitions tend to be reductive, for a subtle abstract concept is often defined purely by means of concrete
examples; and the repeated use of such terms as "tous," "toujours," and "jamais"
further reinforces the conclusive and final nature of the definitions.[13] Flaubert's
concept of the dictionary here contrasts sharply with that of Louis Lambert for
whom dictionary words were living beings and the lexicographical process served
to narrate their adventures, trace historical origins, and reconcile dualities of inner
self and outer garment.

In resorting to such a "definitional" style, Flaubert's narrator is suggesting that
Emma's reading process is essentially analytical and disintegrative in nature; it is, in
fact, a process of morcellation. In reading, Emma breaks down abstract and general
concepts into a multiplicity of concrete and specific images that she takes literally,
as real and concrete objects rather than as metaphorical representations of an
intangible ideal. Furthermore, these images are randomly associated, creating the
ironic impression of a collage; they have no meaningful relationship to one another,
but remain separate and isolated. And Emma's imagination is incapable of performing the necessary synthesis that would reunite these fragmented details into a
unified and coherent whole.

The narrator's definitional style further suggests that Emma, far from assimilating the fictional worlds and characters of her novels, remains an outside spectator. For example, her reactions to her novels are formulated not in her own
language but in a connotative discourse whose images are the anonymous and
common currency of an entire literary tradition. Emma has not absorbed this
language into her own being; it remains external to her, the property of the *on*
rather than the *je*. Moreover, this discourse is essentially a nominal style that
foregrounds nouns both as terms proposed for definition and as the definitions
themselves. This nominal style contributes to our sense of Emma's detachment
from her visions and fantasies as it focuses on objects as objects rather than on
Emma's relationship to them or on their relationship to one another. Objects
and figures seem to be imprisoned at a great distance from her, frozen like the
forms on the decorated plates that have become permanently engraved in her
imagination.

Although Emma's pose as a detached contemplator is only implicitly suggested
in the narrator's description of Emma's reading process, it is explicitly remarked
upon throughout chapter 6 and in later episodes of the novel. Indeed, in chapter
6 Emma does not so much read texts as look at pictures of religious and romantic
scenes; she may be seen contemplating the holy pictures of her missal, the engravings on tissue paper of her novels, the decorated plates that record the story of
Mlle. de la Vallière, or, finally, the memorial picture that consecrates her mother's
memory. This detached pose of a viewer of pictures, coupled with the distanced
perspective from which Emma reads her romances, clearly testifies to her inability
to maintain an active relationship with her texts or pictures. What eventually

happens, then, is that Emma draws the romantic plots and characters she reads about out of the realm of fiction into the real world. As a consequence, any identification that occurs during the reading process is one of vague potentiality (what *might become* of her *if* she were to come across such a romantic situation in real life) rather than one of actuality (what she imaginatively *becomes* by fully merging with the characters of her fiction). Thus an immeasurable gap remains between Emma and her readings; for her, reading involves no union of subject and object, it leads to no insights into, or greater consciousness of, the self.

If the narrator's *discours* explicitly mocks the *bas romantique* literature that Emma reads and the seriousness with which she accepts its depiction of erotic intrigue and adventure, it also constitutes an implicit critique of Emma's reading as an aesthetic process. In his appraisal of her reading, Flaubert's narrator denies from the very beginning the earlier hopes of Louis Lambert that through reading humankind would be able to trace the origins of self and culture, reconcile those dualities that were tearing it apart, and recover wholeness of being. On the contrary, Emma's reading reflects Flaubert's belief in the failure of such Romantic aspirations and the triumph of purely mechanistic modes of thought in the post-Romantic period. For Emma Bovary, there is no reconstitution of the organic, only continued fragmentation and morcellation that will eventually lead her to seek solace in Dionysian intoxication.

Because Emma's reading process is so flawed—disintegrative rather than synthetic, literal rather than metaphorical, distanced rather than involved, passively accepting rather than critical—she is unable to sustain any imaginative activity around her books for very long. So instead of immersing herself in situations portrayed in her novels, Emma draws these situations out of the fictional realm and seeks them in real life. In her reading she comes across a remarkably diverse set of images of women, and in her life she applies them all to herself. On the one hand, she accepts images of women as passive and languorous, in contrast to men, who are active and aggressive: women wait, languish, look out of windows, and are persecuted, while men gallop on horseback, travel, and lead a life of adventure. On the other hand, she is also fascinated by remarkable women like Mary Stuart and Joan of Arc, singled out by history for a special destiny. Emma applies these two images of woman to herself simultaneously, constructing an image of self as both extraordinary and passive. The narrator makes it clear to us, however, that Emma is quite unlike this picture she has formed of herself. She is not remarkable: her education has been mediocre; her artistic endeavors—piano playing, drawing, singing—are amateurish; her waltzing at the ball at the château de la Vaubyessard is undistinguished. Nor, however, is she passive: she has already revealed her energetic nature by rebelling against the discipline of the convent. Emma's simultaneous application of contradictory models of imitation to herself serves further to complicate her quest for identity.

Later in Yonville when Emma meets Rodolphe, she believes that she has at last met the ideal lover of her novels and that her romantic dreams will soon be fulfilled. She forgets about reading, choosing instead to act out the part of the adulterous

heroine: "Alors elle se rapella les héroïnes des livres qu'elle avait lus. . . . Elle devenait elle-même comme une partie véritable de ces imaginations et réalisait la
longue rêverie de sa jeunesse, en se considérant dans ce type d'amoureuse qu'elle
avait tant envié" (p. 167).[14] In truth, however, Emma continues to misread life—her
own and others'—just as she has misread literature. She "reads" Rodolphe "disintegratively" and "literally," focusing on details of dress (his riding clothes, for example), of physique (his black hair curling over his forehead), of language (the
disconnected romantic clichés he glibly spouts) rather than on his whole self, and
she accepts these surface signs as Rodolphe's true self rather than looking to the
cruder reality that lies beyond them. Through such a misreading Emma manages to
keep the real Rodolphe at an immeasurable distance, hidden and out of reach.

But if Rodolphe is not the romantic hero that Emma assumes him to be,
neither is she a typical romantic heroine. Indeed, Emma is already moving beyond
the feminine models proposed in her romances; she becomes increasingly aggressive in her behavior toward Rodolphe and tries, by showering him with gifts and
planning their elopement, to dominate him: "Cependant ces cadeaux l'humiliaient.
Il en refusa plusieurs; elle insista, et Rodolphe finit par obéir, la trouvant tyrannique
et trop envahissante" (p. 195).[15] Rodolphe's final abandonment of her is caused in
large part by such aggressive behavior.

When Emma later embarks on an affair with Léon, she once again believes, as
she had with Rodolphe, that she will at last become a romantic heroine and act out
the passions of her novels rather than merely read about them. But Emma has now
truly transcended all of these literary models. She has become such an exceptionally
aggressive woman that, as with Lamiel, a reversal of roles occurs between the two
lovers: "Il devenait sa maîtresse plutôt qu'elle n'était la sienne" (p. 283). This affair,
too, involves a mutual misreading, for just as Léon falsely sees Emma as
"l'amoureuse de tous les romans, l'héroïne de tous les drames, le vague *elle* de tous
les volumes de vers" (p. 271), Emma misinterprets the surface signs of Léon's
physical appearance and believes him to have a sensitive and poetic soul.[16] As with
Rodolphe, then, the affair is doomed from the start.

When the affair wanes, Emma instinctively turns back to books, searching for
a new literature and new models of imitation. Romances with their images of
delicate and passive women will no longer suffice; nor will religious texts with their
bland pieties and appalling ignorance of the world. Instead, Emma turns to texts that
depict highly active situations and call for a highly active reader response: "elle lisait
jusqu'au matin des livres extravagants où il y avait des tableaux orgiaques avec des
situations sanglantes. Souvent une terreur la prenait, elle poussait un cri, Charles
accourait. 'Ah! va-t'en! disait-elle' " (p. 295). At such moments Emma seems to have
achieved that identification with text and that unity of self that has eluded her.[17] But
the attempt to bring such extravagant situations into real life only leads to renewed
disappointment, as Emma discovers when, the morning after the mid-Lent ball, she
finds herself in the company of prostitutes and men who do not have enough
money to pay for their pleasure.

If Emma continues to the very end to misread the men she meets and the relationships she establishes with them, she does come—however unconsciously —to reject for herself that initial image of women as passive and languorous. Although Emma fails to achieve the stature of a Mary Stuart or a Joan of Arc, she eventually displays a degree of activity and energy extraordinary for a woman in her time. She becomes increasingly aggressive in her attitude toward her husband and lovers, adopts increasingly "masculine" (in the words of the narrator) modes of dress and behavior, and moves from the status of passive reader to active writer as she becomes increasingly productive in her writing of love letters.[18]

In this portrayal of Emma's final development through adultery, Flaubert's narrator continues Stendhal's exploration of the antiromantic tendency of the modern novel, particularly as it relates to female characterization; for Emma bears a striking resemblance to Stendhal's earlier heroines, Mathilde de la Mole and Lamiel. Like them, she is a reader who, in her reading, chooses strong female figures as specular images with which to identify. Like them, too, she relies on these figures as models of imitation when turning to real life in quest of self-fulfillment; Emma, in particular, is given to servile imitation and plagiarism in her excessive reliance on literary models. But as in Stendhal's novels, literary imitation ends up by becoming free invention, as Emma breaks through the restrictions imposed upon women by nineteenth-century society to pursue a course of open adultery and frenetic sexuality. She too becomes an exemplar of Nietzsche's Dionysian poet and Baudelaire's "poète hystérique." She is truly an intoxicated and excessive being who expresses herself in "drunken outbursts of desire," in a "whole pantomime" of frenzied activity. Like Mathilde and Lamiel before her, she uses the tools of culture, books, to move out into the wild and engage in forms of behavior that directly threaten the stability of the patriarchal social system. She asserts her liberation from tradition and convention, particularly in the area of sexuality, as she abandons herself to her immoderate sexual desires. From a naive young woman hunted by Rodolphe, the aggressive male who displays his rifle and hunting trophies on the walls, she becomes, at least for a time, a huntress engaging in wild copulation and transgressing all conventional norms of social behavior.

But Flaubert's portrait of Emma as a Dionysian artist is, of course, an ironic one that categorically denies the possibility of heroic action in nineteenth-century France. For Emma is an example of the Dionysian artist whose excessive subjectivity incapacitates her for true artistic creation. In all of her actions, Emma is continually saying "I" and losing herself in her own selfish passions and desires; she is unable to move out of herself and perceive herself objectively. Her frenzied moments of activity are followed by uncreative moments of lethargy and torpor. Neither is Emma's time of childbirth one of creativity; it is rather one of frustration and disappointment, as Emma believes that the birth of a daughter will simply lead to a sterile repetition of the conventional patterns of restriction that patriarchal society has imposed on women rather than to the creation of a new lifestyle of freedom and exploration of the wild. Finally, in her relationship with both Rodolphe and Léon, the forgery involved in her hysteria becomes fully apparent. In her love affairs, she impersonates the role of adulterous heroine adapted from her books and assigns the role of romantic lover to Rodolphe and Léon. In so doing, she creates an entire semiotic system composed of iconic signs; there exists a prescribed language of love, code of behavior, and mode of dressing; every object in the rooms she inhabits with her lovers receives a specific iconic interpretation. But both Rodolphe and Léon become increasingly unwilling to accept such interpretations; they ultimately reject her rhetoric of hysteria and break off the relationship.

Flaubert makes it clear that Emma's excessive Dionysian tendencies, unaccompanied by the countervailing force of the Apollonian, cannot overcome the cultural decadence of nineteenth-century France. He ultimately leaves the reader with a very negative assessment of French culture at midcentury, as the only effective artist figure who is opposed to Emma, and who ultimately triumphs over her, is the pharmacist Homais. Indeed, just as Emma is a caricatured version of the Dionysian poet, so is Homais a caricature of Nietzsche's "theoretical man." As a pharmacist, he considers himself a true scientist. Interested not only in the pharmaceutical but also in agronomy and in questions of climate, he examines these disciplines in the light of the laws of physics and the teachings of science. Claiming to be a rationalist, he firmly believes that human progress can be achieved by means of science and derides religion as superstition, the Bible as pure fable. The only god he believes in is the god of Socrates, Voltaire, and the Encyclopedists. He is opposed to displays of "drunkenness," indeed to any manifestation of irregular behavior such as that exhibited by the Blind Man. Despite Homais's scientific pretentions, however, Flaubert's narrator reveals the pharmacist to be nothing but a buffoon, a man of pseudoscience, dominated by his own superstitious beliefs and given to eccentric forms of behavior. And yet it is Homais and his form of artistry—not Emma—that ultimately triumph. Whereas Emma's rhetoric of hysteria fails to convince anybody of the validity of her adopted roles, Homais effectively manipulates the people around him both through his spoken and written speech. As at the end of The Bacchae, the Dionysian woman's exploration of the wild is doomed to failure, and we are left to witness the reassertion and triumph of patriarchal authority.

As with Lamiel, then, Emma's Dionysian excesses can only lead to self-destruction and to a form of dismemberment suggestive of that of the god Dionysus; unlike Stendhal, Flaubert had little compunction about killing off his heroine. Overpowered by a male-dominated society whose primary texts are money and legal edicts, Emma finally succumbs to its pressures, goes mad, and gives in to the same fragmentation of mind and spirit that characterized Corinne's madness:[19]

> Elle resta perdue de stupeur, et n'ayant plus conscience d'elle-même que par le battement de ses artères, qu'elle croyait entendre s'échapper comme une assourdissante musique qui emplissait la campagne. Le sol sous ses pieds était plus mou qu'une onde, et les sillons lui parurent d'immenses vagues brunes, qui déferlaient. Tout ce qu'il y avait dans sa tête de réminiscences, d'idées, s'échappait à la fois, d'un seul bond, comme les mille pièces d'un feu d'artifice. . . . La folie la prenait.   (p. 319)[20]

In her death agony, morcellation of body joins that of mind to signal the failure of the Romantic aspiration toward unity and synthesis, and to pave the way for the triumph of "theoretical man" in the person of Homais.

NOTES

[1] Gustave Flaubert, *Correspondance*, ed. Jean Bruneau (Paris: Bibliothèque de la Pléiade, 1980), 2:219. "*Louis Lambert* begins, like *Bovary*, with an entrance into boarding school, and there is a sentence that *is the same*" (translation mine).

[2] Gustave Flaubert, *Madame Bovary*, ed. Claudine Gothot-Mersch (Paris: Editions Garnier, 1971), p. 25. All page references in the text are to this edition. Translation: ". . . too clever to have anything to do with farming." *Madame Bovary*, trans. Francis Steegmuller (New York: Modern Library, 1957), p. 27. Page references following the English translations of the novel are to this edition.

[3] " 'Did it ever occur to you that this wicked book might fall into my children's hands? It might just be the spark that . . . It might sully the purity of Athalie! It might corrupt Napoleon!' " (p. 284).

[4] ". . . seeking in their pages vicarious satisfactions for her own desires" (p. 65). ". . . reject[ing] as useless everything that promised no immediate gratification" (p. 41).

[5] For a detailed account of Charles's education, see Tony Tanner, *Adultery in the Novel* (Baltimore: Johns Hopkins University Press, 1979), pp. 242–249.

[6] ". . . 'bliss,' 'passion,' and 'rapture'—words that had seemed so beautiful to her in books" (p. 39).

[7] "The metaphors constantly used in sermons—'betrothed,' 'spouse,' 'heavenly lover,' 'mystical marriage'—excited her in a thrilling new way" (p. 40). For a more detailed discussion of Emma's eroticized religious reading, see Victor Brombert, *The Novels of Flaubert: A Study of Themes and Techniques* (Princeton: Princeton University Press, 1966), p. 54.

[8] "Later, reading Walter Scott, she became infatuated with everything historical and dreamed about oaken chests and guardrooms and troubadours" (pp. 41–42). "She pored over the interior decorating details in the novels of Eugène Sue; she read Balzac and George Sand" (p. 65).

[9] For a different interpretation of Emma's imaginative process, see Lawrence Thornton, "The Fairest of Them All: Modes of Vision in *Madame Bovary*," *PMLA* 93 (October 1978): 982–991.

[10] "Behind a balcony railing a young man in a short cloak clasped in his arms a girl in a white dress, a chatelaine bag fastened to her belt; or there were portraits of unidentified aristocratic English beauties with blond curls, staring out at you with their wide light-colored eyes from under great straw hats" (pp. 42–43). "Then there were sultans with long pipes swooning under arbors in the arms of dancing girls; there were Giaours, Turkish sabres, fezzes. And invariably there were blotchy, pale landscapes of fantastic countries: pines and palms growing together, tigers on the right, a lion on the left, Tartar minarets on the horizon, Roman ruins in the foreground, a few kneeling camels" (p. 42).

[11] For a general discussion of Flaubert's "heterogeneous style," see Jonathan Culler, *Flaubert: The Uses of Uncertainty* (Ithaca: Cornell University Press, 1974).

[12] "They were invariably about love affairs, lovers, mistresses, harassed ladies swooning in remote pavilions. Couriers were killed at every relay, horses ridden to death on every page; there were gloomy forests, broken hearts, vows, sobs, tears and kisses, skiffs in the moonlight, nightingales in thickets; the noblemen were all brave as lions, gentle as lambs, incredibly virtuous, always beautifully dressed, and wept copiously on every occasion" (p. 41).

[13] Gustave Flaubert, *Dictionnaire des idées reçues*, ed. Lea Caminiti (Paris: Nizet, 1966). The following examples will help to illustrate the points made above. "Albatre" follows "airain" (p. 49), and "Descartes" follows "dent" (p. 68) because of contiguity of sign not significance. "Blondes" are defined as being "plus chaudes que les brunes" (p. 56), but equally "brunes" are "plus chaudes que les blondes" (p. 58). "Cognac" is labeled as being simultaneously "très funeste" and "excellent dans plusieurs maladies" (p. 63). "Inspiration" is defined not as a poetic process but rather in terms of those things that provoke it: "choses qui la provoquent: la vue de la mer, l'amour, les femmes" (p. 93). "Alcoolisme" is stated to be the "cause de *toutes* les maladies modernes" (p. 51), and "institutrices" "sont *toujours* d'une excellente famille qui a éprouvé des malheurs" (p. 92).

[14] "She remembered the heroines of novels she had read.... Now she saw herself as one of those *amoureuses* whom she had so envied: she was becoming, in reality, one of that gallery of fictional figures; the long dream of her youth was coming true" (p. 183).

[15] "But he found her presents humiliating, and on several occasions refused them. She was insistent, however, and he gave in, grumbling to himself that she was high-handed and interfering" (p. 214).

[16] "He was becoming her mistress, far more than she was his" (p. 316). "She was the *amoureuse* of all the novels, the heroine of all the plays, the vague 'she' of all the poetry books" (p. 303).

[17] "She would read till morning—lurid novels full of orgies and bloodshed. Sometimes, in sudden terror, she screamed; but when Charles ran in she dismissed him: 'Oh, get out' " (p. 328). See also Leo Bersani, "Flaubert and Emma Bovary: The Hazards of Literary Fusion," *Novel* 8 (Fall 1974): 25.

[18] Naomi Schor makes this point in her provocative article, "Pour une thématique restreinte: Ecriture, parole et différence dans *Madame Bovary*," *Littérature* 22 (May 1976): 30–46. Schor's article deals mainly with Emma's emergence as a writer and treats her reading process only very briefly.

[19] See Tanner for a discussion of Flaubert's "morselized" descriptions of Emma's physical being, *Adultery in the Novel*, pp. 349–465.

[20] "She stood there in a daze. Only the pulsing of her veins told her that she was alive: she thought she heard it outside herself, like some deafening music filling the countryside. The earth beneath her feet was as yielding as water, and the furrows seemed to her like immense, dark, breaking waves. All the memories and thoughts in her mind poured out at once, like a thousand fireworks. . . . Madness began to take hold of her" (p. 355).

Nathaniel Wing

EMMA'S STORIES: NARRATIVE, REPETITION AND DESIRE IN *MADAME BOVARY*

—Eh bien! reprit Homais, il faudrait en faire une analyse.

    Car il savait qu'il faut, dans tous les empoisonnements, faire une ana-
lyse...   (295)

Qu'on n'accuse personne.   (294)[1]

Flaubert's use of narrative in *Madame Bovary* demystifies in many ways the desires which motivate Emma's stories, her fantasies, dreams and her extended fictions of escape and romantic love. Emma's narratives, her protonarratives (fantasies and dreams), her letters to her lovers, the account of her financial ruin told to Lheureux, Binet, Rodolphe and others in the last desperate moments of her life, can be read as repeated and unsuccessful attempts to give order to desires which are destabilizing in their effects and ultimately unattainable. Emma's narratives of desire presuppose closure, bringing on, paradoxically, the death of desire, which cannot live on images of fulfillment, but only on displacements and deferrals.

    The division between language and experience is a major concern of the novel. Emma's stories oppose the events which constitute her world, yet lack the force to transform that world. One can attribute Emma's difficulties throughout the novel, then, not just to her foolishness and to the mediocrity of her milieu (although Flaubert clearly treats ironically the shop-worn topos of provincial adultery) but to the more general problems of desire and its realization, and of language and illusion.

    Throughout the novel desire, narrative and writing in general produce corrosive effects. These are figured most directly and powerfully, perhaps, during Emma's agony, with the likening of the taste of poison to the taste of ink, and later in the same sequence when the narrator describes a certain black fluid oozing from Emma's mouth. Only a very limited reading, however, would link Emma's desires and her narratives unequivocally to an ultimately mortal alienation of the desiring

From *The Limits of Narrative: Essays on Baudelaire, Flaubert, Rimbaud and Mallarmé* (Cambridge: Cambridge University Press, 1986), pp. 41–77.

subject and to writing as death. However demystifying its narrative, the novel *is* a story about desire, with "characters," organized with extraordinary control at certain points of the text by a narrator whose production of fiction must necessarily be interpreted not only as a denial but also a repetition of Emma's relations to narrative and ... to desire. Once again, what are the possible meanings of that famous statement which Flaubert may or may not have made "Madame Bovary, c'est moi"?

While this chapter focuses on the context and the order of Emma's narratives, it will also re-examine the general problematic of writing in the novel, in the hope that the subject of Emma's narratives will implicate the performance of narrative in the novel itself and, ultimately, the performance of the critical text as well. If Emma is a figure for the writer at a certain point in the history of the novel, this figure does not function exclusively as an uncomplex emblem of the deluded Romantic in an already post-Romantic moment.[2] It may be suspected that the demystification of Emma's narratives does not in fact validate without reserve the control of an enlightened narrator whose understanding transcends the dilemmas of Romantic subjectivity and Romantic literary stereotypes. In many ways, of course, that control is exercised with remarkable force, yet an omniscient narrator is caught in an intricate web of repetition and difference which includes and radically exceeds the logic of identification between narrator and protagonist; includes and exceeds a simple demystification which would deny altogether the links between protagonist and narrator.

An omniscient narrator in *Madame Bovary* is only one among several figures through which narrative is articulated. One of the most fascinating aspects of the novel is the dispersal and fragmentation of authority for narrative. As Barthes has noted, it is impossible to establish with certainty in any comprehensive sense "who speaks" as narrator in this text or from what "point of view."[3] Point of view in *Madame Bovary* can be characterized only by its instability and indeterminacy. It alternates between an omniscient narrator, who knows the motivations of all the protagonists and the truths of the world in which they are placed; a limited point of view, circumscribed by the thoughts and feelings of a particular protagonist; and the even more limited scope of certain minor figures in the text, spectators who have no immediate connection with the major protagonists. The frequent use of free indirect discourse, with its blurring of distinctions between reported speech and narrative, is another complex amalgam of narrative authority.[4] The resulting indeterminacy of point of view, as Culler has demonstrated, is one of the major features of the novel.[5] Those passages which organize narrative according to one or another point of view are countered by others which function in a very different way. The "impersonality" of Flaubert's text, then, is not a distanced objectivity, but a mix of modes of presentation which prevent the reader from identifying a consistent pattern or, to use Rousset's term, modulation. Objectivity is not the absence of narrative authority but a dispersal of that authority which makes it ultimately resistant to recuperative interpretation.

This chapter will question how authority for narrative, both the story of the novel, and Emma's stories framed by the main narrative, is assumed and at the same time problematized. An examination of the composition of Emma's narratives elucidates the ways in which those narratives ironically construct the subject as radically different from what she would be. My assumption is that both narrative form, as well as the stereotypes of narrative content, are necessary to the assertion of desire and intimately related to its failures. The dissolution of the protagonist will be interpreted through perceptible shifts in her relations both to the fictions of desire, the narrative *énoncé,* and to narrative form, both *énoncé* and *énonciation,* as means of ordering and appropriating objects of desire. Finally I will ask how the account and the interpretation of Emma's narratives implicate at once narrators and the reader, as producers of stories: the narratives of desire and the allegories of interpretation.

In a broad sense, *Madame Bovary* gives considerable attention to questions of reading and writing; it narrativizes the interpretation of narrative. The effects of narrative are never merely limited to an explicit content, a subject's relation to the objects of desire, but always open up the more troublesome problematic of how narratives attempt to organize and control desire, how they interpret and construct "reality" and the desiring subject.[6] The power of narrative ordering as a means to fulfil desire and attain knowledge is a ubiquitous motif in this novel. That power fails consistently, as I have suggested, for the effects of fiction-making are quite different from those projected by the desiring subject.

The very control which encourages metanarrative commentary is itself prob-lematized, as in the opening pages of the second part of the novel, when a statement, rare for its explicitness, speaks of the aporia of fictions. The comment serves as a sweeping demystification, yet it doesn't simply write off narrative, for it is set in a transition between the first and second parts of the novel and serves as a preface to a major section of the story. Following a realistic description of the countryside and the village of Yonville, just prior to Charles's and Emma's arrival at their new home, the narrator states simply:

> Depuis les événements que l'on va raconter, rien, en effet, n'a changé à Yonville. La drapeau tricolore de fer blanc tourne toujours au haut du clocher de l'eglise; la boutique du marchand de nouveautés agite encore au vent ses deux banderoles d'indienne; les foetus du pharmacien, comme des paquets d'amadou blanc, se pourrissent de plus en plus dans leur alcool bourbeux, et, au-dessus de la grande porte de l'auberge, le vieux lion d'or, déteint par les pluies, montre toujours aux passants sa frisure de caniche.   (68)

There is a curious complex of meanings here, the sort which will interest me throughout this study. First, a narrator announces in a traditional manner that a new story sequence is about to be related. In an equally traditional fashion, the state-ment is proleptic; it alludes to the conclusion of the story, known to an omniscient narrator who will relate it to the reader. A moment "beyond narrative" is also posited here, when the main story will have been told and events will return to a meaningless repetition of the same (*toujours, encore*). Narrative, according to this passage, seems to be invested with a significance which is superior to "reality." The world of Yonville after the story, "outside" of narrative, is set against narrative as an endless and seemingly meaningless repetition, which is figured by random motion, the weather vane turning in place, the pennants flapping in the wind, and by the degeneration of the bottled foetuses.

One can also interpret the first sentence of the passage in a very different way, however, as signifying something like: "Events occur, nothing changes." The narrative signified would then be undercut as ultimately insignificant. Thus read, this passage denies the closure of the story about to be told before it is narrated, as it sets these events against an insignificant post-narrative "reality." While establishing demarcations between story and non-story, the comment problematizes the meaningful difference produced by narrative. I have said that the passage serves as a preface to a section of the novel, and at the same time suggests much about the inconsequentiality of the story; things are further complicated, however, because this is not the *beginning* of the story, but the opening of the second of three major sequences. Whatever is being said about stories in general must be applied retrospectively to the first part of the novel. The commentary which seems to set itself outside of the main narrative is already framed by the earlier narrative, which can be read as a *commentary* on the metanarrative statement. What is at issue here is less the knowing control over the story by an omniscient narrator who demystifies the fiction from a privileged position, than the impossibility of narrating and at the same time placing oneself outside of the rhetorical operations of fiction. The passage thus becomes engaged in a crisis of narrative whose terms it reiterates in an inevitable play of repetition.[7]

I have already hinted at some of my conclusions about the operations of desire, narrative and interpretation, which can be ordered tentatively in terms of the two statements quoted at the beginning of this chapter. Both quotations are taken from the last pages of the novel. The first is uttered by Homais, panicked when he discovers that Emma has taken poison: "Eh bien! reprit Homais, il faudrait en faire l'analyse. Car il savait qu'il faut, dans tous les empoisonnements, faire une analyse; ..." (295). In this moment of crisis, the pharmacist unhesitatingly turns toward his science to determine what action must be taken to save Emma from herself. Rapidly moving events prevent Homais from performing his diagnosis, but the critic faced with unsettling problems of interpretation is not subject to such constraints. If we are to analyze the reasons for Emma's destruction in terms of the workings of narrative and accept the guidance of an ironically illusive and sophisticated narrator, we must also accept the tutelage of the pharmacist, that other patron of the analytic process. The imperative to analyze and to achieve interpretive validity allies us unwittingly, yet unfailingly, with Homais.

The other statement informing my reading is a fragment of Emma's suicide letter, which Charles has torn open as Emma lies convulsed on her bed: *"Qu'on n'accuse personne..."* (294). At the very moment when it becomes a most urgent concern, we are told in a curiously ambiguous fashion that interpretation is to be suspended. In what ways does Emma's statement serve as an antidote to Homais's disastrously inadequate imperative to undertake analysis? What, in fact, are we being asked not to evaluate? the immediate responsibility for Emma's death? her adultery? or perhaps in a more sweeping sense, those wider issues I have raised—the destructive effects of Emma's relations to fiction? This imperative regarding interpretation, however, is literally suspended, broken by deletion marks in the text. I will return later to the interpretive space opened up by those marks, but let us note for the moment that Homais's and Emma's statements, taken together, point to radically different and incompatible positions concerning the finality of fiction and the necessity for interpretation.[8] The first aims at masterly control and is killing in its effects; the second invites the suspension of judgment and is powerfully productive of interpretation. Inevitably, the reader is engaged by these two imperatives, simultaneously; interpretation circulates between Homais's inept, but nonetheless murderous authority, and Emma's call for the suspension of the interpretation.

Learning Narrative: A Story of One's Own

The first part of the novel establishes certain constants in Emma's relation to her desires and the law of the father, which will be repeated throughout the text, and through reiteration, modified. From the outset, Emma's desires are articulated within another's story: paradoxically "her" story is explicitly spoken or already composed by another. In its simplest form, she is the silent and passive object of the story of another's desire, the alienated object of masculine appropriation.

Some of the major preoccupations of the text concerning language and desire, that language is always inadequate to desire, that the language of desire is never unique, but always a common and alienating discourse, are figured early in the novel by the account of Charles's stammering attempts to ask for Emma's hand. This passage marks Emma's entry into the discourse of desire. It is paralleled, as we shall see, by an extensive sequence at the end of the novel which explicitly links the economy of romantic desire with the economy of bourgeois capitalism, when Emma tells the story of her ruin to the men who directly or indirectly contributed to its design. In Part One of the novel Emma undergoes what might be called an apprenticeship to narrative, in which she acquires an individual "voice" for her desires and elaborates them in narrative fictions. Although this section ends with the classic impasse of feminine desire, the "silence" of hysteria, Emma emerges in Part One from the position of a passive voiceless object of desire, to an active fiction making "subject." She theorizes about love, passion and happiness, and composes stories of fulfilled desire. There is an earlier pre-narrative moment, however, which informs all of Emma's subsequent relations to narratives and to desire. Charles attempts to tell Emma's father of his wish to marry her:

> Maître Rouault, murmura-t-il, je voudrais bien vous dire quelque chose. Ils s'arrêtèrent. Charles se taisait.
> *Mais contez-moi votre histoire!* Est-ce que je ne sais pas tout! dit le père Rouault, en riant doucement.   (23, italics added)

The formulation of desire here, early in the text, is associated significantly with the ability to compose a story. Charles, of course, has difficulty with stories throughout the novel, and that is part of the reason why his demand is relayed to Emma by her father. There are further implications of this episode, however, which are worth exploring. Throughout the novel Charles will remain deprived of the status of acting subject in the stories of desire. In terms of Emma's stories, he is the silent institutionalized opponent. There is more at issue, however, than Charles's silence and his ultimate exclusion from the stories of desire. Here the figure of the prospective husband and that of the father are conflated in a manner which *Emma* never fully overcomes, in spite of the transformations of Charles's role later in the narrative from subject to opponent. The story of feminine desire remains linked consistently with the figure of the father, for the voice of the father always reverberates in the voice of the lover. The "position" Emma occupies here, as determined by the possessive adjective *votre*, and by her role as the object of a story in which the male formulates desire through the voice of the father, or functions as his symbolic equivalent, remains constant throughout the novel. Even as Emma becomes the teller of stories, she can exercise that role only in imitation of this initial model, within the structure of masculine desire.[9] The chapter ends with a paragraph in which the first sentence confirms the displacement of Emma as a subject of her desire: *"Emma eût, au contraire, désiré se marier à minuit, aux flambeaux, mais le père Rouault ne comprit rien à cette idée"* (24, italics added). The sentence derives as much meaning from its syntax as from its semantic content; the adversitive *au contraire*, which interrupts the verbal structure interrupts the language of Emma's desire, which in asserting itself against the father (lover) becomes disintegrated, deferred.

Shortly after her marriage, at the end of chapter 5, Emma's disappointments take the form of speculation about the full meaning of the words of love; they remain in a pre-narrative mode:

> Avant qu'elle se mariât, elle avait cru avoir de l'amour; mais le bonheur qui aurait dû désulter de cet amour n'étant pas venu, il fallait qu'elle se fut trompée, songeait-elle. Et Emma cherchait à savoir ce que l'on entendait au juste dans la vie par les mots de *félicité*, de *passion* et *d'ivresse*, qui lui avaient paru si beaux dans les livres.   (32)

From the outset, Emma's experience of desire is linked to the elusive meanings of words; access to pleasure and knowledge will "take place" in language. Language is doubly deficient, however; on the one hand it is always the discourse of the other ("ce que *l'on* entendait par les mots . . .") never the unique property of the desiring subject. On the other hand, the words mark a radical flaw in the system. Scandalously, they require but utterly lack reference. This dilemma, as critics have shown, is a key element of *bovarysm*, a desire/writing which maniacally seeks the *mot juste* without the ultimate guarantee of a reality which would validate the relations of signification. In a general sense, the object of desire in Flaubert's novels retreats under the proliferation of the signs which are necessary to its representation.[10]

These words also have a particular relation to narrative: they mark a pre-narrative moment for Emma, in which the signifiers of desire are presented as pure nomination, not yet engaged in a verbal sequence. This moment is in many ways similar to the intransitive position which Anna O., in Breuer's famous analysis, assumes in her reveries, at one stage in her treatment. During her "absences," Anna murmurs the impersonal "tormenting, tormenting." Anna has lost the position of grammatical subject; she repeats an impersonal form with no immediate link to the first person, standing outside any narrative ordering of a fantasm.[11] Emma, too, at this point in the story has not yet appropriated a discursive form which will be charged with giving meaning to the signifiers of desire. The experience of desire here is the interpretation of the already spoken or written, which the subject cannot know until she assumes a relation to narrative.[12]

The retrospective account of Emma's emotional formation, in chapter 6 of the first part of the novel, is the story of her first seduction, the seduction by romantic fiction. The terms which refer to Emma's readings have significant erotic implications not simply in their themes, but in reference to the act of reading itself. The narratives of desire are invested with erotic intensity not only because of their content, but also because they are read in secret. Of reading keepsakes it is said: "Il les fallait cacher, c'était une affaire ..." (35). Erotic transgression thus becomes linked from the outset with concealment and an intimate relation is established between narratives of desire and secrecy.

Emma not only fantasizes by imitating the stereotypes of romantic fiction throughout the novel, but her imaginings imitate the second-rate copy. Her representation of romantic fiction will be associated not only with erotic intensity, but also with the dissolution of energy. The texts which establish the models of desire are themselves set in a structure of destructive repetition. Emma reads the classics of romantic fiction, yet she reads with even greater pleasure the second-rate reproductions of romantic stereotypes; keepsakes and popular novels. By interiorizing the stereotype it becomes a fantasm, which Emma assumes as her personal history. The text does not repress the knowledge of the repetition, which implicates an omniscient narrator as well as the protagonist; it becomes one of the major motifs of the novel. In demystifying Emma's blindness to her engagement in these repetitions, the narrator assumes a largely sadistic role, which we may suspect is the effect of a powerful nostalgia for the lost power of now obsolete stories of desire, still painfully contemporary.

The relation of desire to language here is similar to that discussed above in the context of Emma's wish to know the meanings of the words of bliss, but there are significant differences. Attention shifts from the static paradigm (metaphor) to the mobile syntagmatic order of narrative (metonymy). Desire, when associated with the nouns which serve as its signifier, can only remain virtual, a possibility forever suspended. When it is articulated as the narrative of fulfilled pleasure, however, desire is linked inevitably with the alienating repetitions of the stereotype. The private strategy of concealment only renders more apparent this alienation within romantic narratives.

Other constants of Emma's relation to desire and narrative are also established jn this chapter. Desire is experienced as an imperative to appropriate objects for personal profit. Emma's personal narratives will later provide the means for that appropriation, but here the motif of the pleasures of reading and the motif of appropriation are simply contiguous, not yet joined explicitly as they will be later in the novel. Certain links between the personally pleasurable and bourgeois economy, however, are already formed in this chapter:

> Il fallait qu'elle pût retirer des choses une sorte de *profit personnel;* et elle rejetait comme *inutile* tout ce qui ne contribuait pas à *la consommation immedédiate* de son coeur, étant de tempérament plus sentimental qu'-artiste. . .   (34, italics added)

Pleasure is set in a system of exchange which conflates the emotional and the commercial, in which the subject seeks to consume the object of desire. Flaubert's correspondence repeatedly underscores implications in this passage that Emma is a perverted emblem of the artist and that her experiences of desire are characteristic of bourgeois sensibility. Desiring, for Emma, is a form of imitation whose object is the recuperation of sense, without difference or loss.

In terms of the novel's narrative order, this chapter is analeptic to the main narrative, its events situated in the protagonist's childhood.[13] Clearly, chapter 6 provides information about attributes of Emma's "character" which will remain remarkably static throughout the novel. Emma will attain maturity as a "subject," however, only when she actively orders the elements of Romantic narratives according to an economic and sentimental schema already set by these earliest reported experiences of literature.

In the remaining chapters of Part One, Emma's desires are confined to a narcissistic silence. She now spins out her narratives as voiceless fantasies. In the opening lines of chapter 7, Emma composes hypothetical stories of travel to far-away places:

> il eût fallu, sans doute, s'en aller vers ces pays à noms sonores où les lendemains de mariage ont de plus suaves paresses! Dans des chaises de poste, sous des stores de soie bleue, on monte au pas des routes escarpées, écoutant la chanson du postillon, qui se répète dans la montagne avec les clochettes des chèvres et le bruit sourd de la cascade.   (38)

Moments of daydreaming such as this, as Genette notes in an excellent study of description and narrative in Flaubert, are doubly silent.[14] The protagonists have ceased to speak to each other; Emma turns toward the world of her dreams. The narrative of the novel is also silent here, immobile, interrupted by a fantasy narrative which suspends the sequence of events in the main story. Emma's narratives, although they intrude upon the sequence of the main story, never acquire the power to take over from that story the initiative for ordering events.

Following this passage, the text focuses specifically on the illocutionary context of communication: Emma's needs are formulated less in terms which characterize a specific object of desire than in terms of a discursive situation.[15] She lacks that *other,* necessary to the circuit of communication:

> Peut-être aurait-elle souhaité faire à quelqu'un la confidence de toutes ces choses. Mais comment dire un insaisissable malaise, qui change d'aspect comme les nuées, qui tourbillonne comme le vent? Les mots lui manquaient donc, l'occasion, la hardiesse.   (38)

This passage opens up questions considerably more complex than the problem posed for Emma by the absence of an interlocutor. On the one hand the role of the other can never fulfill the function which Emma desires, for the other is to be always elsewhere and different from what the subject wishes. The images and the stories of desire, furthermore, are to be located beyond a particular and immediately accessible reality, a particular time and space contemporary to the subject, yet they can be constructed only with the aid of what they attempt to reject: reality ... *another* reality. As for the formation of images and stories of pure desire, a further paradox makes itself felt. From the outset, there is a fundamental problem: these things, objects of desire, are lacking, and the elements which might constitute objects are heterogeneous, disparate, incapable of acquiring a stable configuration. Language cannot fix them, nor can they be generated by "reality" to be retrieved by language.[16]

Emma's attempts to arouse passion in herself pursue an illusive, provisional and ultimately inadequate solution. She develops theories about desire, narrative explanations of the empty signifiers. She repeats passionate verse in the manner of a sentimental catechism:

> d'après des théories qu'elle croyait bonnes, elle voulut se donner de l'amour. Au clair de lune, dans le jardin, elle récitait tout ce qu'elle savait par coeur de rimes passionnés ...   (41)

Theory, for Emma, is auto-erotic, a solitary gesture directed toward narcissistic fulfillment. Knowing pleasure is repeating *by heart* the language of another's passion.

The major "event" of Part One, the trip to the chateau de Vaubyessard, the dinner and the ball, appears to provide the occasion or access to the passion about which Emma had mused earlier. She remains excluded, however, from the language of potential partners in communication. What she wishes for most fervently is a passionate interlocutor, yet, in the conversations which take place in this sequence, she occupies an unmistakably marginal position; the language of the people at the chateau is incomprehensible, foreign to her. Emma is excluded because she is ignorant of the meanings of the speaker's words who "causait Italie":

> A trois pas d'Emma, un cavalier en habit bleu causait Italie avec une jeune femme pâle, ... Ils vantaient la grosseur des piliers de Saint-Pierre, Tivoli, le Vésuve, Castellamare et les Cassines, les roses de Gênes, le Colisée au clair de lune. Emma écoutait de son autre oreille une conversation pleine de mots qu'elle ne comprenait pas.   (48)

Her alienation is also figured by the space in which she is caught, a space between two centers of desire. Although the swirling movements of her dance with the Vicomte transform the swirling, formless malaise (*qui tourbillone comme le vent* ...) into intense pleasure, Emma is excluded from the verbal articulations of desire which she seeks to know. Two passages specifically underscore the link between silence and the enforced solitude of Emma's desire. In the first, Emma composes a brief narrative about a cigar case of green silk, which Charles finds by the road on their return to Tostes. Emma supposes that its owner is the Vicomte; her fantasy narrative transforms the case into a fetishized object:

> A qui appartenait-il? ... Au vicomte. C'était peut-être un cadeau de sa maîtresse. On avait brodé cela sur quelque métier de palissandre, meuble mignon que l'on cachait à tous les yeux, qui avait occupé bien des heures et où s'étaient penchées les boucles molles de la travailleuse pensive. Un souffle d'amour avait passé parmi les mailles du canevas; chaque coup d'aiguille avait fixé là une espérance ou un souvenir, et tous ces fils de soie entrelacés n'étaient que le continuité de la même passion silencieuse.   (53)

A cigar case here, is not "just" a cigar case. Once again, Emma's silent narrative is both erotic and the reproduction of the fabric of another text; she composes her story upon the already woven surface of a fetishized object. Paradoxically, however, in seeking a sense which would attain the continuity of "authentic" passion, meanings become a play of surface effects, incapable of evoking the desired presence. The fiction of desire, quite literally, is a fabrication which affirms distance, not presence; "Elle était à Tostes. Lui, il était à Paris, maintenant; là-bas!" (53). The desired moment of absolute presence (*maintenant*) is deferred, and metaphorized as spatial disjunction (*là-bas*).

Emma's taste for stories is not easily satisfied, however, and the inadequacies of this narrative produce more fiction, generated by a word which, in its very emptiness, can accommodate all meaning:

> Comment était ce Paris? Quel nom démesuré! Elle se le répétait à demi-voix, pour se faire plaisir; il sonnait à ses oreilles comme un bourdon de cathédrale; il flamboyait à ses yeux jusque sur l'étiquette de ses pots de pommade.
>
>   ...
>
> Paris, plus vaste qu'un océan.   (53–4)

This passage maintains a certain structural symmetry with the end of chapter 5, in which Emma had speculated on the meaning of the words *félicité, passion* and *ivresse,* yet there are meaningful differences between the two contexts which are due to the increasing importance of narrative to Emma's desire. The passages are similar in that each is an act of denomination, the terms in each case being devoid of semantic substance. The word Paris here must be referential, but is meaningful only as a figure. *Paris* is as empty a signifier as the words of passion, yet a fantasmatic geography has replaced the atopical terms of bliss, and Emma's imaginings move closer to narrative. The term *Paris* justifies the fantasmatic representation of desire, for it has historical, topographical reference, but it only functions effectively as a signifier which can accommodate the projections of desire when it becomes detached from that reference.

The act of naming is followed by another debauchery of reading, similar to that in the retrospective chapter 6. In the later episode, Emma subscribes to "feminine" reviews and studies descriptions of Parisian decors in E. Sue, Balzac and George Sand; "y cherchant des assouvissements imaginaires pour ses convoitises personnelles" (54). The same desire to consume the text and the same relation between desire and writing of both the first (Balzac, etc.) and the second order (*le journal de femmes*) are asserted as before. Emma takes the realist project literally; if the word is able to represent adequately the essence of things, then that essence is available to appropriation as language. Emma wants writing without difference, a desire figured here by her turning away from the symbolic mode of romantic narratives toward realist description and, beyond that, toward the iconic figure of a map of Paris. She buys a map and traces imaginary walks through the city:

> Elle's s'acheta un plan de Paris, et du bout de son doigt, sur la carte, elle faisait des courses dans la capitale. Elle remontait des boulevards, s'arrêtait à chaque angle entre les lignes des rues, devant des carrés blancs qui figurent des maisons.   (54)

Like Félicité, in "Un Coeur simple," who asks to be shown the house of her nephew on a map of Cuba, Emma's interpretation of the map seeks the real, where there is only the surface of an iconic figure. Her misreading in this passage allegorizes the separation between figures of desire and referents. Emma's finger on this fetishized surface of the map attempts an impossible coincidence between her imaginings and the abstract surface on which desire has been projected.

It is at this time that Emma begins to wear an open house coat, buys paper and a blotter and dreams of *Charles* becoming a famous writer: "Elle s'était acheté un buvard, une papeterie, un porte-plume et des enveloppes, quoiqu'elle n'eût personne à qui écrire" (56). Emma fills the space of lack not by writing herself, but by displacing the feminine subject in favor of a masculine proper name, which is to assume phallocentric mastery and circulate within a bourgeois economy: "Elle aurait voulu que *ce nom de Bovary, qui était le sien,* fût illustre, le voir étalé chez les libraires, répété dans les journaux, connu par toute la France" (58, italics added). At the very moment when Emma might begin to write, her enclosure by the bourgeois family permits access to writing through the name of the husband, which can circulate only in accordance with the laws of commerce. Emma has effaced feminine difference in favor of the workings of the *non(m) propre.*[17]

Emma has come full circle; having gained access to narrative as the medium of desire she now refuses the role of the writing subject and in her fantasies seeks to give over that role to a man. The "solution" takes the form of denial and displacement; it produces a re-emergence of desire in the symptoms of a "nervous disorder": "Elle devenait difficile, capricieuse ..." "Elle pâlissait et avait des battements de coeur" (62, 63). This sequence, then, repeats regressively the order of Emma's initiation to narrative; from symptom, to fantasm, to the nominal terms (*félicité*, etc.) to narrative ... the silenced narratives of desire have been reconverted into the symptoms of hysteria. At the end of Part One of the novel, Emma can give voice to her desire only through the "silent" metaphor by which she is strangled: "Elle eut des étouffements aux premières chaleurs..." (59).

Denials, Repetitions and "Bad" Ironies

As we saw earlier, the first chapter of Part Two contains a curious observation by an omniscient narrator which announces that the events about to be told are ultimately inconsequential. Having suggested that this metanarative comment must be read not only in terms of its authoritative detachment from the story, but also as already interpreted by the fiction of the first part of the novel, we can now consider some further implications of this passage. That statement would seem to refer to the "emptiness" of Flaubert's subject, to Emma's radical superficiality and to the bankruptcy of bourgeois, romantic desire, yet a reader attentive to the questions raised above will speculate on other possible resonances of this statement. These remarks establish the existence of a demystified tale, a story assumed to be by an omniscient which works in opposition to Emma's mystified stories. There is an implied contrast between two types of narrators, those who understand the aporia of fiction and those who are blind to its illusions. We are well aware of Emma's tenacious and desperately deluded belief in the power of her stories to change things and to appropriate the objects of her desire, and so her place in this opposition would seem to be securely established. Although they do not erase it entirely, ironic effects are considerably more complex than this opposition would suggest.

The account of the arrival at Yonville and the description of the setting, an introduction in the realistic manner, are written from the point of view of an omniscient *on*, which would seem to strongly reinforce mimetic illusion. Even as it is asserted most securely, however, that illusion is undercut. Situated at the end of a narrative/descriptive passage immediately preceding the arrival of the Bovarys at Yonville, the passage serves as a conclusion to a prefatory sequence. It thus has the effect of a denial which affirms and sets an omniscient narrator in a homologous relation to Emma.[18] It is not possible, however, to dissociate completely that narrator's stories from a belief in the finality of narrative which, ultimately, re-sembles Emma's faith. The telos of stories re-emerges even in deconstructive narratives, even in fictions which allegorize the aporia of meaning. We must consider, then, the doubling effects between an omniscient narrator and the central protagonist not only from the perspective of sadistic control. The schema is also strongly masochistic, for the relations between narrator and story inevitably re-produce the same dilemmas ironized in the account of Emma's fictions. The very assertion of a lucidly controlled relation to narrative cannot resist yielding ultimately to narrative's seductions.

Much has been written about Emma's relation to language in Part Two of the novel, particularly about the importance of literary stereotypes in her exchanges with Léon, her second lover.[19] The couple's conversations repeat the already worn language of Romantic love, ironically exposing as a delusion the desire for a transparent language of fulfilled self-expression. Their exchanges require, yet cannot locate, an "original" language. Conversations are played out in a phatic register and the contact there established dramatizes a radical lack at another level.[20] The couple's conversations, the fragments of Romantic texts which they repeat, are linked to an economic mode of exchange: "Ainsi s'établit entre eux une sorte *d'association, un commerce continuel de livres et de romances"* (93, italics added). Emma, even as a desiring subject, is appropriated by the discursive structures of a system against which passion asserts itself.

The stereotype, as Felman, Gaillard and others have shown, sets the would-be unique subject in a depersonalized language, a common currency, in the very moment at which he or she seeks fulfillment.[21] The language of singular experience is the stereotype of Romantic passion, which promises the possession of the desired object, as indicated by these exclamations following Emma's first amorous encounter with her first lover, Rodolphe:

> Elle se répétait; "J'ai un amant! un amant!" se délectant à cette idée comme à celle d'une autre puberté qui lui serait survenue. Elle allait donc posséder enfin ces joies de l'amour, cette fièvre de bonheur dont elle avait désespéré.
>
> (·151–2)

As Emma fantasizes about her emotions, a cascade of the empty terms of passion burst forth: "Elle entrait dans quelquechose de merveilleux où tout serait passion, extase, délire . . ." (152).

Emma's identification with Romantic heroines, their language and the imitation of a *type* of adulterous lover further erodes her difference:

> Alors elle se rappela les héroïnes des livres qu'elle avait lus, et la légion lyrique de ces femmes adultères se mit à chanter dans sa mémoire avec des voix de soeurs qui la charmaient. Elle devenait elle-même comme une partie véritable de ces imaginations et réalisait la longue rêverie de sa jeunesse, en se considérant dans ce type d'amoureuse qu'elle avait tant envié.   (152)

Through identification with these heroines and their voice, Emma is effectively deprived of her own status as first person subject; *je* becomes homologous with *elle(s);* the self is multiplied as other(s). As she finally "possesses" what she desires, Emma is herself possessed by those she imitates ("des voix de soeurs *qui la charmaient"*).

In registers which are superficially distinct, though similar at a more abstract level, both Rodolphe and Lheureux, the merchant (*marchand de nouveautés*), know and exploit the links between desire, narrative and appropriation. Lheureux's astuteness ("c'était un homme habile") consists in anticipating the conjunction of appetites which Emma's frustrated love for Léon in fact produces: "Les appétits de la chair, les convoitises d'argent et les mélancholies de la passion se confondirent dans une même souffrance . . ." (101). This conjunction between erotic desire and commerce becomes more and more intimate later in the book, and, as we shall see, it has far-reaching consequences.

In this section of the novel, the episode which works out most fully this equivalency between the social/commercial and the private/sentimental is, of course, the famous scene at the *Comices agricoles*. As Rodolphe presses Emma with his passionate language, the orators at the fair extol public and commercial achievements. The irony in this sequence stems not so much from the discord between Rodolphe's and the orators' voices which alternate in the passage, and from the contrast between private, sentimental values and public virtues, as from their underlying similarities; the register of sentimental exchange is not essentially different from that of the *comices*. In the collapse of an apparent opposition, public and private stereotypes which are superficially opposed are revealed as sustaining the circulation of similar values.

Rodolphe, for his part, knows something of the value of words and understands that seduction is a question of language.[22] His observations following one of his first encounters with Emma serve as a cruelly ironic echo of Emma's earlier wish to know the meaning of the three words of desire:

> Ça baille après l'amour comme une carpe après l'eau sur une table de cuisine. Avec *trois mots de galanterie* cela vous adorerait j'en suis sûr! Ce serait tendre, charmant! ... Oui, mais comment s'en débarrasser ensuite?
>
> (122, italics added)

Once again, and in a vulgarly dramatic manner, Emma is reduced to an impersonal status (*ça, cela*) alienated from even the minimally individual form of the subject pronoun. These brief musings, in fact, contain the entire narrative of the affair, whose end is proleptically announced at its beginning: "Comment s'en débarrasser ensuite?" Like the stories of romantic passion, it is a story already well known and one which pre-supposes the necessity of narrative closure even at its outset. The hint here that Rodolphe's schemes have much to do with narrative plotting as a repressive strategy of containment is confirmed at the end of the affair. Rodolphe's remarks, then, have a particularly rhetorical resonance; naming Emma for what she was, he provides a clear temporal demarcation and a neat narrative closure; "C'était une jolie maîtresse!" (187).

Whenever Emma enters into a "new" relation with stories or writings, her role as subject is already codified, determined by the discourse, and it is invariably an alienated role. The chapter which precedes mention of Emma's impulsive correspondence with Rodolphe ("Souvent même, an milieu de la journée, Emma lui écrivait tout à coup ..." 174) contains a passage about the "bad ironies" of adultery, which she pursues so avidly, and suggests that letter-writing can be interpreted as one of those ironies:

> Elle se repentait, comme d'un crime, de sa vertu passé, et ce qui en restait encore s'écroulait sous les coups furieux de son orgueil. Elle se délectait dans toutes les ironies mauvaises de l'adultère triomphant.   (173)

In fact, Emma's letters are never part of the novel and so we must look elsewhere for signs of their content and of their effect upon the couple. The principal result of these letters, as the opening passage of chapter 12 indicates literally, is to generate presence. This passage is almost a parody of Emma's insistent desire that writing produce a presence susceptible to appropriation; her letters summon Rodolphe to her side, but what really counts is the production of more narrative. Disgusted by her life with Charles, Emma writes Rodolphe impulsively, in the middle of the day, calls Justin to deliver the note, and Rodolphe appears . . . to listen to Emma's stories, her plans to escape:

> Rodolphe arrivait; c'était pour lui dire qu'elle s'ennuyait, que son mari était odieux et l'existence affreuse! . . .
>
> . . .
>
> Elle soupira: "Nous irons vivre ailleurs . . . quelque part . . ."
>
> (174)

On one level, letter writing is a "bad irony" of adultery, a liberty required by the transgression, exemplified elsewhere by other episodes such as the lovers' meetings in Charles's consulting room. The ironies are "bad" in other and more powerful senses, however, in that they subvert the control of the subject in the very exercise of her desires, according to patterns already elucidated. The permutations are many, but the operative figure here is ironic reversal, in which the difference between marriage and adultery is virtually effaced. The lovers' passion loses energy and becomes a "domestic flame" (159). In pursuing her desires, Emma loses all control as subject, and becomes subjugated to her lover:

> avec cet supériorité de critique appartenant à celui qui, dans n'importe quel engagement, se tient en arrière, Rodolphe aperçut en cet amour d'autres jouissances à exploiter . . .   (179)

The fantasy narratives which anticipate Emma's new life with Rodolphe in a different country undergo a similar transformation; the signifier of absolute difference comes to symbolize an indifferent continuity. Emma's fantasies about her life with Rodolphe are contrasted with Charles's dream of future happiness, in a passage which follows immediately the account of Charles's dreams of domestic enjoyment for himself, Emma and Berthe, their daughter. Charles's projects center on the accrual of capital and the preservation of the family:

> Il pensait à louer une petite ferme aux environs, . . . Il en économiserait le revenue, il le placerait à la caisse d'épargne: ensuite, il achèterait des actions, . . . il voulait que Berthe fût bien élevée . . . Il se le figurait travaillant le soir . . . Enfin, ils songeraient à son établissement; on lui trouverait quelque brave garçon dans un état solide; il la rendrait heureuse; cela durerait toujours.
>
> (182)

Emma's dreams, however, appear radically different, as the narrator suggests: "elle se réveillait en d'autres rêves." The contrast is elaborated through an opposition

between the diegetic space of the narratives, familiar and local for Charles, picturesque and foreign for Emma:

> Souvent, du haut d'une montagne, ils apercevaient tout à coup quelque cité
> splendide avec des dômes, des ponts, des navires, des forêts de citroniers
> et des cathédrales de marbre blanc ... Et puis ils arrivaient, un soir, dans un
> village de pêcheurs ... C'est là qu'ils s'arrêteraient pour vivre ...
>
> (183)

While Charles's dreams are static, Emma's are full of energy and movement: "Au
galop de quatre chevaux, elle était emportée dupuis huit jours vers un pays nouveau, d'où ils ne reviendraient plus." Charles dreams of producing and conserving
capital and of containing sexual energy within the social and economic unit of the
family. Emma, on the other hand, fantasizes endless leisure. The very absence of
social context in Emma's dreams of Romantic bliss, however, points to an ideological repression, underscoring once again the alienating effects of her fantasm; the
desiring subject, in her dream of plenitude, is invaded by the depersonalized representation of bliss. However different they may seem, Emma's fantasies of appropriating the objects of fulfilled desire are congruent to Charles's desire to
control emotional and monetary capital. The end result, for each, is the death of
desire, a final and meaningless continuity. For Charles, this is an eternity of domestic
bliss (*cela durerait toujours*) and for Emma ... the eternity of an exotic life do-
mesticated by familiarity:

> Cependant, sur l'immensité de cet avenir qu'elle se faisait aparaître, rien de
> particulier ne surgissait: les jours, tous magnifiques, se ressemblaient comme
> des flots; et cela se balançait à l'horizon infini, harmonieux, bleuâtre et couvert
> de soleil.   (183)

Emma's letters, like her dreams, also suffer a radical loss of meaning, as in the scene
in which Rodolphe rereads some of her communications, along with those of
former mistresses, just before he writes her to break off their affair. The process
of loss is complex; on the one hand, in the letters from Emma which Rodolphe
rereads, sentimental expression has been contaminated and replaced by the practical. The letters are likened to business letters; and again the sentimental and the
commercial are conflated. Filled with details of their projected trip, the letters are
"courtes, techniques et pressantes *comme des billets d'affaires*" (188, italics added).
Rodolphe never gets around to reading the others ("les longues, celles d'autrefois"),
he is distracted by mementos of other past loves; bits of hair, old bouquets and the
like, dusty fragments, fetishes no longer charged with erotic energy. These objects
are only capable of evoking fragmentary memories of his former loves:

> A propos d'un mot, il se rappelait des visages, de certains gestes, un son de
> voix; quelquefois, pourtant, il ne se rappelait rien.
>   En effet, ces femmes, accourant à la fois dans sa pensée, s'y gênaient les

unes les autres et s'y rapetissaient, comme sous un même niveau d'amour qui
les égalisait.   (188)

The memory of Emma is already caught in a play of imitation and repetition when,
before reading her letters, Rodolphe looks at her miniature portrait and is unable
to assert the primacy of his recollections of the original, over the copy:

> Il y avait auprès, se cognant à tous les angles, la miniature donnée par Emma;
> sa toilette lui parut prétentieuse et son regard *en coulisse* du plus pitoyable
> effet; puis, à force de considérer cette image et d'évoquer le souvenir du
> modèle, les traits d'Emma peu à peu se confondirent en sa mémoire, comme
> si la figure vivante et la figure peinte, se frottant l'une contre l'autre, se fussent
> réciproquement effacées.   (187–8)

The dramatic posturing in the picture suggests that the Emma represented is once
again playing a role, miming a stereotype of a woman in a portrait. The model, in
short, isn't very original. The integrity of a unique individual subject, the "original,"
is seen here only as a figural inscription, with no priority over the copy, both figures
suffering a similar "effacement." Neither the writing subject nor her letters survives
the passage into a representation which was to have assured enduring communication. Emma's texts become absorbed into the general anonymity of the signs
which bear the traces of past loves. One signifier can be arbitrarily substituted for
another in the impersonal and now random discourse of spent passion. The portrait and the letters have become figures in an anaphoric series of fragments.

Repetitions become more frequent at the end of the second part of the novel,
the most extensive play of repetitions being set forth in the episode at the opera.
This scene thematizes repetition in its *mise en abyme* structures, as Emma recon-
structs her own personal past in the story of Lucie de Lammermoor, and in the
content of the stories superimposed within the episode. The introduction at the
end of the sequence, of a "new" narrative, as Emma's and Léon's re-acquaintance
inaugurates a "new" affair, leads to a further chain of repetitions. The concentration
of repetitions in this scene is preceded, moreover, by a number of others; the first
and most obvious is Emma's desperate return to reading in order to distract herself
from Rodolphe's rejection. After receiving his letter, Emma falls ill with a nervous
disorder which repeats the episode of her hysteria at the end of the first part of
the novel. Although the mysterious sickness is attributed by Homais to an allergic
reaction to apricots, contained in a basket sent by Rodolphe in which his letter has
been concealed, her symptoms are not allayed by the diet prescribed, but by a
religious conversion. The "cure" is effected by providing for the displacement of
Emma's repressed desire onto religion, as it was in her childhood at the convent.
Once again Emma's fantasies are sustained by frequenting second-rate texts, imitations of the great romantic religious writings sent to her by a bookstore special-
izing in devotional literature: "C'étaient de petits manuels par demandes et par
réponses, des pamphlets d'un ton rogue dans la manière de M. de Maistre,..."

(200). As before in Emma's childhood, the devotional and the sentimental merge in a voluptuous language, now more intensely erotic:

> Quand elle se mettait à genoux sur son prie-Dieu gothique, elle adressait au Seigneur les mêmes paroles de suavité qu'elle murmurait jadis à son amant, dans les épanchements de l'adultère.   (200)

Emma's sentimental excesses are once again judged by the family to be threatening and, as at the end of the first part of the novel, the remedy proposed is a trip. Although the excursion to the opera is not purely analogous to the move from Tostes to Yonville, structural homologies do exist: a change of scene sets the stage for a new affair. In one sense this trip is an ironic deformation of Emma's failed project of escape with Rodolphe to an exotic refuge. The irony is complex, however, for the trip to Rouen produces results considerably different from those intended. The "cure" does not put an end to Emma's nervous disorder, but aggravates the "malady" in ways unforeseen by any of the participants. The excursion is intended to establish closure by arresting the symptoms of malady/desire, yet it will provide the basis for a "new" sequence, which repeats the same desires, and plays out virtually the same fantasy narratives, the same deferrals of satisfaction, the same uncontrollable effects of writing.

The Theatre and Her Doubles

The scene at the opera is crucial to an interpretation of narrative repetition in the novel: Emma's musings, interpretation and fantasy projections dramatize a dilemma repeated throughout Flaubert's writings; the absolute impossibility of ever being original, and the persistent desire for the unique. The writer, as it is said in the early novella, *Novembre,* wishes to attain the impossible originality of the mythical romantic genius, yet he remains a copyist, whose writing reiterates fragments of the already written:

> Oui, il ma' semblé autrefois que j'avais du génie, je marchais le front rempli de pensées magnifiques, le style coulait sous ma plume comme le sang dans mes veines; . . . parfois des idées gigantesque me traversaient tout à coup l'esprit, comme, l'été, ces grands éclairs muets qui illuminent une ville entière, avec tous les détails de ses édifices et les carrefours de ses rues. J'en étais ébranlé, ébloui; mais quand je retrouvais chez d'autres les pensées et jusqu'aux formes même que j'avais concues, je tombais, sans transition, dans un découragement sans fond; je m'étais cru leur égal et je n'étais que leur copiste!
>
> ("L'Intégrale," 254)

The episode at the opera is one of the most cohesive of the sequences in the novel which are devoted to Emma's fiction-making. Though more complex in the structure of its narrative composition and in the stratification of various levels of interpretation, the passage recalls in certain ways Rodolphe's contemplation of Emma's portrait. The relations between an "original" and its imitation by figural transposi-

tions once again efface the "original." Subjective identity, primary meaning or uniqueness of desire, make no sense whatsoever. To read the scene at the opera,
however, as an unproblematically ironic dismissal of a naive dreamer, unable to
maintain even the most rudimentary distinctions between "fiction" and "reality," as
we surely do to some extent, is to dismiss both the complexity of Emma's interpretations and the more troublesome implication that Emma's confusions may in
fact inhere to all fiction-making.

The chapter begins under the emblems of repetition, which provide necessary
descriptive details (the name of the opera, and the principal singer) and which serve
at the same time as a sign of the importance of repetition in the following episode:
"A l'angle des rues voisines, de gigantesques affiches répétaient en caractères
baroques: *Lucie de Lammermoor* . . . Lagardy . . . Opéra . . . etc." (206). As an enactment and interpretation of repetitions, the episode engages some of the central
questions of the novel. The sequence repeats the major sentimental themes of
Emma's life, but more important to our interests, it raises the issue of the interplay
of repetition in desire, narrative and interpretation. Once again, as Emma attempts
to order her desire as a story she is alienated by the discourse in which she seeks
to locate herself. This passage suggests that the desire for narrative and for its
interpretation is not easily assuaged even as mystifications and mis-readings are
revealed in Emma's fictions.

Emma's interpretations of the opera, *Lucie de Lammermoor,* enact a rereading of the novel by Scott, which she knows from her youth. Her emotions in this
scene are again set in an intertextual network; she asserts her subjectivity by
rereading a literary text. The fiction on stage, however, is not the "primary" text for
Emma, but is arrived at by the detour of a memory of the prose. These two fictions
are also supplemented by Emma's memories of her own life, which become a text
superimposed on the other two fictions. This superimposition undercuts not only
esthetic distinctions, those between narrative prose and stage performance, but in
a more radical subversion, disrupts the boundary between fiction and "reality,"
source and text. Although the episode presents Emma's relations to fiction as
fraught with naive illusions, exemplified most dramatically by her confusion between the actor Lagardy, who performs the fiction, and the off-stage character,
Lagardy, who becomes the subject of her own fantasy, the text also presents
Emma's readings and narratives in a highly complex textual network.

The recapitulative structure of the scene retraces and reiterates the stages of
Emma's sentimental history and re-enacts a repetition which provides the narrative
"starting point" for the third section of the novel. She enters the theatre like a child
("elle eut plaisir comme un enfant . . ."),[23] rereads the libretto of the opera through
the memories of her own childhood, becomes caught up in the music, recalls the
earlier emotions for Léon and the affair with Rodolphe, and finally, exits from the
theatre before the third act . . . the third part of the opera, and the third section of
Flaubert's novel. The scene is thus at once a retrospective narrative, the story of a
hypothetical past and a proleptic vision.

Emma first reconsiders her past life, then quickly supplements the fiction performed on stage by her own modalized, hypothetical narrative of a past which might have been. In this ideal past, Emma once again yields to the sure control of a man and to an economy of sentiment, which the term *placer* suggests is linked to a bourgeois, commercial exchange:

> Ah! si, dans la fraîcheur de sa beauté, avant les souillures du mariage et la désillusion de l'adultère, *elle avait pu placer sa vie sur quelque grand coeur solide,* alors la vertu, la tendresse, les voluptés et le devoir se confondant, jamais elle ne serait descendue d'une félicité si haute.   (210, italics added)

The *placement* or investment which Emma fantasizes in a nostalgic past is in fact arrived at as a complex series of *dis*placements; as she finds her own story represented by Lucie's role. This displacement generates a fantasized personal past which transforms the desiring subject into an object of masculine desire. Emma, the spectator, identifies with the actress, imposes on the dramatic role a fictional personal past, and then imagines this twice displaced figure of her desire as the desired object of the actor Lagardy. Emma has become a disabused interpreter, however, who knows the deceptiveness of words. *Virtue, tenderness, voluptuousness* and *duty,* converge in a single word, *félicité,* whose meaning she now recognizes to be generated by the deceptions of art:

> Mais ce bonheur-là, sans doute, était un mensonge imaginé pour le désespoir de tout désir. Elle connaissait à présent la petitesse des passions que l'art exagérait ... Emma voulait ne plus voir dans cette reproduction de ses douleurs qu'une fantaisie plastique bonne à amuser les yeux, et même elle souriait intérieurement d'une pitié dédaigneuse ...   (210)

Paradoxically, as a disabused reader, Emma is doubly vulnerable to self-deception, for she once again becomes caught up in the seductions of fiction: "Toutes ses velléités de dénigrement s'évanouissaient *sous la poésie du rôle qui l'envahissait...*" (210, italics added). The role takes over, in spite of Emma's initial lucid resistance; it is a means of access to the "real." This desire to possess the real produces more than a simple confusion between the "real" and the performance; it composes the real through the only terms available to the desiring subject, the figures of fiction: "entrainée vers l'homme par l'illusion du personnage, ell tâcha de *se figurer* sa vie ..." (210, italics added). The effort to appropriate the "real" (*entrainée vers l'homme*) is given over to the suspect operations of fiction, the figures of narrative fantasy:

> Ils se seraient connus, ils se seraient aimés! Avec lui, par tous les royaumes de l'Europe elle aurait voyagé de capitale en capitale, partageant ses fatigues et son orgueil, ramassant les fleurs qu'on lui jetait, brodant elle-même ses costumes ...   (210)

The shift from a discourse on the person of the protagonist to the artifices of fiction making is marked by the term *se figurer,* and by a description of a primitive text-making, as Emma imagines herself embroidering the actor's costume. The text

appears to have reproduced "reality," as the narrative tenses shift from the hypothetical past conditional, to the imperfect, recounting Lagardy looking at Emma, and
finally to the present: "il l'aurait regardé. Mais une folie la saisit: il la regardait, c'est
sûr! Elle eût envie de courir dans ses bras ..." (211). This moment of confusion
between fiction and the textual "reality" is thematized as a moment of madness
(*une folie la saisit*). Madness, for Emma, is the inability to maintain distinctions which
she knows are essential; the figural and the referential commingle, beyond control.
If madness is the desired confusion between the operations of fiction (which
maintain the vitality of desire) and "reality" (a moment of "sure" communication),
then "sanity" can only be restored by reinstating the differences which desire would
seek to obliterate. Paradoxically, then, the moment of communication which would
be the fulfillment of desire, is its death; the possession of the "incarnation of love
itself" is madness. The falling curtain, however, restores Emma to her senses, by
reinstating the difference between stage and spectator, and in the wider sense, by
re-establishing conventional barriers which are the conditions upon which desire
can live.

If narrative organizes desire according to a deluded ideal of subjective control
and intelligibility, and if these lies of fictions are known to Emma, she will nonetheless deny what she has come to understand; that denial, as we have seen,
engages her once again in a narrative of desire. At this moment Léon appears, and
Emma seems to move definitely outside of the complex and confused web of
fictions, to turn away from rhetoric, toward an object of desire represented as real.
This rejection of fiction is signaled in several ways. First, Emma abruptly denies her
earlier fascination with the Opera. As Léon joins Emma and Charles in the theatre,
he asks Madame Bovary if the spectacle interests her and she replies: "Oh! non, pas
beaucoup." She also finds the mad scene excessive, artificial: "la scène de la folie
n'intéressait point Emma, et le jeu de la chanteuse lui parut exagéré" (212). Emma's
lack of interest in madness is deceptive. She had been seized by madness at the
moment in which the boundaries of meaning are disrupted. This is the brief instant
of transgression, which is quite different from the representation of madness on
stage. The theme of madness is contained by the discourse of reason, which
radically reduces its otherness. Emma's confusion between "reality" and fiction,
however, conceals a profound insight into the negativity of "reality," which is only
accessible to her through the operations of fiction. Her folly is not only that the
stage becomes "real" for her and that the place of the spectator becomes a fiction,
but that even within these reversed polarities each position is at once fictive and
"real." Emma believes firmly in the divisions between fiction and reality, yet the
locus of both the "real" (offstage) and of the fictive (onstage) accommodates
indiscriminately the other term. Emma constantly seeks to maintain thresholds
between fiction and "reality" and to go "beyond" fiction to "reality"; what she fails
to understand is that the interest is not what lies "beyond" but in the instability of
the threshold.

Emma rejects the representation of a madness which is not madness, but
becomes caught up in a different kind of uncontrolled play at the very moment

when she appears to reject fictions with the greatest lucidity. In deflecting her attention from the theatre to Léon it would appear that she re-enters the world of real passion. At this moment, however, when the distinctions between fiction and reality seem the clearest, the desiring subject becomes caught up in a most impersonal play of language and enters a network of substitutions. Léon takes the place of Lagardy and of Rodolphe and of all the vaguely characterized men she has fantasized. Indeed, beyond its obvious meaning, Léon's remark about Lagardy, suggesting that he will soon put on another show ("Il donnera bientôt une autre représentation"), can be read as preface to the third section of the novel which introduces another performance in which Léon, not Lagardy, will act out an already well-established narrative, in a sequence no less rigorously structured than the opera. We are far from the madness of the earlier scene, but this repetition, in its un-rationality goes beyond an untroubling feminine "folly."

Repetitions and Their Ends

The third part of the novel opens with observations by an omniscient narrator about Léon's experiences with women, which prepare for the first extended, intimate conversation between Emma and her companion. Léon's decision to possess Emma places her in a series of conquests, homologous to the series of the figures of Emma's desire in which the clerk himself has already taken a place. Léon's resolve is made possible by his repeated successes, yet its price is the wearing away of emotional spontaneity: *"sa timidité s'était usée* au contact des compagnies folâtres..."* (215, italics added). The passage suggests once again that the pursuit of desire is an affair of language. Léon's initiative is not sparked by an explosion of erotic energy, the prelude to a passionate act, but begins in a more calculated manner as a speech act: "Il fallait, pensait-il, *se résoudre* enfin à la vouloir posséder" (215). The overtures to seduction begin not in the stirrings of the heart but by setting a certain register of discourse. Léon's disabused choice of a rhetoric of seduction appropriate to his partner ("on ne parle pas·à l'entresol comme au quatrième étage" 215) further heightens the alienation produced here by the couple's relation to language. As in earlier conversations, the exchange is structured as an imitation of imitations. Now included in this web of repetitions is an inevitable imitation of Emma's earlier affair; in giving herself to Léon, as Sartre has noted, Emma parodies herself.[24] Léon mirrors Emma's melancholy which itself is set in a web of repetitions:

> Pour se faire valoir, ou par une imitation naive de cette mélancholie qui provoquait la sienne, le jeune homme déclara s'être ennuyé prodigieusement tout le temps de ses études. (216)

In contrast to their first conversations in Part One of the novel, both speakers now consciously exploit literary stereotypes; they order and edit their narratives for rhetorical effect:

Car ils précisaient de plus en plus les motifs de leur douleur, chacun, à mesure qu'il parlait, s'exaltant un peu dans cette confidence progressive. Mais ils s'arrètaient quelquefois devant l'exposition complète de leur idée, et cherchaient alors à imaginer une phrase qui pût la traduire cependant. Elle ne confessa point sa passion pour un autre; il ne dit pas qu'il l'avait oubliée.

(216–17)

The literary character of the conversation becomes increasingly evident, as Léon recalls having found an Italian engraving of a Muse in a print shop:

Il y a sur le boulevard, chez un marchand d'estampes, une gravure italienne qui représente une Muse. Elle est drapée d'une tunique et elle regarde la lune, avec des myosotis sur sa chevelure dénouée.   (217)

The representation seemed to him a likeness of Emma: "Elle vous ressemblait un peu" (217). This Muse is emblematic of the stereotypically fictional mode of the lover's exchange and allegorizes the inevitability of imitation. The passage is unmistakably caustic in its demystification of Romantic love and of the alienating effects of language. Even as the narrator ironizes the devaluation of passion through its language, however, he comments, in an intensely nostalgic remark, on the destructive inadequacy of language, "car c'est ainsi qu'ils auraient voulu avoir été, l'un et l'autre se faisant un idéal sur lequel ils ajustaient à présent leur vie passée. D'ailleurs, la parole est un laminoir qui allonge toujours les sentiments" (218). This nostalgia for an ideal language and a true narrative which would coincide entirely with personal history has many echoes elsewhere in the text and produces significant implications about an omniscient narrator's own relation to narrative. As we shall see, the register of irony is extended considerably by such statements.

The depersonalization of Emma and her lover in Part Three is executed even more relentlessly than earlier in the novel, as are the links between alienation and male narcissism. Critics have noted that as Léon recognizes Emma when she arrives at their rendezvous in the cathedral in Rouen he identifies her not by name, but by the impersonal pronoun: "C'était elle!" (224). A few pages later, the famous carriage scene produces an even more forceful displacement. The episode is the account of the first sexual encounter between Emma and Léon, the most intense of subjective experiences, according to their rhetoric of romantic love. Emma and Léon roll through the streets of the city in a journey whose only purpose could be determined by the untold action which occurs within the vehicle, yet that essential interior is never described. On entering and leaving the carriage, Emma is presented in the most impersonal terms. Hesitating to get into the carriage, she is persuaded, "determined," by a word:

—Eh quoi! réplique le clerc. Cela se fait à Paris!
    Et cette parole, comme un irrésistible argument, la détermina.   (227)

At the end of the sequence it is not Emma who emerges from the carriage, but simply "a woman": "Puis vers six heures, la voiture s'arrêta dans une ruelle du

quartier Beauvoisine, et une femme en descendit..." The loss of an identity pre-
sumed necessary to sentimental exchange is underscored also by a crucial lacuna in
the sequence. The scene "within" is never described; the protagonists disappear
into a *lourde machine* (227), which is at once the erotic couple and the carriage.[25]
The reader's interpretation of the goings on within the carriage is entirely dependent on the surface effects of meaning. The text omits what the situation would
seem to require most. Far from a euphemistic suppression, this absence points
again with sadistic insistence to the destructive effects of certain "machines": the
carriage (*la lourde machine*) takes its place with the rolling press (*le laminoir*).

At the height of their passion in Rouen, during Emma's first visits, the couple's
intense pleasure is described as a commingling of selves in a pleasurable *possession,*
which, as earlier in the sequence with Rodolphe, leads to the domestication of
passion.

> Ils étaient si complètement perdus en la possession d'eux-mêmes, qu'ils se
> croyaient en leur maison particulière, et devant y vivre jusqu'à la mort, comme
> deux éternels jeunes époux.   (246)

The alienating effects of a will to appropriation of the other becomes more and
more apparent in this passage; there is an eventual equivalence between the lovers
and the objects of a bourgeois décor. An insistent series of adjectives in the
following passage blurs the distinction between possession of the other and possession of the objects which surround the lovers: "Ils disaient notre chambre, notre
tapis, nos fauteuils, même elle disait mes pantoufles, un cadeau de Léon, une
fantaisie qu'elle avait eue" (246). The passage sets up a metonymic equivalence
between Emma and the objects on which Léon lavishes his attention.[26] His admiration for Emma's soul is equated in a comic repetition of a symbolist correspondence, with an object, her lace. "Il admirait l'exaltation de son âme et les dentelles
de sa jupe." This displacement is pursued further, as "Emma" becomes for Léon a
series of roles, which, like his mistress's lace, figure Léon's desire:

> D'ailleurs, n'était-ce pas *une femme du monde,* et une femme mariée! une
> vraie maîtresse, enfin?
>   Par la diversité de son humeur, tour à tour mystique ou joyeuse, babil-
> larde, taciturne, emportée, nonchalante, elle allait rappelant en lui mille désirs,
> évoquant des instincts ou des réminiscences. Elle était l'amoureuse de tous les
> romans, l'héroïne de tous les drames, le vague elle de tous les volumes de
> vers. Il retrouvait sur ses épaules la couleur ambrée de *l'Odalisque au bain;* elle
> avait le corsage long des châtelaines féodales; elle ressemblait aussi à la *Femme
> pâle de Barcelone,* mais elle était par-dessus tout Ange!   (246)

The apparently meaningful diversity of these characterizations paradoxically underscores the radical reduction of the protagonist to a series of equivalent figures.
Finding and naming the object of desire, beyond the apparent diversity of Emma's
temperament "la diversité de son humeur" leads to the inscription of the letter of
Léon's desire: "c'était le vague *elle*/c'était le vague L." The pronoun not only breaks

away from the construct which is Emma's personality, as she comes to signify all idealized woman, but, at the same time, though a homonymic play suggests the letter which signifies the desiring male: Léon: L.

The play of the letter becomes caught up in the "bad ironies" noted earlier in the sequence with Rodolphe. Within transgression, the defied norms reassert themselves. In this sequence Léon becomes Emma's mistress: "Il ne discutait pas ses idées; il acceptait tous ses goûts; il devenait sa maîtresse plutôt qu'elle n'était la sienne" (258). Léon, as mistress, is also caught up in a reversal of the sense of the pronoun and letter: elle : L :: L : elle. This is not the circulation of differences in a bi-sexual love which disrupts oppressive sexual polarities; on the contrary, relations of dominance and appropriation within a certain schema of desire establish sexual non-difference on a masculine model. These transformations reaffirm enclosure, instead of producing destabilizing effects which would open up new possibilities for the erotic intensities of difference.[27]

The passage we have been reading deals in the most direct way with narrative and desire; Emma asks Léon at each rendezvous to recount the story of events which have occurred since their last meeting and she asks him to write love poetry in her honor ("des vers pour *elle,*" italics added):

> Il fallait que Léon, chaque fois, lui racontât toute sa conduite, depuis le dernier rendez-vous. Elle demanda des vers, des vers pour elle, *une pièce d'amour* en son honneur; jamais il ne put parvenir à trouver la rime du second vers, et il finit par copier un sonnet dans un keepsake.   (258)

This entire passage is a complex of repetitions, of imitations of imitations, whose effects include not only a depersonalization of the desiring couple, as the poetry of love is (re)written as a copy, but the disruption of difference, as the desiring male takes on the role of a passive mistress. Far from breaking with the ideology which underlies the relations between appropriation and desire in the novel, the reversals in this passage reinstate the same relations without effecting any violence to the schema itself.

An episode immediately preceding the account of Emma's financial ruin underscores once again the exhaustion of meaning within the stereotypical discourse of Romantic passion. As in the sequence with Rodolphe, the illusion of difference is exposed, and the language of desire suffers a radical loss of sense, figured in this passage by the conjunction of music and *vacarme* and by the literal resonances of the term *platitude,* a leveling effect:

> son coeur, comme les gens qui ne peuvent endurer qu'une certaine dose de musique, *s'assoupissait d'indifférence au vacarme* d'un amour dont il ne distinguait plus les délicatesses.
>
> Il se connaissaient trop pour avoir ces ébahissements de la possession qui en centuplent la joie. Elle était aussi dégoûtée de lui qu'il était fatigué d'elle. *Emma retrouvait dans l'adultère toutes les platitudes du mariage.*
>
> (269, italics added)

Characteristically, Emma seeks a literary solution in response to this dilemma. She has now acquired Rodolphe's knowledge regarding the difficulties of endings: "Mais comment pouvoir s'en débarrasser?" Rather than bringing the story to an end as Rodolphe had done earlier, she continues to write love letters to Léon, believing that writing is *appropriate* to her role. The role survives beyond passion and writing produces desire in the absence of the lover. It is no longer a question in this passage of exchanging letters, however, as it had been in the correspondence with Rodolphe. There is no mention of Léon's participation. These letters are Emma's final effort of appropriation and, as throughout the novel, the inability of writing to seize upon the meaningful object of desire simply produces more desire and more writing. Emma's letters now dispense with the figure of her correspondent altogether; her texts produce "another man," spectre of her desire. By repeating literary models in an interplay of image and displacement, the wished-for transparency of a fixed meaning has been replaced by an uncontrollable supplementarity:

> Mais, en écrivant, elle percevait un autre homme, un fantôme fait de ses plus ardents souvenirs, de ses lectures les plus belles, de ses convoitises les plus fortes; et il devenait à la fin si véritable, et accessible, qu'elle en palpitait émerveillée, sans pouvoir néanmoins le nettement imaginer, tant il se perdait comme un dieu, sous l'abondance de ses attributs.   (270)

Emma experiences the most intense sensations of pleasure as she evokes this ideal lover: "Elle le sentait près d'elle, il allait venir et l'enlèverait tout entière dans un baiser. Ensuite elle retombait à plat, brisée: car ces élans d'amour vague la fatiguaient plus que de grandes débauches" (270). The other, object of desire, is most powerfully "real" as a purely anonymous verbal construct.[28] Emma is caught by the force of her own words; the potentially limitless profusion of attributes is capable of generating an endless sequence of metonymic figures for her desire. While Emma believes in the power of words to represent an attainable object, she loses touch here; the object becomes "real" only when it is entirely displaced from "reality." Reality is subjugated to the law of desire by a radical break with that reference which was to have been the ultimate validation of Emma's language. It is precisely at this point that the ideological underpinnings of Emma's mystified relation to language become most explicit; the question of writing and of Emma's place in a narrative, shifts from stories of romantic desire to the complex financial schemes of Lheureux in which she has become entangled. One kind of writing is substituted for another; in "exchange" for her letters to her lover Emma receives subpoenas and notarized documents, the following paragraph tells us. The "commerce" she originally established with Léon is displaced by a more literally commercial affair. Once again Emma is situated in a story already composed and she must now narrate her desires in opposition to an inescapable narrative enclosure.

At the end of the novel, Emma recounts to several men the story (*son récit*) of her financial ruin; she speaks to Lheureux (272), all the bankers of Rouen whom she knows (275), Léon (275), Maître Guillaumin (280), Binet (284), and finally to Rodolphe (287). As indicated explicitly in the episode in which Emma visits Rodolphe, she approaches each of these encounters with an awareness of the problems facing the story teller, the problem of beginnings and the wider question of narrative order and content: "Que vais-je dire? Par où commencerai-je?" (286). These narratives are surprisingly congruent to Emma's stories of Romantic desire, although the relation between the teller and knowledge has been inverted. Emma's stories attempt to transmit knowledge, rather than to acquire it, but they are nonetheless similar to the sentimental narratives in their attempt to reappropriate what has already been lost. Just as Emma's stories of passion are repetitions of literary stereotypes in which the desiring subject has already been displaced, this story of financial ruin has already been composed, as the episode with Maître Guillaumin indicates specifically. Emma cannot escape the literal resonances of the term *situation*. The tale of her circumstances places her, encloses her, or one might say sites (cites) her:

> Monsieur, dit-elle, je vous prierais . . .
> —De quoi, madame? J'écoute.
> Elle se mit à lui exposer *sa situation*.
> Maître Guillaumin la connaissait, étant lié secrètement avec le marchand d'étoffes, chez lequel il trouvait toujours des capitaux pour les prêts hypothécaires qu'on lui demandait à contracter.
> Donc, il savait et mieux qu'elle *la longue histoire de ces billets* . . .
> (280, italics added)

The effects of Emma's writing in this sequence are clearly more tangible than her romantic fantasms; by signing promissory notes she has provided a capital for Lheureux. Once again, Emma, as the teller, is the already told. Her value as a "subject" is measured more precisely here in terms of the arbitrary monetary system, which can function only in the absence of individual specificity. There are significant differences however, between the stories of erotic desire and the narrative of capital. While the secret operations of sentimental discourses are always discontinuous with the "real," the exchange in which the story of Emma's ruin is played out is an underlying reality. The similarities between the two types of narratives, Romantic/erotic and capitalist, suggest a fundamental congruence between their aims and their operations. The terms of Romantic desire are apparently gratuitous, yet they are not dissimilar from the system of exchange in which Lheureux's cupidity is played out. Paradoxically the story of Emma's ruin has realized the goals of all of Emma's narratives: appropriation and closure. That stable sense is lethal, however, for, when achieved, it allows no possibility of repetition and metonymic displacement, which are the vital forces of desire and narrative. Emma turns desperately to narrative invention as a way out, near the end, but to no avail: "Il faudrait inventer une histoire qui expliquât les choses à Bovary. Laquelle?" (285). Emma's suicide follows immediately her submission to the position she has been forced to assume in the "intrigue" composed by Lheureux and Guillaumin; another system of desire flourishes on the bankruptcy of Emma's desires for romance. The triumph of Lheureux's plot dramatizes ironically the death of the subject, at issue implicitly, as we have seen, in all of Emma's fantasms and narratives. Emma's suicide, in a sense, is tautological, after the fact; it ironically validates as a stereotypical act what has already taken place in the dual registers of the sentimental and the economic.

Commentators have often remarked that the description of Emma's death recalls in grotesque detail the ultimately destructive consequences of her fascination with writing. The first effects of poison come to Emma as the taste of ink: "Cet affreux goût d'encre continuait" (293). The realistic details of the episode in which Emma's body is being dressed for burial have metaphoric resonances which repeat the same association between death and writing; black liquids pour forth from her mouth: "Il fallut soulever un peu la tête, et alors un flot de liquides noirs sortit, comme un vomissement, de sa bouche" (307).

The novel does not end with Emma's death, however; I can best interpret here the issues I have addressed by returning to Emma's last words, which counter in their ambiguity the apparently killing effects I have just been considering. Her last utterance is a suicide note, the only letter whose contents are ever presented directly in the novel. The fragment included in the text, "Qu'on n'accuse personne . . ." has extensive repercussions, as suggested earlier. The most striking effect of this imperative against interpretation, of course, is to serve as a powerful incentive to interpret. If the narratives of Emma's desire are to be read allegorically as commentaries on fiction, making this statement invites us to return to our interpretations once again and to reconsider the problem of the connections between Emma's deluded narratives and the status of the novel itself as writing. Just as the principal sequences converge on the death of the major protagonist, questions of responsibility and irresponsibility are introduced in a way which invites speculation on problems of interpretive finality and the effects of deconstructive narratives in this text. The registers of ethics and rhetoric are inextricably intertwined here. Emma's simple melodramatic statement generates a complex series of questions. First, the identity of the pronoun *on* can be read as addressing the surviving protagonists, the reader, and perhaps obliquely, an omniscient narrator as well; every interpreter is a potential accuser, and Emma's last clichéd utterance, may, in fact, loosen the paranoiac constraints of a certain kind of criticism and put in question once again the often sadistic authority of an omniscient narrator. Whom might one accuse? Who is the accusor and what is the accusation? On an ethical level, this novel, which so relentlessly exploits the ironic topos of adultery is a criticism of both the repressions of bourgeois society and the impasses of Romantic passion, and is not to be read as an apology either for marital fidelity or or adultery. Equally clearly, it is unlikely that the remaining protagonists will attribute Emma's death to a murder plot. Rather than interpreting this statement exclusively in ethical or hermeneutic terms, it is perhaps more productive to read this fragment as a statement about readability and interpretive authority and to further extend our considerations of the ways in which interpretations and narratives are deconstructed by the texts.

Emma's narratives subvert their own telos, as we have seen. They take place in a story which, in so far as it is validated by the authority of an omniscient narrator, necessarily repeats the delusions it ironizes throughout the novel. Irony is produced not only by the controlled performance of a narrator demystifying Emma's relation to stories, but will also include reverberations of the same desires and impasses in the performance of the deconstructive narrative. The text thus contests narrative performance ... in the performance of narrative. The story of the delusions of stories is not outside the delusions it re-cites. If Emma's narratives attempt to create an ordered "subject" (both an "I" and a topic), and attempt to give substance to the words of desire, the omniscient narrator's story, as a narrative, is also caught up with the complex of desires which motivate stories. The relentless construction of a distance between an omniscient narrator and the protagonist not only validates the differences between them but also makes it necessary to account for their distressing similarities. Whatever sadistic elements there may be in the narrator's relation to the protagonist, there is also a reflexive masochistic component as well, for the novel both reveals the deluded relation with Emma's stories and the law and at the same time problematizes the relation of its own writing to the law.

Perhaps the most interesting and elusive irony of the novel is not that which marks the *distance* between the protagonist's dispersed subjectivity and the dispassionate effacement of an omniscient narrator, but an irony which, beyond the differences between narrator and heroine, reasserts similarity between them. Flaubert's realism is radically different from Emma's corrupted romanticism principally because it rejects without illusion or concession certain relations with desire, representation and appropriation which remain constant in Emma's fantasies, stories and loves. The story proceeds from the knowledge that the dispersal of things and the dissolution of the self is not to be remedied by language or by repeating as one's own the already constructed stories of romantic passion, yet the novel attests to a generalized, irremediable dispersal and dissolution of forms and the self from which an omniscient narrator is no more exempt than is Emma. The novel is a construct; its relentless pursuit of form is the chosen defense against the impasses of desire and the failures of romantic topoi. A lucid detachment from Emma's struggles, however, cannot resolve the displacements and dissolution, any more than can Emma's narratives of escape to the perfect shore. The fragmentation and consequent depersonalization of narrators is a strategy which is made in response to the problems I have been discussing, yet it is a "solution" which consistently raises questions about the authority of narrators. While demystifying Emma's narratives as fetishistic, like the fetishist, an omniscient narrator repeats the denial of castration which he "knows" to be deluded. Readers have shown that Emma stands in a particular relation to castration; her failed apprenticeship to writing is an attempt to become a "man," to reserve castration, to attain an effective power over meaning and refuse her relation to lack.[29] I would like to pursue further the question of Emma's relation to castration and to conclude with some speculative remarks about authority, narrative and desire.[30]

Freud's essay on fetishism has much to say about incompatible views on important subjects, subjects which are not dissimilar to those I have been discussing either in their contradictory force or in their importance.[31] The fetishist, Freud tells us, denies the fact of castration, the child's reluctant acknowledgment that the mother does not possess the phallus, and with the fetish object seeks a substitute for an inadmissible lack. The refusal is not an absolute refusal of the "reality" of castration; in fact, that "reality" is acknowledged. At the same time that the child admits the lack, however, it is denied by the erotic investment in the fetish. The power of the fetish to endure, its resistance, as Derrida shows, is produced by the way in which incompatibles are linked, so that they never attain the resolution of decidability.[32] In one sense, there is a powerful difference between an omniscient narrator's and Emma's relations to narrative and to castration; Emma persists in believing in the finality of narrative and submits to her belief, while that belief is consistently problematized by an omniscient narrator, by the plurality of narrative points of view and by other means discussed earlier. The novel constantly raises questions not only of Emma's relation to the law, but of the subjects of writing, desire, the law and the aporia of meaning. The deconstruction of the Romantic narratives of desire is not a "simple" ironic dismissal, however, for recopying the narratives not only reaffirms their persistent fascination, as the narrator in *Novembre* had already told us, but it also suggests the extent to which all narratives call in question the subject's relation to an impossible meaningful completion. Inevitably, the ironic treatment of narratives serves as an alibi for a fetish: reasserting the power of narrative and the impossible desire to make meaningful as one's own the empty words of bliss.

NOTES

[1] All references to *Madame Bovary* are to the Garnier edition (Paris: Garnier, 1961). References to Flaubert's other writings are to the *Oeuvres complètes* (Paris: Seuil, "L'Intégrale," 1964).

[2] Of the many studies which treat the problematic of language and writing in Flaubert, and in particular in *Madame Bovary*, I have found the following to be most valuable: Charles Bernheimer, *Flaubert and Kafka: Studies in Psychopoetic Structure* (New Haven and London: Yale University Press, 1982); Leo Bersani, *A Future for Astyanax* (Boston-Toronto: Little, Brown, 1976), 89–105; Victor Brombert, *The Novels of Flaubert* (Princeton: Princeton University Press, 1966); Dominick LaCapra, Madame Bovary on Trial (Ithaca and London: Cornell University Press, 1982); Jonathan Culler, *Flaubert: The Uses of Uncertainty* (Ithaca, NY: Cornell University Press, 1974); Alain de Lattre, *La Bêtise d'Emma Bovary* (Paris: Corti, 1980); Françoise Gaillard, "L'En-signement du réel," in *La Production du sens chez Flaubert*, ed. C. Gothot-Mersch, Colloque de Cérisy (Paris: Union Générale d'Editions, 10/18, 1975), 197–220; "La Représentation comme mis en scène du voyeurisme," *Revue des Sciences Humaines* vol. 154, no. 2 (1874), 267–82; Jean Rousset, *Forme et signification* (Paris: Corti, 1962), 109–33; Jean-Paul Sartre, *L'Idiot de la famille*, II (Paris: Gallimard, 1971), 1611–20; III (Paris: Gallimard, 1972), 178–201; Naomi Schor, "Pour une thématique restreinte: Ecriture, parole et différence dans *Madame Bovary*," *Littérature* 22 (1975), 30–46; R. J. Sherrington, *Three Novels by Flaubert* (Oxford: Clarendon Press, 1970); Tony Tanner, *Adultery in the Novel* (Baltimore and London: The Johns Hopkins Press, 1979), 233–367; Albert Thibaudet, *Gustave Flaubert* (Paris: Gallimard, 1935); Anthony Thorlby, *Gustave Flaubert and the Art of Realism* (London: Bowes and Bowes, 1956). Most of these analyses, in so far as they offer any extended study of Emma's stories, treat them as framed by the narrative of an authoritative narrator. Although that perspective must be taken into account, this chapter will focus more directly on Emma's stories and will trace their effects on a general interpretation of narrative in the novel. Reversing the conventional perspective produces unanticipated effects which lead to a re-examination of framing, desire and the impulses of power in narrative.

[3] Roland Barthes, *S/Z* (Paris: Seuil, 1970), 146: "Flaubert . . . , en maniant une ironie frappée d'incertitude,

opère un malaise salutaire de l'écriture: il n'arrête pas le jeu des codes (ou l'arrête mal), en sorte que (c'est là sans doute la *preuve* de l'écriture) *on ne sait jamais s'il est responsable de ce qu'il écrit* (s'il y a un sujet *derrière* son langage); car l'être de l'écriture (le sens du travail qui la constitue) est d'empêcher de jamais répondre à cette question: *Qui parle?"*

[4] For a discussion of the combination of impersonal narration and *erlebte Rede*, or free, indirect discourse in *Madame Bovary* see Hans Robert Jauss, "Literary History as a Challenge to Literary Theory," *New Literary History*, II, No. I (1970), 7–38.

[5] Culler, 109–22.

[6] The troublesome word "reality" will assert itself frequently in my text. I will define my uses of the term here to avoid the repeated intrusion of cumbersome definitions in the course of my discussion. On the one hand, the term will refer to what the fiction designates as real, what is generally understood as an *effet de réel*. See Roland Barthes, "L'Effet de réel," *Communications*, II (1968), 84–9. In other instances the meaning of the term will be closer to what Lacan has called *le Réel*, which, precisely, cannot be named and resists symbolization. The *Real* can only be approximated by narrative in asymptotic fashion, as Frederic Jameson has noted: "Imaginary and Symbolic in Lacan: Marxism, Psychoanalytic Criticism and the Problem of the Subject," *Yale French Studies*, 55/56 (1977), 338–95, esp. 383–95. Very often in reading *Madame Bovary* it is not possible to assert with any confidence which of these two senses is appropriate and much of the force of the novel is generated by this indeterminacy.

[7] Gauillard, "L'En-signement du réel": "on ne peut triompher de l'écriture qu'en s'absorbant en elle: par un mouvement vertigineux de répétition en abîme, il faut être le livre en recopiant le livre que l'on recopie dans le livre," 201.

[8] Naomi Schor's very suggestive article, "Pour une Thématique restreinte," discusses the similarities between Homais and Emma, both of whom aspire to be writers. It should also be noted that, as interpreters, Emma and Homais are set in opposition to each other at the end of the novel. On the legal implications of a stable narrative signified see LaCapra, Madame Bovary *on Trial* and the final chapter of this book.

[9] Luce Irigaray, in *Speculum de l'autre femme* (Paris: Minuit, 1974), 9–162, discusses the displacement of a feminine libidinal economy and the imposition of masculine mimetic models of desire in the Freudian theory of sexual difference. In Freud's analysis of the early relation between the daughter and her mother, the young girl's role is determined by that of the male child; the daughter is said to understand her sexual difference as a lack, a defect, an absence of the phallus. The terms in which Irigaray discusses this suppression of feminine difference and its assimilation by the story of masculine desire are strikingly pertinent to this crucial passage in *Madame Bovary*: "Laissée au *vide*, au *manque* de toute représentation, re-presentation, et en toute rigueur aussi mimésis, de son désire (d')origine. Lequel en passera, dès lors, par le désir-discours-loi du désir l'homme: tu seras ma femme-mère, ma femme si tu veux, tu peux, être (comme) ma mère = tu seras pour moi la possibilité de répéter-représenter-reproduire-m'approprier le (mon) rapport à l'origine . . . Mais disons qu'*au commencement s'arrêterait son histoire,* [l'historoire de la fillette] pour se laisser prescrire par celle d'un autre: celle de l'homme père," 47.

[10] See de Lattre's discussion of the "paradox of the image," *La Bêtise . . . ,* 20.

[11] Laurent Jenny, "Il n'y a pas de récit cathartique," *Poétique,* 41 (février, 1980), 1–21. "Cette douleur impossible, c'est celle, pour un sujet, de ne pouvoir se conjuguer au noyau verbal de son fantasme, dans la syntaxe d'une narration," 7.

[12] Paradoxically, Emma seeks a fully expressive, unmediated language of desire by imitating, as if they were "her own," the stories of others' passion. In the most fundamental way, the possibility of appropriating meaning for the self is determined as a process of censorship imposed by discourse. The language of "self-expression" imposes what Pierre Bourdieu has called *euphémisation:* "Toute expression est un ajustement entre un *intérêt expressif* et une *censure* constituée par la structure du champ dans lequel s'offre cette expression, et cet ajustement est le produit d'un travail d'euphémisation pouvant aller jusqu'au silence, limite du discours censuré." "La Censure," in *Questions de sociologie* (Paris: Minuit, 1980), 138.

[13] Gérard Genette, *Figures* III (Paris: Seuil, 1972), 90.

[14] Genette, "Silences de Flaubert," *Figures* (Paris: Seuil, 1966), 223–43.

[15] On illocutionary speech acts, see Mary Louise Pratt, *Toward a Speech Act Theory of Literary Discourse* (Bloomington, London: Indiana University Press, 1977), 80–1.

[16] de Lattre, La Bêtise . . . , 20–1.

[17] C. Clément, H. Cixous, *La Jeune Née* (Paris: Union Générale d'Editions, 10/18, 1975), 144–7: Irigaray, *Speculum,* 165–82.

[18] The term *denial* is used in Freud's sense; the subject formulates a repressed desire or thought, while denying that desire (*Verneinung*, translated in French as *dénégation*).

[19] Tanner, *Adultery in the Novel*, 292–6.

[20] The phatic function in language establishes, prolongs or discontinues communication. In Jakobson's terms, it is the "set for contact." R. Jakobson, "Linguistics and Poetics," in *Style in Language*, ed. Thos. Sebeok (Cambridge, Mass.: M.I.T. Press, 1960), 350–77.

[21] S. Felman, "Gustave Flaubert: Folie et cliché," in *La Folie et la chose littéraire* (Paris: Seuil, 1978), 159–213; Gaillard, "L'En-signement," 198–9.

[22] On narrators' strategies of textual seductiveness, see Ross Chambers, *Story and Situation: Narrative Seduction and the Power of Fiction* (Minneapolis: University of Minnesota Press, 1984).

[23] See Tanner, *Adultery in the Novel*, 207.

[24] Sartre, *L'Idiot de la famille*, II, 1284: "la vie apparaît à Flaubert comme un cycle de répétitions involutives: tout recommence toujours mais en se dégradant sans cesse. Ainsi appliquerait-il volontiers aux événements d'une vie individuelle la remarque que fera Marx, un peu plus tard, touchant les grandes circonstances de l'Histoire: les faits se reproduisent; la première fois ils sont vrais et tragiques, la second burlesque:..."

[25] See Sartre, *L'Idiot* ..., II, 1276–82. The dehumanizing of the protagonists in this passage is seen by Sartre as a failure to present a correspondence between a microcosmic segment and a macrocosmic totality. "c'est la mort de l'illusion: il n'y a plus de personnages, juste des figurants manipulés par un cinéaste," 1285.

[26] The couple's relation to the decor is clearly fetishistic. On the importance of fetishistic structures of substitution in *L'Education sentimentale* and in *Bouvard et Pécuchet* see Bernheimer, *Flaubert and Kafka*, 102–17. I discuss fetishism in *Madame Bovary* in the concluding pages of this chapter.

[27] Clément/Cixous, *La Jeune Née*, 155–69. Cixous speaks of a bi-sexuality which does not nullify differences, but animates and proliferates them. Reversals of sexual roles in this passage of *Madame Bovary* function in a radically different manner; they underscore the polarization of sexuality, according to a schema dominated by masculine desire.

[28] In commenting on this passage, Bernheimer notes its symmetrical relation to the passage I quoted earlier in which Emma becomes the "loving woman of all novels, the heroine of all dramas..." What Emma considers "real about the figure is precisely its function as a stimulus for metaphoric attribution." *Flaubert and Kafka*, 62.

[29] See N. Schor, "Pour une thématique restreinte," 43–4.

[30] See Charles Bernheimer's excellent study, *Flaubert and Kafka*, which contains interesting discussions of fetishistic structures in *L'Education sentimentale* and *Bouvard et Pécuchet*. Bernheimer distinguishes between two types of fetishes. The first is analogous to Emma's attachment to the cigar case discussed above in this chapter; examples are Frédéric's attraction to Madame Arnoux's shoes, the hem of her dress and the fur trim of her velvet coat. The second type of fetish is linguistic: "they are the codes of social discourse, discourse systematized into self-contained ideological structures.... What precisely do the clerks fetishize? They replace the code of clichés that initially served to cement their relationship ... with a succession of books. Each of these books contains a specialized vocabulary, a hermeneutic code, that they adopt and cathect with Erotic energy," 109–10.

[31] S. Freud, "Fetishism," transl. J. Strachey, *Second Edition*, XXI (London: Hogarth Press, 1961), 149–57.

[32] J. Derrida, *Glas* (Paris: Galilée, 1974), 252–4; "La consistence, la résistance, la restance du fétiche est à mesure de son lien indécidable à des contraires. Le fétiche—en général—ne commence donc à exister qu'en tant qu'il commence à se lier à des contraires. Ce double lien, ce double ligament définit donc sa structure la plus subtile."

Bruce E. Fleming

AN ESSAY IN SEDUCTION, OR THE TROUBLE WITH *BOVARY*

Madame Bovary is surely one of the most troubling of the members in good standing of the pantheon of World Literature. Even when we have put it down, it continues to itch: what, we wonder, is this book really about?—surely not (we think) this wretched woman and her melodramatic end. And this sense that neither the characters nor the plot can, in fact, really be the point of this work feeds our impulse to grasp after meta-theories. Perhaps, we suggest, the work is about the relation of art to life (and is thus the story of a female Don Quixote), or is about inaction (and is thus the story of a Mrs. Hamlet), or mirrors the modern world or bourgeois society, or expresses a state of boredom or ennui, or—remembering Flaubert's desire to write a book about "nothing"—is only about words. Our impulse with such theories, at any rate, is certainly to talk more in terms of negatives than positives: what is absent, what is not done, what cannot ever have been. Yet none of these suggestions, I think, does justice to our experience of reading the work. For I would characterize this as being one of extraordinary passivity coupled with a sense of overwhelming inevitability: we must, that is, wait at every moment for the author to tell us what comes next—though when we have it, that something seems almost frustratingly logical.

My suggestion is that we can best explain such a perception by considering the work as an essay in seduction. By essay I mean seeing it not so much as the arrangement of particular people and events but as an illustration of logically possible permutations on a given state, a kind of thesis novel without a thesis. And seduction is like desire (a concept more common in contemporary analysis) in that both imply the lack of something; yet unlike desire, seduction is nothing more than a pattern of forces of which we ourselves are part, not a relationship with a defined other. And it is precisely the lack of a definition of people as substantial entities that characterizes *Madame Bovary*. (For an analysis of the novel in terms of desire see René Girard's work on deceit and desire in the novel, 63f.)

A number of other commentators, including Erich Auerbach and Tony

From *French Review* 62, No. 5 (April 1989): 764–73.

Tanner—whom I will be considering here—have offered theories that take as their point of departure this sense of there somehow being a hole at the center of this book. Yet it seems the unavoidable tendency of such theories that begin with the perception of something missing in *Madame Bovary*, to find the meaning of the novel in precisely the fact of lack, to make coherence of incoherence. And this, it seems to me, is to deny away the perception of centerlessness or absence that produced these theories in the first place. It is just this reader experience that *Madame Bovary* does not, at the level of character and plot, "make sense" that I am concerned with preserving; my hope is to offer a meta-theory that explains our sense of what is missing in the work without at the same time explaining it away.

In terms of character, moreover, the presupposition of such theories is that the second Mrs. Charles can be analyzed exactly as if she possessed the same coherence that we ascribe to living human beings as a presupposition of their comprehensibility. The incoherence and absence that these theories perceive in Emma is, as a result, taken as a quality of personality—as Aristotelean analysis allows us to understand a character whose very lack of consistency constitutes his consistency, or the way Lacanian analysis makes "sense" of the lack in a character such as Hamlet. The one thing that such analysis forbids us to conclude is that Madame Bovary simply doesn't make sense. And this is precisely what I am claiming here.

Nonetheless the impulse of these commentators to speak in terms of char-acter and plot with regard to the novel is, I think, perfectly understandable. For the book produces what I will be calling here a "character-effect" and a "plot-effect," the illusion of character and plot without their substance. These effects are char-acterized by, respectively, the pasting together of opposing qualities of character, and the alternation of actions between diametrically opposite poles of action. All of these, in turn, are strung together by the most tenuous chain of all, what I call mere temporality—the structure of "and then, and then, and then."

These notions can be clarified by an appeal to E. M. Forster's discussion in *Aspects of the Novel* (86). Emma is not, to be sure, what Forster would call a "flat" character (one characterized by a recurring tag action)—but this does not mean she is a "round" one either. Instead, she is the easiest and most simplistic devel-opment on a flat character—someone who is a pasting together, front to back, of diametrically opposed character traits. And Forster arrives at a concept similar to what I call "mere temporality" by making a distinction between story—that is, succession—and plot, which involves causality. An example of the first for Forster is: "The king died and then the queen died." An example of the second would be: "The king died; and then the queen died of grief." And it is in this first category that, I believe, *Bovary* falls. (Seymour Chatman suggests that the mind has a natural tendency to see the first as the second, 45–46.)

Yet I think we arrive most ineluctably at the conclusion that neither Emma nor the world she lives in "make sense" by avoiding it as long as possible: by asking repeatedly of Emma and the actions that mark turning points in her life the one question we may legitimately ask both of real people and of characters in novels

that aspire to the same status of coherence: "why?" It is the consistently disappointing results of doing so that drive us to the conclusion that the question itself is
illegitimate.

The first major change in her life was the move from the convent (on which
the period at her father's farm may be taken as an added post-script) to married
life. Why, we ask, did she marry Charles? And to this question I do not believe we
have an answer. To be sure, we are told that she had tired of the adolescent
fantasies of romantic novels and visceral religion. Clearly she was (so to say) fallow
ground, ripe for the next logical step of a relation with another person. Yet we
never have any indication that marriage in general, or her marriage with Charles in
particular, was the result either of rational choice or of pressure from either her
father or her situation. The conversation between father and daughter regarding it
is, after all, as unseen by us as it is by Charles, and the bride remains impassive at
the wedding and the morning after. Of Emma's motivation here, that is, we know
only that she has no other pressing interests. And this means only that the subsequent event *could* follow upon the first—not that it was in any sense probable. The
events of convent, farm, and marriage are related only by the link of temporal
succession: first one thing happens, then the next. (Charles' reactions here, as
always, are a lack of reactions—all based on the fact that he understands nothing,
sees nothing. And this should no more be confused with insensitivity than Emma's
lack of a motivation for acting should be confused with boredom—for it represents
the absence of an entire faculty, not a defect in an extant one.)

Since Emma was never in love with Charles, she is in no position to fall out of
love with him; her relation with another man is not (causally) produced by her
married life—instead, once again, it merely follows upon it. She falls in love with
Léon because, so to say, he is there in the novel to fall in love with. For this is the
first swing of her pendulum of passions that is the pattern of her life. It is followed
by a swing in the opposite direction: she becomes domestic, virtuous. (The oscil-
lations are not so wide now as they later become, the extremes of her behavior
less extreme.) At this point Léon grows discouraged, and leaves; Rodolphe reaps
what Léon, as well as the guest at the ball, have sown. And when Léon returns to
Emma's life it is only to carry out the pattern of this same oscillation which Emma
had in the meantime already lived out with Rodolphe.

At no point, however, do we have a sense of *why* things happen. We can, to
be sure, always identify that which—using Aristotelean terms—we may call the
efficient cause, but never the final one. That is, given that things do happen, we can
give the reasons why they have done so. What we cannot do, however, is explain
why they *should* do so, or predict for the future. And this substitution by Flaubert
of a series of efficient causes for a final one contributes to the production of what
I am calling the "plot-effect." If, for example, we ask why it was that Emma was
seduced by Rodolphe, we may give the efficient causes: his position, the smell of his
haircream, the fact that he is an attractive male. What we cannot answer is the
question of why Emma is susceptible to *this* seduction, at *this* time. Why does she
retreat into virtue at the end of the affair? The efficient cause is surely her disgust

with Charles' bungling of the club-foot operation. But why should exasperation with Charles produce *this* result, *this* swing back of the pendulum? It is this question which is never posed and never answered. The same is true of the affair with Léon: after the carriage ride, she regrets and becomes virtuous. Why? We cannot say. For she hasn't hesitated to compromise herself with Rodolphe, and not for a moment did she feel guilty about it. The answer seems to be merely: because the choices at any one time are limited to the two extremes of virtue and vice, and we have not had the latter in a while.

The character-effect with respect to Emma's two lovers is produced by a similar combination of opposites. Clearly Rodolphe is somewhat brutal—made so, Flaubert suggests, by his contacts with the demi-monde. Yet he is clearly involved emotionally with Emma, and he too has a capacity for tenderness—both of which are suggested by the scene in the moonlight before their projected flight. But his drops of water for tears on the final letter, as well as this letter's ruthlessly rational composition, represent the opposite trait of brutality. So too for Léon, who also seems simply a combination of admirable and despicable (or at least pitiable) traits. Playing a role, happy to have "une vraie maîtresse" yet also involved emotionally, he is at once both exploiter and exploited. The equivalent for Léon of Rodolphe's letter is his engagement to another woman, which takes place off stage, and enters the action only in the form of the printed announcement.

In effect, Emma has the same affair twice. To be sure, Flaubert manages to give this repetition what seems to be the overall connection of a logic tighter than that of mere temporality by limiting the affairs to two (so that the second "re-writes" the first to an appreciable degree, as a third or subsequent ones would not), by the trick of framing one around the other, and by suggesting that she has begun to tire of the second as she had not done of the first. Yet though Flaubert may tell us that she is tiring (just as he tells us earlier that she is bored with her life)—this does not mean that we need believe it; no character in fiction forgets sooner than Emma, or learns less from more experiences. And through this relatively slight formal re-arrangement of material the pendulum of involvement and withdrawal ticks back and forth. We can, in fact, imagine it ticking through a third affair, a fourth, a hundredth. For if Emma is capable of forgetting the first affair enough to have a second one, why is she not capable of a hundred and first? It seems that she dies simply because she has had affairs with all the available men that Flaubert has introduced, and because she has nowhere else to borrow money—given that her relations with the outside world are defined in terms of these two means of contact. The logical possibilities are exhausted, so the heroine must disappear.

There is yet another phenomenon in the book that contributes to the sense that we are, in fact, dealing with a coherent human being in Emma: the alteration of divergent narrative points of view offered in the text with no attempt at rec-onciliation. For this bundling together of points of view encourages us further to fill in the vacant areas between them, to ascribe knowledge to characters who have none and logic to situations that lack it. An example of this is the passage where Flaubert describes Emma's reading in the convent as a child (35–36). First we are made conscious of the book as an object by a reference to it in physical relation to Emma's body, as if from a point in the air not far from her face: "Elle frémissait, en soulevant de son haleine le papier de soie des gravures." We then move to the objects portrayed in the picture: "C'était, derrière la balustrade d'un balcon, un jeune homme" and so on; upon this follows a summarizing, non-physical description passage where we have a précis of both the portrayed world and the fact of its portrayal in Emma's: "ou bien les portraits anonymes des ladies anglaises à boucles blondes". At this point the sentence takes on the air of being mere objective fact, offered in present tense and in the second person: "qui vous regardent avec leurs grands yeux clairs" and so on. We then find ourselves once again on the level of perception, but one offered in a grammatical impersonal: "On en voyait d'etalées dans des voitures, glissant au milieu des parcs" etc. And the passage which follows continues in this constant alteration of pictured world and the manner of picturing— fingers that are turned up like pointed slippers, the virgin forest that is (an ironic aside) "bien nettoyée"—and the subsequent paragraph ends up back in Emma's room where the dormitory is silent and the light falls from the lamp over her head.

The most important result of this flickering point of view is that by following it we acquire a great deal of knowledge about Emma's situation. Moreover we get this knowledge, so to say, on the sly—so that we are encouraged to forget that Emma does not know as much as we. And it is this that contributes to the illusion of a substantial character. This is perhaps clearest during the moment when Emma, realizing that Léon is growing weary of her, sits by the convent wall and regrets her childhood (263–64): "Elle n'était pas heureuse, ne l'avait jamais été. D'où venait donc cette insuffisance de la vie, cette pourriture instantanée des choses où elle s'appuyait?" Up to this point in the text we can imagine that these sentences are an indirect discourse rendering of her thoughts, taking over from the direct quote ("se disait-elle") of the preceding paragraph. But finally the paragraph arrives at the following sentence: "Chaque sourire cachait un bâillement d'ennui, chaque joie une malédiction, tout plaisir son dégoût, et les meilleurs baisers ne vous laissaient sur la levre qu'une irréalisible envie d'une volupté plus haute." And by this time it is clear that we have left Madame Bovary's head and are in another world entirely— though, because of the progression of the paragraph from direct discourse, to indirect, to an abstract level, we are unlikely to be aware of having done so. The result is that we half-attribute these reflections to Emma, almost believe her to be a creature that can change from within rather than being subject to (because defined by) the merciless force of chance.

Jean Rousset has analysed this phenomenon; some of his observations are similar to my own. For example, he points out that in the processes of shifting the point of view "Flaubert at times fills out Charles's usual perceptions, just as he sometimes puts in Emma's mind reflections or shades of irony that couldn't possibly be hers" (444). Yet Rousset explains this mixing of points of view as the effect of Flaubert's alternations between the structure of, on one hand, the traditional novel and, on the other, the anti-novel that it seems he wanted to write—his discovery during the act of writing that he was "the greatest novelist of inaction, of ennui, of stagnation" (457). From my point of view, however, it seems unlikely that this can be the almost accidental result of something that crept up on the author unawares, given its major role in the production of the so rigorously produced character-effect in the work. This effect seems far too calculated and, under the circumstances, logical, to be merely the result of misjudgement on Flaubert's part.

Erich Auerbach makes a similar point about what Emma knows and does not know, though also with different conclusions from mine. He is considering the scene where Emma sits with Charles at table and is overwhelmed with disgust. He quotes Flaubert, then comments: *"Toute l'amertume de l'existence lui semblait servie sur son assiette*—she doubtless has such feelings, but if she wanted to express it, it would not come out like that; she has neither the intelligence nor the cold candor of self-accounting necessary for such a formulation" (484). Auerbach, that is, agrees that the expression of these things is beyond Emma, that it represents a point of view out of her reach. Yet his argument, as I suggested above, is that this very fact characterizes Emma's life, and her character. His commentary on this passage continues as follows: "The way in which language here lays bare the . . . very wretchedness of [her] life . . . excludes the idea of true tragedy . . . she is always being tried, judged, and . . . condemned" (490). Yet I think Auerbach is being too forgiving, too ready to explain. Flaubert does in fact clearly say *it seemed to Madame Bovary* that all the bitterness of existence, and so on. It will not do to have so ready as justification, for the fact that it can seem nothing of the kind, that Flaubert is condemning Mme Bovary for not doing what he says she is in fact doing.

It is the loyalty of these commentators to the notion that Mme Bovary is the simulacrum of a coherent human being that I perceive to be the greatest flaw in their analyses. Commentators influenced by Lacan, such as Tony Tanner, take the same point of departure (unsurprisingly: Lacan was, after all, a psychologist). This seems most easily shown in one of Tanner's parenthetical asides: "If we may speak in Sartrean terms for a moment we may say that Emma yearns towards a dream of Being engendered by the Nothingness of her existence and experience—the vagueness of the terms is itself a part and symptom of her plight" (338). *Emma yearns, her plight:* we are still in the realm of an analysis of character and situation that presupposes a coherence, on the personal level, in Emma's incoherence. Moreover, Tanner's treatment of the oscillation between extremes of Emma's actions, which I have been considering here, is in psychological terms as well (308).

Our experience in reading this book is one of passivity: if at any point we put our finger in the novel and look up, we stop the action utterly. This, I proposed, was the result of the fact that the characters are merely a bundling together of opposite qualities, their actions merely an alternation between extremes. The best way to take account of these facts is by considering the book as an essay in seduction. For in the situation of seduction, neither the object nor the originator (subject) of the relation need be defined off from the other—cannot, in fact, be so defined if the relation is to continue—and neither of these, in turn, can be defined off from the sentiment that links them. (In a Lacanian analysis of language of desire we at least have a clear notion of what it is we lack.) Certainly no particular action towards the attainment of the goal is implied, for action requires both separating out the goal and conceptualizing the distance between ourselves and it—a distance which we may then set about removing. The distance itself, however, must remain, ill-defined though the components may be; when there is no longer any distance between the poles of a situation of seduction the relation is at an end.

In my consideration above I repeatedly asked "why?" If we continue using "wh-" words in questions we may compile a list of some of the principal sorts of seduction—all of which are to be found in *Madame Bovary*. First, there is seduction of place—which answers the question *where?*—produced when we imagine in- herently other a place, a country, or a way of life linked to these. Secondly, we may find seductive a time other than that in which we are situated (answering the question *when?*), thus fixating either on the future as a time inherently better or more beautiful than the present, or losing ourselves in the past as a never-to-be- repeated idyll. Third, there is seduction by *what* we are not, as adolescents and children have crushes on people simply because they are adults, or dress well, or have a position they admire—or as we imagine certain situations, positions in life to be inherently more attractive than our own. Last—though not of course least— there is sexual seduction, which I view as seduction by *whom* we are not. For sex (I avoid a lengthy consideration of the psychology and philosophy of sex) is at least to some extent based on our narrowing of the distance between ourselves and a being which is at once complementary to ourselves and irrevocably Other, a being that defines us, limits us—and at the same time completes us.

Now, all of these are situations where the half-attained, the half-ourselves- and-half-other, is held (for greater or lesser periods) in a state of tension. And this, from the point of view of the person in the relation of seduction, means: held from us by constraints as various as our age and sex, the geography of our position on the globe, the strictures of our society, or the ineluctable nature of time itself which moves in one direction only. Thus we may proceed to a consideration of the relevance of these types of seduction in the case of Emma Bovary by considering the things which constrain her. To these we will find corresponding a list of things (as best they can be differentiated from their situations) which seduce her. (This correspondence will hardly be on a one-to-one basis, since it is her situation as a whole that ultimately constrains her in all its aspects.) In no particular order, then, I suggest the following list of those factors which constrain, confine, and render unhappy that most unhappy of modern heroines.

First, Emma is out of place physically. In a word, she is far too pretty for her surroundings, not as much the *paysanne* as would be appropriate in a world still defined by a correspondence between rank (and the freedom from manual labor it implied) and physical beauty. This fact is remarked by Rodolphe as well as by the marquis who invites the Bovarys to the ball. Second, she is out of place with her tastes and refinements. These tastes were partly acquired at the convent; partly, it seems, they are her natural inclination. (It is, after all, her flourishes with house and table that Charles finds so devastating.) Third, she does not love her husband, and feels both his presence in the house and her role as his wife to be a constraint. (We may legitimately ask if she could have loved any husband—but the answer to this is the same as that given repeatedly above: we do not know.) Fourth, she hates small towns, and is forced to live in one. Fifth, there is the suggestion that Emma may find monogamy itself constraining—which in turn is linked to the sixth sort of constraint, namely, that Emma finds being a woman in itself limiting. Both of these last find expression in her thoughts concerning the birth of her daughter: a man, she reflects, is free; when she is displeased with Léon she thinks that he is "mou comme une femme". And her fascination with the act of breaking marital bonds is evident ("J'ai un amant! J'ai un amant!").

Thus with these constraints in mind, we can list some of the seduction to which Emma is prey. Clearly she is seduced by place. She dreams constantly of the two paradigmatic dream-lands of the Romantics, Scotland and Italy, and fantasizes her life with Rodolfe in a haze of crags and fountains, fruit and fishermen worthy of the worst of Byron. Nor need she look so far: Paris seems heaven itself, even Rouen possesses at first an air of the mystical and mythical. And if we are interested in co-ordinating constraints with seductions, we may see here elements of four and five from the list above, as well as possible traces of two.

Second, she is seduced by time: she (like all Romantics) is taken by the Age of Chivalry; she dreams of her own childhood, or she dreams of the future with Rodolphe, of a second ball, of something, anything, that is to happen—like Prufrock, waiting for a knock upon the door. Time past and time future—both seem desirable. Third, she is seduced by position, by the (asexual) sense of what people are. This is clear in her reaction to the drooling old duke at the ball, as well as (to a large extent) to the tenor Lagardy—which kind of seduction, moreover, plays a role at least conceptually separable from the sexual one in her two affairs. She gives in to Rodolphe because his hair has the same smell as that of the guests at the ball, and gives in to Léon as a partial transference of her feelings for the tenor. Thus each of the two sexual affairs (and we may call sexual seduction the fourth sort of seduction) is mediated by a seduction of position.

The fifth sort of seduction operative here is that of art itself—or at least, of its romantic, dreamy variety. This is one of the most critically remarked varieties of seduction at work here, to the point where we frequently forget that by the time Emma agrees to marry Charles, she has voluntarily put away the books to which she was addicted, finding them tiring. To be sure, the subsequent opera and ball each have about them some of the elements of this seduction by art and artifice—but at some point this dissolves into other sorts of seduction relations: we recall that Emma has already become bored with the second act of *Lucia* in the presence of Léon. Thus this sort of seduction does play a role in the work, but it is just as clearly only one sort of seduction among many. And lastly, it is clear that for a time in her childhood Emma was seduced by the crystalline perfection of the world of religion—or at least by its visual and tangible manifestations. This too has received more than its fair share of attention, undoubtedly because of the ironic contrast between crude piety and the intellectual pretensions of religion found more strongly in other works of Flaubert (for example "Un Cœur Simple").

Thus my claim is that Emma is not a character with a personality at all, but rather a walking textbook of seductions. It is this fact which, I suggest, is the source of our problems in conceptualizing as discrete entities either the character or her actions—for the first takes definition from the second; neither can be separated from the other. On the other hand, I think it is undeniable that if we feel nothing else for Emma, we feel at least sympathy—and that this is the source of what is after all our great willingness to follow the exploits of a creature otherwise so vacuous. But this is as it should be. For seductions imply constraints, and it is with the *constraints* limiting Emma that we sympathize, not with the character so limited. In fact, I would suggest that we feel these constraints the more acutely precisely because of the vacuity of that which they constrain.

The work gives us, thus, the outlines of actions, the skeletons of persons, and a game of connect-the-dots for actions; it is an airy world of girders and armatures rather than even the constructions of people. Yet this too is as it should be, precisely because it is a world defined by seduction—the book an essay upon it. Commentators like Auerbach and Tanner see Emma as a fly caught in a spider's web of society and the world around her. Instead, I think she is herself the diaphanous threads, her motions merely tremblings in the wind as of the web itself, her life its own prison: that force field of locked longing and frozen wants, that purgatory of desire unenunciated which constitutes seduction.

WORKS CITED

Auerbach, Erich. *Mimesis: The Representation of Reality in Western Literature.* Princeton: Princeton UP, 1953.

Chatman, Seymour. *Story and Discourse: Narrative Structure in Fiction and Film.* Ithaca: Cornell UP, 1978.

Flaubert, Gustave. *Madame Bovary.* Paris: Garnier, 1961.

Forster, E. M. *Aspects of the Novel.* New York: Harcourt, Brace, and World, 1927.

Girard; René. *Deceit, Desire, and the Novel: Self and Other in Literary Structure.* Baltimore: Johns Hopkins UP, 1965.

Lacan, Jacques. "Desire and the Interpretation of Desire in *Hamlet.*" *Yale French Studies* 55/56 (1977): 11–52.

Rousset, Jean. "*Madame Bovary:* Flaubert's Anti-Novel; An Aspect of Flaubert's Technique: Point of View." *Madame Bovary: Backgrounds and Sources, Essays in Criticism.* Paul de Man, ed. New York: Norton, 1965. 439–457.

Tanner, Tony. *Adultery in the Novel: Contract and Transgression.* Baltimore: Johns Hopkins UP, 1979.

William VanderWolk

MEMORY AND THE TRANSFORMATIVE ACT IN *MADAME BOVARY*

As Flaubert moved from the first *L'Education sentimentale* toward the production of *Madame Bovary,* memory acquired a more complex role in his work. The
movement begun in his early twenties from autobiography to the elimination of
personal memories culminated in *Madame Bovary,* the ultimate impersonal novel.
Paradoxically, Flaubert became even more concerned with his own interior existence as evidenced in his travel notes and in *La Tentation de Saint Antoine.* Rather
than a separation of author and work, we see a fusion of the two that obliterates
the visibility of the man and solidifies his presence in the work. Instead of searching
for clues to understanding in Flaubert's biography, the reader must now rely
primarily on the texts themselves. This was certainly Flaubert's intention in statement on authorial presence. The personal memories became completely transformed into fiction.

In *L'Education sentimentale* it was already clear that memory as a theme had
become an increasingly important substitute for authorial visibility. In *Madame
Bovary* memory is an essential structural device as well as a principal theme of the
novel. As chronological time passes, Emma clings increasingly to the past for sustenance, and with each successive disillusionment, her nostalgia for the past increases. Emma's fascination with and dependence on the past recalls Flaubert's own
and thus provides the reader with a clear indication of the author's involvement in
his character.

Emma is never allowed to escape her past in favor of the present. She is
continuously drawn back to memories of her youthful readings of romance and
intrigue just as she is haunted by the blind beggar and his song of love and death.
By looking at themes related to memory, idealization of the past, the destructive
nature of time, confusion of past and present, the illusory quality of memory that
results in *bovarysme* and doubling, one sees that memory is a vital thread in the
weave of the novel and a clear link with the author himself.

From *Flaubert Remembers: Memory and the Creative Experience* (New York: Peter Lang, 1990), pp.
67–129 (abridged).

Finally, memory guides us to the overriding theme of Flaubert's major novels: literature supercedes life. For Flaubert, the beauty and truth of literature were superior to daily life, yet the attempt to craft the real world in the mold of literature produced nothing but despair. A life based on literary models was not spontaneous but derivative and, therefore, fundamentally unfulfilling. The role of both memory and art in the lives of the characters and in Flaubert's own life illustrates this theme. While Emma is able to become the heroine of the romantic novels she remembers from her youth, Flaubert, through his memory, creates characters into whom he can disperse himself. The metaphysical planes on which they operate, however, yield opposing results: Emma is destroyed by self-delusion while Flaubert has become immortal. Although memories may create great fiction, fictional memories as the basis of existence create only chaos. By actually entering the work, Flaubert necessarily gives it substance as well as form and transforms *Madame Bovary* from "un livre sur rien" into a novel of form *and* ideas.

From the beginning of *Madame Bovary,* despite Flaubert's assertions to the contrary, it is clear that Flaubert's own memories will come into play in the novel. The very setting of the story injects a personal note into the work, for Flaubert's contempt for country life rivalled Emma's. He tells Louise Colet about growing up in the country: "Nous étions, il y a quelques années, en province, une pléïade de jeunes drôles qui vivions dans un étrange monde.... Nous tournions entre la folie et le suicide. Il y en a qui se sont tués... plusieurs qui se sont fait crever de débauche pour chasser l'ennui" (*Corr.* II, 15). However exaggerated a picture of Flaubert's youth, this description reveals an attitude about the country and about his past, and such negative memories remained with him throughout his life.

In the same letter, written in 1851, Flaubert reveals his desire to write about that past which he has just described: "Si jamais je sais écrire, je pourrai faire un livre sur cette jeunesse inconnue, qui poussait à l'ombre, dans la retraite, comme des champignons gonflés d'ennui. Le secret de tout ce qui vous étonne, chère Louise, est dans ce passé de ma vie interne que personne ne connaît" (*Corr.* II, 15). *Madame Bovary* is not, strictly speaking, the story of Flaubert's youth, but it is the story of the crushing boredom he knew as a youth, an ennui always associated in his memory with the country.

Flaubert thus undertook, at the urging of Maxime du Camp and Louis Bouilhet, an exercise in style, a more realistic work than his previous one, *La Tentation de Saint Antoine.* Flaubert was determined to put none of himself into the novel, but coming to the work with the memories cited above, Flaubert could not avoid personal inclusion. He states his goal as: "Nul lyrisme, pas de réflexions, personnalité de l'auteur absente ..." (*Corr.* II, 40), but after one year of work, he admits: "C'est difficile d'exprimer bien ce qu'on n'a jamais senti" (*Corr.* II, 180). In spite of his efforts to use imagination as his only source of material and inspiration, his memory remained a potent creative force without which his imagination would not function. Just as Jules "n'est lumineux qu'à cause du contraste d'Henry" (*Corr.* II, 29), Flaubert's imagination is fertilized by his memory.

Memory and the Dictates of Desire

From the beginning of the novel, it is clear that Flaubert has endowed Emma with his own disdain for the emptiness of country life: "Elle eût bien voulu, ne fût-ce au moins que pendant l'hiver, habiter la ville, quoique la longueur des beaux jours rendît peut-être la campagne plus ennuyeuse encore durant l'été..." (I, 582). Although Flaubert sequestered himself at Croisset to write, it was not the bucolic peacefulness of the countryside that drew him but the utter isolation from humanity that the provinces afforded. Emma, on the other hand, marries Charles, in part, to escape the monotonous routine of her father's farm. That which she desires is elsewhere. But once in Yonville, she is quickly disillusioned by the mediocrity of her new life and by her husband, whose answer to everything seems to be "c'est bien assez bon pour la campagne" (I, 588). It is perhaps good enough for the country but not for her.

It is not surprising that Emma attempts to compensate for the emptiness of her present by projecting herself into a world of dreams and desires. But the formulation of her desires is based on deceit. Instead of particularizing her own needs, she uses an Other to form her desires. René Girard in *Deceit, Desire, and the Novel,* finds Emma guilty of "external mediation" (9), allowing literary characters to be the models of her desire. In the famous chapter devoted to Emma's life at the convent school, Flaubert describes her introduction to Romantic novels. An old woman tells the girls stories, sings them "des chansons galantes du siècle passé," and reads to them from novels containing an endless series of "amours, amants, amantes" (I, 586).

Emma begins reading these novels on her own because they respond to the needs of her character. She is portrayed as "plus sentimentale qu'artiste, cherchant des émotions et non des paysages" (I, 586). Her reading is not the cause of her sentimentality but a logical extension of it. As Ion Collas correctly points out, the influence of art on character is "negligible. Books may function as outlets for pre-existing tendencies, may even help shape aspirations that have germinated in the psyche. But they are not capable of producing desires *ex nihilo,* still less character traits, a whole attitude toward life" (13). The illusions of her reading afford the emotional variety, adventures, and personal satisfaction which her convent life lacks. It is later, when the memory of these readings becomes the focus of her desire, that Emma relinquishes her own personality and becomes the disciple of fictional desires.

The canon of Emma's reading is virtually an historic array of the movement of Romantic literature, from the primitive idyll of *Paul et Virginie* to the historical events of Sir Walter Scott to the fictionalized character of Mademoiselle de la Vallière in Dumans' *Le Vicomte de Bragelonne.* In each fiction she finds a catalyst for her own image making, finding herself, as Léon is later to say, "mêlée aux personnages; il semble que c'est vous qui palpitez sous leurs costumes" (I, 602). History also presents Emma an image of ideal eras populated by glorified figures and it is in these figures that she finds a model. Joan of Arc, Agnès Sorel, Héloïse,

La Belle Ferronière are all women whose deaths and loves—whether of God or man—propelled them into the realms of "félicité, de passion, et d'ivresse" (I, 586) that Emma so eagerly seeks. Her image of fiction and history is sustained in music and art as she sings melodies that afford a glimpse of "l'attirante fantasmagorie des réalités sentimentales" (I, 587) and gazes at hidden prints of exotic scenes populated by idealized lovers in medieval garb. Like Frédéric Moreau of L'Education sentimentale, her adolescent desires have their foundation in these art forms, and she devotes herself to their worship, never acknowledging the distance that exists between herself and the fictional heroines. Emma's will is stronger than Frédéric's, however, for while he accepts the deceit of one illusion and moves on to the next dream, she, "a woman subject to the influence of an unresolved past" (Collas 53), abandons herself to the worship of her fictional models.

The repercussions of Emma's adolescent reading in her adult life are different from the effect of Romantic novels on Frédéric or, indeed, on Flaubert. Unlike them, her dreams are passive; theirs, initially, are active. She wishes to be written as the heroine; they wish to create. She creates none of her fantasies. For Girard, Emma has surrendered "the individual's fundamental prerogative: [choosing] the objects of his own desire" (1). Without controlling the source of her desire, Emma allows the emotion of created fiction to control her.

Although Naomi Schor agrees that Emma practices "external mediation" in her desire to transform the read word into lived experience, she proposes Emma to be "the portrait of an artist, but the artist as a young woman" (15). Through the love letters she writes, using the epistolary form of eighteenth-century novels as her model, Emma seeks not a lover but literary fame. Thus, Schor explains, what Emma "lacks in order to write are neither words nor pen but a phallus" (17). What I also propose she lacks are essential characteristics that allow Flaubert, using similar raw materials, to become an author: the differentiation between self and fictional memory and the impersonality of the written text. Her sex and her sensibility are what render Emma a failed artist and maintain her role as a character rather than a creator.

Emma's appearance as a character in a novel is a recurring motif in the work, and she is not the only one who sees herself in that role. Léon, equally as sentimental as Emma, has the same vision: ". . . elle allait rappelant en lui mille désirs, évoquant des instincts ou des réminiscences. Elle était l'amoureuse de tous les romans, l'héroïne de tous les drames, le vague 'elle' de tous les volumes de vers" (I, 664). Léon, like Emma, takes the figure of reality and metamorphoses it into Art. Ironically enough his desire for her effectively dissects her into portions, each of which has an artistic equivalent. He rediscovers the hues of Ingres' "Odalisque au Bain" in her shoulders, the waist of the feudal chatelaines Emma envied in her convent fantasies in Emma's slender torso, the Romantic figure of Musset's "Femme Pâle de Barcelone" in her appearance. He transforms her from the living into a legend: ". . . elle était par-dessus tout Ange!" (I, 664). Yet Léon's poetic imagination does not outlast his bourgeois desire for comfort. As he changes his desires from metaphors to mundane matters, he abandons Emma in the realm of illusion.

There is no place for Emma in the present. Even in her moments of greatest happiness when it seems as if she has found one of the "certains lieux sur la terre [qui] devaient produire de bonheur" (I, 588), she sees herself in a fictional world, a world that is very much a part of her past. Emma's inability to capture or be captured in the present is a problem Flaubert saw as afflicting everyone: "Le Passé nous mange trop. Nous ne sommes jamais au Présent qui seul est important dans la vie" (*Corr.* II, 413). Flaubert set about seizing a piece of the present by stopping time through art, but even he felt that his life was not confined to its spatial and temporal limits. He occasionally thought of himself as reincarnated, not from an unknown life but from a life he had read about. He calls such a sensation "le frisson historique."

In *L'Education sentimentale* Madame Arnoux makes Frédéric the central character of a novel, but the situation differs from Emma's. Madame Arnoux fictionalizes her desire for Frédéric, using the heroes of her reading as a guide. She does so because her desires cannot be fulfilled in the real world. Emma, on the other hand, finds the physical expression of her desire in the sensual pleasure of loving Rodolphe and Léon. But her emotional desires, created by her readings, are unsatisfied in her present reality and lead her back to her memories. Psychoanalysts see such regression as a normal function of the human mind. Otto Fenichel writes: "Whenever a person meets a frustration, there is a tendency for him to long for earlier periods in his life when his experiences were more pleasant, and for earlier types of satisfaction that were more complete" (159).

Both Emma and Frédéric Moreau depend on Art as a means of ego-fulfillment. In doing so, however, they rely on the reality of their lives in different ways. For Madame Arnoux, fiction or image-making offers a substitution for a denied reality. She uses the outer world as a framework for a representation of her inner desires in fiction. While she does so, she recognizes the illusion of her fiction-making. Emma, on the other hand, avoids the usual process of mimesis. Instead of the outer reality providing a framework to which the fictive reality of Art is compared, Emma's reading becomes a presence of its own, a reality divorced from the framework of life. Emma illustrates the threats of the imagination as "essentially always a cliche, since it articulates the real by impoverishing it—however rich or extravagant its articulations may be" (Bersani 167). For Emma the literature, art, and music of her youth constitute the reality and frame by which she judges life. Reality becomes a poor substitute for a denied ideal. The relational framework between reality and the illusion of art has become reversed. Hallucination has closed the gap between the real and the text, just as Félicité's map of Cuba represented the actual island to her. That which is true is written; that which is lived is not real until it is transformed into a written framework.

As Emma pursues her metaphysical desire, memory becomes the agent of transformation. It acts as a sense of detachment—artistic detachment from the experience—which allows that experience to retreat into time. The imagination, then, is able to recreate that moment of past time within the framework of her ideal. The abstractions of experience are transmuted by memory into the concrete images of her desire. Memory, in Emma's terms, is an agent of destruction and renewal. The more her framework of life relies on the deceptions of Art, the more detached from reality she becomes. Yet at the same time, her memory, which is the repository of her written framework, provides the necessary catalyst to turn experience into meaningful existence.

The Transformation of Reality

Love does not become concrete until Emma has given it a written manifestation. Just as Frédéric and Madame Arnoux's love was based on what is or is not said between them, Emma finds a way to strengthen and, in a sense, legitimize her love for Rodolphe and Léon through past novels, exchanged letters, and even prayer. By placing her love in an artistic context, it is transformed from the abstract into the concrete. Although her feelings of love are authentic in the present, a gap remains between Emma and the concept, and consequently, she wonders whether she has found true love. Once memory provides a framework and once the feelings have become part of a word-construct (novel, letter, prayer), the gap between Emma and her love disappears, and she becomes convinced of its reality.

Emma, the voracious reader of novels does not attempt to write one, as Frédéric and Flaubert do. Instead, she depends on letters to express her feelings on paper. Throughout her affairs with both Rodolphe and Léon, she exchanges letters with her lovers in order to bridge their physical separation; but the letters also serve the important purpose of concretizing their love in Emma's mind. Thus, it is significant that Rodolphe chooses to end their relationship with a letter. It is an act of cowardice, but it is also more devastating to Emma than the spoken word would have been. If Rodolphe had said the words to her, her emotions would have preserved the distance between her and reality and she might easily have denied hearing the words. As she has not denied the possibilities of her adolescent reading, she cannot deny the written word. Rodolphe's letter drives her to the brink of suicide.

Letters play an even larger role in Emma's liaison with Léon for she uses them not only to render the love real but to prolong it after it has waned. After the first passion dies and she finds in adultery "toutes les platitudes du mariage" (I, 672), she continues to write to him out of habit. In her writing, Léon takes on a new dimension, becoming a fictional character composed from her memories and her reading: ". . . en écrivant, elle percevait un autre homme, un fantôme fait de ses plus ardents souvenirs, de ses lectures les plus belles, de ses convoitises les plus fortes" (I, 672). Even though she cannot clearly imagine him in this blue dreamworld, she feels as close to him as ever and closer than she has in some time. When she finishes the letter, ". . . elle retombait à plat, brisée; car ces élans d'amour vague la fatiguaient plus que de grandes débauches" (I, 672). Not only does this phantom lover mean more than Léon, but her written union exhausts her more than actual lovemaking. Her memory and imagination, reinforced by her reading, have transformed him into the ideal lover. She is seduced by her creation rather than by the man.

Emma's transformation of Léon in her letters parallels Flaubert's rendering of his memories in literature. Just as Léon is more interesting as a vague entity, Flaubert's vague memories are often the richest source of literary material. In her analysis of Flaubert's "mémoire vulgaire et créatrice," Bollème writes: "Ce n'est pas tant le souvenir de sa vie qui l'intéresse, mais plutôt, ce qui est différent ... [cela crée] un regret qui précisément efface le souvenir précis et la chose, pour les faire renaître l'un et l'autre plus vivace et plus vraie" (40). This new reality grows not out of the memory of an object or event but out of its combination with other memories. That which Flaubert retrieves from his memory is an impression, an impression which, for him, remains incomplete until it is transformed into words. For Emma, the process is the same: the real lover leaves her unsatisfied, but the reconstructed "fantôme" fulfills her desires.

The concretization of memory through words is taken to the extreme when Emma turns to religion for comfort after Rodolphe has abandoned her. The details of Rodolphe fade but the desire remains, and Emma readjusts her external mediator from the legions of adulterous women to the religious heroines of her convent reading. Using prayer as the new language, Emma's imagination tailors her memories to suit her desires. In memory, through the power of imagination fired by her desire, she can constantly enjoy the sensations she seeks, for remembered objects can be changed to resemble objects of desire. To find a substitute ecstasy in faith that she found in Rodolphe's arms, she murmurs to God the same words she used with her lover.

Emma does in fact create a new world, but in the absence of a direct response from God, she must build her religious world around her memories of reading and lost love: "Emma se comparait à ces grandes dames d'autrefois ... qui ... se retiraient en des solitudes pour y répandre aux pieds du Christ toutes les larmes d'un coeur que l'existence blessait" (I, 647). These images of women link her current conversion to her days of adolescent religious fervor in the convent at Rouen. She is transported to the times when "elle avait rêvé la gloire sur un portrait de La Vallière" (I, 647) in the small inn outside the convent which used painted china depicting scenes from the life of Louis XIV's mistress. The chipped and fading plates glorified religion and associated it with "les délicatesses de coeur et les pompes de la Cour" (I, 586). Before the fictions of the Romantic novels, Emma had been seduced by the drama of religion even to the extent of fictionalizing sins in order to prolong her time in the confessional. As she had used religion as the mediator to satisfy her adolescent cravings. Emma turns to religion and the words of prayers to replace amorous sensations that had been provided by her liaison with Rodolphe.

Emma's life, then, follows a pattern that Flaubert clearly developed, both here and in other works such as *Novembre* and the two *Education sentimentale*. The protagonist, bored with youth and country life, dreams of a new life of love, adventure, and fulfillment. Imagination is aided by reading novels and historical accounts. In reality, however, life destroys all of his youthful illusions. Through memories, the protagonist is able to recreate reality in an attempt to find some meaning in her life, but such attempts inevitably fail. The realization of the failure of her life again comes through memories of that life which has been a series of disappointments. Once they have come to such an impasse, Flaubert's protagonists cope with it in varying ways: Emma commits suicide; the protagonist of *Novembre* dies for no apparent reason, presumably without a fight; and Frédéric Moreau accepts his lot. Only Jules finds an active way out of life's emptiness: he, like Flaubert, turns to artistic creation as a means of expressing his memories, and through them, finds meaning in his life.

Many of Flaubert's protagonists attempt to create Art; all but Jules fail. The protagonist of *Novembre* writes the story of his youth but at a certain point finds nothing more to say; Emma paints and plays the piano, but her "piano lessons" are an excuse to rendezvous with Léon in Rouen; Frédéric renounces writing, music, and painting out of laziness and the frustration of not being able to capture the ideal, either in life or in Art. The inevitable end of these artistic ventures is failure since none of the characters wishes to create a reality apart from himself. Instead of putting their reconstituted memories on paper or canvas, they try to live through them so that their acts of imaginative creating are acts of self-transformation. Yet unlike fiction or creations of art, personal re-creation is subject to the mutability of time. Thus, when Frédéric and Emma wish to immobilize their life in an act of creative fiction-making, they fail, since the present, always in the process of be-coming the past, does not allow the creation the temporal immutability afforded fiction. ⟨. . .⟩

The Transubstantiation of Time

The inevitable result of a concentrated effort on the part of Flaubert's char-acters to unify past and present is a confusion of the two of them. Throughout Flaubert's works, characters mix past and present, memories and hopes, dream and reality. Such confusion is particularly clear in the characters who turn simulta-neously toward the past and the future since their rejection of the present affords them no clear point of delineation between past, present, and future. It is through them, Jules, Emma, and Frédéric, that Flaubert shows us the flow of time, a move-ment that cannot be halted by assigning the word "present" to a specific moment. By the time the label is affixed, the moment has passed, taking its place in the past. Just as memories color one another, the past and future color one's present and blend with it, creating a temporal melange. The present can never be isolated from that which precedes or succeeds it.

Flaubert was always conscious of the movement through life from dreams of the future to memories of the past, a movement that permitted very few moments of union between experience and consciousness. In 1852, just after the death of a friend, the artist Pradier, Flaubert reflected on this question: "Je pourrais déjà faire un volume nécrologique respectable de tous les morts que j'ai connus. Quand on est jeune, on associe la réalisation future de ses rêves aux existences qui vous entourent. A mesure que ces existences disparaissent, les rêves s'en vont" (*Corr.* II, 101). A month later, in a letter to Louis Bouilhet, he penned a maxim to describe life: "Espérer, tout est là, espérer et mourir, telle est la vie" (*Corr.* II, 133).

The flowing together of past and future reduces the present to a continuous repetition of meaningless activities. Daily activities, no matter how diverse, are only an interruption of life's important functions: dreaming, remembering, and dying. Flaubert writes to Louise Colet: "notre activité n'est qu'une répétition continuelle, quelque diversifiée qu'elle ait l'air." (*Corr.* II, 424). When one becomes aware of the gap between the present and past or future, one's very existence comes into question. Flaubert found that "Quelque chose d'indéfini vous sépare de votre propre personne et vous rive au non-être" (*Corr.* II, 424). This idea is translated in his texts through characters, such as Frédéric, who do not so much exist as remember and dream.

In *Madame Bovary* past, present, and future often mix, to the detriment of the characters' lives. Emma's dreams of the future and memories of the past both increase her unhappiness in the present. Facing the past and future at the same time, Emma condemns her present to a virtually non-existent state, and the result is a life of conflicting dreams. In the days before meeting Rodolphe, Emma, because of her nature and her reading, is trapped between fantasy and memory: "Elle avait envie de faire des voyages ou de retourner vivre à son couvent. Elle souhaitait à la fois mourir et habiter Paris" (I, 594). Unlike Charles who escapes feeling like two people by immersing himself in his present (love, work, routine), Emma is two people without a present. She is unable to capture the present because it is fleeting, and it does not hold the promise of the future or the security of the past.

Even in Emma's most triumphant moments, when it seems as if she has found the love she was seeking, the past intrudes on the present and gives it an unreal quality. At the Comices, when her desire for Rodolphe is being awakened, old desires are rekindled and the Vicomte and Léon appear in her memory: "Elle crut voir [Léon] en face, à sa fenêtre, puis tout se confondait, des nuages passèrent; il lui sembla qu'elle tournait encore dans la valse au bras du vicomte, et que Léon n'était pas loin, qu'il allait venir . . . et cependant elle sentait toujours la tête de Rodolphe à côté d'elle" (I, 624). The present, which should have been a privileged moment, the beginning of Emma's fulfillment, is reduced to a melange of sensations, past and present. We see a similar process in *L'Education sentimentale* where Frédéric often thinks of one woman while in the presence of another. By mixing present and past, the present is denigrated to the point of insignificance.

Before his marriage to Emma, Charles also occasionally found past and present blending together. During the ride to the Rouault farm to repair the farmer's leg, Charles falls in and out of sleep: "il entrait dans une sorte d'assoupissement où ses sensations récentes se confondant avec ses souvenirs, lui-même se percevait double, à la fois, étudiant et mari, couché dans son lit comme tout à l'heure, traversant une salle d'opérés comme autrefois" (I, 578). Until he meets Emma, Charles' whole life is lived in a half-slumber in which his unhappy past mixes with the dull routine of the present. After his marriage to Emma, he becomes one of the rare Flaubert characters who can thrive in the present. But even Charles is doomed to unhappiness, for the claim of his present is upset by his wife's death, and he ultimately finds himself living in the past.

There are, however, moments when past, present, and even future come together to reinforce the intensity of the present experience. When Emma and Léon find each other again in Rouen, their happiness is augmented by their memories and hopes: "Ils venaient de se joindre les mains; et le passé, l'avenir, les réminiscences et les rêves, tout se trouvait confondu dans la douceur de cette extase" (I, 654). Flaubert does not allow these moments to last, and soon the present is once again usurped by the past or the future. Emma protests that she has grown too old to fulfill her dream of loving Léon, and in a sense she is correct. Although she still possesses certain illusions, she has experienced enough that the present can never again free itself from the past. Léon also recognizes this and knows that any new relationship must take their past into account: "C'est ainsi qu'ils auraient voulu avoir été, l'un et l'autre se faisant un idéal sur lequel ils ajustaient à present leur vie passée" (I, 653). Their future together depends on reviving and attaining this past ideal, and like so many of Flaubert's characters, they will fail because of the destructive nature of time.

The pervasive and ultimately insidious role of the past is, ironically, particularly evident in beginnings. Charles' courtship of Emma consists of each one talking about the past, especially of their youth when the dreams that control Emma's adult life were born. At the Comices, Rodolphe strengthens his argument that he and Emma were meant for one another by basing their mutual attraction on the past: "Rodolphe en était venu aux affinités ... le jeune homme expliquait à la jeune femme que ces attractions irrésistibles tiraient leur cause de quelque existence antérieure" (I, 624). Each beginning is tainted by the intrusion of the past, and this foreshadows the failure of the present to stand alone and to live up to the past memories and dreams of the future.

When the past becomes too great a part of a character's life, she often tries to eliminate the memories from her consciousness. Emma plunges into marriage in order to escape the boredom of her youth in the country; Homais wants to eliminate the memory of his reprimand; Charles desperately tries not to think about the botched club-foot operation; Félicité tries to forget her lost love as fervently as Madame Aubain attempts to conserve the memory of hers. In each case, the character is unsuccessful; either the memory is too strong to be eliminated or material reminders keep it present in the character's mind.

Similarly, certain characters attempt to eliminate the history that surrounds them. Léon is assailed by the past when he and Emma meet in the Rouen cathedral. For Emma, the cathedral is the home of all of the mysteries of her faith, but for Léon, irritated by the guide's insistence, it is a place whose past threatens to rob him of his future with Emma: "Léon fuyait; car il lui semblait que son amour, qui depuis deux heures bientôt, s'était immobilisé dans l'église comme les pierres, allait maintenant s'évaporer telle qu'une fumée ..." (I, 656). The cathedral represents an immobile, historical text, "un autre livre, un livre antérieur" that Léon finds menacing (Butor 104). Léon desires to leave the context of history, indeed to leave time altogether, to allow his love to flourish. He manages to step from one temporal context to another by entering the timelessness of the fiacre, but he also is eventually brought back to temporal reality. Inevitably, time will lessen his passion for Emma, and his love will become as fixed in the past as one of the stones of the cathedral.

Flaubert experienced the same frustrations; he was continually thwarted in his attempt to eliminate himself and his past from his works. He concluded that we are a composite of what we are, what we were, and what we dream of being, and not even the dispassionate author can eliminate his memories from his work or his consciousness. He wrote to Louise Colet in 1846:

> Ne nous accrochons-nous pas toujours à notre passé si récent qu'il soit? Dans notre appétit de la vie nous remangeons nos sensations d'autrefois, nous rêvons celles de l'avenir. . . . Je me suis toujours défendu de rien mettre de moi dans mes oeuvres, et pourtant j'en ai mis beaucoup. . . . J'ai imaginé, je me suis ressouvenu et j'ai combiné. (*Corr.* I, 302).

As the author blends memory and imagination to create the material for his work, many of the characters in Flaubert's fiction do the same, not to create Art but to better cope with reality. In Emma's case, her imagination is nurtured by her reading and her boredom. In order to fill the void that is her present, she must invent a new world, one which is invariably based on her memories and dreams. After Léon's departure from Yonville, Emma depends on the memory of him for stimulation: "Dès lors, ce souvenir de Léon fut comme le centre de son ennui. Elle se précipitait vers lui et les réminiscences les plus lointaines comme les plus immédiates occasions, ce qu'elle éprouvait avec ce qu'elle imaginait . . . elle ramassait tout, prenait tout, et faisait servir tout à réchauffer sa tristesse" (I, 616).

Emma's memories are more vivid than the actual experience because of the strength of her desire and the embellishment of imagination. Imagination helps her conserve the past which fills a void in the present. The worlds Emma creates from memory and imagination are insufficient to fill the void she feels, and so the ultimate victor is the present, the empty time which, through memory or dreams, she has tried so hard to escape.

This present differs from the one that is subservient to the past and future. It is the exterior present, the character's, or indeed Flaubert's present combined with the world around him. It is the world of Homais, of Monsieur Dambreuse, a Balzacian world of routine and habit that was Flaubert's nightmare. It is the world Flaubert virtually exited in 1844, but which his characters never escape. For Flaubert "notre. activité n'est·qu'une répétition continuelle" (*Corr.* II, 423–24), and "la vie n'est tolérable qu'à la condition de n'y jamais être" (*Corr.* II, 255). Flaubert may have been able to leave the present world through his writing, but Emma, Frédéric, and Félicité must remain, and much of the tension of each work finds its source in the characters' inability to function in their own worlds.

The Present as Victor

This triumph of the real and present world is most evident in *Madame Bovary*, for Emma is rebelling against the boredom of her reality in everything she does. Her desire to travel, to escape the countryside, leads her to marry Charles; she reads and dreams to escape the tedium of Tostes and Yonville; she takes lovers as much out of boredom as desire; she commits suicide to evade the crushing reality of her life. Her present lives up to memories and dreams only in privileged moments such as the ball and her first betrayal. At the ball she begins to think of the farm where she grew up, "mais aux fulgurations de l'heure présente, sa vie passée, si nette jusqu'alors, s'évanouissait tout entière, et elle doutait presque de l'avoir vécue" (I, 592). The remainder of the time, Emma must retreat into her past in order to live because her goals do not coincide with those of the people around her.

It is those people who triumph in the world of the novel: Homais is *élu*, Emma is *exclue*. Homais trumpets his belief in "nos devoirs de citoyen et de père de famille" and in "les immortels principes de 89" (I, 600) while rejecting the mystical side of religion to which Emma clings so desperately in times of despair. Both Emma and Homais are treated ironically, as Claudine Gothot-Mersch notes in her introduction to the novel: "Flaubert ne prend point parti; il renvoie dos à dos Emma et M. Homais. . . . Il se montre impartial dans la mesure où il condamne tout le monde" (lxii). Flaubert may condemn *élus* and *exclus*, but it is the former who ultimately triumph by simply continuing their narrow lives. Flaubert reserves the grimmest irony of all for the final sentence: "Il vient de recevoir la croix d'honneur" (I, 692). Homais, the most mocked figure of all, emerges, if not triumphant, at least eternal.[2]

Emma's inability to integrate herself into her present is a problem of quantity as well as quality. The events of the present overwhelm her with their number and insignificance. After Rodolphe's departure, she becomes particularly aware of the routine nature of life in Yonville because the memories which had been a refuge are now too painful: "ce qu'elle aimait autrefois, à présent lui déplaisait. . . . Et Emma quotidiennement attendait, avec une sorte d'anxiété, l'infaillible retour d'événements minimes, qui pourtant ne lui importaient guère" (I, 646). The present, from which she has always felt excluded, nevertheless comes to dominate her existence through the sheer weight of the number of small, habitual events of which it is composed.

Emma's memories, which "semblaient élargir son existence" (I, 654), can be destroyed by the routine of everyday life. After Léon's departure for Rouen, "l'amour peu à peu s'éteignit par l'absence, le regret s'étouffa sous l'habitude ... il fut de tous côtés nuit complète, et elle demeura perdue dans un froid horrible qui la traversait" (I, 616). This victory of the present over memories and illusions is the cruelest aspect of Emma's existence. Homais' success and the failure of her lofty dreams are condemnations of the two characters and of all of us for allowing the superficial present to govern our lives. The "infaillible retour" which Emma lives daily is far from the "retour" that Jules saw in nature. For Jules, nature's cycles provided the basis for the formulation of beauty and truth, and the expectation of the rebirth of the seasons was an inspiration to create Art; but for Emma, recurrence means emptiness, and the return of each insignificant daily event brings her one step closer to death.

Diana Knight makes a valid distinction between the terms repetitious and repetitive. Repetitious words or events lose importance with each occurrence while repetitive experiences or phrases have equal or more importance each time (66). Both are present in Emma's life: the repetitious moments become dominant over the repetitive, meaningful experiences such as her Thursday meetings with Léon in Rouen. Descriptions of Emma's boredom abound in the text, while her successive disappointments in love create another type of insidious repetition. Collas writes: ". . . the composition of *Madame Bovary* is based on the inexorable repetition of one and the same experience. All the episodes of Emma's life have as their common denominator a fundamental emotional void that reconstitutes itself with almost monotonous regularity" (51).

The narration of the Thursday visits is iterative, Flaubert describing an event that took place several times. The meeting with Léon is thus valorized in its uniqueness and minimized when compared with the sheer weight of repetitious experience. The result is the crushing defeat of meaningful experience at the hands of an empty, bourgeois routine. Consequently, life becomes nothing more than the anticipation of death.

Chronological time is erosive, destroying both life and memory, and it ultimately creates in Flaubert's characters a desire for nothingness, seen in Emma's suicide. In this context memory no longer represents a means of escaping life in the present but rather a means of preserving any life at all. Because of Emma's and Frédéric's inability to find a meaningful life in the present, their desires are rarely fulfilled until it is too late. Homais finds satisfaction because his horizons are relatively limited; but Emma's vast expectations preclude any change for mundane fulfillment. When Emma and Léon begin their affair, Emma is no longer the woman whom he worshipped, and Emma has far surpassed the young law clerk in her knowledge and desires for sensual and emotional gratifcation.

The result of failed aspirations is a chasm Emma cannot fill. She and Léon are able to unite their bodies but not their minds. Flaubert explains the problem in an authorial comment from the first *Education sentimentale:*

Dans le développement comparé d'une passion, d'un sentiment, et même dans la compréhension d'une idée, l'un devance toujours l'autre, et le second est arrivé au point culminant que le premier l'a déjà dépassé ou est déjà revenu en arrière. Les âmes ne marchent pas de front commes des chevaux de carrosse attelés à la même flèche, mais plutôt elles vont l'une après l'autre, s'entrecroisant dans leur chemin, se heurtant, se quittant, et courent éperdues comme des billes d'ivoire sur un billard; on adore telle femme qui commence à vous aimer, qui vous adorera quand vous ne l'aimerez plus, et qui sera lassée de vous quand vous reviendrez à elle. L'unisson est rare dans la vie, et l'on pourrait compter le nombre des minutes où les deux coeurs qui s'aiment le mieux ont chanté d'accord. (I, 343)

This is a rather fatalistic outlook, as if Flaubert believed that the emotions of two people coincide only by chance. Indeed he did believe this, and his other works substantiate such a pessimistic view. The moments in which "deux coeurs chantent d'accord" are rare and very brief. Emma's spiritual unions are illusory. She believes that she has experienced such a privileged moment with Rodolphe, but she cannot see inside his heart. She comes closer to an "accord" with Léon, but it is more of a mutual agreement that they missed their chance when their hearts were more innocent.

As a result of unfulfilled desires, Emma compares her present unhappiness and frustration with what she perceives as a happy past. She has a penchant for reconstructing the past in a favorable light, so that the memories, influenced by imagination, are far more pleasant than was the actual experience. Such comparisons of past and present lead to a deepening of the present despair and drive her even closer to destruction. Emma, who ironically was unhappy much of her youth, finds a wealth of happiness in her memory when she compares it to life with Charles. Her first source of imagined happiness was literature, and real life can never live up to fiction:

> Avant qu'elle se mariât, elle avait cru avoir de l'amour; mais le bonheur qui aurait dû résulter de cet amour n'étant pas venu, il fallait qu'elle se fût trompée.... Et Emma cherchait à savoir ce que l'on entendait au juste dans la vie par les mots de "félicité," de "passion," et d' "ivresse," qui lui avaient paru si beaux dans les livres. (I, 586).

At each stage in her life she finds something superior in a previous period (the convent, the ball, conversations with Léon). These memories serve only to destroy any possibility of Emma adapting to her present, and in this capacity, contribute significantly to her demise.

Flaubert presents a direct contrast to Emma in the person of Charles. His marriage to Emma marked the dividing line between a happy present and a miserable past: "Jusqu'à présent, qu'avait-il eu de bon dans l'existence?" (I, 585). Charles' memories are of solitude, penury, and an empty marriage to the widow Dubuc. Emma brought him her youth and beauty, and his world had no need to extend beyond her. The difference between Charles and Emma is thus one of limits: his world and his needs are restricted to that which is within reach; Emma seeks the unattainable.

As early as age eighteen Flaubert recognized the danger of comparing past and present. In a letter to Ernest Chevalier in 1840, he writes:

> il y a des jours ... où l'on est triste ... où l'on se hait, où l'on se mangerait de colère. Ce qu'il faut faire c'est de ne pas penser au passé, c'est de regarder l'avenir ... sans écouter la voix plaintive des tendres ... souvenirs ... Il ne faut pas regarder le gouffre car il y a au fond un charme inexprimable qui nous attire. (Corr. I, 64)

This is the love-hate relationship Flaubert has with his own memories, and it is translated into Emma, Frédéric, Félicité, and others. There are times when Flaubert would like to ignore his past, but "ma curiosité impitoyable demande à tout creuser et à fouiller jusqu'aux dernières vases" (*Corr.* I, 224). Memory can only be avoided by the superficial, represented by Homais and Dambreuse. The rest, particularly those whose past seems idyllic, such as Emma and Djalioh, must live with, and suffer with, their memories. For the latter two characters, the only way to rid themselves of their suffering is self-destruction.

NOTES

[1] Emma may be seduced by her creation, but it is the act of writing that is the real agent of the seduction. Naomi Schor explains:

> As Freud demonstrates in *The Poet and Daydreaming*, the fictive character, like this composite being who is sketched by Emma's pen, is the product of all the unsatisfied desires of its creator. Transcoded into psychoanalytic terminology, the 'phantom' that Emma perceives is a phantasm. Moreover, writing, such as Emma practices it (such as Flaubert practiced it), is a solitary pleasure: the phantasmic scene is one of seduction. The pleasure that Emma experiences in rewriting Léon, in giving herself a lover three times hyperbolic, is intensely erotic.   (19)

The end product of Emma's writing is death, the natural result of such a renunciation of lived experience, and a fitting consequence of an experience known as "la petite mort." Happily for us, Flaubert, with the aid of his memory, was able to avoid the fate of his character.

[2] Schor sees Emma as Homais' equal, however, in the realm of the written word:

> But if on the communication axis Homais wins out over Emma, who, it must be remembered, does not shine as a decoder ... when one turns to that delayed communication which is writing, the balance of forces is equalized. Certain readers, unaware of Emma's scriptural activities, will perhaps be surprised at this affirmation. It is, however, in the area of writing that the Emma/Homais rivalry turns out to be the most violent; it is to the extent that they practice two different forms of writing that their sexual opposition becomes significant ... Compared to [Homais'] journalistic logorrhea, what has Emma published? Nothing, but she does write. What, to my knowledge, has escaped critical notice is the thematic and structural relationship between *Madame Bovary* and the first *Education:* the Emma/Homais couple is a new avatar of the Jules/Henry couple ... Emma is the portrait of an artist, but the artist as a young woman, and it is this difference, this bold representation of the writer as a woman which disconcerts, which misleads, and which, for these reasons, must be examined.   (14–15)

WORKS CITED

Bersani, Leo. *Balzac to Beckett: Center and Circumference in French Fiction.* New York: Oxford University Press, 1970.

Bollème, Geneviève. *La Leçon de Flaubert.* Paris: Les Lettres Modernes, 1964.

Collas, Ion. Madame Bovary: *A Psychoanalytic Reading.* Geneva: Droz, 1985.

Fenichel, Otto. *The Psychoanalytic Theory of Neurosis.* New York: Norton, 1945.

Flaubert, Gustave. *Correspondance.* Ed. Jean Bruneau. Paris: Gallimard, Bibliothèque de la Pleïade, 1973. [Abbreviated in the text as *Corr.*]

———. *Madame Bovary.* Ed. Claudine Gothot-Mersch. Paris: Garnier Frères, 1963.

———. *Oeuvres complètes.* Paris: Seuil, 1964. [All citations to *Madame Bovary* are taken from this edition.]

Girard, René. *Deceit, Desire, and the Novel.* Baltimore: Johns Hopkins Press, 1965.

Knight, Diana. *Flaubert's Characters.* Cambridge: Cambridge University Press, 1985.

Schor, Naomi. *Breaking the Chain.* New York: Columbia University Press, 1985.

Michael Danahy

MADAME BOVARY: A TONGUE OF ONE'S OWN

As soon as Emma Bovary feeds herself a handful of arsenic, we read: "Puis elle s'en retourna subitement apaisée, et presque dans la sérénité d'un devoir accompli" [Then she returned suddenly calmed down, and almost in the serenity of a duty accomplished].[1] Suicides have a special language all their own, according to the poet Anne Sexton: "Like carpenters they want to know which tools / They never ask why build."[2] This chapter examines not only how Emma Bovary learned to speak such a language, her tools in trade as it were, but also the uncarpenterlike question that Flaubert precluded her from asking: Why should she build her own coffin? Who did or indeed could hold such awesome power over her to define so fatal a "duty" and set in motion the morbid process by which self-destruction came suddenly to be swallowed so dutifully? To what order of obligations has she been subordinated? Psychically and socially, what forces make this choice incumbent upon her? To whom, in short, does she owe such mortal obedience?

To the men in her life. And these include, besides the obvious ones in the novel, her narrator first of all. So vividly does Emma live in Flaubert's imagination that he is led to react to her as if she were real. Archetypally construed, his words "Madame Bovary, c'est moi" take on a new meaning. As Annis Pratt explains it, the male who "journeys from the day-to-day world of society into a different reality, that is nevertheless translatable in cultural terms ... encounters his 'shadow,' which represents a collection of antisocial tendencies, his opposite or wicked self, himself as a self-hater and social rebel."[3] This figure must be repressed by the owner's "good citizen persona" for a number of reasons. As a man moves from the realm of the personal down into the collective unconscious, "the shadow changes sex, merging alarmingly with his buried feminine side." This shadow and anima together embody a "terrible mother," who compels its owner to "struggle with this powerful feminine component of himself; his goal is to absorb her import, master her autonomous control over his impulses, and then return, a reborn psyche, to

---

From *The Feminization of the Novel* (Gainesville: University of Florida Press, 1991), pp. 126–58 (abridged).

everyday life." This tension is the crux of the narrator's adventure in *Madame Bovary*.

Because Emma functions as Flaubert's anima, she draws upon herself the narrative animus that we will explore.

But the narrator is not the only "good citizen persona" to silence this terrible mother. The other men in Emma's life include her critics and commentators. They, too, share in the narrator's adventure. I will show how the critical myth of the novel has been used to discredit her, equating her femininity with fictionality,[4] and why the tools of this myth have been made to work as mechanisms of oppression against what she represents.

The Second Empire piously prosecuted Flaubert for outrage to public manners and morals, and not entirely unlike these operatives of the imperial government, commentators on the novel have severely circumscribed the heroine's attempt to articulate what Mary Daly has called the unspeakable human emancipation from "the eternal circle of separation from and return to infantile dependence."[5] In the "feminine mode of existence," according to Daly, the only possibility of transcendence—and Emma achieved this form of it—is separation from the home of her parent only to return to paternalistic dependence in the home of a husband. The woman who believes that she needs men to be happy has therefore been enlisted unwittingly in her own reenslavement even as she embarks on a program of emancipation.

In the crisis that precedes and dramatically provokes her death rattle, three images flash through Emma's disturbed mind, invading and overwhelming her: Papa Rouault, Lheureux, and Rodolphe. This threesome, Male Parent, Money Man, and Playboy, are the father figures in her life, a demonic trinity invested with the fullness of ultimate powers and authority. Between the image that Emma receives and the impulse on which she acts, between the explosion that shatters her mind into the thousand pieces of a fireworks display and the implosion of her self-immolation, Flaubert's text has established an immediate, startling, onrushing connection without stating where or what this connection is. Does it ring in the death knell, for instance? Is it a romantic fantasy of the Apocalypse? But other men, too, Husband and First Love, Charles and Léon, have compelled her to lethal allegiance and help turn one of Emma's few successful attempts at anything in life, "un devoir accompli" [a duty accomplished], into the inevitability of dying. They turn what could be into what should be, the desperate choice of a suicidal gesture into an obligation.

What the textual connection between Emma's image and her impulse makes us realize about these men is that Emma has internalized as her own their sense of her worthlessness in failing to live up to male-centered standards and the prefabricated roles that they have prescribed for her, roles that she "should have" played better all along. But now it is too late. They will not help her out. Already having said no to her in words, they loom large and speechless in her imagination, only to condemn her silently to the lonely romanticism of an apocalyptic fantasy and the well-constructed realism of her carpenter's death. Her suicide is marked in its every phase by ex-communication. To understand this bizarre psycholinguistic process, we first need to understand how communication normally worked for her.

The author makes this difficult, however. In a realistic novel, presumably we should go directly to the dialogues to discover *in vivo* how people communicate with each other. One might listen to what the men say straight out to and about Emma and the way it is said in order to learn about the norms and expectations that they express and convey, the rules and roles that they are prescribing for her. But in Flaubert's case, something—his hatred for the ugliness of plain language perhaps—led him to avoid either showing or telling readers outright what the characters were saying to each other, out loud, or to themselves. Thus, the narrator blurs the distinction between reporting discourse indirectly in a narrated summary or directly in a dramatic or dialogue form. His sense of style led him away from a more or less verbatim record of ordinary utterances and to other means of characterization. Chief among these is *le style indirect libre,* which becomes at various times a peculiarly Flaubertian shorthand for transcribing both voiced and unvoiced speech, mingling verbal interactions, pronouncements, interior monologues, musings, and the like. But the narrator's mélange remains so subtle that the reader is often hard-pressed to understand what is being said by whom and to whom. The meaning of the words often slips away or evaporates. "Evanescent" is Claudine Gothot-Mersch's evocative word for this curious effect.[6] That ambiguity can prove both fascinating and rewarding, despite the difficulty it presents to deciphering the implications of speech.

In his writing, therefore, Flaubert embedded chunks of his characters' utterances, and it becomes the reader's task to unearth the buried fragments of spoken speech and reactivate their muffled intonations. This exercise involves determining voice more than it does point of view, as is customary among Flaubert critics, and it proves akin to Flaubert's own exercise as he submitted his sentences to the test of his "gueuloir" ["screech room, yelling place"], reading them aloud at the top of his lungs, declaiming them in different registers, sounding different notes in different keys, listening keenly for their undertones and overtones. Through the work of our own "gueuloirs," we must amplify the resonances and catch the reverberations of an oral discourse silenced into writing. Stephen Ullmann has noted the close connection between intonation and *style indirect libre,* in which the narrator can retain not only the emotive and expressive features of a character's speech, but the very inflexions of the spoken language.[7] In examining microscopically several of Flaubert's sentences, we shall see how the narrator transcribed the inflexions of Emma's voice in a way that actually deprived her of a tongue of her own. In the histrionics of these sentences, and the speech acts that they imply, one can hear everything but the histrion, Flaubert's own narrating voice. One may hear verbal cues, nonverbal nudges, all the innuendoes of interaction patterns. Flaubert's style was finely tuned to register or resonate with the rules of discourse that a society may find it imperative and in its best interests to leave only in an indirect form. These rules may have been unannounced and unstated, but they were not unarticulated, not unknown, and not inoperative. Recording only indirectly the utterances in which they are inscribed keeps the code secret; they require careful listening to catch the echoes of the voices cited, their overtones, and the secret of the code itself. Thus, Flaubert's style does contain the traces that we are after of the verbal and nonverbal interaction patterns, the communication system. We shall see that the language Emma caught from others, like a bad cold, was the death of her; she ceased to live when she ceased to talk back.

Each of the male figures in Emma's life articulates and enunciates a set of norms by which she is to be measured and her conduct evaluated. What they say to her, what they say about her, and the way it is said contain tacit but specific behavioral cues; and Emma's self-expectations, as well as the norms she herself uses to interpret and evaluate her own performance, her ideals and her feelings, come not from her reading or her powers of illusion and self-delusion, but from the tacit male utterances that circumscribe her possibilities. To the extent that Flaubert's novel deserves its subtitle, *moeurs de province,* it is a novel of the manners and morals inscribed in and by a male-dominated society. If Paris prefigured, in 1857, the possibility of any one of a number of fundamental changes, then an artist could represent in its purest form the provincialism of one sex continuing to dominate the other and engender the existence of both of them only outside this figure.

While only the written and fragmentary residue of many speeches that men would make to women survive in Flaubert's textual transcription of this society, these remnants nonetheless truly constitute the verbal markers of a male-dominant culture. By this I mean that it is not enough to claim that these gender-based verbal markers reflect the culture depicted by Flaubert. Rather, they delimit what is defined as culture; manners and morals of any kind reside only within the limits enunciated by these verbal markers. The society that Flaubert portrayed relied on standards of judgment, norms, customs, and values that were imposed according to gender. But, more than that, the narrator is structured by his own structuring and creates for himself a gender. Indeed, as I shall show, the narrator himself relied on the same standards of judgment. Rules of discourse are patterned to serve first and foremost the needs of males. The men are uniquely privileged to determine and enunciate the norm and the normal; this privileging of the male, more than a portrait of a society that made it possible, was due to choices on Flaubert's part, the active collusion of his own narrative strategies. In creating his own community of readers, implied or fictional, but sensitive, comprehending, and attentive, he encoded a male-dominant gender-based scale of values.

Emma, for her part, internalizes the role-model demands that originate with men and are of greater utility to them than to women in general or her in particular. But how did it come about that she internalized the men's norms and incorporated the sense of worthlessness that eventually ended as the swallowing of poison? To give her a start in life, her father purchases for her "une belle éducation" from the Ursuline Convent in Rouen. Not only is it costly, but it is one for females far above her station, that of a farmer's daughter. As an investor, the father is soon enough disappointed with the results, not of the schooling per se but with the returns he had expected afterward. "Mlle Rouault ne s'amusait guère à la campagne maintenant, surtout qu'elle était chargée presqu'à elle seule des soins de la ferme" [Miss Rouault was hardly enjoying the country now, especially since she had been assigned to do the farm chores almost by herself] (339). The conversational tone, the rhythm, and the stress patterns of the sentence read like a perlocutionary speech act meant to convey indirectly someone's attempt at getting the listener to do or feel something by what is implied as a spoken speech. But who is speaking or listening to whom? Here we are apt to do not a double, but a triple take. If Emma alone was "sounding off," the placement and stress pattern especially of "surtout" and "presqu'à elle seule" ring with a huffy tone of indignation at exploitation perhaps or resentment at doing the barnyard drudgery. But do the words summarize an attitude, Emma talking only to herself out of self-pity, or do they dramatize Emma complaining out loud to gain sympathy and perhaps relief from a listener? But the sentence also has the ring of someone mimicking the exaggerated laments of a rather more lethargic than overworked young girl, a hostile parent's way of taunting her into silent submission. The name calling with which the sentence starts, "Mlle Rouault," may be a jibe directed against the snobbery of her "high-falutin" ways. The tone of feigned indulgence in the word "guère" perhaps mutes the patronizing jeer of a parent talking to a child who is talking back. But, finally, what if the narrator, *sotto voce,* is "sounding out" his two characters, probing them to show their limits, or is his, too, a heckling voice in a medley of voices? Then he would be indulging in rather facile sarcasm.

All of the above? none of the above? Nothing in the context permits us to decide or get a fix on any of the potential speakers. Given the interplay of irony and empathy, proximity and distance, we cannot locate or situate the voice. The overall effect of the sentence is uncanny, and, in the final analysis, only a kind of disconcerting indeterminacy characterizes the mingling of voices, their intonations and modulations. This kind of choral sentence recurs throughout the book. Like the sentences from a Robbe-Grillet film uttered by more than one speaker, this polyphonic utterance weirdly disconcerts because all its dissonances belong to no one in particular and least of all to the narrator who made them.

This single uncanny sentence transmits no one message but a style of interaction and therefore harmonizes two voices entwined in domestic conflict. Thanks to the narrator, in its tonal ambiguities, as it reverberates with irony, the discordant voices are discernible at the same time. First the voice of Emma, disdainful of her lot, conniving for sympathy, self-pitying, and resentful about her father's expectations, and second that of Le Père Rouault, equally disdainful, echoing Emma's voice the better to mock her. The tones of a sorely vexed father commingle with the ring of sarcasm meant to shame the pretentious girl into conformity.

Thus, the sentence resounds with three statements:

1. What you are supposed to feel is: Gratitude
2. The reason why you are supposed to feel it is: the schooling
3. And what you are supposed to do now is:
   —stay down on the farm
   —be cheerful or keep still, in either case, stop complaining
   —do the work assigned

Although the astute and prosperous peasant might have predicted his own dissatisfaction, he directs his disappointment against the daughter for not doing and feeling what she should have.

Since the death of her mother, Emma has had no other mirror in which to seek or see an image of herself. Clearly, she can find no basis for self-esteem in the way Rouault labels her "malade." From her childhood and upbringing, Emma begins, and not without justification, to feel like a misfit and is made to feel that way. Jean Baker Miller clarifies the role of this kind of labeling.

> For a woman, even to *feel* conflict with men has meant that something is wrong with her "psychologically" since one is supposed to "get along" if one is "all right." The initial sensing of conflict then becomes an almost immediate proof that she is wrong and moreover "abnormal." Some of women's best impulses and sources of energy are thus nipped in the bud. The overwhelming pressure is for women to believe they must be wrong: they are to blame, there must be something very wrong with *them*.[8]

The casual consent that Emma's father gives for her marriage is another of the many ways that he has to voice the criticism "you are not worth having around as a housekeeper, and you are certainly not worth paying a large dowry to be rid of, your future welfare is not worth bothering about." It is precisely at the time of Emma's wedding that the narrator invents a bit of biography: Le Père Rouault had had a firstborn son who died long ago, leaving him only with Emma and nostalgia for the lost male heir. This bit of fiction is rarely noted at all in the secondary studies of the novel, let alone its connection with the degrading paternal mirror.

For her marriage, Emma requests a midnight torchlight ceremony. What motivates her father's response is not a farmer's down-to-earth concern about money nor reluctance to indulge fantastic whims or capricious excesses. Rather, in flatly saying no to her, he is saying that his own fantasies, not hers, are the ones worth paying for. His banquet for forty-three persons lasting sixteen hours is no more sensible or pragmatic than any of Emma's wishes, but hers are the ones to be categorized, here as elsewhere, as the ridiculous desires of an eccentric "malade." In a similar fashion, critics generally dismiss Emma's ideas for her wedding ceremony as romantic fantasies absorbed from novels that have corrupted her imagination with clichés. Yet her choice for the nuptials is really her way of asserting that she is no longer a part of the social group from which she came. Its presence at her wedding disturbs her. She has been educated far above it and is marrying out of it. Offended at the tawdry wedding banquet, she need not be labeled a spoiled child, spiteful, disappointed, and resentful at the failure of a gratuitous and girlish pipe-dream. Her father has helped instill but not fulfill certain needs, and one must recognize that he has not followed through on what he has encouraged her to expect, namely a certain ambiance. He does what she wants only when it does not disturb or compete with what he wants.

It is all too apparent, therefore, that from her father she has learned that she should hide both what she was and what she is becoming. Having fostered in her the education, tastes, and sensibility of an upwardly mobile middle-class lady, he expects Emma nonetheless to set these aside. She should not be unhappy, mal-adjusted, or unappreciative of farm life, including the boorish habits he has, like spitting on the andirons. He has the last word and he enunciates what is normal and what is normative. This interaction pattern, reinforcing negative self-images and low self-esteem, recurs with all the other men who make an impact on Emma.

As a wife, Emma is seldom at a loss to know what she "should" and "should not" do.[9] The list of what Charles tells her is long: She should go horseback riding with Rodolphe for her health, she should work more in the garden for her health, she should go to the theater in Rouen for her health, she should hug her daughter Berthe for her health. After the disastrous clubfoot operation on Hippolyte, she should of course be more accepting, understanding, less bitter, more calm and caring. What she also learns, on the other hand, is that she should not be so sensitive.

At one point she avoids Charles "qui lui aurait fait des observations sur ce qu'elle s'apprêtait de trop bonne heure" [who would have made remarks about the fact that she was getting ready too early]. When he does risk "une observation" about the household muddle, he musters no greater strength than to suggest in various ways what she should do or be, think or feel. She should not read so many novels, because she should get more exercise. So at this point, he simply cancels her subscription to her book club. Nor should she take the expensive piano lessons. Yet he acquiesces in spite of the financial distress that he knows he is risking. Later, like the subscription, he cancels the power of attorney that he had previously given her, with the reprimand that she should not have used it as she did, as he let her.

In all these ways Charles tolerates and reinforces the negative images that Emma has of herself, signaling that she and her behavior should not be the way they are. At one point, for instance, Emma's mother-in-law initiates an argument in which she heaps considerable abuse upon her; the cue from Emma's husband is that she should apologize first, for it is she who should have been more docile and defer-ential. But the narrator has already made clear the extent to which Emma resents the norms dictated to her in her conjugal state; it resounds in her sarcastic imper-sonations of Charles's mother. Emma "répétait qu'il fallait économiser, puisqu'ils n'étaient pas riches, ajoutant qu'elle était très contente, très heureuse, que Tostes lui plaisait beaucoup, et autres discours nouveaux qui fermaient la bouche à la belle-mère" [repeated that they had to economize, because they were not rich, adding that she was very content, very happy, that she liked Tostes very much, and other new speeches that shut the mother-in-law up] (385). Thus, she has learned to heckle women verbally, as her father had done, as her narrator does.

Charles further signals that she ought to be at least as happy as he in becoming a parent. The good wife should be not just a mother but motherly. She, on the other hand, alone dares to utter, if only in whispers to herself, a truth that is otherwise unspeakable in her time and place.

Elle souhaitait un fils; il serait fort et brun, et s'appellerait Georges.... Un homme, au moins, est libre.... Mais une femme est empêchée continuelle-ment. Inerte et flexible à la fois, elle a contre elle les mollesses de la chair avec les dépendances de la loi. Sa volonté, comme le voile de son chapeau retenu par un cordon, palpite à tous les vents, il y a toujours quelque désir qui entraine, quelque convenance qui retient.   (406)

[She desired a son; he would be strong and dark and would be named Georges. . . . At least a man is free. . . . But a woman is constantly hindered. Inert and pliable at once, she has against her the weaknesses of the flesh and the subordination of the law. Her will, like the veil of her hat held down by a tie string, flutters in all the winds, there is always some desire which pulls, some propriety which restrains.]

Reproachful labels like "confused heroine" authorize readers to invalidate Emma's point of view here and disregard the implications of her suffering.[10] The rhetorical parallels, the present tense, the image all suggest a plaintive defensive self-indulgence, but also something more, the voice of a woman who sees her situation in a gender-based society with an amazing degree of self-knowledge and who challenges the manners and morals of this restrictive situation. Yet the voice is deprived of the authority to utter another story about the future the way it could be. Instead, like the speaker herself, whose face is covered, the message is veiled, clothed in an image of feminine apparel that could not more adequately or intimately represent a woman's status. And the narrator does not have his readers hear the heroine speaking in any other way, except from beneath the veil.

Richard Bolster's study of independent feminist voices of the nineteenth century led him to conclude that "la plainte de Madame Bovary est celle de toute une génération de femmes" [Madam Bovary's complaint is that of an entire generation of women].[11] This point certainly puts in a new light Flaubert's own remark that his heroine was suffering and crying throughout the villages of France.[12] In the passage just cited, the language of Bovarysme has once again blended with another voice in what Graham Falconner has called "the rhetoric of ambiguity."[13] Once again it is difficult to know who is talking to whom, but someone is making a clear-headed statement about real social conditions and registering the perception not of an incurable romantic but of an astute commentator. For a woman, language is no more than a form of clothing, both instrument and image of imprisonment.

In Emma Bovary's time, "confinement" often referred to a woman's being pregnant. Emma accepts maternity, as she was expected to, but not as she was expected to, in the conventional frame of mind. The pregnancy is for her own fulfillment, not for the men and their motives. A male son will enable her to experience vicariously the freedom given to them in the real world. Thus, when told the sex of the newborn, she passes out without replying to Charles at all.

As a role or a concept, the mother who wants sons is, of course, the invention of a culture in which women are depotentiated and living their potential in projections on the envied and beloved male offspring. On the other hand, Emma also seems to believe that the birth of a daughter will simply lead to a sterile repetition of the conventional patterns of restriction that patriarchal society has imposed on women rather than to the creation of a new life-style of freedom and exploration of the world.[14] And as time goes by, she does not delude herself with the patriarchal idea of motherhood that would make her indispensable to her daughter. She does not want to base her self-esteem merely on doing for others, nor does she see herself as limited to this role. She shows the self-assurance needed to seek avenues of fulfillment beyond its narrow and prescribed limits.[15]

In contemporary society, we are more willing to admit that the relationship with one's child need not be the primary one in a mother's life. While Emma was strong and curious enough to break out of the traditional mold of good mother, she lacked the terrible strength to survive as a "bad" mother.[16] Homais and the Curate, who serve as narrative caricatures of opposing points of view on every issue of importance in the man's world of religion and politics, unite to speak with one voice on this issue. A mother ought constantly to monitor her child; anything else, the idea that Emma need not do this, they would and did call reprehensible in their consistent desire to impose female role models.

So Emma dared risk the consequence that would come in her society from not being the wife and mother that she "should" be, from feeling that children are not enough for an educated adult woman. The courageous side of Emma's emancipation has escaped the appreciation even of the novel's very controlled and highly self-conscious author. Thus, Flaubert saw such an attitude with the cold eyes of irony as little more than silly romantic bravado in Emma. But her implicit courage did not escape the notice of another Flaubert, the artist, who was able to share his sense of this side of Emma in society.[17]

Emma lives out to its real, logical, and bitter conclusion the emptiness of the institutions of marriage and the masculine norms that go with it. Just as she speaks only in forms of discourse that are alien to her own voice, her attempt to find happiness through child rearing is an alienated attempt to articulate an aspiration. Alienated, because its justification was not in and for herself but in and through another being. Critics have quite unfairly emphasized what a pitifully inadequate mother she is rather than the dehumanizing and unrealistic norms imposed on women by the social institution of nineteenth-century motherhood and the gender-based patterns of discourse. One critic, for instance, takes her child's dirty ears as an indictment of Emma's character, reading them reproachfully as a sign of slovenliness and selfish withdrawal from a world of dirt into a world of illusions.[18]

From her lovers Emma learns that she should not be so intense in her reactions, so sensuous and voracious. Shut up by men in the world of immanence and sensuality, she is then reproached for it and told again that she should not be what she has become. Rodolphe, for instance, uses all the verbal tactics of an experienced ladies' man: "you should not be so timid, you should be yourself, uninhibited," and so on, with intercourse the only end in view. Satiated rather easily, he quickly asserts that she should not visit him as frequently as she does, she should not be so imprudent as to compromise herself. And thrice in a row he stands her up to let her know that she should not be so complicated and moody. She should be less crazy, less impulsive and possessive, more normal as he defines it for her but based on his experiences, more patient, less agitated, less agitating. In the letter he writes finally to dismiss her, she is told that she should have been "une de ces femmes au coeur frivole comme on en voit" [one of these women frivolous at heart such as one sees], as Rodolphe criticizes that delectable exaltation of hers that has given him so much trouble.[19]

With Léon Emma learns that she should be circumspect in her gestures and purchases. She should not pay for the dinners in fancy restaurants. She should not interfere with his work. Nor should she be so lascivious in so profound and secretive a way, so wanton, so aggressive and sexually uninhibited, so lusty and encompassing. It comes as no surprise finally when he fails to help her obtain money on the grounds that she should take care of her own affairs.

Many literary critics in effect concur with Emma's lovers because they share the same hidden models of what is appropriate. Thus, their discourse also becomes richly perlocutionary. We may learn from Sherrington, for instance, that Emma's impressions are suspect and her view of her lovers deformed.[20] She should be more perspicacious, more balanced, perhaps more broadminded. Even more un- wittingly like the men in Emma's life, one professor, *en pleine Sorbonne* [in the Sorbonne itself], denounced her sexual activity for the benefit of his audience as "impudeur déchaînée" [indecency unbridled].[21] Rather than examine the gender- ized paradigms and canons that coerce Emma (and her readers) to settle for what she gets—that is, accept inadequate lovers and nurture the growth of others— commentators instead attribute her destiny to second-rate self-delusions or inade- quate distorted views of reality on her part. With this collusion from criticism, when the so-called subordinate shows signs of initiative and assertiveness, the sensuality that frightens the dominant group is invalidated as neurosis, maladjustment, and the like.

From Homais and Bournisien Emma learned that she should be saved more easily, that is, in a manner that spares them great effort. Each, of course, has a different formula for success in the salvation that she is supposed to find. But in both cases, for her own good, she is not allowed to recognize her sensuality, nor should she be so complicated or frustrated. The norm is happily to adjust. "Moi," Homais intones, "je trouve que les mères doivent instruire elles-mêmes leurs enfants" [As for me, I think mothers should teach their children themselves]. In the name of science he persuades Emma that she should help save the young Hippolyte. She has her own motives for yielding to Homais's instances, but she does comply by influencing Charles to operate on Hippolyte's clubfoot. The hideous results of the operation move anyone who reads the novel. But what is less obvious is that earlier, as a result of a bruise that Berthe received, Homais had expounded the theme that parents must be prudent enough to prevent physical harm from hap- pening to the young. Thus, the narrator enables us also to take the measure of Homais's discourse, its emptiness and incongruity, its grotesqueness and barbarity, in the inhumane absurdity of its one-sided norms.

The name of the local curate may remind one of Boursin cheese, obese bovines, and country bumpkins. The principle that this Bournisien impresses upon Mme Bovary, when she desperately comes to him for advice and solace, is "le devoir avant tout" [duty first]. Not only does he fail utterly to sense the frantic needs and feelings that echo so strongly in her pleas for help, but he tells her first of his duties and then suggests that she should go home to her husband and take some tea. It seems as if it is she who is at fault and as if it is within herself that the malfunction is to be found. So preoccupied is he with the most vulgar of material realities that he locates the problem in her lower digestive tract. After recommending the tea, which is the French equivalent of two aspirin in these cases, he adds reassuringly, "ça vous fortifiera, ou bien un verre d'eau fraîche avec de la cassonade" [that will fortify you, or perhaps a glass of cold water with some brown sugar].

In its liturgy, its dogmas, and its sacraments, the church proclaimed that the needs of one's flesh and the needs of one's spirit could be integrated and fulfilled by the bonds of matrimony. Indeed, this ideal had become conservative and middle class by the middle of the nineteenth century.[22] Emma's initial youthful acceptance of it can hardly be labeled eccentric or abnormal. On the other hand, because the priest would have her more fully embrace the very roles that had begun to nauseate her, his prescription can only worsen the situation. The narrative irony makes it clear that, not unlike psychiatrists of today who want only for their clients to adjust, the spiritual counselor here has authority to speak but without knowledge of what he is talking about. The same authority figure will tell her once again what she should do: "Elle devait joindre ses souffrances à celles de Jésus Christ et s'abandonner à la miséricorde divine" [She should join her sufferings to those of Jesus Christ and throw herself on divine mercy] (706). This time she is on her deathbed.

Between these two interchanges, Bournisien remains at a loss to handle the religious fervor that Emma experiences after her nervous collapse. Not knowing how else to handle the matter, he reduces it to a disturbance based on gender difference; thus, he writes to the diocesan bookstore for "quelque chose de fameux pour une personne du sexe, qui était pleine d'esprit" [something great for a person of the opposite sex, who had many brains] (521). When he receives a jumbled assortment of pious books, pamphlets, and polemical tracts in vogue, he simply hands the confusing array of readings over to Emma, not caring himself to help her avoid the excesses of devotion that prompted him to write in the first place. Instead of pursuing the matter through spiritual dialogue, each afternoon he takes a swig of cider with Charles, toasting "au complet rétablissement de Madame" [to Madam's complete recovery].

The moneylender's discourse is far more overtly callous. Lheureux lies to Emma, pressures her, and leads her on with IOU's, and when she has the money to pay her debts, he advises that instead she should trust him, get her husband to sign power of attorney over to her, and sell his property. The reason that he gives for doing so is again cast in the language of duty: She should spare her bereaved husband from practical problems while he is mourning the death of his father. When Lheureux has finished bleeding her, he turns his advice unscrupulously around, telling her that it is her own fault after all, if she cannot liquidate the debts.

She should not have let it go so far, he rationalizes, but now she must be fair to him and pay the debt. "A qui la faute ... Tandis que je suis, moi, à bûcher comme un nègre, vous vous repassez de bon temps" [Whose fault is it ... While I'm working like a black man, you're out having a good time]. And when Emma refuses to make love with the notary who has connived with Lheureux to defraud her, the notary suggests only that she should have asked for his help earlier in making more profitable speculations and investments.

Because Emma has internalized standards for measuring personal worth that belong properly to the men in her life, the answer is inevitable to Lheureux's cynical taunting question: "A qui la faute." Why, Emma herself is at fault. Her death by poison is the perfect dramatization of this process of psychic swallowing, for it symbolizes both the norms ingested and the morbid self-esteem that results from them. One of her reactions with Rodolphe typifies this process. When he expresses concern for the social obligations at which he had earlier scoffed, she absorbs his judgment whole and organic, without questioning the ultimate motives of his speech. Hence, "peu à peu ces craintes de Rodolphe la gagnèrent" [Rodolphe's fears gradually overwhelmed her] (476). Here she impersonates Rodolphe on the basis of what he says to her and what she in turn says to herself, as elsewhere she used physical objects to impersonate him, putting his pipe in her mouth for instance.

Similarly, with the other men when they voice a feeling, expectation, or duty, she is actually absorbing as her personal fate the identity, the roles, the behavior (including attitude and affect) that social discourse imposes on her as a woman. Madame Bovary's discourse, as we find it controlled and freely reported by the narrator, is but a series of impersonations, not the authentic talk of one person directly to another. Thus, she has learned to impersonate who or what she is supposed to be. "Elle s'étonnait parfois des conjectures atroces qui lui arrivaient à la pensée, et il fallait continuer à sourire, s'entendre répéter qu'elle était heureuse, faire semblant de l'être, le laisser croire?" (424) [She was sometimes astonished at the awful conjectures that came to her mind, and she had to go on smiling, listen to herself repeat that she was happy, pretend to be so, let people believe it?]

Grammatically, the sentence does not read like a question, and there would be no question mark if we were merely reading about a situation that the narrator alone were directly or indirectly summing up. Yet the punctuation is undeniably, mysteriously there. To read over the passage and beyond it, without pausing to notice its oddity, is easy to do in the middle of a long and complex novel. It is, however, also not to hear a medley of three different voices speaking at once in three different ways. At some intuitive level of artistic awareness, the narrator is impersonating Emma impersonating others in the novel, her antagonists. So intensely and directly is the narrator involved here in Emma's animus that it rises to the surface, asking to be heard. By casting her resentful questions in the forms and the words of others' affirmations, however, the narrator is nonetheless able at the same time to disguise his own voice. And all that is left in print is a kind of echo chamber, in which Emma internalizes against herself the angry feelings and words that she does not direct against those around her, her words and their words that she hears and reiterates. Thus, Emma herself is the echo chamber of the real world and of what others say (stereo) typically to people like her in that world.

In a fundamental sense, moreover, Emma takes upon herself, takes as her very self, the qualities of passivity and animality that pass for the female essence in general. When she accepts as her own or impersonates what is socially ascribed as her norm and her gender identity, she is made to do so from two sides, both by the narrator and by the other men of the novel acting in complicity to deny her access to language as identity and a way of articulating the self. In men's writing, the female is made "unsound." Emptied by this complicity of her individuality as a thinking, feeling, speaking human being, Emma nonetheless makes it known in public just how unlivable are the norms and expectations built in to the social institutions around her. Concluding that her self is worthless, unspeakable, she trashes it. So perfectly, in effect, has she internalized the consciousness of the oppressors that she becomes that oppressor in her own case.

George Sand's heroine does the same thing, but only up to a point, as we shall show. Madame Bovary, on the other hand, dramatizes her own inability to survive in her community as a free agent or to become an individual endowed with liberty. The opposite of failure for Emma is not worldly success or happiness, material well-being or sexual gratification, but liberty. If we examine the use of the word throughout the book, we find that what Charles called "un acte précieux de sa liberté" [a precious act of his liberty] was to play dominoes at night in one of Rouen's sleazy bars. Emma has a definition far less pitiful; her yearning encompasses freedom in all of its physical, social, moral, and even spiritual ramifications. But she, too, associates the concept with a masculine life-style and quality of life, with masculine pursuits and pastimes. "Et cette idée d'avoir pour enfant un mâle était comme la revanche en espoir de toutes ses impuissances passées. Un homme, au moins, est libre" [and this idea of having a male as a child was, in her wishes, like the revenge for all her past inabilities. A man, at least, is free]. An editor working for a stage producer might be tempted to put this last sentence in quotes. Its simple syntax, the monosyllables, and the punctuation all bespeak a conversational tone which would indicate that Emma is supplying her own words, directly, dispassion- ately, and objectively cited by the narrator. Even at this point, however, the source or authority for the utterance is indeterminate. The narrator could instead actually be mimicking the character's voice in a travesty of her. With the next sentence, the narrator begins clearly to intervene and take over. And the tone modulates as he begins to blend in his own voice, his own words, and structures. A man has freedom because he can "parcourir les passions et les pays, traverser les obstacles, mordre aux bonheurs les plus lointains" [explore passions and countries, overcome obstacles, bite into the most faraway pleasures] (405). Is there only irony in these undulations or perhaps not also the hint of sympathetic vibrations? At any rate, Emma knows what the supplier of her words is talking about. The three active transitive verbs and three very general direct objects suggest what women lack: power, pleasure, and mobility. These characterize Emma's jealous understanding of the freedom that locomotion gives to men.

For the most part, therefore, Emma confronts the facts: Being free goes with having money, and both are still based on gender. Whether liberty designates an ideological concept or the quality of life, both French romanticism and the Revolution had redefined it in terms of positive law. Civil society had recently and loudly proclaimed its intent to make liberty available and support it as a form of personal fulfillment. Gone, in other words, were the negative values formerly associated with the word in favor of new and powerful connotations. But not gone were the gender-based patterns of association. Not only is Emma painfully aware of this, that being *libre* has not been extended to women, but she is lucid in using the adjective to qualify men only. To Rodolphe, she says astutely, realistically, "Il me semble pourtant que vous n'êtes guère à plaindre ... Car enfin ... vous êtes libre, riche" [Still, it seems to me that you are hardly to be pitied ... for you are, after all, free, rich] (452). And she plainly understands that the linguistic equivalent attributed to women for equivalent behavior is "libertine."[23] The kind of concrete personal physical freedom that Emma wants is available with impunity only to men.[24] When she does not scruple to spend francs "libéralement," she is harshly judged as mannish by her community and the narrator. Repeatedly, in fact, she is labeled as acting "à la façon des hommes" [like men], because they see her taking so-called liberties in the way that she walks, talks, thinks, dresses, and smokes.

There is no need, within this framework, to glamorize Emma's suicide as one woman's desperate, courageous, but hopeless attempt at emancipation. All can agree that her death is no more humanly desirable or dignified than her life. But on the other hand, and without justifying or glorifying her suicide as an existential or feminist revolt (which it could never be), we need not trivialize it either, as do her critics both within and without the novel, by interpreting her problematic behavior only in the narrowest terms of yet another "duty" that she has, namely to continue to live within the confines of the gender models made available to her. How self-deluded or deceptive is Emma, when she sees herself dragging on a useless existence? Rather than *Bovarysme* this sense of futility is an accurate, undistorted reflection of the guilt feelings that she suffers from not fulfilling the norms that she has internalized. Because the value that she assigns to herself accurately reflects the estimates of those around her, she concludes that abuse is what she deserves. To imagine herself maltreated seems the only way of easing her mind "elle aurait voulu que Charles la battît, pour pouvoir plus justement le détester, s'en venger" [she would have liked Charles to beat her so she could more justifiably hate him, take revenge on him]. This sense of unworthiness governs all that she says, for instance, both before and during the love tryst at the Rouen Cathedral. The mislabeled misfit becomes a self-appointed victim, when the accumulated burden of unworthiness for not being a good daughter and daughter-in-law, wife, mother, and mistress—all the roles prescribed for being a good woman—makes her unbearable to herself.

In the final analysis, Emma Bovary's death is no pretext for ironic intertextual references to previous literary conventions, Flaubert's self-conscious literary parody of Chateaubriand, for example, or other famous romantic death scenes from novels or church ritual books. Nor is it Emma's silly attempt to imitate or intertextualize great death scenes from literature she knows. Nor the narrator's satire on one kind of bookish imagination. One finds a number of preposterous explanations for the decision. According to Leo Bersani, "Emma Bovary kills herself because of her failure to find a situation worthy of her vocabulary."[25] But from the brief discussion of the word *libre* above, the important challenge in her life is not to know the literary meaning of "bliss," "passion," or "ecstasy," but to be denied a tongue of one's own. Her suicide is perhaps the only thing that Madame Bovary can call her own. Although there is no vocabulary in the book that we can call properly "hers," Bersani's point is correct in a sense. He sees it, however, as a universal problem, a spiritual problem, and a trivial problem in Emma's case, or as a particularized problem, whereas others—Mary Daly in theology, Jean Baker Miller in psychology, and Christiane Rochefort in the novel—show how the excommunication from language is none of these, but a gender-based phenomenon.

As if no one wanted to acknowledge that the concatenation of such problems is *real*, commentators generally stress Emma's capacity to produce fictions and suffer from their unreality. Bersani can even write that "her sickness is purely imaginary,"[26] falling prey to a process well known in social psychology as blaming the victim. The failure of scholars to appreciate the physical and moral horror of Emma's dying results from a systematic unwillingness to assess the interrelationship of the men in her life and their masculine norms in producing her situation, the denial of a tongue of one's own.

On the other hand, the imperial government that stupidly put Flaubert on trial for outraging public manners or morals showed no such readiness to discount Emma's problems. Taking the novel seriously, they paid it the indirect homage of treating it as "ideological crime."[27] Dominick LaCapra wonderfully demonstrates that the prosecution of Flaubert constituted a case of "scapegoating," by which he means the anxiety-ridden sense that an event or series of events constitutes a fundamental challenge to the norms, values, and ways of life assuring the solidarity of the group. Emma should not have been unhappy enough to make apparent the inadequacy of the cherished social norms as a way of achieving personal fulfillment. But she was and what she expected of herself in trying to live up to these norms was, when all is said and done, unspeakable and unlivable. Emma's suicide puts in doubt the scale of values and the social practices tacit in the novel. LaCapra would limit the conflict in values to one of marriage, family, and property versus adultery and shows how the defense, the prosecution, and even modern critics of the novel hold the same fundamental values in common. What I am arguing, on the other hand, is that the scope of the ideological crime is even wider, an indictment not just of class but of gender as patriarchy had culturally constructed and articulated it. Patriarchy retaliated with a counterindictment of the portrait that was only too convincing, offering, as it did, a fearful example of the systematic manner in which the values sacred to "nos aieux, nos pères, ou nos proches" [our forefathers, our fathers, or our neighbors] created and destroyed women like Emma Bovary.[28]

Emma's potential elevates her above the dull masculine sobriety of her surroundings, but she inevitably falters, given nothing but their sense of her duty to cling to. Who on earth of either sex could reconcile the contradictions and conflicts that Emma confronts? The successful integration of love with marriage, of sensitivity and cultivated emotions with the banality of housework, of an active sensory pathology with mystical yearnings, of superiority in mind and body with inferiority of social circumstance, of moral integrity with monotony, of esthetic taste with practical budgeting are the masculine ideal of what women should be in Emma's society. The humanly impossible is demanded of women, and sex-role models and norms are the vehicle of these demands, as Simone de Beauvoir argues.

> Woman is shut up in a kitchen or in a boudoir, and astonishment is expressed that her horizon is limited. Her wings are clipped, and it is found deplorable that she cannot fly. . . .
>
> The same inconsistency is deployed, when, after being enclosed within the limits of her ego or her household, she is reproached for her narcissism, her egotism with all their train: vanity, touchiness, malice, and so on. She is deprived of all possibility of concrete communication with others.[29]

Beauvoir's remarks aptly evoke the discourse typical not only of the men in Emma's fictional life, but of her critics and commentators as well. In various ways both groups reckon her failure as personal, which it is clearly not, for the standards by which it is measured are not personal but sex-linked. The norms by which Emma lives to acquire the sense of failure with which she dies cannot be properly called her own at all, because in the society depicted, no merely mortal female had the superhuman range of abilities that would be required to integrate the divergent factors Beauvoir mentions into patterns of behavior. Thus, to discard one's up-bringing, to renounce one's sexuality, to be easily saved by the ready-made answer, these are all expectations of herself but are not self-given or self-supportive but meant for the benefit of those around her.

There is a final factor at work in Emma's utter deprivation of a tongue of her own: the voice of the implicit narrator and the viewpoint he chose. The experience endured by Doris Lessing in 1962 when she published *The Golden Notebook* may clarify this issue. Carolyn Heilbrun explains how the viewpoint chosen for writing the novel accounts for the negative critical reactions and the drubbing Lessing received at the hands of the critics. "Lessing had assumed that the filter 'which is a woman's way of looking at life has the same validity as the filter which is a man's way.' "[30] For the same reasons, the viewpoint chosen by Flaubert has actually prompted the drubbing of Emma at the hands of her commentators for over a century now, that is to say, the extent of negative critical reactions to the heroine. And this drubbing is not unlike the physical one that she thought she deserved from Charles and the emotional one that she incurred from the men in her life. With the Flaubertian narrator, gender identity and experience control and color the point of view in the novel; he, too, discredits the woman's filter. Despite the pretensions of Flaubert and many scholars to a neutral or objective point of view, his (and theirs) is not only gender-based but resolutely biased. As R. J. Sherrington has pointed out, most critics, reacting to the novel as if it were a sex object, "were content to fondle it or walk on it."[31]

We have already noted instances when the narrator adopts an ironic distance to view Emma's behavior; the manner she sometimes has of dressing, walking, and doing her hair in a bob are seen as unduly mannish.[32] This point of view does characterize the community around her, but just as certainly there are times when the narrator cannot claim this shield for his own viewpoint. The tone can become particularly harsh or flip, when we read, for instance, that "Léon devenait sa maîtresse, plutôt qu'elle n'était la sienne" [Leon was becoming her mistress, more than she was his]. Here, as elsewhere and not infrequently, the narrator is passing judgment even though no witnesses are present who might serve as the upholders of sex-role conventions and to whom, as vehicles, the narrator might attribute these orthodox standards. When the narrator is not putting words in someone else's mouth, the opinions are no one's but his own. The irony in such cases is directed at Emma's behavior patterns not just because these are bourgeois or pretentious or in poor taste but also because her behavior is regarded either as typically feminine or the opposite, not feminine enough, not very feminine at all. It is very much the kind of irony that men practice on women for infringing their standards. In the following example, when Emma sweet-talks Charles into letting her go to Rouen, there is once again no anonymous community of townsfolk on hand to serve as a mouthpiece. Instead, the narrator alone may be held to account for the standard of judgment implied and applied. What is said directly reflects his own initiative and attitude. "Et voilà comment elle se prit pour obtenir de son époux la permission d'aller à la ville, une fois la semaine, voir son amant" [And that's how she went about getting permission from her husband to go to town once a week to see her lover]. One can hear Flaubert chuckling in his *gueuloir* [scream room] at the *blague supérieure* of the opening flourish, the periodic rhythm of the phrasing, and the clincher, the climactic rhetorical parallel, permission from the husband to see the boyfriend.

The narrative pose of offhanded cleverness and the amused indifference or indignation belie a normally male tone of voice and point of view in handling the bantering repartee reserved for the subject of cuckoldry. The same kind of demeaning, trivializing persiflage reverberates in the narrative handling of Emma's religious and esthetic experiences. In *La Princesse de Clèves*, it was acceptable for a heroine to bolster her ego by spiritual practices and to buttress the self thereby against the stress of erotic involvement. But that novel about a woman was written by a woman. In Flaubert, admittedly of a different historical period and social class, one finds a far less sympathetic treatment of the heroine's religious impulses or esthetic sublimations. When he moralizes that Emma "se sentait au coeur cette lâche docilité qui est, pour bien des femmes, comme le châtiment tout à la fois et la rançon de l'adultère" [felt in her heart that cowardly docility that, for many women, is like both the punishment and the price for adultery], the narrator obviously thinks of himself as very much the nineteenth-century enlightened male. Whether or not one appreciates the smug humor, the reader recognizes the voice of experience in the use of the demonstrative adjective, the coy parenthetical generalization, and the clever paradox about that scarlet letter A.

The sole adult whom the narrator obviously admires is the good Dr. Larivière. And among the qualities for which he is praised is this one based on gender: He was paternal with the poor. Likewise, the narrator assures us that "son regard ... vous descendait droit dans l'âme" [his gaze ... penetrated right into your soul]. Who is this *vous* but an all-male audience of Larivière's medical students? Having described Homais's and Bournisien's all-night vigil beside Emma's corpse, the narrator refers to "cette gaieté vague qui nous prend après des séances de tristesse" [that vague gaiety that overcomes us after melancholy occasions]. This "nous" that has recurred from the opening pages of the novel happens to be "we men," not, as it could be, "we humans." Maxims uniting the reader and the narrator as "nous" are, to say the least, odd for Flaubert, but recurrent. So, too, are the occasions when the narrator speaks of the effects that love has on "vous." The *vous* he talks to in these lapses of stylistic control and finesse are men, for the remarks generally reflect the way men look at women rather than the other way around. Thus, his maxim that "une demande pécuniaire, de toutes les bourrasques qui tombent sur l'amour" [of all the squalls that love endures, a demand for money] is the coldest and most devastating refers to a masculine experience interpreted from a masculine point of view, for the simple reason that women are the ones put in the position of having to ask for money, while it is men upon whom the demand falls.

At times, the narrator comments negatively on the men in Madame Bovary's life. He constantly ridicules Homais, Bournisien, and Lheureux, for instance. But here it is a question of failures to achieve standards of intelligence or originality that a certain kind of man expects both of other men and of women. The standards are those that a privileged male, but not necessarily a female, would set. That is, the narrator, even in speaking against the representatives of nineteenth-century middle-class provincial French manhood, speaks in the name and by the authority of an elite that is also male. To speak with the voice of women or from the point of view of women would require a kind of impartiality or reciprocity that the narrator never achieves. He is writing for the 98 percent male members of a spiritual and cultural elite, the same one, as Professor Moreau has suggested, that Baudelaire wrote for and that appreciated the caricatures of Champfleury, Duranty, and Daumier similar to the verbal ones Flaubert was drawing.[33] The objectivity of Flaubert and his impassibility, hailed from the very year of the novel's appearance by Barbey d'Aurevilly, appears diminished, much less neutral and impersonal, once we have examined the stereotyping and sex-role models reflected in various narrative judgments. The problem lies always in determining whose values are called objective and which ones are at stake.

The sexually partisan viewpoint of the narrator is disclosed not only stylistically, but in another, more fundamental way: in the very ordering of events. The way in which the narrator sets reality up, by structuring the plot sequence, carries out a double function. When Flaubert makes the timing of events, their progression and sequence, seem inevitable and irreversible, on the one hand, he is authorizing or legitimizing Emma's feeling of helplessness to change the given order of things; on the other hand, in presenting her failure as an inevitable chain of events, he is also shielding the men in her life, providing alibis for the parts they actively play in her undoing.

At one point Flaubert had planned to make Léon and Emma lovers before Emma and Rodolphe became lovers. By contrast, in the definitive narrative sequence, the affair with Rodolphe intervenes between the platonic relationship first established between Emma and Léon and the subsequent unplatonic liaison consummated by the couple. Because of this intervention, Emma is doomed, before the fact as it were, by the very logic of the structure the narrator imposed on the events. The aspirations first roused in Emma by Léon go unfulfilled, until redirected toward Rodolphe. But, given the marked differences between the two men, she will not at first be sensitive to the gratifications that Rodolphe brings, nor could she possibly have found in him what she had begun to seek after. But the sequencing also ensures that she will no longer appreciate that which Léon offered once and might have offered again. This is because Rodolphe's initiation of her into adultery changes her so definitively and to such an extent that any subsequent escapade with Léon will leave her unsatisfied. She is all the more frustrated because she enjoys with Léon neither the physical union she hoped she would nor any longer the platonic, if not simpler, pleasures that indeed she had enjoyed in the first place.

Most often, it is Emma's sense of her own helplessness to change the given order of things that critics intend to speak of when they discredit her view of the world as unreliable, subjective, warped. Coming from Charles at the end of the novel, the claim "C'est la faute de la fatalité" [Fate is to blame] rings hollow, but Emma's judgment of herself as doomed to frustration and failure is strikingly confirmed by the objectivity that is inscribed in the order of events in the plot. To discount her perceptions as a distorted or falsified picture of reality and impugn their credibility is, therefore, to miss an important point and evade a necessary conclusion. Even Justin, the boy who loves Emma in an innocent adolescent way, shows the reader how quickly and easily the male learns that his filtered version of reality will prevail. Like all the other men in her life who do nothing to reverse or retard her downfall, he does not reveal what he knows about the poison Emma took because the truth would have compromised him for letting her into the druggist's supply room. Instead he keeps silent to protect himself from charges of complicity. Although he is the one who might have saved her in the end, he is but the final instance of the fact that the male filtering of reality is always the last word.[34]

When the narrator presents her failure as an inevitable chain of events, he, too, is making it difficult, but this time for the reader, to "read" the men in Emma's life and their complicity in the events. Once again, however, the appearance of inevitability fostered by the narrator cannot utterly obscure the truth of the other story that informs his narrative. While internal pressures brought Emma to a low level of self-esteem, the negative self-image is not, on account of its subjectivity, in error. Rather, when Emma poisons herself emotionally, first ingesting failure as her fate, this experience is consistent with reality as the narrator has set it up. Contrary to the prevailing views of most male critics, Emma has internalized fate as her own failure, when clearly it is not. Her downfall is due, on the one hand, to society and, on the other, is a function of the textual ordering of events that comes with the narrator's built-in sexual bias and the "good citizen persona" repressing a shadowy figure of the self.

Despite the masculinized psychology that informs the narrator's point of view and the sexually partisan basis of the narrator's judgments, which invite "us" and "you" to evaluate Emma's behavior, the narrator presents enough information objectively enough to allow for a view of it that differs from his and relies on norms that differ from his. Her suicide is the most striking example of what the controlled narrator harshly judges in one way while the artist and deep seer enable us to see in another way.[35] There are others—when, for instance, the reader recognizes the importance and the validity of Emma's reactions: "Elle aurait voulu battre les hommes, leur cracher au visage, les broyer tous" [She would have like to thrash men, spit in their faces, grind them all to bits] (603). Similarly, the narrator furnishes the information enabling us to disagree with his own manner of speaking of the decisions Charles makes after Emma's death. The narrator suggests that "Elle le corrompait par delà le tombeau" [She was corrupting him from beyond the grave], as if to put the weight of corruption again on the female, charging her finally with an archetypal responsibility that a mere mortal cannot have, and hinting at the mythical female power or impact of the anima. The responsibility does not, cannot belong here, but what Flaubert wrote obscures Charles's role and denies his part in letting the memory of Emma guide him in decisions of his own making.

Madame Bovary's suicide is then the most extreme form of self-denial, but it is only that: the last of many such acts of self-denial to which she is brought. It is to the narrator's credit that he has the courage to show the hideous reality of such a principle. As a woman defined, supported, and circumscribed by men, and norms formulated outside the self, she had come to practice self-denial in vain attempts to live up to heteronomous expectations. The surprise would be for her to accomplish such a task and integrate into her life all the norms by which she has denied herself. Thus, her failure to do so need not be evaluated as less than can be expected of human nature, for, on the contrary, it is all that can be expected. In a very real way, Emma embodies the abstract truth that no one can happily and successfully achieve the degree of self-denial in question. This portrait of feminine frailty is not the mirror of human nature at its most paltry and puny.

NOTES

[1] Gustave Flaubert, *Madame Bovary*, in *Oeuvres complètes*, ed. A. Thibaudet and R. Dumesnil, 2 vols. (Paris: Gallimard, 1951), 1:613. Subsequent citations from the "Pléïade" edition will be indicated by page number in the text.

[2] Anne Sexton, "The Barfly Ought to Sing," *Tri-Quarterly* (Fall 1966): 90.

[3] Annis Pratt, "Spinning among Fields: Jung, Frye, Lévi-Strauss and Feminist Archetypal Theory," in *Feminist Archetypal Theory*, ed. Estella Lauter and Carol S. Rupprecht (Knoxville: University of Tennessee Press, 1985), pp. 101–2.

[4] Jonathan Culler rightly questions such an identification, especially when it comes to explaining Emma's corruption and downfall by her novel reading. But the special affinities claimed between the female sex and the genre of prose fiction are attributed to Flaubert, rather than to literary historians. To explain

the nature of fiction, hence its principle of interpretation, Culler prefers the concept of indeterminacy; other explanations, he feels, are category mistakes, interpreting the right things with the wrong principles. *Flaubert: The Uses of Uncertainty* (Ithaca: Cornell University Press, 1974), pp. 143–46.

[5] Mary Daly, *Beyond God the Father* (Boston: Beacon Press, 1976), p. 25.

[6] Claudine Gothot-Mersch, "Sur le narrateur chez Flaubert," *Nineteenth-Century French Studies* 12, no. 3 (Spring 1984): 347.

[7] Stephen Ullmann, *Style in the French Novel* (New York: Barnes and Noble, 1964), pp. 109, 116. On this basis, I would suggest that Roland Barthes's name for this typically Flaubertian technique is misleading. In *Le Plaisir du text* (Paris: Seuil, 1973), he calls it "la citation sans guillemets" [quoting without quotation marks] (p. 57), but the place where citation normally takes place is in print, not out loud.

[8] Jean Baker Miller, *Towards a New Psychology of Women* (Boston: Beacon Press, 1976), p. 131.

[9] As Tony Tanner points out, Emma is forever reminded not of her name but of her role in life. "Ma femme, ma femme," Charles calls out when he enters the house and does not see her. Tanner, *Adultery in the Novel* (Baltimore: Johns Hopkins University Press, 1979), p. 256, shows in detail how Emma, through no fault of her own, could never be happy with Charles; see pp. 237–50.

[10] Victor Brombert, *The Novels of Flaubert* (Princeton: Princeton University Press, 1966), p. 57.

[11] Richard Bolster, *Stendal, Balzac et le féminisme romantique* (Paris: Les Lettres Modernes, 1970), p. 9.

[12] Flaubert, *Correspondance* (Paris: Conrad, 1926–33), 3:291.

[13] Graham Falconner, "Reading *L'Education sentimentale:* Belief and Disbelief," *Nineteenth-Century French Studies* 12, no. 3 (Spring 1984): 333.

[14] Carla Peterson, *The Determined Reader* (New Brunswick, NJ: Rutgers University Press, 1986), p. 173.

[15] The alternative to condemning Emma for not feeling what she "should have" felt as a mother is suggested by Ellmann's discussion of childbirth. She insists that "uterine accomplishment" is often only a detached and fleeting impression. It is legitimate not to define oneself by the products of one's cellular multiplication. Moreover, Patricia Branca points out that historically the demands of the new concept of motherhood emerging in the nineteenth century could not be met fully by anyone at the time, because the new means of coping with the changing and increased role demands—the medical, social, and economic means—were often outstripped by the pressures and ideology to do so. See her *Women in Europe Since 1750* (New York: St. Martin's Press, 1978), pp. 121–28.

[16] See Leslie Rabine, *Reading the Romantic Heroine* (Ann Arbor: University of Michigan Press, 1985), p. 8. The work of Claire Goldberg Moses, in *French Feminism in the Nineteenth Century* (Albany: SUNY Press, 1984), shows that Emma's rejection of motherhood was consistent with, if not informed by, feminist views of the time. On the social background, see, for example, pp. 136, 165.

[17] Rabine, in *Reading the Romantic Heroine,* has outlined and applied the theory of this kind of reading for a "poly-" or "multiple logic" in texts where the voice of women is otherwise suppressed. She speaks of the sexual conflict between different levels of text: "Women's silenced voice gives evidence of itself not in overt utterances, but in the conflicts between levels and elements of the text that disrupt the dominant narrative voice" (p. 8).

[18] Brombert, *The Novels of Flaubert,* p. 84.

[19] Margaret Tillett comments sensitively on the impact on Emma of Rodolphe's final denial and betrayal. See her *On Reading Flaubert* (London: Oxford University Press, 1961), p. 32.

[20] R. J. Sherrington, *Three Novels by Flaubert* (Oxford: Clarendon Press, 1970), p. 98.

[21] Pierre Moreau, *Flaubert:* Madame Bovary (Paris: Centre de Documentation Universitaire, n.d.), p. 22. Moreau goes on to consider Emma's "nostalgie d'âme" which he calls her "mal"—not her quality or her character or her temperament or even her problem, but her sickness or, if you will, her evil. Moreau's choice of the word "mal" recalls the label also used by Emma's father.

[22] As Nancy K. Miller puts it in "Writing (from) the Feminine: George Sand and the Novel of Female Pastoral," in *The Representation of Women in Fiction,* ed. C. Heilbrun and M. Higonnet (Baltimore: Johns Hopkins University Press, 1983), p. 128, *Madame Bovary* is the nineteenth-century novel that supplies the intertext for the "rhetoric of elision" which figures respect for *the sacred unsaid* of marriage.

[23] The narrator applies the rather pejorative words "libertin" and "libertinage" in four out of six cases to the ways in which women may or may not behave. See *A Concordance to Flaubert's* Madame Bovary, ed. C. Carlut, P. Dube, and J. R. Dugan (New York: Garland Publishing Co., 1978).

[24] Edgard Pich, "Littérature et codes sociaux: L'Antiféminisme sous le Second Empire," in *Mythes et réprésentations de la femme au dix-neuvième siècle,* ed. Claude Duchet (Numéro spécial du

Romantisme) (Paris: Champion, 1976), points out that Emma "manifeste certains aspects de la volonté d'émancipation de son époque." See pp. 177–78.

[25] Leo Bersani, Balzac to Beckett (New York: Oxford University Press, 1970), p. 142.

[26] Ibid., p. 155.

[27] Dominick LaCapra, Madame Bovary on Trial (Ithaca: Cornell University Press, 1982), p. 24. LaCapra demonstrates, in fact, that both the prosecution and the defense shared the same values, the point at issue being only whether the novel undermined them or not.

[28] The defense rested by insisting that the novel really was consistent with the patriarchal values and norms of Bossuet and Masillon. The defense therefore referred to Charles as "admirable" to sustain its point that the novel did not invite disrespect for the values that the male judges might deem necessary for proper social order. There is no doubt as to the gender stereotypes of Flaubert's contemporary readers, for whom Emma was a paragon of female mental hysteria. See Moreau, Flaubert, pp. 32–33. Both camps—those who found Charles an excellent man and those who found the book immoral because he and the other guardians of established values were not excellent enough—held in common the same gender stereotypes. And what of critics of our own day?

[29] Simone de Beauvoir, The Second Sex, translated by H. M. Parshley (New York: Vintage Books, 1974), p. 673.

[30] Carolyn G. Heilbrun, "The Profession and Society, 1958–1983," PMLA 99, no. 3 (May 1984): 408.

[31] Sherrington, Three Novels, p. 152.

[32] Naomi Schor, Breaking the Chain: Women, Theory, and French Realist Fiction (New York: Columbia University Press, 1985), pp. 23–24.

[33] Moreau, Flaubert, p. 67.

[34] Most critics, since the first publication of the novel, have not seen it this way, of course. Sainte-Beuve, for instance, privileging the male's power to articulate reality, simply defined Justin's criminal complicity out of existence; he labeled Justin's concealment of Emma's poisoning as "silent love," although a timely disclosure of the information might have saved her life. Sainte-Beuve likewise considered Justin the only devoted, disinterested character in the book. See Madame Bovary, ed. Paul de Man (New York: Norton, 1965), pp. 335–36.

[35] Again Rabine articulates the theory of this kind of reading. The dominant masculine voice of the narrator seduces readers into accepting the interpretations or limited range of interpretations offered by the voice of the narrator. We automatically agree to see what the dominant masculine voice shows us and to ignore what it masks, because the narrator tells his story through codes of interpretation which readers have already internalized and which seem natural (Reading the Romantic Heroine, p. 18). This does not mean that "another story" does not exist, because the story exceeds the frame, described by the "charm of the narrator's voice."

CONTRIBUTORS

HAROLD BLOOM is Sterling Professor of the Humanities at Yale University and Henry W. and Albert A. Berg Professor of English at the New York University Graduate School. He is a 1985 MacArthur Foundation Award recipient, served as the Charles Eliot Norton Professor of Poetry at Harvard University (1987–88), and is the author of twenty books, the most recent being *The American Religion* (1992). Currently he is editing the Chelsea House series Modern Critical Views and The Critical Cosmos, and other Chelsea House series in literary criticism.

FRANK D. McCONNELL is Professor of English at the University of California at Santa Barbara. He has written *The Spoken Seen: Film and the Romantic Imagination* (1975), *Four Postwar American Novelists: Bellow, Mailer, Barth, and Pynchon* (1977), *Storytelling and Mythmaking: Images from Film and Literature* (1979), and *The Science Fiction of H. G. Wells* (1981), and has edited *The Bible and the Narrative Tradition* (1986).

BARBARA SMALLEY is the author of *George Eliot and Flaubert: Pioneers of the Modern Novel* (1974). She is a Associate Professor of English at the University of Illinois at Urbana.

CHARLES BERNHEIMER is Professor of Comparative Literature and Romance Languages at the University of Pennsylvania. He has written *Flaubert and Kafka: Studies in Psychopoetic Structure* (1982) and *Figures of Ill Repute: Representing Prostitution in Nineteenth-Century France* (1989) and, with Claire Kahane, has coedited *In Dora's Case: Freud—Hysteria—Feminism* (1985; rev. 1990).

MARGARET LOWE wrote several articles on Flaubert prior to her death in 1982, some of them collected in *Towards the Real Flaubert* (1984). She was the editor of *On Teaching Foreign Languages to Adults: A Symposium* (1965).

SARAH WEBSTER GOODWIN is Professor of English at Skidmore College (Saratoga Springs, NY). She is the author of *Kitsch and Culture: The Dance of Death in Nineteenth-Century Literature and Graphic Arts* (1988) and is the coeditor of *Feminism, Utopia, and Narrative* (1990), *The Scope of Words: In Honor of Albert S. Cook* (1991), and *Death and Representation* (1993).

CARLA L. PETERSON is Associate Professor of English and Comparative Literature at the University of Maryland. She is the author of *The Determined Reader: Gender and Culture in the Novel from Napoleon to Victoria* (1986).

NATHANIEL WING is Professor of French at Louisiana State University. He has written *Present Appearances: Aspects of Poetic Structure in Rimbaud's Illuminations* (1974) and *The Limits of Narrative: Essays on Baudelaire, Flaubert, Rimbaud, and Mallarmé* (1986).

BRUCE E. FLEMING is Professor of English at the United States Naval Academy. He is the author of *An Essay in Post-Romantic Literary Theory: Art, Artifact, and the Innocent Eye* (1991) and *Caging the Lion: Cross-Cultural Fictions* (1993), and has published fiction and essays in many literary journals.

WILLIAM VANDERWOLK is Professor of Romance Languages at Bowdoin College. He is the author of *Flaubert Remembers: Memory and the Creative Experience* (1990).

MICHAEL DANAHY, Professor of French and Chair of Foreign Languages at the University of Wisconsin at Stevens Point, has written *The Feminization of the Novel* (1991), which was awarded the Chinard Prize.

BIBLIOGRAPHY

Adams, Robert M. "The Ordinary in Front of the Infinite: Flaubert and Others." In *Nil: Episodes of Literary Conquest of the Void During the Nineteenth Century.* New York: Oxford University Press, 1966, pp. 62–85.

Ahearn, Edward J. "The Magic Cigar Case: Emma Bovary and Karl Marx." In *Women in French Literature,* ed. Michael Guggenheim. Saratoga, CA: Anma Libri, 1988, pp. 181–88.

Babuts, Nicolae. "Flaubert: Meaning and Counter-Meaning." *Symposium* 40 (1986–87): 247–58.

Bart, Benjamin F. "Aesthetic Distance in *Madame Bovary." PMLA* 69 (1954): 1112–26.

———. *Flaubert.* Syracuse: Syracuse University Press, 1967.

———. *Flaubert's Landscape Descriptions.* Ann Arbor: University of Michigan Press, 1956.

Bersani, Leo. "Flaubert: The Politics of Mystical Realism." *Massachusetts Review* 11 (1970): 35–50.

———. "Flaubert and Emma Bovary: The Hazards of Literary Fusion." *Novel* 8 (1974): 16–28.

———. "Flaubert and the Threats of Imagination." In *Balzac to Beckett: Center and Circumference in French Fiction.* New York: Oxford University Press, 1970, pp. 140–92.

Black, Lynette C. *"Madame Bovary:* The Artist and the Ideal." *College Literature* 12 (1985): 176–83.

Bloom, Harold, ed. *Gustave Flaubert's* Madame Bovary. New York: Chelsea House, 1988.

Buck, Stratton. "For Emma Bovary." *Sewanee Review* 65 (1957): 551–64.

———. *Gustave Flaubert.* New York: Twayne, 1966.

Butler, R. "Flaubert's Exploitation of the 'Style Indirect Libre': Ambiguities and Perspectives in *Madame Bovary." Modern Languages* 62 (1981): 190–96.

Church, Margaret. "A Triad of Images: Nature as Structure in *Madame Bovary."* In *Structure and Theme:* Don Quixote *to* James Joyce. Columbus: Ohio State University Press, 1983, pp. 61–80.

Collas, Ion K. Madame Bovary: *A Psychoanalytic Reading.* Geneva: Librairie Droz, 1985.

Cross, Richard K. *Flaubert and Joyce: The Rite of Fiction.* Princeton: Princeton University Press, 1971.

Culler, Jonathan. *Flaubert: The Uses of Uncertainty.* Ithaca, NY: Cornell University Press, 1974.

———. "The Uses of *Madame Bovary." Diacritics* 11, No. 3 (Fall 1981): 74–81.

Dauner, Louise. "Poetic Symbolism in *Madame Bovary." South Atlantic Quarterly* 55 (1956): 207–20.

Duncan, Phillip A. "Charles *Bovaryste:* Romantic Prefiguration in *Madame Bovary." South Atlantic Bulletin* 44, No. 4 (November 1979): 11–19.

Festa-McCormick, Diana. "Emma Bovary's Masculinization: Convention of Clothes and Morality of Conventions." In *Gender and Literary Voice,* ed. Janet Todd. New York: Holmes & Meier, 1980, pp. 223–35.

Furst, Lillian R. "Gustave Flaubert: *Madame Bovary,* 1857." In *Fictions of Romantic Irony.* Cambridge, MA: Harvard University Press, 1984, pp. 69–92.

———. "The Role of Food in *Madame Bovary." Orbis Litterarum* 34 (1979): 53–65.

Gans, Eric. Madame Bovary: *The End of Romance.* Boston: Twayne, 1989.

Genette, Gérard. "Flaubert's Silences." In *Figures of Literary Discourse*. Tr. Alan Sheridan. New York: Columbia University Press, 1982, pp. 183–202.

Gervais, David. *Flaubert and Henry James: A Study in Contrasts*. London: Macmillan Press, 1978.

Ginsburg, Michael Peled. *Flaubert Writing: A Study in Narrative Strategies*. Stanford: Stanford University Press, 1986.

Goodhand, Robert. "Emma Bovary, the Baker's Paramour." *Rice University Studies* 59, No. 3 (Summer 1973): 37–41.

Goodwin, Sarah Webster. "Libraries, Kitsch and Gender in *Madame Bovary.*" *Esprit Créateur* 28 (1988): 56–65.

Gray, Eugene F. "Emma by Twilight: Flawed Perception in *Madame Bovary.*" *Nineteenth-Century French Studies* 6 (1977–78): 231–40.

Greene, Robert W. "Clichés, Moral Censure, and Heroism in Flaubert's *Madame Bovary.*" *Symposium* 32 (1978): 289–302.

Griffin, Robert. *Rape of the Lock: Flaubert's Mythic Realism*. Lexington, KY: French Forum, 1988.

Haig, Stirling. *Flaubert and the Gift of Speech: Dialogue and Discourse in Four "Modern" Novels*. Cambridge: Cambridge University Press, 1986.

Hollahan, Eugene. "Irruption of Nothingness: Sleep and Freedom in *Madame Bovary.*" *Studies in Philology* 70 (1973): 92–107.

Knight, Diana. *Flaubert's Characters: The Language of Illusion*. Cambridge: Cambridge University Press, 1985.

Kovel, Joel. "On Reading *Madame Bovary* Psychoanalytically." In *The Radical Spirit: Essays on Psychoanalysis and Society*. London: Free Association Books, 1988, pp. 31–52.

Lapp, John C. "Art and Hallucination in Flaubert." *French Studies* 10 (1956): 322–34.

Leblanc-Maeterlinck, Georgette. "In Madame Bovary's Country." Tr. Alexander Teixeira de Mattos. *Fortnightly Review* 91 (1909): 862–75.

Levin, Harry. "—But Unhappy Emma Still Exists." *New York Times Book Review*, 14 April 1957, pp. 1, 4.

Lowe, A. M. "Emma Bovary, a Modern Arachne." *French Studies* 26 (1972): 30–41.

Lytle, Andrew. "In Defense of a Passionate and Incorruptible Heart." *Sewanee Review* 73 (1965): 593–615.

Maurois, André. "Gustave Flaubert: *Madame Bovary.*" In *The Art of Writing*. Tr. Gerard Hopkins. New York: Dutton, 1960, pp. 116–35.

Mitchell, Giles. "Flaubert's Emma Bovary: Narcissism and Suicide." *American Imago* 44 (1987): 107–28.

Muir, Edwin. "Emma Bovary and Becky Sharp." In *Essays on Literature and Society*. Enl. and rev. ed. London: Hogarth Press, 1965, pp. 182–94.

Muller, Herbert J. "Gustave Flaubert." In *Modern Fiction: A Study of Values*. New York: Funk & Wagnalls, 1937, pp. 121–35.

Nadeau, Maurice. *The Greatness of Flaubert*. Tr. Barbara Bray. New York: Library Press, 1972.

Newton, George. "The Liberation of Emma Bovary." *European Studies Journal* 3 (1986): 9–16.

Pace, Jean. "Flaubert's Image of Woman." *Southern Review* 13 (1977): 114–30.

Peterson, Carla L. "The Heroine as Reader in the Nineteenth-Century Novel: Emma Bovary and Maggie Tulliver." *Comparative Literature Studies* 17 (1980): 168–83.

Peyre, Henri. *"Madame Bovary."* In *Varieties of Literary Experience,* ed. Stanley Burnshaw. New York: New York University Press, 1962, pp. 331–52.

Porter, Dennis. "Gustave Flaubert's Middle-Class Tragedy." *Forum for Modern Language Studies* 13 (1977): 59–69.

Poulet, Georges. "The Circle and the Center: Reality and *Madame Bovary." Western Review* 19 (1954–55): 245–60.

Ramazani, Vaheed K. "Emma Bovary and the Free Indirect Si(g)ns of Romance." *Nineteenth-Century French Studies* 15 (1986–87): 274–84.

Riffaterre, Michael. "Flaubert's Presuppositions." *Diacritics* 11, No. 4 (Winter 1981): 2–11.

Roe, David. *Gustave Flaubert.* New York: St. Martin's Press, 1989.

Rothfield, Lawrence. "From Semiotic to Discursive Intertextuality: The Case of *Madame Bovary." Novel* 19 (1985–86): 57–81.

St. Aubyn, F. C. "Madame Bovary Outside the Window." *Nineteenth-Century French Studies* 1 (1973): 105–11.

Sartre, Jean-Paul. *L'Idiot de la famille: Gustave Flaubert de 1821 à 1857.* Paris: Gallimard, 1971–72 (rev. 1988). 3 vols. Tr. as *The Family Idiot: Gustave Flaubert 1821–1857.* Tr. Carol Cosman. Chicago: University of Chicago Press, 1981–91. 4 vols.

Schmidt, Paul H. "Addiction and Emma Bovary." *Midwest Quarterly* 31 (1989–90): 153–70.

Schor, Naomi. "For a Restricted Thematics: Writing, Speech, and Difference in *Madame Bovary."* In *Breaking the Chain: Women, Theory, and French Realist Fiction.* New York: Columbia University Press, 1985, pp. 3–28.

————, and Henry F. Majewski, ed. *Flaubert and Postmodernism.* Lincoln: University of Nebraska Press, 1984.

Sherrington, R. J. *Three Novels by Flaubert: A Study of Techniques.* Oxford: Clarendon Press, 1970.

Shukis, David T. "The Dusty World of *Madame Bovary." Nineteenth-Century French Studies* 7 (1978–79): 213–19.

Spacks, Patricia. "Women and Boredom: The Two Emmas." *Yale Journal of Criticism* 2, No. 2 (Spring 1989): 191–205.

Starkie, Enid. *Flaubert: The Making of the Master.* New York: Atheneum, 1967.

Steegmuller, Francis. *Flaubert and* Madame Bovary: *A Double Portrait.* 1939. Rev. ed. New York: Farrar, Straus & Giroux, 1968.

Stein, William Bysshe. *"Madame Bovary* and Cupid Unmasked." *Sewanee Review* 73 (1965): 197–209.

Thorlby, Anthony. *Gustave Flaubert and the Art of Realism.* New Haven: Yale University Press, 1957.

Thornton, Lawrence. "The Fairest of Them All: Modes of Vision in *Madame Bovary." PMLA* 93 (1978): 982–91.

Topazio, Virgil W. "Emma vs Madame Bovary." *Rice University Studies* 57, No. 2 (Spring 1971): 102–13.

Turner, Alison M. "Why Emma? Subtlety and Subtitle in *Madame Bovary." Romance Notes* 20 (1979–80): 51–57.

Wagner, Geoffrey. "Emma Bovary: The Usurper." In *Five for Freedom: A Study of Feminism in Fiction.* London: George Allen & Unwin, 1972, pp. 138–82.

Weinberg, Harry H. "Foci of Convergence in *Madame Bovary." Language and Style* 16 (1983): 468–77.

————. "The Function of Italics in *Madame Bovary." Nineteenth-Century French Studies* 3 (1974–75): 97–110.

Wiedner, Elsie M. "Emma Bovary and Hedda Gabler: A Comparative Study." *Modern Language Studies* 8, No. 3 (Fall 1978): 56–64.

Williams, D. A. *Psychological Determinism in* Madame Bovary. Hull: University of Hull Publications, 1973.

Williams, John R. "Emma Bovary and the Bride of Lammermoor." *Nineteenth-Century French Studies* 20 (1991–92): 352–60.

Williams, Michael V. "The Hound of Fate in *Madame Bovary." College Literature* 14 (1987): 54–61.

Williams, Tony. "Champfleury, Flaubert and the Novel of Adultery." *Nineteenth-Century French Studies* 20 (1991–92): 145–57.

Winders, James A. "Modernism, Postmodernism, and Writing: Style(s) and Sexuality in *Madame Bovary."* In *Gender, Theory, and the Canon.* Madison: University of Wisconsin Press, 1991, pp. 72–93.

Wright, Doris T. "Madame Bovary's Long Tresses." *College Literature* 15 (1988): 180–88.

ACKNOWLEDGMENTS

"*Madame Bovary* by Gustave Flaubert" by C. A. Sainte-Beuve from *Selected Essays* by C. A. Sainte-Beuve, translated by Francis Steegmuller and Norbert Guterman, © 1963 by Doubleday & Co., Inc. Reprinted by permission of Doubleday, a division of Bantam Doubleday Dell Publishing Group, Inc.

"*Madame Bovary* by Gustave Flaubert" by Charles Baudelaire from *Baudelaire as a Literary Critic* by Charles Baudelaire, translated by Lois Boe Hyslop and Francis E. Hyslop, Jr., © 1964 by The Pennsylvania State University Press. Reprinted by permission of The Pennsylvania State University Press.

"In the Hôtel de la Mole" by Erich Auerbach from *Mimesis: The Representation of Reality in Western Literature* by Erich Auerbach, translated by Willard R. Trask, © 1953 by Princeton University Press, renewed 1981. Reprinted by permission of Princeton University Press.

"Flaubert: The Riches of Detachment" by Albert Cook from *French Review* 32, No. 2 (December 1958), © 1958 by The American Association of Teachers of French. Reprinted by permission of *French Review*.

"*Madame Bovary:* The Tragedy of Dreams" by Victor Brombert from *The Novels of Flaubert: A Study of Themes and Techniques* by Victor Brombert, © 1966 by Princeton University Press. Reprinted by permission of Princeton University Press.

"*Madame Bovary:* The Seriousness of Comedy" by Harold Kaplan from *The Passive Voice: An Approach to Modern Fiction* by Harold Kaplan, © 1966 by Harold Kaplan. Reprinted by permission of the author.

"The Anxious Imagination" by Leo Bersani from *Partisan Review* 35, No. 1 (Winter 1968), © 1968 by Leo Bersani. Reprinted by permission of the author.

"Emma Bovary, a Man" by Mario Vargas Llosa from *The Perpetual Orgy: Flaubert and Madame Bovary* by Mario Vargas Llosa, translated by Helen Lane, ©1975 by Mario Vargas Llosa, translation © 1986 by Farrar, Straus & Giroux, Inc. Reprinted by permission of Farrar, Straus & Giroux, Inc.

"The Novel of Awakening" by Susan J. Rosowski from *Genre* 12, No. 3 (Fall 1979), © 1979 by the University of Oklahoma. Reprinted by permission of *Genre*.

"Aspects of the Novel" by Dominick LaCapra from Madame Bovary *on Trial* by Dominick LaCapra, © 1982 by Cornell University Press. Reprinted by permission of Cornell University Press.

"The Parody of Romanticism: Quixotic Reflections in the Romantic Novel" by Frederick Alfred Lubich from *European Romanticism: Literary Cross-Currents, Modes, and Models,* edited by Gerhart Hoffmeister, © 1990 by Wayne State University Press. Reprinted by permission of Wayne State University Press and Gerhart Hoffmeister.

"The Lexicography of *Madame Bovary*" (originally titled "Félicité, Passion, Ivress: The Lexicography of *Madame Bovary*") by Frank D. McConnell from *Novel* 3, No. 2 (Winter 1970), © 1970 by Novel Corp. Reprinted by permission of *Novel*.

INDEX